D1629521

INTERTWINED LIVES:
P.N. HAKSAR AND INDIRA GANDHI

INTERTWINED LIVES

P.N. Haksar and Indira Gandhi

Jairam Ramesh

**SIMON &
SCHUSTER**

London · New York · Sydney · Toronto · New Delhi

A CBS COMPANY

First published in India by Simon & Schuster India, 2018
A CBS company

Copyright © Jairam Ramesh, 2018

1 3 5 7 9 10 8 6 4 2

Simon & Schuster India
818, Indraprakash Building,
21, Barakhamba Road,
New Delhi 110001

www.simonandschuster.co.in

Hardback ISBN: 9789386797261
eBook ISBN: 9789386797278

Typeset in India by SÜRYA, New Delhi

Printed and bound in India by Replika Press Pvt. Ltd.

Contents

This is in memory of Lovraj Kumar and Abid Hussain,
two distinguished civil servants who had been influenced by P.N. Haksar
and who, in turn, encouraged me hugely

... incorrupta Fides, nudaque Veritas,
quando ullum invenient parem?

When shall Loyalty unshaken & candid Truth,
ever find a peer to him?

—Horace 24th Odes, Book 1, Poem 24

A Note on Names

I have stuck to the names of places as they existed during the 1960s and 1970s. Their new names are shown below.

Name in Book	*Name Now*
Bangalore	Bengaluru
Bombay	Mumbai
Burma	Myanmar
Calcutta	Kolkata
Ceylon	Sri Lanka
Dacca	Dhaka
Gauhati	Guwahati
Gurgaon	Gurugram
Madras	Chennai
Orissa	Odisha
Peking	Beijing
Pondicherry	Puducherry
Poona	Pune
Simla	Shimla
Trivandrum	Thiruvananthapuram

Chou En-lai used in the book later came to be written as Zhou Enlai.

Haksar used Bangala Desh and Bangla Desh in some of his notes. I have used Bangladesh consistently.

Indira Gandhi is referred to as Indira Nehru during the pre-1942 years.

Haksar: Who & Why?

IT WAS 8 JANUARY 1985.

After having been sworn in as India's prime minister eight days earlier, Rajiv Gandhi was in his office in South Block, the stately British-era edifice in New Delhi. His appointment just ahead of noon was with someone who had once been India's most powerful civil servant.

This man had been close to the prime minister's family for decades, both personally and professionally. He was not given to displaying much emotion in public. But uncharacteristically that day, he broke down on entering the prime minister's chamber. He had much to say. But he couldn't say much. This was because past memories had overwhelmed him.

This was the very room which he had first entered on 15 October 1947 to join the newly created Ministry of External Affairs and Commonwealth Relations, just eight weeks after India became independent. This was the very room where he frequently met India's first prime minister, Jawaharlal Nehru. This was the very room where he met India's third prime minister, Indira Gandhi, almost daily between May 1967 and January 1973 and often between January 1975 and March 1977. This was the very room he had walked out of after taking leave of India's fourth prime minister, Morarji Desai, on 31 May 1977, to start a new life outside government service.

This is the life story of that distinguished man who had crafted many turning points in the life of the nation in the late 1960s and early-1970s.

This is the chronicle of a man who was born in what was to later become part of Pakistan. He grew up in central India and studied in Allahabad and later London, where he befriended Feroze Gandhi and Indira Nehru in the late 1930s. He went through an active communist phase first in London and then on his return to India in Nagpur. Thereafter, he became a lawyer and a diplomat. He emerged as Indira Gandhi's ideological compass and moral beacon from May 1967 to January 1973, guiding her through her magnificent achievements: the nationalization of banks, coal and oil refineries, the abolition of privy purses, the victory over Pakistan in the war of December 1971, the creation of an independent Bangladesh and subsequent agreements to bring durable peace to the subcontinent, India's emergence as a major agricultural, space and nuclear power, the integration of Sikkim into the Indian Union and strengthening planning and the public sector to rebuild the economy.

This is also the saga of a man who drifted apart from Indira Gandhi, choosing to leave her side on his terms even though she would continue to consult, and sometimes entrust, him on special and sensitive assignments. He bravely opposed the Emergency from the inside and offered protection and solace to its bitterest critics; and while he paid the price for it, he did not ever speak or write against her. In fact, he may well have been kept on by her successor but he declined. With his days of power and influence behind him, he became an elder statesman, responsible, among other things, for the beginning of the process of reconciliation between India and China in May 1987. He later played a key role in the selection of a prime minister in May 1991, headed a large number of academic institutions and became the champion of many worthwhile public causes.

All biographies of Indira Gandhi do speak of this man. One such well-known author has written:[1]

> Of him it was rightly said that, at a critical juncture in modern Indian history he was "not only the most powerful civil servant but also the second most powerful person in the country" ... He did "not derive all his authority from Indira Gandhi. He contributed in no small measure to her own dominance."

This man was a mentor to many from different walks of life. His circle of close friends was unusually large and included scientists, economists, civil servants, diplomats, artists, authors, journalists, musicians, social activists and politicians. People—both the high and mighty as well as ordinary men and women who did not even know him—would write in and he would make it a point to reply. At the height of the India–Pakistan war on 9 December 1971, he found time to write to a middle-level manager of a government soap factory in Bangalore thus:

> I have your letter of November 24. I have received a sample of your Mysore Sandal Soap and I shall be glad, in due course, to place an order.

This man's unusual gift for friendship was pithily captured in one of J.R.D. Tata's letters to him in which the famed Indian industrialist wrote:

> … As I am sure you are aware, I have retained a deep feeling of respect and regard for you even though, as you also may know or have guessed, I was unresponsive to many of Mrs. Gandhi's policies, in the formulation of which you must have played an important role!

One part of him was true scholar, steeped in Sanskrit, Urdu, Hindu and Persian, with some knowledge of Bengali, French and German. He had a deep knowledge of the myriad traditions that have gone into the making of India. He made notable contributions to the cultural life of the country as well. He saw the celebration of India's many diversities as being essential to its advancement. He was unflinching in his commitment to secularism which, he believed, meant that the Indian *state* should have nothing to do with religion.

Described as 'the very embodiment of the hope that does not flag, the faith that does not waver and the self-confidence that strengthens the weak and cautions the strong',[2] this man was Parmeshwar Narain Haksar or Haksar Saheb as Indira Gandhi and his colleagues would very often call him or PNH as he would also be known. He was a legend once upon a time. He is all but forgotten today, recalled only by a dwindling generation of Indians. But, for the person he was and what he stood for, for what he did and accomplished, for the unflinching courage of his convictions and for the manner in which he advised a prime minister during a most turbulent period, he deserves to be rescued from growing obscurity and oblivion.

Haksar first had *power*. He wielded it with a high-minded sense of social purpose.

He then had *influence*. He exercised it to advance the national interest.

In the final decade of his life, Haksar had *voice*. He raised it to remind the citizens of this country of their heritage, of the threats that the Indian Republic faced from within and from outside.

This is not a book on India's recent political and economic history. It is, instead, the story of an extraordinary man who did much to shape that history. It is really his own story that emerges from the remarkable archive he left behind.

Notes

1. Malhotra (2004).
2. This is from Gopal Gandhi's notes for a draft speech for President K.R. Narayanan on the occasion of Haksar's first death anniversary in November 1999. Gandhi very graciously made available this draft to me.

I. The Katni Kashmiri
(1913–1929)

This section covers the first sixteen years of Haksar's life, from birth till the time he entered college. He was born in what was to later become part of Pakistan and grew up mostly in small towns in central India. It was when he was seven that he first set his eyes on a three-year-old Indira Nehru. His formal schooling was to begin when he was 13 and three years later he moved to Allahabad for higher education.

Haksar's immediate family with him (standing left), probably 1930.

HAKSAR WAS AT THE UNIVERSITY OF KASHMIR IN SRINAGAR IN THE SUMMER of 1981. The eminent economist and former finance minister of Jammu and Kashmir (J&K) Haseeb Drabu was a student there and was present when he spoke. He recalls that the vice chancellor, Waheeduddin Malik, insisted on introducing and referring to him as Mr Haskar. When PNH's turn came to speak, he gently chided the vice chancellor saying that his name was Haksar, not Haskar and went on to elaborate: *Hak* from one of the most common Kashmiri cuisine items (green leaf) and *Tchar* from a worm that feeds on the green leaf. It may well have been tongue-in-cheek since the consensus view is that the Haksars hail from Hakchar, which was the name of a village in the Baramulla district in Kashmir Valley.

Haksar was, in his own words, a 'non-Kashmiri speaking Kashmiri', the only member of the so-called 'Kashmiri cabal' around Indira Gandhi[1] to be so. He was certainly conscious of his heritage although the first time he visited Kashmir was only in June 1968 when he was 55 years old and was at the peak of his power as Indira Gandhi's secretary. Unlike the two other Kashmiri bosses of his—Jawaharlal Nehru and his daughter—PNH had no special emotional fascination for his ancestral land.

An autobiography, the noted historian Ramachandra Guha once said, is a pre-emptive attack on a future biographer.[2] From that perspective, I have an advantage since Haksar wrote no autobiography that covered his entire life. Just as he was about to leave the Government of India on 23 April 1977 after three decades of distinguished service, he replied to a Calcutta-based publisher, O.K. Ghosh, who had approached him saying that 'a bird had whispered in my ears that you are thinking of writing your memoirs':

> I have your letter of April 4. The bird which whispered in your ears that I was thinking of writing my memoirs actually whispered that advice in my ears also. Writing memoirs is a hard thing. And for one who has been so close to men and events, it is difficult to acquire the calm philosophical detachment without which memoirs tend to become egotistical.

Over the next 20 years, many people would urge him to write his life story. But that was not to be. During the penultimate year of his life, on 5 January 1997, Haksar was to confess to one of these persistent persuaders, Sudesh Pai:

> I lack a strong ego to follow in the footsteps of my very dear friend B.K. Nehru. Autobiographies should, in my view, be a reflection of the evolution of one's consciousness rather than deeds of valour.

But thankfully, he has left behind a part autobiography which does precisely what he said should be done in such writings.[3] In a delightful account of his childhood and boyhood, Haksar describes the evolution he went through in the first 16 years of his life, appropriately titling the chapters 'Larvae', 'Pupa' and 'Breaking Out of Cocoon'. To place this evolution in its long historical context, he begins with a description of his family lineage in some detail.

He tells us that he was part of the Kashmiri Brahmin community that had migrated from the Kashmir Valley to the plains of North India in the late-18th and early-19th centuries in the aftermath of the Afghan rule in that region (1753–1819). Some scholars,[4] however, believe that the trigger for such a migration was not just religious persecution but also the desire of an enterprising lot to exploit expanding service opportunities outside the Valley.

Haksar recounts his lineage, tracing his ancestry from his mother's side to Raja Dina Nath, Maharaja Ranjit Singh's finance minister who had signed the Treaty of Amritsar in 1846. This accord had ceded the best part of Punjab to the British and led to the creation of the kingdom of Jammu and Kashmir under Gulab Singh, one of Ranjit Singh's generals. He traces his ancestory on his father's side to Swaroop Narain Haksar who was Dewan of Bundelkhand of the Central India Agency in the middle of the 19th century. His mother's side was largely in undivided Punjab and his father's side mostly in central India, but members of both lines had a presence in Delhi as well.[5]

PNH was born on 4 September 1913 in Gujranwala, now part of Pakistan's Punjab. Gujranwala has produced many notable personalities, the most distinguished of whom must surely be Maharaja Ranjit Singh himself. Unlike two Indian prime ministers—I.K. Gujral and Dr Manmohan Singh, who were also born in what became Pakistan in August 1947—Haksar was never remotely sentimental about the place of his birth. This is perhaps because he never stayed in Gujranwala, having very soon rejoined his father in central India.

PNH's father Jagdish Narain Haksar was in the judicial service and served in a variety of places including Nagpur, Sakoli (which is situated some 100 km northwest of Nagpur) and Katni (an important railway junction about 80 km away from Jabalpur). It was in Nagpur in December 1921 that PNH got his first glimpse of the person with whom his name would come to be inextricably linked decades later. This is what he writes:

> In the evenings when everyone gathered, I heard new words like azadi and swaraj. I heard accounts of how Jawaharlal Nehru, who could have lived like a prince, had sacrificed everything for this *azadi*; and of his father Motilal, descriptions of whom made him appear to me like some sort of fairyland king, abandoning a life of luxury and his anglicized ways for his beliefs. Their names assumed a measure of reality for me when

a little child, perched on the shoulder of a servant, came to our house. My mother lavished attention on this girl and told me that she was the daughter of Kamala, Jawaharlal's wife, and that she held Kamala's mother in great esteem and affection. *I have few other recollections of that child except that her eyes seemed to get bigger and bigger the more my mother fussed over her.* [italics mine]

Haksar has another colourful description of a young Indira Nehru in his autobiography and this relates to 1927 when he was in Delhi visiting relatives along with his mother. He was at the family residence of Indira's maternal grandparents and recalls listening to her grandmother express concern on Kamala Nehru's health. Indira's name would be mentioned often and referring to his mother Haksar writes:

> ... and when the name Indu was mentioned she turned to me and asked whether I remembered seeing that little child who visited us at our home in Nagpur. I did remember, and the name Indu was connected with a memory of a face with large, round eyes.

Two other persons mentioned in Haksar's autobiography are of special interest since they went on to play a crucial role in his later life. One is Rajendra Narain Haksar, his father's younger brother, also known as Inderbhai. He was particularly close to PNH and became famous in July 1975 when he was arrested during the Emergency at the ripe old age of 84 in an action widely regarded as Sanjay Gandhi's revenge on PNH for thwarting his ambitions to emerge as the 'Henry Ford of India'—but more on that later.

The second person was someone who Haksar met in 1929 at his elder sister's wedding in Delhi. He writes about an aunt of his thus:

> She was extraordinarily warm and affectionate towards me and I felt a kind of attachment with her which I easily transferred to her two little daughters, Kamla and Urmila, aged nine and seven respectively. Kamla and Urmila had contrasting characters. Kamla was calm, placid and self-willed. Urmila, on the other hand, was effervescent, with a quality of impishness about her.

In August 1952, a 39-year-old Haksar was to marry that 'impish girl' now a 30-year-old Urmila Sapru. The wedding, held in Bombay in his elder sister's house and fixed at short notice, was very low-key and was to cause quite a furore in the Kashmiri Pandit community since the two were second cousins—Urmila Sapru's maternal grandfather and PNH's paternal grandfather were brothers.

ॐ

There is really nothing in his autobiography that would presage Haksar's ideological positions of the 1930s and early-1940s. That was to come from his Allahabad and London experiences. But his appreciation of the composite culture of India came early at the age of 14. He writes of his visit to Delhi in 1927:

> I recall my first visit to Urdu Bazar and the Jama-i-Masjid ... I liked the assemblage of people, but could not respond to the idea of a single God for I like the Hindu pantheon with its millions of gods. As for my reaction to the Jama-i-Masjid, I stood before it spellbound. The sharpness of my identity as a Hindu, Kashmiri Brahmin, blurred and Imtiaz's message that we are, after all, humans, enabled me to absorb the Jama-i-Masjid and its congregation ...

Haksar's boyhood was comfortable and, by the standards of the day, certainly privileged. He came from a family that had produced men who were pillars of the establishment. But he started formal schooling only when he was 13 years old in Katni, now in the state of Madhya Pradesh. Until then, his father educated him in Urdu, his mother in Hindi and a special tutor in Sanskrit. By the time he was ready to go to college, he was proficient in all three languages with more than passing knowledge of Persian as well. He graduated from a municipal high school in Katni in 1929 with distinction in Sanskrit. That was the year he left for Allahabad for further studies. He writes that originally he wanted to study medicine because he had been impressed by a Dr N.B. Khare who was known to his father in Nagpur and served the community caringly to which PNH was a witness.[6]

Haksar's proficiency in Sanskrit and deep knowledge of its rich literature, which he retained through his long life, had its uses at crucial moments of his professional life. Decades later, C.V. Ranganathan, India's Ambassador to China during 1987–1989 recalled:[7]

> Two days before I arrived in May 1987, Mr. P.N. Haksar came as special envoy of Prime Minister Rajiv Gandhi accompanied by Mr. V.V. Paranjpe. The evening of my arrival we were invited to a fabulous dinner by the late Prof. Wu Xiaoling, a close friend of Mr. V.V. Paranjpe and a great Sanskrit scholar. *During the dinner Mr. Haksar and Prof. Wu Xiaofing recited verses from Kalidasa's Meghdoot in Sanskrit.* Mr. Haksar had by then finished rounds of discussions with then Premier Zhao Ziyang and senior Chinese officials. The message conveyed by Mr. Haksar was that India was prepared to be forward-looking, that India did not consider China to be an adversary and that both countries must make efforts to put the past behind … [italics mine]

Finally, two of Haksar's abiding passions appear to have been developed in his childhood itself. In his later life, he would become famous not just as a civil servant but also for his culinary skills as well as his expertise as a photographer. Apart from other things, his cooking would create close bonds between him and Feroze Gandhi and Indira Nehru in London in the late 1930s. It would also lead him to extol the virtues of cooking to his successor P.N. Dhar, in the prime minister's Secretariat who had later joined the United Nations in New York. PNH was to write to PND, as Dhar was popularly called, on 28 December 1978:

> … I am so glad that you have taken to cooking. I hope you find it wholly absorbing. I discovered its magical qualities long time ago. Without such an integrative process which brings together mind, heart, and body, one tends to fall apart. And, this we should endeavor to avoid if only to survive to have the last laugh.

A year before he passed away, Haksar was to reminisce in his foreword to a coffee table book brought out in 1997 by Indian Airlines to mark the 50th anniversary of India's independence:

... I am rather pleased that this book includes a chapter on "Indian Cuisine". I personally attach as much importance to Indian cuisine as to dance, music, science, technology, etc. Each preparation is a complex interaction between a large number of variables ... There is also the human hand that cooks, the nose which smells, eyes which sees and the palate which tastes. Ultimately a dish emerges with a distinct name and flavour ...

As for his other childhood hobby, on the morning of 18 March 1972, while on a river cruise near Dacca with the prime ministers of India and Bangladesh, he would take stunning photographs of Indira Gandhi. A December 1987 report in a magazine called *Society* reads thus:

Haksar's Steam Boot Scoop

"My main interest has always been human faces, whether masked or unmasked", declared P.N. Haksar (the career diplomat and once a Principal Secretary to Mrs. Gandhi) as he exhibited a collection of 150 pictures from his personal album clicked by him over four decades ... What stood out was the collage of Mrs. Gandhi's various moods he captured as he had caught her unaware. "This was in '72 when I accompanied Mrs. Gandhi to Bangladesh. We were all on a steamboat and it was a chance of a lifetime. In fifty minutes, I took fifteen shots of Mrs. Gandhi with a telephoto lens."

Haksar was to remain in touch with some of his classmates from Katni. One of them, Lakhan Singh Solanki, who had settled down in that town after having been a Congress legislator in Madhya Pradesh, was to write to him on 22 June 1995:

This is probably the last letter of mine as I have passed 86 years and have entered 87th year of my life and now I am physically unsound and unhealthy. Accordingly I have prepared myself to pass away from this world to save my self from troubles ... I take pride that I have such high-grade personality like you who has been my class fellow in Katni and now holds India-level status.

Eight days later, Haksar was to admonish Solanki:

> Recalling the old times when you were saturated with vibrant energy and
> sometimes full of innocent mischief, I cannot imagine that you should
> have allowed yourself to fall into despair. You and I must live out of sheer
> bloody-mindedness ... So I won't let you fall into a state of despondency.
> You must rise and shine.
>
> I was very grief-stricken when I received a letter from the son of our
> friend N. Vaman Rao. I did not know that he had passed away. Perhaps
> you do not know that I have become blind and have lost my eyesight
> way back in 1987. My wife passed away in 1989 but I am not torturing
> myself by self-pity. You and I cannot do that out of sheer sense of pride.

Notes

1. At one time between 1970 and 1972 she had P.N. Haksar, P.N. Dhar, T.N. Kaul, D.P. Dhar and R.N. Kao in her inner-most orbit.
2. This was during the Fifth Sharada Prasad Memorial Lecture delivered in New Delhi on 16 April 2016.
3. Haksar (1989).
4. Pant (1987).
5. There is still a Haksar Haveli in Old Delhi which once belonged to Shiv Narain Haksar whose brother was PNH's paternal grandfather. The Kauls lived next door and asked Shiv Narain for the use of his courtyard for the marriage of their daughter with Jawaharlal Nehru in February 1916.
6. Dr Khare was to go on to become the first prime minister of Central Provinces and Berar in August 1937 as a Congressman but lasted only 11 months. In the early 1950s he became the president of the Hindu Mahasabha.
7. Ranganathan (2002).

II. Radicalization in Allahabad
(1929–1935)

This section covers the next six years of Haksar's life which were spent in Allahabad, two years in an intermediate college and the next four at the famous university in that city. His academic performance was very ordinary. But this was the time when he became politically conscious and was drawn to Communist ideology. He wrote about a part of this period but that manuscript has remained unpublished.

The killing of Chandrashekhar Azad in the-then Alfred Park in Allahabad on 27 February 1931 which Haksar witnessed and that radicalized him.

1918 HAS GONE DOWN IN HISTORY AS THE YEAR IN WHICH WORLD WAR I came to an end. But this was also the year of the Spanish Flu that has been described as being the 'worst epidemiologic disaster' and the most 'devastating pandemic' of modern times.[1] The pandemic swept across the world in two spells and within 12 months had extracted a death toll estimated at between 20 million and 50 million globally. The maximum mortality, recently re-estimated at a little below 14 million, occurred in pre-partition India.[2]

In an unpublished manuscript of these student years in Allahabad Haksar writes that he, along with his mother and siblings, was making one of his periodic visits to his uncles in undivided Punjab in 1918. This time they were in Lyallpur which was soon swept away by the virulent influenza epidemic. He and his sister were badly affected and from the window of the room in which he was kept, he could see hundreds of dead bodies being carried on shoulders. He was being treated, as were many others, by a Dr Kishen Singh who appeared to him to have 'an air of immortality about him', and who went about his job with great poise. This evidently had left a deep impression on a very young Haksar. Much later as recounted in Haksar's autobiography, Dr N.B. Khare was to have a similar impact. Thus, Haksar appears to have dreamt of becoming a physician from an early age primarily because of these two doctors.

He arrived in Allahabad on 8 July 1929 to join the Government Intermediate College. His subjects of study were physics, chemistry and biology. But his dreams of becoming a doctor were dashed on the very first day in college which Haksar recalls as having been on 10 July 1929. He passed by an empty room which was the biology laboratory. What happened next is best described in his own hilarious words:

A surge of curiosity possessed me. Entering that room, I found a large basin of frogs. I looked at these ugly slimy creatures. Some day, I thought, I would have to cope with them … With great exertion of willpower [I] stretched the palms of my hands to catch a frog. My stomach turned. But I persisted. Ultimately I got one frog in my hand. I hastened to lay it upside down on the dissecting table. Somehow, I managed to pin down the creature. Then I applied the scalpel. The frog, collecting all the will to live, let itself loose and fell flat on the floor. Its bulging eyes looked accusingly at me. I could not stand the sight of blood. My stomach turned and I vomited. *The thought that one could not become a physician without dissecting frogs, guinea-pigs and other creatures added to my agony. My dream of becoming a physician was thus shattered.* [italics mine]

Haksar thus decided to give up biology and substitute it by mathematics. He completed the course two years later and graduated with a creditable second division.

∾

As Haksar was about to graduate from intermediate college, three specific events in quick succession were to have a profound impact on his life.

The first was on 1 February 1931 when Mahatma Gandhi addressed a public meeting in Allahabad. Haksar admits he was a bit disappointed by his speech and writes:

[I] was thunderstruck by the response it evoked among thousands upon thousands of people who had assembled to hear him … The people's response to Mahatma Gandhi was in the nature of some supernatural phenomenon and I have still not resolved the question that arose in my mind at that time, namely, whether it signified greatness of the Mahatma or large-heartedness and compassion of our people. Obviously they had faith in Gandhi.

The second event was the funeral of Motilal Nehru in the city five days later. Haksar was outside the patriarch's house when his body was brought out. Katherine Frank, one of Indira Gandhi's well-known biographers who had spoken at length with PNH in the mid-1990s, writes:[3]

He [Haksar] had not seen her [Indira Gandhi] for ten years. She was tall, painfully thin, pale as death. Her eyes were deeply shadowed and even larger than he remembered.

Haksar himself recalls that day as being important as that was the first time he set sight on Jawaharlal Nehru—'a mixture of myth and legend'. He was transfixed and the fixation was to last a lifetime. He also remembers Indira Nehru 'standing in one corner looking utterly forlorn and disheveled'.

The third event—and the most transformative of all—took place on 27 February 1931. This was when Chandrashekhar Azad, the iconic revolutionary, not even 25 years old, was ambushed in Allahabad's Alfred Park by the British authorities. Rather than give himself up, Azad killed himself. Haksar was, by his much later recollection to his daughter, a witness to this colossal tragedy from the window of a nearby house. A few weeks after Azad's martyrdom, three of his fellow revolutionaries, including the iconic 23-year-old Bhagat Singh, were executed by the British in Lahore.

What lay behind this martyrdom? In 1928, the British government set up a commission under the chairmanship of Sir John Simon to report on the political situation in India. The Congress had wanted Indians to be

15

included as members but the Simon Commission was all-British. There were widespread agitations against the Commission when it came to India and, on 30 October 1928, the famed Congress leader Lala Lajpat Rai had led a protest march in Lahore. The police resorted to a lathi charge in which Lajpat Rai was injured. He died of a heart attack 20 days later.

A revolutionary anti-British organization of which Singh and Azad were the leading lights—Hindustan Socialist Republican Association (HSRA)—vowed to avenge Lajpat Rai's death and killed a senior British police official in Lahore on 17 December 1928. Singh and Azad were involved in this killing. Four months later Singh along with his compatriots threw two bombs from the public gallery into the chamber of the Central Legislative Assembly in New Delhi. They were arrested and sentenced to death for the earlier shooting of the police officer.

In his unpublished manuscript, Haksar is reverential towards Gandhi and speaks of the tremendous impact the Mahatma had on him. But in his published autobiography Haksar recalled that his family had not been carried away by Gandhi, and that as an 11- or 12-year-old boy he had listened to one of his grand-uncles lamenting thus:

> Gandhi, a Bania and a vegetarian, could not lead the country. India, he said, had always been conquered by non-vegetarians ... Father seemed to agree. My grand-uncle said that Gandhi's leadership would turn us into goats. This filled me with alarm and I feared that Gandhi practised some sort of magic.

That magic was evidently seen first-hand by Haksar in Allahabad. While he had grown up in an environment where Gandhi's name did not evoke awe, it is clear that by the time he was to turn 18, he had decided to explore Gandhi through his writings. But this exploration also coincided with a growing fascination with Bhagat Singh and Chandra Shekhar Azad as well, because of their heroism and courage. It is conceivable that PNH's attraction for communism began with the death of these two revolutionaries who were only a few years older than him.

Bhagat Singh and Chandra Shekhar Azad were not formally members of the Communist Party of India (CPI) which had been founded in December 1925. But there is little doubt that they were deeply influenced by Marxist ideology. One of Haksar's seniors in Allahabad University was Rajeshwar Dayal, who later became foreign secretary in 1967. In his memoirs,[4] Dayal writes:

> Gandhi's civil disobedience movement largely fell on deaf ears in the University. But what really thrilled the students was the cold courage and self-sacrifice of the revolutionaries, the votaries of violence. The Communists attracted a certain following.

Allahabad University had been started in 1887 and it emerged as one of India's elite institutions. Known at one time as the 'Oxford of the East', it was to be the alma mater of generations of lawyers, scientists, jurists, historians and civil servants. Haksar enrolled for his Bachelor of Science degree there in mid-1931. Muir Hostel used to be the prized abode in the University of Allahabad which admitted only first divisioners. But he applied to it even though he had obtained a second division in intermediate college. He was interviewed by A.N. Jha, the warden of the hostel who was to later become a legend of sorts. Muir Hostel was to be re-named after him. The interview lasted for more than an hour and Haksar recalls Jha asking him whether he was in some way related to Sir Tej Bahadur Sapru and the Nehrus. The recollection continues:

> I said that one of my cousins was the daughter of Kailash Narain Haksar who was married to Sir Tej's son and that another cousin of mine named Rajan was married to one R.K. Nehru. I did not quite understand the purpose of the question. I suppose it was part and parcel of our cultural expression in which community and kinship are considered relevant.

It is hard to avoid the conclusion that Haksar got admitted into Muir Hostel on the strength of his family connections. His academic record thereafter was lacklustre for he ended up getting his undergraduate degree in a third division. In comparison, some of his contemporaries in the university who were to later on become his close colleagues performed much better. It is, however, possible that Haksar's poor result was the outcome of his spending more time learning to be a revolutionary and following in the footsteps of Bhagat Singh and Chandra Shekhar Azad.

Haksar was not deterred by his poor undergraduate performance and continued in Allahabad University. The records of the Ministry of External Affairs and Commonwealth Relations for the year 1947 available in the National Archives reveal that he had a Master of Science (MSc) degree in mathematics. But there is no authoritative evidence supporting the award of that degree in the archives of Allahabad University itself. I cannot resist drawing the conclusion that he may well have enrolled for an MSc in mathematics but no degree was conferred on him.

PNH completed his stay at Allahabad University by mid-1935. His passport, issued at Pachmarhi with number 3896 is dated 7 October 1935 and a duplicate copy is available in the India Office Records in the British Library, London. It is valid till 7 October 1940 and has this description of him:

Height: 5 ft 8 and a half inches
Colour of Eyes: Dark Brown
Colour of Hair: Black when oiled, Brownish when dry

He set sail for the UK in late-1935. Haksar's wife was to say this about his departure in her own memoirs published in 1972:[5]

That autumn, my favourite cousin, to whom I had got very attached, left for the U.K. I did not shed tears but I was extremely sad. All that I had of his comforting presence now were few words, hurriedly scribbled, in Hindi, in my favourite album—"Love truth" or "love truly". It could be interpreted either way, Love the Truth! Be truthful!

Notes

1. Spinney (2016).
2. Chandra (2016).
3. Frank (2002).
4. Dayal (1998).
5. Haksar, Urmila (1972).

III. Student Molotov in London
(1935–1942)

This section covers the next seven years of Haksar's life as a student of anthropology and law, communist worker, and agitator for India's independence under the tutelage of the redoubtable V.K. Krishna Menon. This is the time when his close friendship with Feroze Gandhi and Indira Nehru got established and when he came into contact with many other Indian students who were also deeply influenced by Marxist ideology.

Haksar (hand on chin) at the Third International Conference of World Student Assembly, Paris, August 1939.

It was end-1935 when Haksar moved to London with the financial support of his uncle. His immediate objective was to sit for the coveted Indian Civil Service (ICS) examination. He registered himself at the University College London (UCL). His UCL dossier reveals the following:

> Haksar first entered UCL in October 1936, studying for the Indian Civil Service (ICS) examination. However, he transferred to a Diploma Course in Anthropology in the 1937-38 academic session and from 1938-39, transferred to the MSc course in Anthropology. He also studied at the London School of Economics, and it does not appear on his student record that he was awarded any degree at UCL and therefore did not graduate.

Haksar appeared for the ICS exam in 1936 but did *not* qualify. The records available in the British Library in London show that his marks in the written qualifiers were much below the minimum amongst the persons selected.

A couple of weeks after he had enrolled himself at UCL, Haksar had an encounter which was to completely overturn his life. Like many Indian students in London, he used to frequent a bookshop called 'Bibliofile', which was located close to the British Museum. Speaking at a function in New Delhi four decades later in November 1976 in honour of Feroze Gandhi, PNH recalled Bibliofile and its owner Dr Sashadar Sinha, saying:[1]

> We were attracted as much by the love of books which he could get us at a discount but even more by his massive intelligence and his remarkable insight into the whole ethos of our country's civilization and contemporary strivings of those days. It was in this Bibliofile and through the courtesy of Dr. Sashadar Sinha that I met Feroze [Gandhi] … From that moment of our acquaintanceship we were drawn unto each other. After that friendship he led me to introduce me to another man, namely Krishna Menon of India League …

Haksar was not the only person introduced to Bibliofile by Feroze Gandhi. On 11 April 1981, Indira Gandhi was to write to Sinha's widow:

> I do remember my visits to The Bibliophile quite well, the interesting people one met there and the exciting arguments. I was introduced it to it by Feroze Gandhi whom I later married.

Sashadar Sinha had come to London in the 1920s and had started the bookshop after studying at the London School of Economics (LSE). That Bibliofile was an important meeting point for Indian students in the late-1930s is evident from the fact that Jyoti Basu, the eminent communist leader who was chief minister of West Bengal during 1977–1996 also mentions it in his memoirs. Sinha was to return to India in 1947 and join the Publications Division of the Government of India.[2]

༃

In his recollection of Feroze Gandhi, Haksar does not mention that his friendship with him, perhaps in the final weeks of 1936, led him not just to Krishna Menon but brought the 'big-eyed' Indira Nehru back into his life. The three—Haksar, Feroze Gandhi and Indira Nehru—became close friends drawn together not just by Haksar's cooking and their Allahabad links but, more importantly, by Krishna Menon and the India League and by their common passion—India's freedom from British rule.

Feroze Gandhi and Haksar were to spend time together once again during 1955–1960 when PNH was posted in the Ministry of External Affairs in New Delhi and Feroze Gandhi was a fiery member of Parliament (MP). No records of their interactions in New Delhi have survived, but in 1977 Harish Chandra Heda, one of Feroze Gandhi's close friends and fellow MP in the 1950s recalled[3] that 'Feroze always looked forward to leisurely chats with P.N. Haksar'.

In London, Haksar was becoming not just an ardent associate of Krishna Menon but was also getting very interested in anthropology. He had started taking courses at the London School of Economics (LSE) with Bronislaw Malinowski, a distinguished anthropologist. In December 1937, he was elected, undoubtedly with the support of Malinowski, as a Fellow of the Royal Anthropological Institute. A testimonial given to him by Malinowski, dated 11 June 1938, has survived in the latter's archives at the LSE and reads thus:

> I have great pleasure in stating my very high opinion of the personal character, the intelligence and general ability of Mr. P.N. Haksar, a student of the University of London (University College). Mr. Haksar has been working with me for a full academic session, and I regard him as one of the ablest students in my seminar, which contains young research scholars from many parts of the world. Mr. Haksar has shown great application as well as clarity of mind and ability of expression. He deserves every support in his scientific work. *Given the possibilities for further training, Mr. Haksar will develop into a prominent scientific research worker in Indian Anthropology.* [italics mine]

Raymond Firth, the very first doctorate in social anthropology from the LSE in the early-1940s, was to write almost half a century later to PNH, sending him greetings for 1996 and recalling:

I still remember a seminar paper of yours in which you explained very clearly how sub-castes improve their position by economic means. It was quite illuminating.

Haksar had done field-work in a small cluster of villages of Khandwa in the-then Central Provinces and Berar (in today's Madhya Pradesh). He had concluded that 'despite its apparent rigidities, castes do change and have changed'. But Malinowski's prognostication of his student's future proved wrong. A few months before getting this 'certificate' from his professor, PNH had been admitted as a student to Lincoln's Inn on 28 January 1938. He was later called to the bar on 25 June 1941. However, Malinowski's class had other impacts on his later life.

One of Haksar's classmates was Jomo Kenyatta, who later went on to become the president of Kenya. PNH was to meet him in Nairobi in September 1970 when he found him living like 'King Kenyatta', as he informed Firth in his letter of 4 January 1996. In 1972, New Delhi and Nairobi were both competing to be the location for the proposed United Nations Environment Programme (UNEP). Ultimately, Kenyatta's friendship with Haksar, Haksar's disdain for UN organizations and India's foreign policy objective of not wanting to needlessly antagonize its African allies ensured India withdrew its candidature gracefully.

A second classmate was Fei Hsiao-tung, who went on to become one of China's leading social scientists at the University of Peking. Haksar sent word to him through an Indian social science delegation that went to China in 1982 and Fei landed up in New Delhi the next year for a conference. Haksar and he picked up the threads from where they had left off 45 years earlier in London. This resulted in Haksar making his first visit to China at Fei's invitation in November 1984.

Haksar would talk of Malinowski with respect all through his life. In a farewell function for him in the UK in early-1967 he was to be referred to as someone who had studied with Harold Laski at the LSE. Haksar was to correct it to say that he had not been Laski's student but Malinowski's. Laski, however, had been a mentor of Krishna Menon and so Haksar would definitely have met and interacted with the well-known Labour Party intellectual.

Did Haksar get a formal degree from the LSE? I asked the LSE archivist and her reply was:

> Unfortunately we do not have a surviving student file and his period at the School was too later for him to appear in the published register of early students.

However, Haksar's archives have papers from the LSE showing that he was on the mailing list of alumni. A 'Dear LSE Graduate' letter dated 17 February 1992 from J.M. Ashworth, the then LSE Director, invited Haksar for a 'presentation ceremony for war-time graduates at the Royal Festival Hall on June 23, 1992' and went on to 'invite all alumni who graduated from LSE during war years to a reception at the School after the ceremony'.

Haksar's London sojourn is important not just because of his establishing a warm personal rapport with Feroze Gandhi and Indira Nehru but also because of his growing involvement with the communist movement. He attended and spoke at the Third International Conference of the World Student Association held in Paris during 15–19 August 1939, less than a fortnight before World War II commenced in Europe. At the conclave funded by the USSR through the Communist International (Comintern) and which had some 300 student delegates from 35 countries participating, he presented a detailed report, the cover page of which reads thus:

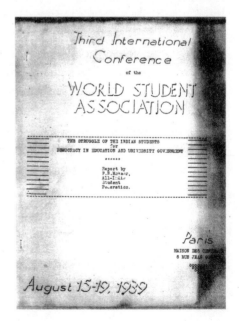

The report resonates well with today's concerns as well. He wrote how the Indian educational system had evolved to suit British colonial interests and lamented the abysmally low levels of literacy in India. He spoke of a charter of students' rights—the right to free education, the right to be provided with qualified teachers, the right to freedom of thought and association, the right to be associated with the internal administration of educational institutions and the right to employment. He ended by declaring that:

> The enemies of students all over the world today are essentially the same … To defeat these forces maximum unity possible must be achieved. The Indian student movement has realized this necessity; both at home and through its members abroad, it strives to establish closer and closer contacts with the student movements in other countries … It is for these movements to demonstrate increasingly their support for the Indian students' demands, for by doing so they will in turn be weakening their own enemies and ensuring their own victory. *Assured of such solidarity, the Indian student movement will throw its entire weight into the struggle against not only the forces of Imperialism in India, but also against the forces of Fascist reaction in the world today.* [italics mine]

Today, the All-India Student Federation (AISF) is affiliated to the CPI but in the late-1930s, its beginnings were different.[4] The AISF was launched at a students' convention held at Lucknow on 12 August 1936. Jawaharlal Nehru inaugurated it and Muhammad Ali Jinnah presided over the function—in itself an unusual combination since by then the Congress and the Muslim League had already become bitter rivals. Initially it was an independent, student-initiated non-political body. But it formally split in December 1940 and it is only after that the AISF came under CPI control which, at that time, definitely meant the influence of the Soviet Union.

Krishna Menon had close links with leading figures of the Communist Party of Great Britain (CPGB), most notably its main theoretician Rajani Palme Dutt. Krishna Menon used the CPGB heavily because it supported the single-point objective of the India League—which was India's complete freedom from British rule. Haksar too moved with CPGB leaders amongst whom James Klugmann was prominent. There is a group photograph of the 1939 World Student Assembly in Paris which shows Klugmann standing next to Pieter Keuneman who later became head of the Sri Lankan Communist Party and Haksar himself.

It was to later come out that Klugmann, who had toured India in 1938, was enmeshed with the Cambridge spy network that had, unknown to others, carried out espionage on behalf of the Soviet Union. His biographer[5] has this to say about Klugmann's activities in the late-1930s:

> ... Klugmann continued agitating on behalf of Indian students' struggle for independence, keeping in contact with Cambridge comrades who organized the Colonial Group there, notably Victor Kiernan and S.M. (Mohan) Kumaramangalam, general secretary of the Federation of Indian Student Societies in Great Britain and Ireland, as well as P.N. Haksar, then at the LSE, who would later go on to be principal secretary to Indira Gandhi.

Klugmann was an indefatigable champion of Indian independence and that is all that mattered to PNH and other Indian students in the UK.

Haksar's intimate circle of Indian friends in the UK consisted of young men and women from privileged backgrounds. Eric Hobsbawm, the distinguished historian, was close to this Indian student network. He was to write in his memoirs almost six decades later:[6]

> Until much later I did not realize how untypical they were of their societies. Those who got to Cambridge, Oxford, and the London School of Economics were the elite of elites of the 'native' colonial population, as soon became evident after decolonization. They were family friends of the Nehrus, like P.N. Haksar of the LSE, who provided cover in Primrose Hill for the courtship of Indira Nehru with Feroze Gandhi and, as civil servant, was the most powerful man in Independent India when I visited him in New Delhi in 1968 ...

As if to confirm Hobsbawm's recollection, on 2 April 1998 some seven months before he passed away, Haksar was to write to Katherine Frank:

> I have read with admiration the way you are tracing the footsteps of Indira. Yes, I was in London from 1935 to 1942. Feroze was there too.

When she arrived in London sometime in January 1941, she and Feroze stayed together in Feroze's flat at 20, Abby Road. I was living very near there in 29, Abercorn Place. We met almost every evening and I cooked for both of them ...

The later half of the 1930s continued to be crisis years for capitalism. The USA was struggling to get out of the Great Depression. The UK economy was in the doldrums. Fascist forces had taken over in Italy and the Nazis were supreme in Germany. In this background, the Soviet Union provided an attractive alternative. It had industrialized impressively in a short span of time. The terrible human cost of Soviet farm collectivization of the early-1930s was not yet in full evidence. Stalin's infamous gulags and mock trials putting to death millions of people in the mid-1930s were yet to be fully known.[7] This was also the period when the Spanish Civil War rallied idealistic youth and, at least, two of Haksar's young English friends—John Cornford and Christopher Caudwell—went to fight for the Republican cause and perished.

The 1930s was also a time when unabashed 'right wingers' of Indian politics of the 1960s, and thereafter, were championing the cause of socialism. The outstanding example of this group of Indians is Minoo Masani, who enjoyed a very warm relationship with both Jawaharlal Nehru and Krishna Menon up to the end of the 1940s but became their bitter critic some years later. Jayaprakash Narayan was another well-known political figure who was Marxist in the 1930s, socialist in the 1940s but later became the leader of a movement in the 1970s that embraced political ideologies he had fought against decades earlier.

The left-wing Indian students who were part of Haksar's world were close to Indira Gandhi as well, the thread binding all of them together being Krishna Menon directly and Jawaharlal Nehru and Subhas Bose indirectly. Two very personal letters from Indira Gandhi to Rajni Patel written in 1939 show the extent of this closeness. For example, on 7 January 1939, she wrote from Almora to Patel in Cambridge:

... As for my health, its is about the same: certainly no worse but not very much better either ... Living up to the expectations which somebody else builds up for one is not at all easy. And what do you mean by 'not get spoilt'? If you mean swollen-headed I can assure you it cannot happen. I know myself too well and my standards are too high for it to happen. I cannot live up to the reputation that Feroze may choose for me, it's probably not the kind of reputation I want and anyway I hate living up to reputations!

Haksar's active communist phase in London coincided with the new policy of Comintern to establish what were called 'popular front' governments all over Europe to fight Hitler, Mussolini and their allies. The heyday of the idea of a popular front was between 1934 and 1939. The historian Kermit McKenzie has described the popular front as:[8]

> An imaginative, flexible programme of strategy and tactics, in which communists were permitted to exploit the symbols of patriotism, to assure their role of defenders of national independence, to check fascism without demanding an end to capitalism as the only remedy, and most important, to enter upon alliances with other parties, on the basis of fronts or on the basis of a government in which communists might participate.

Haksar came of age in London when the popular front idea was at its peak. He remained a 'popular frontist' all his life. He was wedded—as indeed was Indira Gandhi—to this mode of thinking about progressive political alliances. It was this political outlook imbibed in England in the late-1930s that led Haksar to welcome communists into the Congress fold and that encouraged Indira Gandhi to keep them on her side between 1967 and 1977.[9]

What exactly was Haksar doing when he was not studying law after being admitted to the prestigious Lincoln's Inn? A report prepared by the intelligence agencies for the Commonwealth Relations Office in April 1951 that identified 'communists and fellow-travellers and sympathisers' in the Indian High Commission in London may provide a clue. One person identified in the 'fellow travellers category' was Haksar who had joined the High Commission in June 1948. The intelligence report available in the British Library has this to say about him during these years:

Studied in UK 1935-1942. Joined Indian Foreign Service 1948. Held important position in FEDIND [Federation of Indian Societies in UK and Ireland] in 1939 and later became leader of secret group of Indian communist students. One time editor of Fedind magazine "The Indian Student"—Communist in tone. Still well disposed towards Communists and critical of his Govt's attitude towards Communism.

That report also identified Patsy Pillay, Haksar's assistant in the High Commission as a communist sympathizer. This must have been because her husband Vella Pillay was a leading anti-apartheid activist and a member of the South African Communist Party. The Pillays were to remain in close touch with Haksar till his death in 1998.

Haksar was clearly under close surveillance for his activities when he was a student in London. Scotland Yard was to report his presence at a function organized by the India League on 5 September 1941 in memory of Rabindranath Tagore, who had passed away a few months earlier. The report of 17 September 1941 available in the National Archives of India reads thus:

> A public meeting in commemoration of the late Rabindranath TAGORE was held under the auspices of the India League at the Conway Hall, Red Lion Square, W.C. on 5th September.
>
> A great deal of publicity had been given to this function and to the fact that M. MAISKY, the Russian Ambassador , was to be on the platform, with the result that the Conway Hall could not accommodate all the people who desired to attend …
>
> The following Indians were identified among the audience: M.R. ANAND, D.V. TAHMANKAR, S. KABADI, K.S.SHELVANKAR, P.N. HAKSAR …
>
> The usual Indian League literature was on sale …

By August 1982, Haksar had lost his left eye and his vision in the right eye was beginning to get impaired. He spent 10 days in the USSR during December 1983–January 1984 at the Moscow Research Institute of Eye

Surgery. There was some relief and on his return, he was to write on 4 February 1984 to one of his close English friends, John Grigg:

> ... I still have something to argue with you about the true nature and character of the Soviet Union—its achievements and its failures. *The dominant theme of the propaganda against the Soviet Union since the 30s of this century right up to the present has been wrong just as the more ardent admirers have been wrong in looking upon the Soviet Union as some sort of God.* There has to be a saner and a more reasoned understanding of the Soviet Union. Can we agree on this? There has to be a similar approach to China ... [italics mine]

Whatever he may have felt in the 1980s and thereafter, the fact remains that in the late-1930s and very early-1940s Haksar was very much a communist. This was not unusual for a young man then for, as rhyme went:[10]

> Breathes there a man with a soul so dead,
> Who was not, in the Thirties, Red?

When Haksar became powerful in the late-1960s, he went out of his way to find jobs for his 'Red' friends of the London days. Older by eight years, K.S. Shelvankar had worked with Haksar for the India League. He was to become India's consul general in Hanoi in 1969 and ambassador in Moscow in 1971. S.S. Dhavan was also older to Haksar by eight years, had studied law at Cambridge and had come under the influence of Krishna Menon. He was to be appointed India's high commissioner in the UK in 1968 and thereafter the governor of West Bengal the very next year.

Mohan Kumaramangalam first became chairman of Indian Airlines in August 1969 and then minister of steel and mines in March 1971.[11] After a long career with Lever Brothers and Hindustan Lever, K.T. Chandy became chairman of the Food Corporation of India in 1967 and of Hindustan Steel a year later. Himmat Sinh of the princely family of Mansa in Gujarat was an MP during 1972–1978. Barring Dhavan who was a distinguished jurist but quite a disaster as a high commissioner to London and governor of West Bengal—Haksar had to literally demand and secure his resignation from both positions[12]—the others were all able men in their own right and made many contributions. But the fact remains that what got them their governmental positions was Haksar's influence in Indira Gandhi's innermost circle and also the fact that she herself was very well acquainted with them from her own UK stay.

There were, of course, other members of the London cabal who did not join Indira Gandhi's government. A number of them came back and became full-timers in the CPI and were to remain bitter critics of Indira Gandhi, albeit close personal friends of both hers and of Haksar. These included Jyoti Basu, Bhupesh Gupta and Indrajit Gupta who became elected political figures and Parvathi Kumaramangalam and N.K. Krishnan who married each other and became trade unionists. Nikhil Chakravarty returned to India married Renu Roy who became an MP from West Bengal representing the CPI. Snehangshu Acharya became a leading advocate of Calcutta but was intimately connected with the CPI first and the Communist Party of India (Marxist) later. Arun Bose became a well-known Marxist economist and teacher in Delhi University.

There were some who were with Haksar in London in the 1930s and went on to do completely different things far removed from politics. Prominent among them was Mulk Raj Anand, one of India's best known authors. On the occasion of Haksar's 75th birthday in September 1988, he was to write:[13]

> I think P.N. Haksar is 'Student Molotov', the kind of studious man who loves books above other things, as Molotov is said to do.[14] I dare not say this to him. *I told Krishna Menon one day, when he asked me, "Why has Haksar not shown up in the India League office for months?" "Oh!" I said, "he is Student Molotov.* He reads too much and has little time to come and do much of the donkey work of putting addresses on envelopes for your circulars". Krishna Menon, who seldom liked other people's sense of humour said: "Have you told him this?" "No!" I said: "there are some things which can only be said behind people's backs". [italics mine]

Actually, Mulk Raj Anand was being less than fair to Krishna Menon. Over a period of four years, Menon sent Haksar off to different parts of the UK to speak about India to trade unions, students and youth, factory workers and social groups like women's associations, religious organizations like the Quakers and Christian Free Church and political bodies like the Fabians, the Independent Labour Party and the League of Nations Union. The India League, of which Krishna Menon was the pivot for well over two decades, has not got the full due as it deserves. Haksar himself was to point out in a radio broadcast on the night of Krishna Menon's death on 6 October 1974:[15]

> *There is a tendency in our country to be inward-looking and to forget altogether the contribution which India League and Krishna [Menon] made towards the cause of our country's freedom.* We say that this struggle for Indian Independence was fought and won by India. Undoubtedly it was fought and won in India; but Indian Independence was the product of negotiations and not of a revolutionary upheaval. It was a product of negotiations between the British on the one side and Indian nationalism on the other. More specifically, it was a result of negotiations between the British Labour Government and the Indian National Congress. *Krishna's dedicated work through India League prepared the British Labour movement to accept Indian Independence...* [italics mine]

On Haksar's death in November 1998, Mulk Raj Anand was to write a moving obituary to his friend of six decades and recall their association in London of the late 1930s:[16]

> ... In those days, British socialist intellectuals like John Strachey, Harold Laski, Dorothy Woodman and George Orwell were helping publisher Victor Gollancz. In view of the rising menace of Hitler's Fascism, the readers of Victor Gollancz's Left Book Club had formed small clubs in their own areas. We, the Indian students, had formed one too which met in small halls in Bloomsbury. *P.N. Haksar, an intense scholar of political and social literature, often led the discussion in the Indian students' book club* ... Sometimes Feroze Gandhi invited our informal club members to a Sunday lunch, to which Indira Gandhi came when ever she was in London ... Chaudhury Rehmat Ali, who sold pamphlets on Pakistan to students, seemed to us a joke. *But I remember P.N. Haksar saying, "This pamphleteer may be a joke but in Uttar Pradesh the big landlords wanted the rich lands of Punjab and they were backing Jinnah".* [italics mine]

That was an early 'class' analysis of the demand for Pakistan by a young Indian Marxist student who would have much to do with that country three decades later.

Notes

1. Haksar (1976).
2. Shaw (2016).
3. Falk (2017).
4. Rajimwale (2000).
5. Andrews (2016).
6. Hobsbawm (2000).
7. Arthur Koestler's *Darkness at Noon* that laid bare what had happened in the USSR in the 1930s would come out in early-1941 but later in the year Stalin would become an ally of Roosevelt and Churchill in World War II.
8. McKenzie (1964).
9. I owe this insight regarding the influence of the popular front idea on Haksar to Srinath Raghavan.
10. I thank Supriya Guha for drawing my attention to this rhyme which had first appeared in the *New Statesman*.
11. The eminent Marxist historian V.G. Kiernan wrote a long tribute to his classmate Mohan Kumaramangalam in February 1974 which captures the world of Indian students of Haksar's generation in the UK of the late-1930s wonderfully well (Kiernan, 1974).
12. Haksar was to write to Dhavan on 28 May 1971 when he was governor of West Bengal: 'When we last met we had discussed certain important matters. My impression was that you had promised to think things over and write to me. I have, therefore, been hoping to hear from you. In the meantime, the need for the change is becoming a matter of high importance and urgency. I hope you will accept my credentials as a person who has endeavoured to safeguard in varying circumstances your interests. I would, therefore, advise you with utmost sincerity and in all friendliness, that you accept the line of action that I had proposed.' Dhavan resigned promptly.
13. Anand in Sarkar (1989).
14. This was a reference to Vyacheslav Molotov, Stalin's foreign minister.
15. Haksar (1979).
16. Anand (1999).

IV. Communist in Nagpur
(1942–1943)

This section covers the only year of Haksar's life when he was a full-time office-bearer of the Communist Party of India (CPI) on his return to India from London in 1942. He became active in Nagpur, mobilizing textile, electricity and other workers. But by mid-1943 he left for Allahabad and his formal association with the CPI came to an abrupt end.

Haksar with two of his earliest Nagpur-based Communist Party of India comrades of the early-1940s: Dhanraj Acharya (right) and S.K. Sanyal (left), Nagpur, May 1974.

HAKSAR RETURNED FROM LONDON SOMETIME IN EARLY-1942 TO THE area he knew well from his childhood. He had been out of India for almost seven years. He had a valued law degree but he had no regular job to which he had come back. However, he had a mission—to propagate the communist ideology amongst the industrial workers in central India. The Nagpur unit of the CPI had been formed in 1937 with B.N. Mukherjee as its first secretary. Mukherjee, a textile worker, was arrested for taking part in the Quit India movement launched on 9 August 1942 by Mahatma Gandhi—his last frontal challenge to the British. By the time the Quit India movement was launched, the CPI was officially supportive of the war effort, the switch having taken place after Hitler's attack on the Soviet Union in June 1941. This did not, however, prevent many communists like Mukherjee from following Gandhi's call.

Haksar was appointed secretary in Mukherjee's place. Decades later on the occasion of his birth centenary in 2013, PNH's daughter Nandita was to recall:[1]

> When he returned to India in 1942 he was carrying secret messages for the Communist Party of India (probably from Rajani Palme Dutt to P.C. Joshi) sewn into the lining of his rather smart coat tailored by a Savile Row tailor, Mark Risner, a comrade.

After he had been recommended for selection to the Indian Foreign Service in June 1948, a police report on Haksar's character was asked for by the authorities concerned. That report is now available in the National Archives and has this to say about his Nagpur stint:

> According to the records of the Criminal Investigation Department, Special Branch United Provinces, Shri Parameshwar Narain Haksar son of Shri J.N. Haksar Retired Sessions Judge Nagpur, was the leader of a Communist group of Indian Students in 1935 and was in touch with prominent members of the Communist Party in Great Britain. On his return to India in July 1942, a few communist books were found in his possession. In the same year he associated with a communist of Nagpur named P.T. Dalal and became the Secretary of the Nagpur District Communist Party. *He continued his association and correspondence with P.T. Dalal upto 1944 but did not take party in any communist or other political activities ...* [italics mine]

The police report was simply filed and Haksar was to be inducted into the Indian Foreign Service (IFS).

One of Haksar's young aides in Nagpur was an 18-year-old A.B. Bardhan who later on became the general secretary of the CPI in 1996 and remained in that position till 2012. Bardhan and PNH went their separate ways after 1943. It was only on 21 February 1974 that the two re-established contact with each other with Bardhan writing to Haksar thus:

> After many, many years—in fact decades, I am writing this short personal note to you ... The present letter is to introduce a close friend of mine

who happens however to be in the Congress and is a very prominent Sindhi social worker of this region ...

Speaking in November 2006 at a Haksar Memorial Seminar in Chandigarh, Bardhan was to recall:

> ... I deliberately call him Comrade ... because the period during which I knew him and worked under him, he was a member of the Communist Party of India and I worked only as his assistant. So, that has been my relation with Comrade Haksar ... To think that he was only a communist in those days of 1942-43, will be doing him a great injustice ...

Another early recruit of Haksar into the CPI cadre was Dhanraj Acharya, who took over as district secretary of the CPI in Nagpur from him in 1943. Acharya came from a poor family, got imprisoned, educated himself and later on became a prominent entrepreneur in Nagpur. One of his later letters to Haksar was dated 17 November 1973 and reads thus:

> Presently all TV manufacturing is located at Bombay and Delhi where many of the facilities and necessary infrastructure is available. It was really a big challenge to our young engineer to produce a set at a place where the struggle is very hard.
> It is because of your good offices that I could get a licence to manufacture TV set at Na   and as a token of my gratitude for your support, I would like to install my first set at your residence and it would be my great pleasure to receive your comments with a word of encouragement and blessings.

By the late-1960s and early-1970s, Acharya had gravitated towards the Congress party. Ironically, that very first television set installed in Haksar's residence was named after the young man who would cause PNH's estrangement with Indira Gandhi—her younger son Sanjay Gandhi.

Haksar's direct and formal association with the CPI would end by mid-1943. Seven years before he passed away, he was to look back on this brief phase of his life in a long letter he wrote to one of his intimate friends Pauline Baines in London. On 24 September 1991 he was to recall candidly:

… You have asked me to share with you how I feel about the great upheavals taking place not only in the Soviet Union but elsewhere too. So far as the Soviet Union is concerned, all of us had invested our own distinctive feelings for love, compassion, justice, liberty, equality, humanism and a vision of a society which we call socialist or communist. Neither you nor I had ever visited the Soviet Union. My first visit took place as recently as in 1971. So, we read through several lines written by persons whom we believed had first hand knowledge … *I must, however, confess that I felt certain amount of unease at that time which became very pronounced when I returned home and found Indian communists mechanically obeying Comintern dictat without any possibility of civilized debate and discussion. I had to part company.* [italics mine]

Was this the only reason why Haksar left Nagpur suddenly? There may well have been personal reasons for his decision. His father was not keeping well and he may have felt the need to take up a 'respectable' job, not knowing when he would be called upon to support his family. As it turned out, Jagdish Narain Haksar passed away just a year later. PNH would cease to be a member of the CPI from July 1943 onward. But he would remain an unrepentant Marxist throughout his life.

Notes

1. Haksar, Nandita (2013).

V. The Allahabad Advocate
(1943–1947)

This section covers the four years that Haksar practised as a lawyer at the Allahabad High Court. Having abandoned a career in the CPI, he took to law practice seriously and earned a name for himself quickly coming to the notice of Tej Bahadur Sapru first, and through him Jawaharlal Nehru. During this period, Feroze and Indira Gandhi were also in Allahabad. Haksar was to see their first-born Rajiv, only a few weeks after his birth in August 1944.

Eminent lawyer and Haksar's mentor Tej Bahadur Sapru (centre) with Jawaharlal Nehru and Kailash Nath Katju. Beginning of the trial of Indian National Army prisoners, New Delhi, November 1945.

THERE IS A SECOND UNPUBLISHED MANUSCRIPT OF HAKSAR AND IT DEALS with his Allahabad years in the 1940s. It is a delightful account of the people who formed part of his life and of how he established himself in the legal profession.

On 13 July 1943, Haksar arrived in Allahabad from Lucknow. With him was his cousin Urmila Sapru. She had got a master's degree in political science from Lucknow University and was going to teach in a college in Allahabad. In her memoirs, she writes of 1943 when she was preparing for her final examinations:[1]

> … And then like a miracle the cousin turned up from nowhere. This was
> the cousin I had been very fond of when we were in Allahabad [between
> 1929 and 1935]. He had left for England in 1935. We had exchanged

letters at first, gradually they had become fewer and far between and had ultimately stopped. Eight years was a long gap. The memory of him was dimmed by the passage of time but somewhere the embers of that childish fond affection were still lying dormant and had not grown cold. Ten days he stayed. What wonderful ten days they were! He brought a whiff of fresh air with him and tales and adventures of far off lands ... We talked and talked. On many a subject did we talk and each time there was something fresh he had to add ...

Haksar had come to Allahabad to be a junior to one of the city's leading barristers Bidhu Bhushan Malik, popularly known as Malik Saheb. On his arrival in the city, PNH got a telegram from Bombay with a job offer from the British company Lever Brothers at what was then a grand salary of 300 rupees a month. The man responsible for this offer was his old London chum K.T. Chandy. Haksar seriously considered the Chandy offer. He writes:

> I had a notion that, once established in the legal profession, I would be my own master. In Lever Brothers, I would be part of a hierarchy of businessmen, with the top echelons reserved for the Britishers. In my encounters with businessmen I had not felt comfortable in their company. Their conversation, interests, passions seemed to have little in common with my own. Temperamentally I could not imagine myself in a hierarchical system. And yet, a bird in hand certainly was worth two in the bush. But what kind of bird was it? Lever Brothers, selling soaps and vegetable oil products in India, did not attract me.

What appears to have clinched the issue was that Urmila Sapru approved of his declining Chandy's offer. That, as Haksar writes, 'was the end of the matter. I felt anchored'. Within less than a year of becoming Malik's junior, however, Haksar was left to fend for himself since his senior had become a judge of the Allahabad High Court in 1944. But he helped PNH enormously in the transition with the result that Haksar enrolled as an advocate of the High Court of Allahabad on 24 March 1944. He was 31 and finally appeared to be settling down.

The two biggest names of the Allahabad Bar then were Tej Bahadur

Sapru and Kailash Nath Katju—both known well to Haksar's family. Sapru, of course, was the unsurpassed titan. Yet, Haksar started his legal career with Bidhu Bhushan Malik. It would appear that this would have created some disadvantage but he was consoled, he writes, by some remarks made in May–June 1944 by one of Tej Bahadur Sapru's assistants—Inderpal Singh. In Haksar's words:

> One day, I was walking down the corridor of the High Court, on my way to the Bar Library when Inderpal Singh stopped me and said: "If you will permit me, sir, I want to say something to you. I want to say that in my view, you will be a success at the Bar. Your name will shine". I was rather taken aback by this remark. I asked Inderpal Singh, "Inderpal Singhji, what made you reach this conclusion…?" He said: "I shall explain to you very simply. *You are the first Kashmiri gentleman who came to Allahabad to practice law and did not fall for an easy way by becoming a junior to either Sir Tej or Dr. Kailash Nath Katju.* Many fall for this easier way and certainly made some money, but remained juniors all their lives … you did very well in joining Malik Saheb … Already the clerks in Allahabad High Court, whose judgments about lawyers have unerring precision, are talking about you". [italics mine]

Haksar valued this testimonial all his life. Malik went on to become chief justice of the Allahabad High Court in 1948 and vice chancellor of Calcutta University in the 1960s. Haksar, it seemed, had impressed not just him but Sapru and Katju as well. In one matter in the district court in Nagpur, in 1945, he appeared as a junior to Tej Bahadur Sapru. And soon thereafter, he appeared as a junior to Kailash Nath Katju in a different matter in the Lahore High Court where the opposing counsel was none other than Tej Bahadur Sapru himself.

Ages later, on 22 September 1979, when he was in complete retirement, Haksar was to write to Malik:

> … you were my greatest benefactor apart from my own uncle who lent me financial support in the critical years when I began life in Allahabad.

But without your generous, warm-hearted and gracious interest in me, I would not have been anywhere. I never really asked the reason why you judged me to be an appropriate person to be the beneficiary of your generosity ... However, the question that persists in my mind is as to why you thought of bestowing on me all the kindness and gifts. Can you throw some light?

Unfortunately, Malik's reply to his protégé's plea is not available.

A few weeks after India had become free from British rule on 15 August 1947, Haksar received a telegram from S. Ratnam, joint secretary in the Ministry of External Affairs and Commonwealth Relations. It is best to describe this in Haksar's own words contained in a letter he was to write to Ratnam on 25 May 1982:

You would, no doubt, be surprised to receive this letter. However, I have been wanting to write to you or even speak to you about it. Somehow I could not. I do apologise for making a trespass on your time, but if you could help me in some way I shall be extremely grateful.

I have in my possession a telegram. I reproduce an exact copy of it.

INDIAN POSTS AND TELEGRAPH DEPTS.

Office Stamp

Handed in a (office of origin)	Date	Hour	ALLAHABAD 26 SEPT. '47
New Delhi	26	18	

PANDIT PARMESHWAR N. HAKSAR CARE R.N.GURTU, BAR AT LAW HAMILTON ROAD, GEORGETOWN ALLAHABAD.

"PANDIT JAWAHARLAL PROPOSES YOU SHOULD UNDERTAKE WRITING HISTORY OF RECENT COMMUNAL DISTURBANCES. SPECIAL TEMPORARY POST UNDER EXTERNAL AFFAIRS MINISTRY WILL BE CREATED FOR THE PURPOSE. PLEASE TELEGRAPH RATNAM JOINT SECRETARY CARE FOREIGN DELHI NEW DELHI. HOW SOON YOU COULD COME HERE TO DISCUSS TERMS ALTERNATIVELY RING HIM UP AT 2639 OFFICE OR 8845 RESIDENCE= FOREIGN"

As you will see, the telegram was issued by you. Two things have intrigued me about this telegram. Firstly who could have possibly suggested to Pandit Jawaharlal Nehru my name for writing the history of communal disturbances? And secondly, who actually asked you to send the telegram? Was it Sir Girija Shankar Bajpai?

Ratnam was to reply to this voice from his past as it were five days later:

Kindly refer to your letter of the 21st instant. I am at the moment an in-patient at the Ganga Ram Hospital after having undergone surgery for a gland ailment. You can well appreciate why I am unable to think back what happened 35 years ago. I shall telephone you as soon as I get home.

We do not know whether Ratnam actually did get to speak to Haksar subsequently. Who suggested to India's prime minister that Haksar should be asked to join the Ministry of External Affairs and who asked Ratnam to send the telegram to Haksar? Sadly, the mystery will remain. Although there is no clinching evidence, the probability points to Tej Bahadur Sapru since he was to write a testimonial a few months later in support of PNH's induction into the Foreign Service.

Haksar did not exactly jump at the opportunity to join the Government of India because his law practice was taking off. In his letter to Malik of 22 September 1979 from which I have just quoted, Haksar had also written:

I vividly recall the telegram I received from Delhi from Pandit Jawaharlal Nehru asking me to come over to Delhi to write [a] history of communal disturbances. I took it to you. I myself was not inclined to give up law practice at its formative stage and go over to Delhi. You however persuaded me to go and even assured me that for a short while, at any rate, my cases would remain adjourned. I still want to know why you encouraged me to go to Delhi which resulted, ultimately, in changing the entire course of my life.

Alas, Malik's reply to this letter too is not available.

On 13 October 1947, Haksar left Allahabad for good and for a life in public service. He was 34 when he joined the Government of India, albeit on a temporary basis initially for a period of six months. Those six months became 30 years. But Allahabad remained in his blood. On 6 August 1982 with his left eye gone completely and living in complete retirement, Haksar was to write to the registrar of the Allahabad High Court:

> … I request you to restore my enrolment as an Advocate. I want to do this for a variety of reasons, including a sentimental one that I should come back at my age of nearly 69 to where I belonged, namely the legal profession …

Notes

1. Haksar, Urmila (1972).

VI. Life in the Foreign Service
(1947–1965)

This section covers the first 18 years of Haksar's diplomatic career that began in October 1947. He had assignments in New Delhi, London, Geneva, Korea, Nigeria and Austria. Of these 18 years, almost half were spent in London alone, in two stints. While in New Delhi, between 1955 and 1960, he worked closely with Prime Minister Jawaharlal Nehru who was also the country's External Affairs minister. However, there was nothing extraordinary in this period that pointed towards Haksar's future greatness.

UN Security Council meeting on Kashmir, February 1948.
Seated (front row extreme left) is N. Gopalaswami Ayyangar. Sheikh Abdullah is seated
extreme left on the second row (with cap). Seated third from left in the third row is Haksar.

New Delhi (1947–1948)

Haksar joined the Ministry of External Affairs and Commonwealth
Relations on 15 October 1947 as an officer on special duty for an initial
period of six months. The prime minister had recruited him to produce a
report on communal disturbances in India. Very soon, a turf battle ensued
with the Ministry of Home Affairs questioning the appropriateness of the
Ministry of External Affairs and Commonwealth Relations, studying what it
considered to be purely a domestic issue that fell fairly and squarely within
its domain. Within a few weeks of his joining, therefore, Haksar was asked
to shift gears and start preparing briefs on the Jammu and Kashmir issue
which had been referred by India to the UN Security Council on 1 January
1948 for mediation after the Pakistani invasion of the Kashmir Valley.

On 7 January 1948, Jawaharlal Nehru wrote to Home Minister Sardar
Vallabhbhai Patel:[1]

> During your absence the Kashmir situation, more specifically in regard
> to the reference to the U.N.O. had developed and we had to take a

number of decisions. We have missed you here because your advice would have been valuable but we could not afford to postpone our decisions owing to the urgency of the matter. A part of our delegation, including Gopalaswami Ayyangar is leaving Delhi this afternoon ...

Our delegation has progressively grown. Apart from Gopalaswami, Setalvad and Abdullah, there will be Colonel Kaul and Haksar of the External Affairs Ministry ... *Haksar has been dealing with these matters in our Ministry for the last 2-3 months and knows all about them. He is a very capable young man and a competent lawyer who had a rising practice in Allahabad.* [italics mine]

A couple of weeks later, on 28 February 1948, Nehru also informed Lord Mountbatten, India's governor-general, of the delegation to the United Nations, writing:[2]

... The delegation will thus consist of: Gopalaswami Ayyangar, M.C. Setalvad, G.S. Bajpai, M.K. Vellodi, a military officer and a public relations officer (B.L. Sharma). There is another very intelligent and bright young man named Haksar whom we sent with the delegation and is still there.

The session took place at Lake Success, New York and Haksar played an important backroom role drafting the statements of Gopalaswami Ayyangar and M.C. Setalvad defending India's position on the accession of Jammu and Kashmir to India in October 1947. More importantly, he was to get to know one member of the Indian delegation well with whom he would have much to do in the 1970s and early-1980s—Sheikh Mohammed Abdullah.

On his return from New York,[3] Haksar faced a high-powered interview board on 2 June 1948 to consider his induction into the newly established IFS. He had recommendations from Tej Bahadur Sapru and Bidhu Bhushan Malik. The interview board comprised, among others, Girija Shankar Bajpai, the secretary-general of the Ministry of External Affairs and Commonwealth Relations, and W.S. Puranik, chairman of the Federal Public Service Commission,[4] with K.P.S. Menon, the foreign secretary also in attendance. Seven candidates were interviewed and four were rejected. Haksar was the only one recommended for regular diplomatic duties as a member of the IFS. According to the files available in the National Archives, the interview board observed the following on him:

> Board were of the opinion that he was of average ability but had capacity for hard work.

It was certainly not a ringing endorsement of his candidature but nevertheless, Haksar was recommended for induction which was to formally take place on 15 January 1949. Incidentally, Khushwant Singh, the noted Indian author and journalist, writes in his autobiography that Haksar was interviewed in London for induction into the IFS by a committee headed by Harold Laski.[5] Singh was clearly mistaken.

PNH would be the second Haksar to join the IFS. His father's cousin S.N. Haksar, senior to him in the hierarchy, had come into the IFS via the ICS. They were poles apart in temperament and ideology but were extremely close otherwise.[6] A decade later, a third Haksar—A.N.D.—would join the IFS. When PNH was at the peak of his power during 1967–1973 he would get many letters from all and sundry claiming to be his classmates in school or college and he would reply patiently to each of them saying that he was 'P.N.' Haksar and not 'S.N.' or 'A.N.D.' Haksar and that he was not their classmate. To make matters more complex, he had another second cousin, also called P.N. Haksar [Prakash Narain]. PNH would get similar letters from people claiming to be classmates of his and he would, without being irritated, write back that perhaps they had mistaken him for the other P.N. who lived in Calcutta. As an example, PNH was to write to one Asaf Ali Baig of Hyderabad on 6 January 1970:

> Your letter addressed to Prakash Narain Haksar has been received by me. I have been trying to remember if we have ever met. Unless my memory fails me completely, I do not recall the pleasure of making your acquaintance. This led me to conclude that you are probably thinking that I am, in fact, Prakash Narain Haksar, which I am not. Prakash Bhai was my cousin—indeed a favourite and most lovable cousin. However, he suddenly died a few months ago in Allahabad. He had settled down in Calcutta and was married to the daughter of the late Dr. K.N. Katju. However, since you are a friend of Prakash Bhai, I would be delighted to meet you when you come to New Delhi.

Ten months later, when he would be mistaken for another Haksar, PNH was to write to one J.N. Chatterjee of Hooghly on 10 November 1970:

> I have received your letter. Quite clearly this is case of mistaken identity as I was never in Djakarta and have, in fact, never visited Indonesia. You may have probably met a very young officer of the Foreign Service, Shri A.N.D. Haksar who was, if I recall correctly, a First Secretary in Djakarta. Be that as it may, I shall be glad to be of any assistance if I can. However, it is by no means clear from your letter what precisely you wish me to do and what actually is your background and experience and your present employment.

Meanwhile, with his assignment on Kashmir having wound down for the present, Girija Shankar Bajpai decided, sometime in May 1948, to post Haksar to South Africa. However, as he was coming out of Bajpai's room after getting that news, he ran into Krishna Menon who had just been appointed as India's high commissioner in the UK. In Haksar's later recollection:[7]

> ... [Menon] informed me that I was to go to London. "I have spoken to Panditji. We shall work there together". Thus it was that I found myself in our High Commission in London.

The memory of having had Haksar work with him at the India League in the late-1930s must have still been fresh in Krishna Menon's mind. Bajpai had told Haksar[8] that after having joined the IFS 'one luxury you can no longer enjoy is to choose your boss; you serve whoever he is'. Haksar was to be that rare individual who the bosses would seek out—first Krishna Menon and years later, Indira Gandhi.

London, Geneva, New York, New Delhi (1948–1952)

So off to London Haksar went. His job was to send periodic reports on the political situation in the UK to the Ministry of External Affairs and Commonwealth Relations and speak to British audiences on what was happening in a newly independent India. But his services were sought elsewhere as well. The most notable example of this was the Diplomatic Conference convened by the Swiss Federal Council at Geneva in August 1949 for the establishment of international conventions for the protection of war victims. Four such conventions were negotiated and finalized. These are known as the (i) Geneva Convention for the Amelioration of the Condition of the Wounded and Sick in Armed Forces in the Field, 1949; (ii) Geneva Convention for the Amelioration of the Condition of Wounded, Sick and Shipwrecked Members of Armed Forces at Sea, 1949; (iii) Geneva Convention relative to the Treatment of Prisoners of War, 1949; and (iv) Geneva Convention for the Protection of Civilian Persons in Time of War, 1949.

Haksar was part of a four-member Indian delegation to the Diplomatic Conference. He was virtually the voice of the delegation and played a key role in drafting the report that led to the fourth of the conventions. His services were lauded explicitly and became part of the official record. But I wonder what he would have made of the fact that his contributions were to be used 56 years later by the US Deputy Assistant Attorney General Howard C. Nielson Jr, in a memorandum prepared on the subject of 'Whether Persons Captured and Detained in Afghanistan are "Protected Persons" under the Fourth Geneva Convention'. In an elaborate 29-page memorandum, Nielsen drew from the records of the Diplomatic Convention and on Haksar's interventions at the 1949 Conference to conclude that:[9]

> ... the provisions of the Fourth Geneva Convention relating to "protected persons" do not apply to persons captured and detained [by the U.S.] in Afghanistan.

In early-1952, Haksar was once again asked by Nehru to join the Indian delegation to the United Nations. The Sixth Session of the General Assembly was meeting in Paris and his performance was notable enough for two commendatory references he received in letters sent to the prime minister. The first was from India's ambassador to France, H.S. Malik, who wrote to Nehru on 9 February 1952:

His services as Adviser were of very great value to the Delegation. A keen student of European affairs; he has at the same time a flair for keeping himself well informed by personal contacts and was most useful for lobbying. Towards the end of the session he also participated in the work of the Ad Hoc Committee over the Arab Refugee question when R.K. Nehru was away.

The second was from B.N. Rau, who was then India's permanent representative to the United Nations. Earlier, he had been the principal author of the first draft of the Indian Constitution in 1946. Rau wrote to Nehru on 26 February 1952 that Haksar was:

Another of our promising young men. Chiefly assisted or representative in the "Ad Hoc" Committee but capable of any work assigned to him. Hard working and extremely competent.

But these accolades were small compensation for the frustration that had begun to overtake Haksar. Of the 132 officers in the IFS in mid-1951, he was 55th in seniority. He was 38 years old then with another 20 years of service left. He found promotional avenues being blocked for middle-aged 'lateral entrants' like him. People of his vintage belonging to the ICS had moved ahead faster than him in the administrative hierarchy. So by mid-1952 he had decided to resign from the IFS and return to law practice. This was to lead to an unusual exchange between the prime minister and two of his colleagues concerning Haksar.

It all started with Girija Shankar Bajpai, who had by then moved as governor of Bombay, writing to Nehru on 8 June 1952:

... Haksar who returned from England yesterday, came for a chat ... [He] is thinking of returning to private life ... My own view is that there are not very many such men in the Service, and that if they are given responsibility and reasonable emoluments, they will be satisfied ... I do not wish to be regarded as meddling in affairs which no longer concern me but thought it my duty to let you have my personal impression regarding Haksar, who I think is one of our most promising men ...

Two days later, Nehru sent Bajpai's letter to K.P.S. Menon, the foreign secretary saying:

I enclose a letter from Shri Girija Shankar Bajpai. I entirely agree with him about Haksar ...

Girija Shankar Bajpai had chaired the interview board in June 1948 recommending Haksar to the IFS with the somewhat scathing observation that he was of 'average ability'. Evidently, that opinion had changed dramatically for Bajpai was to write a second time to the prime minister on 25 June 1952, asking him to persuade Haksar to withdraw his resignation and resume his political and diplomatic work in London with the newly appointed high commissioner, B.G. Kher:

... As Haksar has only recently returned, I recognize that he may find it inconvenient, if not impossible, to go back at once. I have little doubt, however, that if he were told that his status and emoluments will both be enhanced and that he was urgently needed in London to assist Kher, his response would be both prompt and favourable ...

Nehru followed Bajpai's advice. He succeeded in his mission and wrote to B.G. Kher on 3 July 1952:[10]

... I had a talk with P.N. Haksar. I have induced him to remain in service and to go back to London at least for some time now. I believe he is going to get married soon. He said he would be able to return about the end of this month. I think that he was very unfairly treated in his grading. We propose to rectify this and to give him the status of a Counsellor ...

Having promised Haksar that the injustice done to him would be rectified, Nehru then took up the matter with the finance minister, C.D. Deshmukh on 5 July 1952:[11]

In a few days time B.G. Kher will take charge in London. He is doing so at a somewhat critical time from the point of view of political talks that have been going on over the very delicate issue of the Korean cease-fire ... Unfortunately the one really competent political adviser we had in London has also come away. This is P.N. Haksar. He is at present on leave in India. He really came away with the intention to retire from the Foreign Service because he had long been feeling that he has had a raw deal. He was one of the rising young barristers in Allahabad when I inducted him, just four years ago, to join the newly started Foreign Service ...

I sent for him a few days ago and have succeeded in inducing him
to remain in this Service and to go back to London as soon as he can.
We have to give him a more responsible position, that of a Political
Counsellor. I hope you agree ...

The finance minister did not take long to reply, writing to the prime
minister six days later and agreeing to the suggestion that Haksar's post
in London needed to be upgraded. Thanks to Bajpai's plea, Nehru's
intervention and Deshmukh's approval, PNH relented. He got married in
August 1952 and returned to London. That he was virtually running the
show in the High Commission on his return is revealed by a letter Indira
Gandhi wrote to Nehru on 17 May 1953 while she was staying with the
high commissioner:[12]

> ... I'm terribly disappointed with Kher Sahib. He is so easily taken in,
> so hedged in with prejudices ... He isn't really interested in politics or
> foreign affairs. He seems quite unaware of currents and cross-currents.
> Somebody—not Haksar—told me that Haksar has to write out the
> simplest things for him.

Not surprisingly when Nehru called all heads of Indian missions in Western
Europe and USA for a four-day conclave in Burgenstock in Switzerland in
September 1953, Haksar was the only non-head of mission present. The
conference had a packed agenda that covered a survey of the world situation,
NATO, European Defence Community, India's relations with individual
countries and specific issues like German Unity, Franco-German relations,
Austrian Treaty, Trieste and American influence in Europe. Haksar was also
asked to prepare the report of the conference and suggestions for follow-up
which he did with his customary meticulousness.

It was at Burgenstock that Charlie Chaplin came to meet Nehru, and
Haksar was to recall this visit seven months before his death, in a letter to
Katherine Frank on 2 April 1998:

> On the last day of the Conference, Charlie Chaplin came to see Nehru.
> It was late in the evening. As he was coming up the steps, I even took a
> photograph of him ... As far as I recall, Charlie Chaplin met Nehru and
> Indira. No one else was present. From casual remarks made by Indira,

I learnt that Charlie Chaplin was full of admiration for Nehru's foreign policy. He also apparently told him the compulsions which led him to migrate from the USA. I have vivid images of various films of Chaplin, e.g. Gold Rush, Modern Times, The Great Dictator, The Circus, etc. etc.

Korea (1953–1954)

1953 was the high point for Indian diplomacy on the world stage. Krishna Menon's indefatigable efforts had resulted in an armistice being declared in the three-year war that had been raging between North Korea supported by the USSR and China on the one side and South Korea supported by the USA, UK and other Western powers on the other. India's role in ending the hostilities has never got the recognition that it deserves and it is only in recent years that some scholars have begun to acknowledge it sufficiently.[13]

One of the follow-up actions to the armistice by the United Nations was the establishment of a Neutral Nations Repatriation Commission (NNRC) which was to decide on the fate of over 20,000 prisoners of war from both sides. India was chosen as the chairman of the NNRC, with Poland and Czechoslovakia representing the communist bloc and Sweden and Switzerland representing the Western world. There was to be a United Nations Command led by an Englishman and a Custodian Force sent by India. Nehru selected Lt General K.S. Thimayya as the chairman of the NNRC and Major General S.S.P. Thorat as the commander of the Custodian Force India (CFI) as it was to be called. Haksar was selected by Nehru as one of the two political advisers in Thimayya's team. Very soon he became the only one since the other person, I.J. Bahadur Singh, had to be repatriated from Korea quickly on health grounds.

Thimayyya became a hero at the end of the NNRC's tenure in February 1954. He was feted—and rightly so—both at home and abroad for having executed a most thankless task courageously. But while in Panmunjom in the Korean Demilitarised Zone for almost six months, Thimayya and Haksar had developed serious differences. It was both a clash of style and substance. Thimayya was a military man through and through while Haksar had more sensitive political antennae. He felt that Thimayya was being excessively solicitous of the Americans and, by extension, of the UN Command. Eric Gonsalves, who was in Thimayya's team as a young Foreign Service officer of three years standing, recalled to me that the differences between Thimayya and PNH stemmed from their backgrounds with 'Haksar being a left-leaning intellectual with the usual LSE background and Thimayya ... a Sandhurst professional ... The main point was India's relationship with China.'[14]

Sometime in February, 1954, Haksar submitted his report on the functioning of the NNRC to Nehru. The report showed that Thimayya was inclined, more often than not, to support the Swedes and the Swiss on the NNRC even when Haksar felt that the Czechs and the Poles had a reasonable request or point to make. He recorded that 'Major General Thorat, and to a certain extent, Lt General Thimayya, always tried to create the impression that they were reasonable people and saw the U.N. point of view but that their political advisers [mainly Haksar] and the Government of India had left them with no alternative except to take up anti-UN attitude'. He added that:

> The Chairman [Thimayya] was particularly inclined to take the U.N. press into his confidence and was in the habit of issuing statements somewhat recklessly which had later to be denied. In point of fact, the number of denials we had to issue constituted a record ... On one occasion the Chairman had arranged to a network of coast to coast broadcast in the United States on the subject of American POWs. By accident, I came to know about it and I had to persuade him not to lend himself to U.N. propaganda. While he agreed to cancel the broadcast he told the press in my presence that he could not broadcast on account of the advice given to him by his Political Advisers.

That the differences between Thimayya and Haksar were not insignificant is shown by this observation made by R.K. Nehru, then foreign secretary (FS), in Haksar's personal file on 28 October 1954:

> I do not think it is necessary to communicate Thimayya's remarks to Haksar. A note, however, might be made to the effect that conditions of work in Korea produced some friction between the officers and I as FS

do not accept the adverse remarks of Thimayya—although I realise that they were made in good faith. I was directly responsible for the Korea operations and I know all about the relations between the officers.

The Commission's reports were all drafted entirely by Haksar and submitted to the UN General Assembly, one in December 1953 and another in February 1954. The Swedes and the Swiss wrote their dissent to certain paragraphs in both reports showing how intensely polarized the NNRC was. At the end of its work, the NNRC was left with 88 prisoners of war who resisted being handed over and expressed a desire to go to neutral countries. On humanitarian considerations, Nehru decided to bring them to India pending a final decision by the United Nations on where they would go. Most left immediately for other countries in Central and South America. Four or five settled down in India and Nehru's government gave them loans to start poultry businesses.[15]

Four years before his death, Haksar would be reminded of his role in Korea by one Colonel Bhupinder Singh to whom he was to write on 24 March 1994:

> I have your letter of March 19. I must confess that I am intrigued by your invitation to me to join the members of the Indo-Korean War Veterans in welcoming the new Ambassador from South Korea … It is of course true that I spent some few months of my life in Panmunjom in my capacity as Alternate Chairman of the Neutral Nations Repatriation Commission of which General Thimayya was the Chairman and General Thorat was the Commander of the Custodian Forces of India. Our task to ascertain the wishes of the several thousands of prisoners of war which the UN Command had handed over to us. A small number of Korean prisoners opted to come to India. I had the privilege of preparing the report on the entire operation which was submitted to the UN. *Be that as it may, I find it awkward to be classified as a Korean War Veteran* … [italics mine]

London (1954–1955)

PNH returned to London from Korea sometime in March–April 1954. This gave him an opportunity of serving under a third high commissioner in five years. This time it was Vijaya Lakshmi Pandit, Nehru's sister. It was the beginning of a warm personal relationship. On 29 March 1955, she wrote to Subimal Dutt, commonwealth secretary in the Ministry of External Affairs and Commonwealth Relations:

... The second matter I wish to mention is the case of Haksar. He is feeling very unsettled and rightly desirous of knowing what his future is to be. I think he would like a change. So far as I am concerned, I find in Haksar a very fine officer. But he has been here a long time and is feeling stale. It is proper that he should have a change ...

Soon thereafter there was indeed to be a change. Haksar was headed back to India after seven years in London. When the time came for him to finally leave London, 'Atticus' wrote about him in the *Sunday Times* on 14 August 1955:

A Regretted Eminence

With the return to New Delhi this week of Mr. Parameshwar Narain Haksar, London's diplomatic and Commonwealth community loses one of its best-liked and admired members. Mr. Haksar, a shrewd and jovial lawyer-turned diplomat, has been at India House as the High Commission's Counsellor on external affairs for eight years.

He has worked with all three High Commissioners—Mr. Krishna Menon, Mr. B. Kher and Mrs. Pandit—and has acquired something of a reputation of an *eminence grise* among his colleagues, though in fact his qualities of warm-heartedness, simplicity and frankness are far removed from anything so sinister.

His new job in Delhi is of a kind that few professional diplomatists like ... But his wide circle of English friends here—and especially in the Foreign Office and the Commonwealth Relations Office—would warmly endorse Mr. Nehru's choice. A first-class senior spokesman in Delhi is becoming indispensable.

This was a handsome tribute to Haksar published in the pillar of the British establishment, the very same establishment that had kept him under surveillance and had painted him as a communist or a fellow-traveller.

Some years after Haksar's death, the noted economist Ashok Mitra was to write,[16] that PNH and the Labour party leader Nye Bevan had been close friends. Bevan is widely recognized to be the chief architect of the UK's much-acclaimed National Health Service and was one of the key players in the wave of nationalizations that took place under Attlee's government during 1946–1950. Haksar had sent three long dispatches from London to New Delhi in 1951 and 1952 on Bevan and his impact on British politics and public thinking. It is clear from these reports that he was a great admirer of Bevan, his way of thinking and his accomplishments. Communism may have attracted Haksar in the late-1930s but in the 1950s he was in thrall of Bevanism. It appealed to him because he saw in it a 'third way' between the inequities inherent in US-style capitalism and the loss of democracy inherent in Soviet-style communism. Bevan was also one of the very few front-line British politicians to consistently demand India's freedom from the 1930s onward.

Haksar's close British friends with whom he would keep in touch over the years included Kingsley Martin, the legendary editor of the left-wing *New Statesman*, John Grigg, a liberal Tory at that time and later to become a well-known media figure, Arthur Gavshon, Roger Toulmin, George Biliankin, Denis Hamilton and Nicholas Carroll, all eminent journalists, Harry and Pauline Baines, a noted artist couple and the social anthropologist Raymond Firth, among a whole host of others. Of Kingsley Martin, PNH was to later recall:

> Kingsley Martin, who was friendly and normally rational, died with a firm belief that Nehru's ethnic origin was the cause of the trouble in Kashmir. I endeavoured to counter this piece of Martinian superstition by facetiously suggesting that on his reasoning the hastening of the liquidation of the British Empire by Lord Mountbatten could be perhaps explained by his Battenberg ancestry and was thus a subconscious and a genetically induced revenge of Germany's defeats in the two world wars ... He accused me of being naughty. But he clung to his own superstition reminding me of the wisdom of the remark that other people's superstitions are facts to be reckoned with.

New Delhi (1955–1960)

In October 1955, Haksar joined the Ministry of External Affairs and Commonwealth Relations in New Delhi. He had been asked by Nehru to organize an external publicity division which would, among other things, keep Indian missions abroad informed of developments back home. One mini-crisis was to develop very soon after US Secretary of State John Foster Dulles issued a joint statement with Paulo Cunha, the foreign minister of Portugal—a NATO ally—on 2 December 1955, making a reference to 'Portugese provinces in the Far East' which India took to mean an implicit acceptance that Goa was an integral part of Portugal. Nehru was livid and spoke at a rally of Goans in Bombay on 4 June 1956 where he criticized Dulles by name for his policy on Goa.

Dulles had taken umbrage at this speech of Nehru's and complained to the Indian ambassador in the USA, G.L. Mehta, that a press release issued by the Indian Embassy had contained a critical reference to him. Mehta then suggested to New Delhi that the 'Embassy should be allowed to exercise its discretion in the presentation of publicity material that is sent from India'. Haksar, in a note sent to the prime minister through the foreign secretary Subimal Dutt on 18 August 1956, disagreed with this approach and said that 'it would be better not to publish any material that the Embassy thought would cause any embarrassment to it rather than censor or modify it'. Dutt agreed with this view as did Nehru who responded to Dutt six days later:[17]

> I agree with you. It is rare that I indulge in personal criticisms. But when I referred to what Mr. Dulles said about Goa, it was not a personal criticism but the obvious reaction to an important public statement.

Dealing with the visits of foreign correspondents to Kashmir had become a big headache for Nehru's government. In mid-March 1957, Haksar submitted a note to the prime minister that foreign correspondents had complained to him about delays and uncertainties regarding permits for them to visit Kashmir. He took up the case of A.M. Rosenthal who much later was to become the editor of the *New York Times*. Haksar told Nehru that 'Rosenthal did not fall into the "malicious" category' and felt that 'it would not be a pretty situation to contemplate if Rosenthal were to write a dispatch in the *New York Times* about the refusal of the Government of India or of the Jammu and Kashmir Government to let him go to Kashmir'.

Nehru replied to Haksar on 25 March 1957 saying:[18]

> ... We realize the difficulties of the Jammu and Kashmir Government in this matter and some foreign correspondents have undoubtedly behaved badly and even maliciously. Yet to refuse foreign correspondents generally is bad. I would unhesitatingly refuse permit in policy to the *Daily Telegraph* and *Daily Express* correspondents—possibly also *Daily Mail*. I am prepared to say publicly ... But such exceptions apart, I would not come in the way of foreign correspondents going to Kashmir even though their going there during election times is a nuisance.
>
> So far as Rosenthal of the *New York Times* is concerned, we think he should be allowed to go to Jammu and Kashmir. Home Minister agrees.

Pather Panchali was a Bengali film made by Satyajit Ray in 1954 based on a novel of the same name by Bibhutibhushan Bandyopadhyay. It was to soon become a classic and win for Ray critical acclaim both in India and abroad. But it had to face a lot of criticism as well, on the grounds that showed grinding poverty and portrayed India in poor light. It was perhaps fine for domestic audiences but the bone of contention was whether it should be the official entry at the Cannes Film Festival in 1956.

Just about two months before he passed away, Haksar was to receive a letter dated 9 September 1998 from Andrew Robinson, the well-known British author:

> I am Ray's Biographer (The Inner Eye) currently working on a second book on Ray. I attach a leaflet for your information.
>
> I am aware of your important role in having Pather Panchali sent to the Cannes Film Festival in 1956 which I would like to mention in the new book. But I have been unable to obtain a copy of your memoirs in which you describe your conversation with Jawaharlal Nehru about the film. Would you be kind enough to send me a photocopy of the relevant pages and any other material you may have published on this episode?

By then, Haksar was very sick and it is no surprise that the letter did not elicit a response. But fortunately his role in this episode has been recorded by Bidyut Sarkar who was a frequent visitor to Haksar's house till the very end. Sarkar writes:[19]

> P.N. Haksar then director of external publicity in the Foreign Ministry first viewed Pather Panchali as a private person. "I saw it with my wife. We were deeply moved by its aesthetic quality, lyricism and sheer beauty ... I did not think in terms of poverty," he recalled years later. His childhood had also been a bit rural. When he was Apu's age, as in the film, he lived in a village Sakoli in central India ...
>
> "In the stillness of rural life, any movement, even if it is of wind, the gentle rain falling on a leaf, or dragonflies dancing over the waters, one is sensitive to it. These were all scenes and sounds I identified with my own past experience", he explained.
>
> ... He met the Secretary of the Ministry of Information and Broadcasting which had put it in the list of films disapproved for showing abroad as it showed India's poverty ... [Haksar] happened to see a few days later Jawaharlal Nehru who was his own Foreign Minister and broached the matter.

This was not all. Nehru then wrote to B.V. Keskar, minister for Information and Broadcasting on 25 May 1956:[20]

> ... It [Pather Panchali] is a first class film and we should give full publicity to it. I gather there is some hesitation about this as it shows Indian poverty. We are a poor country and we should not be ashamed of it, except that we should get rid of poverty.
>
> I hope that your Ministry will help in giving full publicity to this film. I gather External Affairs Ministry are buying some copies from the West Bengal Government.

ॐ

In March 1958, Haksar was appointed to a six-member committee set up to revamp the public information system of the United Nations. Also on this committee were members from Egypt, Uruguay, UK, USA and USSR. The committee submitted its report, the principal author of which was

Haksar, in late-August 1958. But there was to be a furore soon thereafter, with correspondents covering the UN alleging that the report legitimized propaganda by member countries under the garb of the UN.

It was left to other members of the group like the Britisher R.A. Bevan to defend the report in the media. Haksar himself kept quiet but was to write to him on 26 December 1959:

> I was rather amused by the Secretary-General's [Secretary-General of the United Nations] initial reaction to the report. The word amused should be interpreted in the truly Anglo-Saxon sense of being an under-statement, for to be quite frank with you, I was livid with anger. But then, as you know I was never an admirer of the Secretary General and his ways but I am glad to find that with the passage of time, the Secretary General has found wisdom in our report. After all knowledge comes but wisdom lingers.

Haksar was to come on to the Board of Directors of the Press Trust of India (PTI) in 1984. Sometime in the early-90s there was a discussion in the Board on demands being made by foreign news agencies to have the freedom to distribute news to Indian outlets without having to go through Indian-owned news agencies like the PTI. It then transpired that the extant policy which was being sought to be overturned was actually Haksar's legacy from his days managing the external publicity of the Ministry of External Affairs. On paper, that policy continues till today, although since 1998 its spirit has been violated giving PTI and Indian agencies no role in regulating content being distributed, as envisioned by Haksar.

The years 1958 to 1960 saw Haksar's promotion as joint secretary in the Ministry of External Affairs dealing with administration. He was the first IFS officer to hold this post which dealt mostly with personnel matters. Subimal Dutt, India's longest-serving foreign secretary between 1954 and 1961 reminisced thus of the late-1950s:[21]

> The Foreign Office did not have full information about the requirements of the various missions abroad. Rules about postings, allowances, etc., had not yet been standardized and there were complaints from many heads of missions and others concerned about their pay, allowances and housing ...

It was therefore decided to have a separate division under a senior officer for dealing solely with administrative problems concerning the Foreign Service personnel. Haksar was considered the most suitable person for this important job. He was patient, sympathetic and objective in dealing with matters concerning postings and promotions ... As Foreign Secretary, I could rely on the advice of a person who had no special favourites ...

As the prime minister's top aide between 1967 and 1973, Haksar would adopt a similar working style.

∾

Nigeria (1960–1964)

On 15 June 1960 Haksar received a personal letter from Subimal Dutt:

I am glad to inform you that the President has selected you to be our first High Commissioner in Nigeria. As you know, we attach considerable importance to our representation in Nigeria and are most anxious that you should assume charge immediately the new independent Nigeria comes into being ...

Allow me to congratulate you on your selection for such an important assignment.

By no stretch of imagination would Nigeria be called a 'glamourous' posting, even more so for someone who had worked directly with Nehru for well over a decade. In fact, five years later when he was posted as deputy high commissioner in London, Haksar confided in a young colleague, Salman Haidar—later to be India's foreign secretary—that while he received congratulations for his London assignment, it had been only commiserations for his Nigeria posting. But Nehru was clear that Africa's largest country deserved somebody of Haksar's calibre.

In fact, there was an earlier incident which may explain Haksar's posting to Lagos. This had taken place on 6 August 1955 when Nehru was inaugurating the African Studies Programme at Delhi University. In his welcome speech, Vice Chancellor G.S. Mahajani had said that when he was asked 'Why study Africa?' his simple answer was because it is there. Nehru was not amused and responded:[22]

It is obviously necessary and desirable for people in India to study Africa, not merely, as the Vice Chancellor said, because it is there, yes as our neighbour. But you ignore the study of Africa at your peril. Let this be understood. It is not a theoretical proposition. It is not an academic matter for you to consider what Africa is. It is of the most urgent importance for us to understand Africa—to understand the rest of the world too, but certainly Africa and her problems and her people more particularly.

With Nigeria's independence in 1960, Nehru clearly put these ideas of his into operation by designating Haksar as India's very first envoy there. Soon after he had taken charge in Lagos on 25 September 1960, there was a demand from Krishna Menon—then defence minister and leader of the Indian Delegation to the U.N. General Assembly of 1960—that Haksar be deputed to Congo which was then in the midst of conflict. Like in 1953 in the case of the Korean War, India was much sought after in the UN for playing an active role in restoring peace in Congo. Nehru turned down Krishna Menon's request on 5 November 1960. His telegram reads:[23]

> ... I am rather doubtful about advisability of sending Mission to Congo soon ... Haksar is good but it would not be right to pull him out of Nigeria at present. This is [an] important post which should not be left vacant.

Developing a warm relationship with Nigerian leaders including Prime Minister Sir Abubakar Tafawa Balewa, Haksar was to stay in Nigeria for four years, establishing a close bilateral partnership in education, industry and railways. Indian experts were brought into Nigeria in various areas but more importantly avenues for Nigerian students to be educated in India were opened. Years later in July 1974, he would be asked as 'the most well-known eminent Indian in Nigeria' by an Indian company, Birla Brothers, to send a message on the occasion of the signing of an agreement for the expansion of a government-owned paper mill in that country.

Austria (1964–1965)

In 1964, Haksar was transferred to Austria. This too was not exactly a blue-chip posting but here again Nehru had his own way of looking at things. On 7 October 1963, Haksar was informed by Rajeshwar Dayal, a secretary in the Ministry of External Affairs, that:

> The Prime Minister has selected you for appointment as our Ambassador to Austria in succession to Shri Arthur Lall who has resigned.

Why did Nehru consider Austria important when the Foreign Service mandarins themselves would have put it in the second rung of postings? I can think of two reasons. First, the Austrians held Nehru in the highest of esteem because it was largely at his intervention with Soviet leaders that Austria had become completely free from the occupation of the Four Powers—USSR, USA, UK and France—in 1955. This fact was always handsomely acknowledged by Austrian politicians. For instance, speaking in New Delhi on 30 January 1980, Austrian Chancellor Bruno Kreisky was to recall:

> In the year when we celebrate the 25th anniversary of regaining our full independence in Austria, I should like to recall once again Prime Minister Nehru, whose Government's willingness to assist us in 1953 during the international negotiation for conclusion of Austrian State Treaty, is still very much in our mind. India was also amongst the first who recognised our neutrality.

Second, Vienna was also the seat of the International Atomic Energy Agency (IAEA) which was becoming increasingly important to India's nuclear policies, and it may have been the case that PNH was selected to strengthen India's presence there. Some evidence for this view could be gleaned from letters from India's two top nuclear scientists on Haksar's transfer away from Vienna for London in mid-1965. The first was from Dr Raja Ramanna, who played a pivotal role in India's first nuclear test in May 1974. He wrote to Haksar on 5 May 1965:

> A few days ago I read in the newspapers with regret that your assignment is being changed and we are to have a new Ambassador to Austria. I was particularly sorry to hear of this as we were just getting the benefits of your stay there and the complex functioning of the Agency was getting under control as far as India was concerned ... I personally was very sorry to hear of the change.

The second was from none other than Homi Bhabha—the father of India's nuclear programme—himself. He wrote to Haksar on 5 July 1965:

> I am writing to convey to you and your wife my deep sympathies on the sudden death of her brother-in-law B.K. Kaul ...
>
> I am sorry you will be leaving Vienna shortly.

Many years later in 2001, three years after PNH had passed away, Raja Ramanna was to recall:[24]

> Vienna had been chosen as the headquarters of the International Atomic Energy Agency (IAEA) and in his capacity as Ambassador he [PNH] had to represent India on its Board. At first Bhabha was suspicious of him because of his loyalty to Krishna Menon, but within a few months Haksar was made a full member with all powers to explain our position on the Non-Proliferation Treaty and the need for atomic power in India. *His position was not easy, because of the tilt of the USA towards Pakistan, and everybody knew of his leftist views, though it was much muted in his professional work.* [italics mine]

Haksar's tenure in Vienna had been cut short and he was posted as deputy high commissioner in London, in the very High Commission in which he started his diplomatic career 17 years ago. This posting appears to have been done because Indo-Brit ties were then in poor shape. Haksar was expected to be the tonic that the High Commission in London required, especially since High Commissioner Dr Jivraj Mehta at 78 was clearly past his prime.

Notes

1. *Selected Works of Jawaharlal Nehru*, Volume 5 (1987).
2. Ibid.
3. Salman Haidar, the noted diplomat who knew Haksar very well, recalled to me that PNH had told him that, on his return from New York sometime in February or March 1948, he had gone to Nehru and expressed his wish to return to law practice in Allahabad. On hearing this Nehru had lost his cool momentarily and told Haksar that national service was far more important than law practice, and that he himself had given up law in Allahabad to join

the freedom movement. Haksar told Haidar that he felt like telling Nehru that while the nation had gained immeasurably from Nehru's sacrifice, the legal profession had not lost much.

4. This was the precursor to the Union Public Service Commission (UPSC).

5. Singh (2000).

6. S.N. Haksar's son Vinit recalls an amusing conversation that took place between B.K. Nehru, then governor of Assam, and S.N. Haksar when PNH was at the height of his power in 1971. It went something like this. B.K. Nehru: 'What is your brother [reference being to PNH] upto? S.N. Haksar: 'Ask your sister [the reference being to Indira Gandhi whose paternal grandfather and B.K. Nehru's grandfather were brothers].

7. Haksar (1979).

8. As recalled by Haksar in Tandon, Prakash (1988).

9. Nielsen (2005).

10. Jawaharlal Nehru Collection, Nehru Memorial Museum and Library.

11. Ibid.

12. Gandhi, Sonia (2004).

13. Barnes (2014).

14. Email correspondence 14 September 2017.

15. Only one of them, Kim Hyeong, now survives. His son too lived in India for over 30 years before bringing his ailing father back for good to South Korea.

16. Mitra (2004).

17. *Selected Works of Jawaharlal Nehru*, Volume 34 (2005).

18. *Selected Works of Jawaharlal Nehru*, Volume 37 (2006).

19. Sarkar (1992).

20. *Selected Works of Jawaharlal Nehru*, Volume 33 (2004).

21. Dutt (1977).

22. *Selected Works of Jawaharlal Nehru*, Volume 29 (2001).

23. *Selected Works of Jawaharlal Nehru*, Volume 64 (2015).

24. Ramanna (2004).

VII. A VVIP Mother's Confidant in London

(1965–1967)

This is the period when the lives of Haksar and Indira Gandhi began to get well and truly intertwined. They had known each other well since the late-1930s and had met off and on but these two years would bring them even closer making him virtually a part of her family. He would be some sort of a local guardian to her sons in the UK. She would become prime minister on 24 January 1966 and immediately draw him in into her innermost circle.

Indira Gandhi with President Lyndon Johnson, Washington DC, March 1966.
Behind Johnson is Haksar (left with dark glasses) and L.K. Jha (right).
Between Indira Gandhi and Johnson, partially visible is Foreign Secretary C.S. Jha.

HAKSAR TOOK OVER AS INDIA'S DEPUTY HIGH COMMISSIONER IN THE UK in May 1965. He was back in extremely familiar haunts after ten years. He was to navigate Indo-British relations through a particularly bad patch when Prime Minister Harold Wilson came out openly in support of Pakistan in its conflict with India in 1965. But perhaps, more importantly, the tenure this time brought Indira Gandhi intimately into his life and vice versa. A friendship forged in London between the two of them in the late-1930s would now blossom luxuriously.

Indira Gandhi's two sons, Rajiv and Sanjay, were both in England.

Rajiv had originally gone to Trinity College in Cambridge University but had later shifted to the Imperial College of Science, Technology and Medicine in London. Sanjay was undergoing a four-year apprenticeship at the Rolls Royce factory at Crewe near London. It was on 10 November 1965 that Indira Gandhi wrote the first of her letters to PNH—at least amongst those that have survived and are available in his archives. She was then minister of information and broadcasting and among her main worries were protecting the legacy of her father and the education of her sons—one of whom was 21 and the other 19. She wrote and the salutation itself says much of their relationship:

Dear PN:
There has been a lack of contact between India and the British public for some years. Several people have written to me that there is a great need for a non-official organization in England to keep in the British public ...

During my last two visits to England, I had the feeling that Britishers of my generation and earlier are prejudiced against India because of their old colonial memories but that a genuine effort to make contacts with the younger generation, who are not anti-India but perhaps merely bored with India, could yield useful results ...

In America we have been able to do a great deal with cultural events ... In Britain too it may be worthwhile to start on these other levels simultaneously with political effort. What do you think of this and what can be done?
Greetings to you and family.
Indira.

P.S.
The state of affairs is quite extraordinary here. Being a shrewd political observer you can probably guess. When I am depressed, which is often, I feel I must quit. At other times, that I must fight it out even if the results are negligible. There is a flicker of light on the horizon—Kamaraj has emerged from his shell and is making forthright and good statements. However, Congress as a party is dormant and inactive ...

As I see it we are at the beginning of a new dark age. The food situation is precarious, industries are closing. There is no direction,

no policy on any matter. The power shortage is acute. Brave words notwithstanding, there is anxiety to go to America, who will I have no doubt give PL 480 food aid and everything at a price. The manner of execution will be deft and subtle that no one will realize it until it is too late and India's freedom of thought and action will have both been bartered away ... [italics mine]
Indira.

This is not just a future prime minister writing to a civil servant. It is almost like two co-conspirators sharing intimate secrets. It is a cry from the heart from a person who thinks of the recipient of her letter as someone special and who can be trusted with her innermost thoughts and worries.

Indira Gandhi was sworn in as India's third prime minister on 24 January 1966. Within a couple of days of her assuming office, it became known that she would visit the USA sometime in March 1966 and a stopover in London was being speculated. PNH must have got wind of what was happening back home since, on 13 February 1966, he wrote an elaborate letter to the new prime minister setting out his thinking on Indo-British ties:

My dear Induji:
... I have, of course, never believed in the elaborate mythology built up about our post-independence relationship with Britain. But between 1947 to almost the time of Khrushchev and, later, Kennedy came to power, the myth served a useful purpose. Indo-British relations and, more particularly our becoming part of the Commonwealth saved us from the Cold War blizzard when it was blowing really fast and fierce. Britain too derived political and economic benefits in withstanding some of the grosser pressures on her ...

Without going into a detailed analysis of Britain's policies in relation to our sub-continent, one need state only the conclusions: Firstly, we have to safeguard ourselves from a purely negative anti-British attitude compounded by anger and frustration ... Secondly, we have to develop direct relationship with the USA as we have developed with USSR, provided we can do this without getting bogged down in a morass of professional and romantic pro-Americanism ...

... We simply must now stop rushing to this country; ... we must maintain over a long period of time an attitude of correct and dignified cordiality; ... we must continue to press for a revision of British policies in the sub-continent ...

I would not suggest our Prime Minister visiting this country—even if invited ... This does not mean we should be nasty or angry or discourteous. Far from it. But we should be firm, cordial, dignified and correct over a long period of time. Apart from this, the visit to the United States must, for the first time, stand by itself ...

Eight days later the prime minister replied to the deputy high commissioner of India in London saying:

Dear PNH:
... I entirely agree with your reactions. In fact, I had been voicing these sentiments to my father in the later years of his life. I entirely agree with you that I should not go to England ... As plans stand now, I shall probably break journey in Paris ...

With greetings,
Indira

Please inform Rajiv and Sanjay of my dates and schedule as soon as you know them. [italics mine]

That very morning of 21 February 1966, Indira Gandhi sent Haksar a second letter which was entirely family-related showing his place in her life. Using the affectionate term by which he was known to close friends and family, she wrote:

Dear Babooji:
Perhaps you may know that my younger son, Sanjay is working in Crewe at the Rolls Royce factory. Up to now he has been happy there and reports from the Crewe people were also good. About a week ago, he began writing that he had learnt everything that the factory had to teach and it is now a question of going over the same thing. He did not think that they would allow him to learn anything new. Therefore Sanjay was wondering about not completing the course but leave at the end of the year or so and perhaps come back to India to set up on his own. I

am writing this in the greatest confidence since Sanjay did not wish me to mention it to anyone.

I have written to Sanjay telling him that I am writing to you. Also that he should come and meet you. He is reluctant to meet new people, but perhaps Rajiv could bring him over. He is a different type from Rajiv—more practical in some ways and yet more shy and diffident in others.

Leaving the factory now would mean that he has no qualifications except that he has practical experience he has gained. I personally feel that this would be a handicap in India, especially as it may not be possible to find a great deal of capital to start him off.

I do not know how much you are in touch with these matters but should be most grateful if you could find out without getting Sanjay involved. One reason may be that he feels cut off and lonely in far off Crewe. If so, is there some course which he could take in London where it would be easier for friends to keep an eye on him. [italics mine]

With good wishes and haste
Indira.

Indira Gandhi's letter to Sanjay Gandhi is not available but senior Indian journalist Coomi Kapoor appears to have had access to it some years back[1] and shared its contents with me based on notes she had made. It appears that this letter must have been written around 21 February 1966:

Haksar is a friend of extraordinary commonsense and competence. Haksar is discreet and rather shy and does not like to butt in on his own. It is up to you to go and meet him. Make a special trip.

Haksar replied to both the letters of the prime minister on 21 February 1966. It is amongst the longest he was to write to her over the next 18 years and is reflective of the manner he would always communicate with her. It mixed the professional with the personal. She was to change after 1973—he remained the same till her death in 1984. She shook him off—he couldn't or perhaps didn't want to. He wrote:

My dear Induji:
I do not think it would be necessary or even desirable to overfly England. That would be, I am afraid, interpreted as an insult. Nothing would be gained by our hurting national pride and outraging national dignity ...

We still need this country's friendship, as, indeed, she needs ours. And we both have to work out a proper balance in our relationship consistent with our interests, our dignity and our self-respect …

If re-fashioning of our relations with Britain is full of difficulties, our attempt to create new foundations for our relations with the United States is no less difficult …

I devoutly and earnestly hope that your visit will provide an opportunity for a review in a fundamental way of relations between our two countries … The crucial question for us is: Can the United States evolve a new policy vis-à-vis India and Pakistan; can the United States also accept the proposition that the greatest contribution India can make towards peace and stability of the world is to continue to function as a self-respecting Democratic State …

Please do not worry about the boys. I know the pointlessness of such an exhortation. My main difficulty has been the lack of any sort of relationship with them. I have now established some sort of personal friendship with Rajiv. He now comes and sits and talks of mice and men. But with Sanjay I have not even begun. Urmila and I are planning to visit him soon. I have also written to him. I would want him to feel that we are interested in him as a person and not merely because of our friendship with his parents.

My own first reactions to his wanting to change are adverse. I feel that he must complete the course. I, of course, do not know what led him to Crewe? Was it his own choice? Was he really interested?

Rajiv is a fine boy. He is, however, still groping, not quite certain what he would really like to do. He appears to be endowed with more than ordinary artistic sensibility. He reacts to colour and design and shapes and forms. He was planning to go home during Easter Vacations. I suppose he must have written to you about it. [italics mine]

As later events were to reveal, Haksar did open a line of communication with Sanjay Gandhi and told him in no uncertain terms that he should complete the Rolls Royce course and not leave at the end of two years as the young man seemed determined to do. The advice of the mother's friend was to rankle and was the first of the negatives against Haksar in Sanjay Gandhi's book. More negatives would accumulate very soon.[2]

Indira Gandhi was about to embark on her first visit abroad to the USA as prime minister—less than two months after she had assumed office. Amidst all her pre-occupations, she found time to reply to Haksar's long missive on 10 March 1966. She actually did more than just reply as the letter would show:

Dear P.N.

Just a line to acknowledge your letter of the 4th. By now you will have known that Wilson invited me to stop in London on my return journey. But as the Moscow stopover has already been finalized, this is not possible. However, I suppose he will come to the airport to see me.

Although I am in London for six hours, I think it is best to stay in a hotel near-by. Otherwise it is too tiring.

I am anxious that you should accompany me to America not only because you will be such a help on various issues of foreign policy, but also because this may give some opportunity to talk about various matters. [italics mine]

Greetings.

Indira.

As I told you earlier, Rajiv and Sanjay are expected to join me in Paris.

This was indeed most unusual. Indira Gandhi was going to the USA with a strong delegation of senior officials plus she had her own cousin B.K. Nehru as India's ambassador in Washington—and he was very well-known to and popular with the Johnson administration. Yet, she wanted India's deputy high commissioner to the UK to be with her when she was in America. She was definitely signaling that he was someone special in her professional and personal scheme of things.

Indira Gandhi went to Washington and met President Lyndon Johnson on 28 March 1966. Haksar was not there with her in that meeting. The next day, she met with US Secretary of State Dean Rusk, and this time he was with her. The discussions were on bilateral relations, food aid and nuclear policy. Indira Gandhi had evidently charmed President Lyndon as B.K. Nehru was to write in his memoirs years later.[3] In an unprecedented gesture Lyndon Johnson, who was at the ambassador's residence for a reception, decided to stay back for dinner. This caused huge complications for the seating arrangements. Finally, Haksar volunteered to absent himself from the dinner so that the US president's presence on the packed dinner table caused no dislocation.

After this, Haksar went back to London and was a spectator to the dramatic events that unfolded in India following the hefty devaluation of the Indian rupee vis-à-vis the US dollar that was announced on 6 June 1966. The devaluation itself had been under discussion for well over a year and it was expected to happen even when Indira Gandhi's predecessor had been in power. But it had proved hugely controversial and that is why it kept getting postponed. Finally, Indira Gandhi, on the advice of her secretary, L.K. Jha, economists like I.G. Patel and K.N. Raj, and political colleagues like C. Subramaniam and Asoka Mehta, had taken the plunge. What had clinched the issue was the promise of some 900 million dollars in aid from the USA and other countries which India could use as it wished. Devaluation was accompanied by considerable loosening of controls on industry.

The moment she had taken these measures, all hell had broken loose within the Congress party with its president and king-maker K. Kamaraj himself highly critical of the devaluation. To make matters worse the aid package did not materialize. Adding to the discomfiture of Congress big-wigs was the fact that elections to Parliament and to state assemblies were less than a year away and their fear was that the devaluation would cost the Congress dearly in the polls—they were to be proved right.

Indira Gandhi had kept L.K. Jha on as her top aide, inheriting him from her predecessor. He had studied economics at Cambridge and joined the ICS in 1936. Conceivably, the political debacle she experienced following the devaluation must have convinced her that she needed somebody with greater political sensitivity and understanding by her side as her top aide.

On 8 September 1966, the mother in Indira Gandhi again manifested itself to Haksar. She wrote to him after having heard from her family friend T.N. 'Tikki' Kaul, then India's ambassador to the USSR that her elder son had some ideas of studying in Moscow:

Dear Babooji:
Tikki's letter has just come. What can I say? I am rather cut off from all that. I can understand Rajiv's desire to do something before returning.

But what about funds? In England he can earn if he takes the trouble but not in Moscow. Even if the tuition is free, would he not need something? And how acceptable would that training be here? What would be the political consequences here? These are some of the questions which come to mind.

I had collected some roubles from royalties but we are not allowed to leave them there and so they have been converted into rupees.

I have trust in your judgment. Please think this out in all its aspects. [italics mine]

Indira.

As India headed to the polls in February 1967, Indira Gandhi resumed her epistolary relationship with Haksar. In the midst of her election campaign in very early February 1967—perhaps the 4th or 5th—Indira Gandhi wrote to him making him a tentative offer:

… I am scribbling this whilst on tour in Rae Bareili. I have been wanting to write to you for some time to thank you for your letter and also to ask you if you would be willing to come to Delhi. The last part is of course premature—I do not yet know my own future let alone the sort of set up which will emerge after the elections. But I thought I should warn you of my thinking …

Haksar sent her a three-page reply on 10 February 1967 which is worth quoting at some length since it reveals much of him and has some contemporary resonance as well, particularly his reference to the cow and its dung:

My dear Induji:

I am most grateful to you that in the midst of it all you should have found time to write … You have been good enough and considerate in asking me if I would be willing to come to Delhi. Yes, of course Yes.

I have just about four more years to go in the Service. I reach the age of superannuation on 4.9.1971. And if I am granted the leave preparatory to retirement, my last working day would be 3.3.1971. If during this short segment of time, I could be of any use to you I would regard such a possibility as an appropriate end to my "working" life.

I am, however, all too painfully obvious of my inadequacies. The only thing which I could perhaps offer would be a non-negotiable loyalty to you and what you stand for and suffer for ...

... The Secretariat in Delhi is a cruel place. I survived it for six years by playing the game according to the rules. And as all kinds of difficulties arise in making senior appointments ... I would beg of you to let me have the first opportunity to make my submission before initiating any action ...

The election results will soon be out ... One has to show accommodation too for those one may not quite approve of. But if the Congress wishes to produce bread for the people, gradually adopt the tractor as its symbol rather than the Cow or the Bullock and do all this while preserving our national dignity and without sacrificing our liberty there is no other choice except one. Otherwise the Cow and its dung will overwhelm us.

All the controversies about private and public enterprise, of socialism and capitalism are somewhat arid ... But if some of our industrialists feel that we can in this latter half of the 20th century have orderly economic growth with political stability by applying the antiquated Manchester School of Economics, they must surely be warned against having a death wish.

Be that as it may, I would most earnestly beg of you to stand as a custodian of our nation's honour and future and not as a party leader and deal with every one face to face and directly. [italics mine]

This was vintage Haksar—free, frank and fearless, ruthlessly honest with his views and opinions. He was being offered a prime position and he was already telling the person making the offer when exactly his last day at work would be. The style of this letter would be the style of his notes to the prime minister over the course of the next five-and-a-half years, and even thereafter.

On 17 March 1967, Jha put up a note to the prime minister:

... I am confirming to the External Affairs Minister that Shri Haksar will be taken in P.M.'s Secretariat in an Additional Secretary-ranking post ... I gather that P.M. has not yet finally made up her mind as to whether

Shri Haksar will take over my post, or whether somebody else would become Secretary to P.M.

On this note of Jha's, Indira Gandhi scribbled the same day:

Haksar should be promoted, if there is no difficulty in doing so.

Two days later she sent down another note to Jha:

Since I have talked to you, I have been thinking over the question of Shri P.N. Haksar's posting. I think on the whole it would be better for him to be Secretary if there is no objection to this. Having someone over him may not be conducive to smooth working.

The ICS bureaucracy just would not give up. On 20 March 1967, Jha replied to the prime minister:

I have discussed with Cabinet Secretary and Home Secretary ... Perhaps it would be more advisable to let him be Secretary but limit his pay to that of an Additional Secretary, at least to start with. After some months, the position could be reviewed.

Finally, Sushital Banerjee, the prime minister's joint secretary, put Haksar out of his misery on 24 April 1967. The letter reveals the bureaucratic machinations that had been going on and that were delaying his appointment:

I hope Gopi Kaul did give you all the information which I had requested him to do when he was returning to Washington. I thought that would have given you firm news about your posting as Secretary to PM. I find that there was a proposition to have you as a Secretary, give you your due place in the Warrant of Precedence, but on the ground of your supposed lack of adequate seniority (!), to allow you the pay of an Additional Secretary for the present, subject to the position being reviewed after six months. This is what had been approved by PM also on the advice of those concerned.

However, when Cabinet Secretary spoke to me about it this morning, I pointed out that under the IFS Pay Rules (as also under the corresponding IAS Rules), you cannot appoint an officer as a Secretary in the Government of India and pay him less than the scheduled pay—i.e. Rs 3500. I am glad to say that Cabinet Secretary readily accepts this position. In fact, he does not seem to have quite grasped the earlier proposal with the result that when Tikki Kaul spoke to him today, he readily confirmed that you would draw pay as a full-fledged Secretary ...

I need hardly add how much we all look forward to having you here. I wonder if you know that you will be the first to stage a break-through for the new generation at the Secretary-level.

Haksar finally joined the prime minister's Secretariat as secretary to the prime minister on 6 May 1967. It was a small secretariat with only a handful of officials many of whom were relatively young, working in a non-hierarchical manner. He was to keep it that way till early-1973. P.N. Dhar who was at his side for slightly over two years and took over from him has written about the remarkable *esprit de corps* Haksar created in the team directly around the prime minister and the high sense of public purpose he inculcated in his colleagues.[4]

Haksar had such an impact on Indian political history that two others were to claim credit for his appointment as Indira Gandhi's secretary. His friend from the early-1930s, fellow IFS officer, fellow Kashmiri and someone who would be part of his life till the very last, T.N. Kaul has written:[5]

In a private conversation on the lawns of her residence, she [Indira Gandhi] confessed to me that she knew little of economics and wondered whom she should have as her Principal Private Secretary. She said she did not want L.K. Jha, who had been Shastri's P.P.S. because he was too far right of her views ... I suggested B.K. Nehru's name but she ruled him out because, as she said: "He is honest and intelligent, sincere and dedicated, but he is too far to the right of me. Besides he is related to me". I told her frankly that if she was probing me for the post, I would not able to last long in it because I was too outspoken and strong-willed ... She then asked if I could suggest someone. I thought for a while and told her that I could not think of a better person than P.N. Haksar whom she knew and whom I had known since my university days at Allahabad in the early thirties. She seemed to agree and asked me to find out if he was willing. I told her it would take some time and she agreed to wait.

This recollection of T.N. Kaul was in 1994, some 28 years after the event. But there is also a letter from him to Indira Gandhi dated 30 April 1966, written from Moscow where he was ambassador:

> I hope to leave this place by the middle of June and go straight to my desk in India without taking any leave. The Soviets have been making anxious enquiries about my successor. I do not know if you have decided on anyone as yet. Rumor has it that C.S. Jha, G. Parthasarathi, V.K.R.V. Rao or P.N. Haksar are in the reckoning. I should be grateful if you could give me an inkling of your thinking on the subject. The Soviets would feel happy with GP or PN—but we have to decide from our point of view while keeping this in mind.

I.K. Gujral, India's prime minister during 1997–1998 is another person to claim credit—at least partially—for Haksar's appointment as Indira Gandhi's Secretary. In a public lecture delivered in 2002, he said:[6]

> In the first year of her premiership she retained L.K. Jha as head of her secretariat but she soon lost her confidence in him, primarily due to devaluation of the rupee that gravely downed her political reputation. Her meticulous search for Jha's successor spotted P.N. Haksar whom she had known from her London days. She discussed his name with some of us in the 'Kitchen Cabinet' as it was called.[7] We did not know Haksar personally since he had spent most of his time serving in the diplomatic missions abroad but we endorsed her choice, when she told us of his political affiliation with the Nehru family.

Gujral was speaking 35 years after the event. Curiously, he does not mention it in his memoirs that came out in 2011.[8] My own view is that while she may well have spoken to T.N. Kaul and I.K. Gujral, she most probably had already made up her mind on Haksar and had used them more as a sounding board. That was her style. She saw him as being on the same ideological wavelength plus she could be assured of his personal loyalty.

Haksar left London for India in very early-May 1967. He had been away for almost seven years. By conventional Foreign Service standards, two of his diplomatic postings—Nigeria and Austria—would be considered not particularly great, even if he had been handpicked for the assignments by the prime minister. His last job in London would definitely be in the top category of posts but PNH had come to it at the age of 52. His immediate predecessor Kewal Singh was 47 when he became the deputy high commissioner in London in 1962 and so was PNH's buddy T.N. Kaul in 1960. Had Indira Gandhi not recalled him when she became prime minister, Haksar may well have ended his service career as high commissioner in London with one more ambassadorship at most—probably the USSR. But that clearly was not to be, thanks to the 'girl with the big eyes' he had first encountered in 1921.

Before leaving London, Haksar caried out a task for a couple who were far removed from the world of politics. Haksar had got to know Roberto Rossellini, the renowned film-maker well when he had come to India in the mid-1950s at the invitation of Nehru to make a documentary on the emerging India. But a huge scandal soon erupted with Rossellini having got involved with a married Bengali woman—Sonali Dasgupta—mother of a five-year-old boy and an 11-month-old infant son. It had taken Nehru's personal intervention to allow Rossellini to complete and also have possession of the film. With Nehru's approval, Sonali Dasgupta was also given a passport to travel to Paris with her infant son where she delivered Rossellini's daughter. The infant daughter, however, had no citizenship— neither of Italy nor France—because Rossellini and Sonali Dasgupta were not legally married. To cut a long and complicated story short, Dasgupta appealed to Haksar without Rossellini knowing about it, writing a seven-page handwritten letter, the sum and susbstance of which was this:

> ... My second request is to register my daughter's birth in your office. When she was born [in 1958] my name was not registered as her mother because I was not divorced. Nor have I "recognised' her in France—where she was born. But there should be a record of the event on the Indian papers too as I am an Indian citizen. I wish to have it done specially because I could recognize my daughter after many obstacles—not coming from the law but from Roberto ...

Earlier, Sonali Dasgupta had been to the Indian High Commission in London in June 1966, but the officials there had been non-cooperative because the child's father was not Indian. Telling Haksar about her experience with his colleagues there, she continued her tale:

> You were in London but I did not come to you then—not to embarrass you as you are Roberto's friend ... But I feel you would understand how earnestly I am trying only to defend our family ... and that my intentions are entirely constructive. I hold no ill feelings no resentments against Roberto because I have learned to appreciate his enormously good qualities. The trouble is that he is a Latin although it is not his fault ...

On 8 April 1967, some three-and-a-half weeks before Haksar would leave London for good, Sonali Dasgupta thanked him 'for the warm hospitality and for making me secure'. She added: 'I have come back home with a lighter heart and more hopes'. A decree had been issued by the Alipore Court of Calcutta recognizing her as the mother of her daughter. But Sonali Dasgupta was not done. She asked Haksar to help her to see her eldest son Raja, who lived with his paternal grandmother in Calcutta saying: 'I have no doubt that Hari [Raja's father] would listen to you'. But she also understood that '... you have more important matters to attend to!'9

That was to be a classic understatement. Indeed Haksar would have many, many more important matters to attend to in New Delhi from a month later but this convoluted Rosellini–Sonali Dasgupta interlude involving their daughter shows what a multi-faceted human being Indira Gandhi's soon-to-be 'conscience keeper' was.

Notes

1.   This could only have been shown to her by Maneka Gandhi, Sanjay Gandhi's widow.
2.   Folklore among PNH's close circle is that he helped Sanjay Gandhi out of many tricky situations at Crewe. These are, I have to say, totally unconfirmable.
3.   Nehru (1997).
4.   Dhar (2000).

5. Kaul (1995).
6. Gujral (2004).
7. A member of this so-called 'kitchen cabinet' was Romesh Thapar—one-time member of the CPI and then the publisher of a monthly magazine called *Seminar*. His wife, Raj Thapar, was to write in her memoirs that it was her husband who suggested PNH's name to Indira Gandhi as her secretary.
8. Gujral (2011).
9. Padgaonkar (2008) is a gripping story of the Rossellini–Sonali Dasgupta relationship. However, Padgaonkar had not consulted the Haksar archives. If he had, he would have found much to add to his narrative.

VIII. A Prime Minister's Alter Ego
(1967–1972)

Haksar took over as secretary to the prime minister on 6 May 1967. The Congress hegemony had ended in the elections held earlier in the year. The country was reeling from two successive droughts. The economy was in deep crisis. The devaluation of the rupee had proved to be a fiasco. Indira Gandhi was under siege from within. Her cabinet was hardly cohesive. This section covers these five-and-a-half years which witnessed great political turbulence but which also saw Indira Gandhi emerge as a world leader in magnificent style. Haksar was her ideological anchor and moral compass in this momentous period.

The Preparatory Years (1967–1968)

Indira Gandhi being hosted by President Tito of Yugoslavia, October 1968.
Haksar is seated second from right.

HAKSAR BEGAN FUNCTIONING AS THE PRIME MINISTER'S SECRETARY IN THE
prime minister's Secretariat from 6 May 1967. Immediately on taking over,
Haksar was confronted with the serious crisis in rice supply from Burma.
No shipments of rice from that country had arrived in India in April 1967
and as against an expected supply of 25,000 to 30,000 tonnes per month
at least for the rest of the year, the supply in May had dwindled to around
7,000 tonnes. Perhaps, the very first thing he did as secretary to the prime
minister was to get her to speak to the Burmese leader, General Ne Win,
and follow it up with a letter requesting for resumption of normal supplies.
Indira Gandhi wrote to Ne Win saying, 'There is no alternative left to us

than to request you to make some relaxation in export of rice from Burma to our country without which our people in some of the States would be subjected to unbearable hardships'. It was this situation with Burma in regard to rice and the earlier situation with the USA in regard to wheat that was to convince her and Haksar that self-sufficiency in rice and wheat production would have to receive over-riding priority.

∾

Eight days after Haksar had joined her, on 14 May 1967, Indira Gandhi sent him an extract of a letter she had received from her younger son Sanjay in Crewe. The extract reads thus:

> I have talked to P.N. Haksar about my future some time back and I didn't get anything concrete out of it. He seems to be of a similar opinion as you are. [He says] "Plans won't work" before even knowing what they are ... As far as staying with Rolls Royce is concerned, I am wasting my time here and have been doing for the last 4 or 5 months. I don't want to continue doing so for 2 more years ... Besides I am not the only apprentice that sits around doing virtually nothing, most of them are in the same boat.

Clearly, Haksar and Sanjay had not hit it off even when the two of them were in the UK. PNH wanted him to study and complete the course in which he was enrolled, whereas Sanjay felt that he had had enough and didn't want to study further; not more than the O.N.C. [Ordinary National Certificate] which he told his mother 'is on the same level as the 2nd year of an Indian University'. Haksar and Indira Gandhi wanted him to get what was called H.N.C. [Higher National Certificate] but Sanjay was not keen on it. This continued lack of chemistry between Haksar and Sanjay would provide the background to the differences that would arise between PNH and Indira Gandhi a year later over Sanjay's business ambitions. These differences would eventually lead to Haksar's voluntary exit in January 1973.

∾

19 May 1967 was the 77th birthday of Ho Chi Minh who was then at war with the Americans in Vietnam. Indira Gandhi greeted him on the occasion much to the annoyance of the US government. The US ambassador to India, Chester Bowles, was asked to lodge a formal protest which he did three days later with Haksar who recorded this note for his colleague T.N. Kaul in the Ministry of External Affairs. Kaul was sending instructions to the Indian ambassador to the USA on how to deal with the fall-out. Haksar wrote on 22 May 1967:

> [You] may consider adding the following as the last paragraph in your telegram:
>
>> Chester Bowles had also called on Haksar to represent against the birthday message. He had asked whether we had been, consistent with our neutral position ... sending similar messages to the President of South Vietnam. Haksar replied by saying that one had to view this matter in its historical perspective. Long before the United States' involvement in Vietnam, we had developed close and cordial relations with Ho Chi Minh personally. Consequently, messages of greetings have been going for a very long time. As for sending messages to the President of South Vietnam, we did not, for a variety of reasons, consider sending messages to Diem and his successors. Haksar had also stated to Bowles that it was not clear to him why this year's message, which has been more or less similar to last year's message, should have caused consternation.

Right through the 1950s, Haksar had taken the position that Ho Chi Minh was more a 'nationalist' than a die-hard communist. Nehru had commended this view to his foreign secretary. In early-May 1968, the prime minister decided to appoint K.S. Shelvankar as India's first consul general in Hanoi. The letter from Haksar to G. Kasturi, editor of *The Hindu* on 5 June 1968 reveals the background to this decision:

> With the commencement of negotiations between Hanoi and the United States, the situation in Vietnam has reached a new stage ... Situated as we are, our country would be affected one way or another by what happens. Our responsibilities arising out of our chairmanship of the International

Control Commission make it imperative for us to take detailed interest in the developments in Vietnam. Impelled by these considerations, Prime Minister felt that we should have in Hanoi a person of substantial calibre and endowed with more than ordinary political sensitivity. Bearing this in mind, Prime Minister felt that Dr. Shelvankar, who is your distinguished representative in London, would be the right choice ... I am sure you will appreciate Dr. Shelvankar's assignment is in national interest. We earnestly hope that you would be prepared to release him from his obligations to the "Hindu" to enable him to take up his assignment as soon as possible ...

Shelvankar, an eminent author, had been very much part of PNH's world in London in the late-1930s but he was also well known to Nehru and Indira Gandhi. He was to serve in Hanoi for two years before moving to Moscow in 1971 and subsequently to Norway in 1975. Two months after Shelvankar was selected for the Hanoi assignment, another key figure from the 1930s circle of UK-based Indian student-communists wrote to Haksar asking what was in store for him. Based in Madras, Mohan Kumaramangalam had already been advocate general of the state and was now one of India's leading advocates. He was in very frequent touch with Indira Gandhi and Haksar. On 24 July 1968, he wrote to Haksar:

> Yesterday Shelvankar met me and told us the good news about your health ... The delay in taking a decision is bound to mount up the difficulties when finally a decision is taken. Hence better—as she told me herself when I met her—to speed it up ... Shelvankar will have told you of my ideas of persuading JP [Jayaprakash Narayan] and C. Subramaniam to initiate two Seminars—one on Indo-Chinese relations and one of Indo-Pak economic relations. I think the present time is most propitious.

Unfortunately, the letter does not mention what job the prime minister had discussed with him but a year later in early-August 1969, Kumaramangalam was to be appointed as chairman of Indian Airlines. He would hold this post till January 1971 and two months later he would contest the Parliamentary elections on a Congress ticket from Pondicherry and win.

∾

Less than three weeks after PNH had taken charge, there was a flashpoint in West Bengal that would have major political impacts. This was the agrarian unrest that got sparked off on 23 May 1967 in Naxalbari at the northern tip of West Bengal which has come to be known in history as the Naxalbari uprising, and has given the word 'Naxalite' to the political lexicon. This was an armed protest by sharecroppers, tenants, small and marginal farmers, agricultural labour and the landless against not just land-owners, but against the machinery of the state itself.

It was hailed in a long and incendiary editorial in the Chinese newspaper *People's Daily* on 5 June 1967 under the title 'Spring Thunder Over India'. The leaders of the insurrection declared in Bengali that Chairman Mao was their chairman and some of them went off to China to meet him and his colleagues. Over the next two years, the armed revolt by the rural 'subaltern' classes was to spread to other parts of West Bengal as well as to states like Andhra Pradesh, Bihar and Orissa. Some parts of Assam, Punjab, Tripura and Uttar Pradesh were also affected.

It was this event more than anything else that concentrated the minds of Indira Gandhi and Haksar on the causes of agrarian distress and unrest. On the one side, the Green Revolution had been initiated to boost production of rice and wheat very quickly, but at the same time there was growing concern that failure to carry out meaningful land reforms was wreaking havoc in the countryside. The Home Ministry was asked to study the causes of agrarian unrest and in October 1969, its report 'The Causes and Nature of Current Agrarian Tensions' was submitted to the prime minister.

It was an attempt to analyze the 'nature of agitations traceable to the existence of discontent or deprivation in the agricultural sector'. Much of what Indira Gandhi was to do, at least in her initial years, could be traceable to the impact of this report which was the handiwork of Home Secretary L.P. Singh and PNH—they had been contemporaries in Allahabad University during 1931–1935. On 31 October 1969, he was to write to Singh:

> Thank you ... for letting me see the excellent paper you got prepared for the Home Ministry on the agrarian problem.

> I may be entirely mistaken, but I gathered a distinct impression that politically difficult agrarian reforms are difficult to implement. The assumption, presumably, is that it would extensively hurt the property rights of the big land owners. I am wondering if any study has been made quantifying the extent of the loss which land owners would, in fact, suffer if land reforms were to be carried out. I know that such a quantification on all Indian basis would be extremely difficult but it may be possible to make a sample survey in one Tehsil in a State. Since the Kosi area in Bihar has attracted considerable attention, a suitable Tehsil in that area could be chosen for a sample survey. I would like to see it established that land reforms are as much in the interest of land owners as provision of housing and other facilities are for the good of an industrial entrepreneur.

This was not a communist revolutionary speaking but more a Gandhian who really wanted land reforms to proceed on the altruistic instincts of the big landlords. This was a theme that Haksar would keep returning to over the next few years.

A month into Haksar's tenure, on 5 June 1967 the conflict in West Asia erupted. It caused great agitation in Parliament. Large sections supported Egypt and the Arab cause. But there were also parties like the Jan Sangh and Swatantra which stood up for Israel, saying that the Arabs had not supported India during its war with Pakistan two years earlier. The first statement made by Foreign Minister M.C. Chagla in Parliament added fuel to the fire since it explicitly mentioned Israel as the aggressor. With differing opinions in her own party, the prime minister was forced to intervene a couple of times to make India's position very clear. PNH carefully prepared her statement in the Lok Sabha of 6 June 1967 in which she said:

> ... I do not wish to use harsh words or use strong language. But on the basis of the information available there can be no doubt that Israel has escalated the situation into an armed conflict, which has now assumed the proportions of a full-scale war ... Our own national interests are bound up with peace and stability in West Asia ... In the Security Council, we

are making earnest efforts for a cease-fire and withdrawal of armed forces
to the positions they occupied on June 4 ...

The conflict had touched a raw nerve in Parliament for another reason
as well—five Indian soldiers (part of the United Nations Emergency
Force [UNEF] contingent[1]) in Gaza had been killed and many others
injured in Israeli artillery and air force attacks which the prime minister
described as 'wanton', 'deliberate' and 'without provocation'. But despite her
condemnation of Israel then, Haksar was to make use of one of his London
contacts to explore supply of arms from Israel to India during its own war
with Pakistan in 1971. However, for now, he urged the prime minister to
proclaim in no uncertain terms, India's commitment to the cause of the
Palestinian people. He also persuaded Indira Gandhi to write a detailed
letter to all chief ministers, which she did on 22 June 1967 explaining
India's political and economic interests in that region.

Sixteen years later, Haksar would be part of an international conclave of
eminent persons that was organized in Geneva to express solidarity with the
Palestinians. However, for the present, his views were nuanced, as is evident
from this note that he sent to the prime minister on 11 August 1967:

> My first reaction was to advise in favour of PM sending a message to the
> All-India Palestine Conference. I felt, however, a little troubled in seeing
> the Palestine question being cast exclusively in a religious framework.
> Even the question of Jerusalem is being viewed from the point of view
> of Islam. In the United Nations as many as 90 members cast their votes
> in favour of restoration of Jerusalem to Jordan. When these nations were
> voting for a resolution, they were not viewing the problem from the
> religious point of view. It is a pity that the organisers of the Conference
> did not think of having a larger framework ... Mobilisation of support
> for Arabs is not merely a question of a mobilising support for Muslims ...
>
> The character and composition of Majlis-e-Mushawarat is also not
> very reassuring. Under its flag extremely reactionary Muslim tendencies
> tend to congregate. For all these reasons I would advise PM not to send a
> message to the Conference. If the organisers of the Conference had made
> some efforts, they could have, I am sure, succeeded in assembling together
> a larger cross-section of Indian nationals who could have joined together
> in denouncing Zionism and its works. This opportunity has been lost.

As for Chagla he resigned as external affairs minister on 5 September 1967. There was speculation that his unequivocal stance on the Arab–Israeli conflict had cost him his job although Chagla himself was at pains to point out that he had quit because of the government's policy on the medium of instruction in universities. On this issue, a few weeks before Chagla's resignation Haksar had told the prime minister on 24 July 1967:

> ... The paper prepared by the Ministry of Education argued adequately and with conviction in favour of University education in our country being imparted through the medium of regional language ... There is, however, no assurance that plans and resources have been made for the development of Hindi/English. One fails to see an awareness, in concrete terms, of the intimate inter-linking of the two problems to which I have referred above.
>
> What I fear is that if we shall go ahead with regionalization of University education, we shall fall seriously behind in the matter of development of link languages. This will produce difficulties from the point of view of national integration ...
>
> ... P.M. may kindly consider restoring a proper perspective to the problem by posing the equal importance of ensuring a pari-passu growth of link languages [English and Hindi].

Evidently, PNH had sympathy for Chagla's concerns. Indira Gandhi took Haksar's advice but Chagla was adamant and refused to take back his resignation.

An unprecedented assault on Parliament took place in 7 November 1966 by cow protection activists. There had been police firing, people had been killed and the home minister, Gulzarilal Nanda, was forced to resign. A promise had been made by the prime minister subsequently that a committee would be set up to examine the matter of having a national law to ban cow slaughter. It took some six months and Haksar's taking over for this committee to be established. On 29 June 1967, it was finally notified with a retired chief justice of the Supreme Court, A.K. Sarkar, as the chairman. It had politicians, spiritual leaders and at PNH's instance three professionals as well—Dr V. Kurien of the National Dairy Development Board (who was to become famous as the 'Amul' man), Dr Ashok Mitra (then Chairman of the Agricultural Prices Commission) and Dr H.A.B. Parpia (director of the Central Food Technological Research Institute).

After the committee had been announced, leading Indian naturalists like Salim Ali and Zafar Futehally who had unfettered access to Indira Gandhi got into the act. They proposed that the Bombay Natural History Society (BNHS) collaborate with the Washington-based Smithsonian Institution to carry out studies on the ecological consequences of India's large cattle population. Dillon Ripley of the Smithsonian Institution wrote to Indira Gandhi on 3 October 1967:

> I personally believe that one of the most important studies that must be undertaken today is an ecological approach to the age-old problem of the impact of cattle on lands in India.
>
> I write at this time with some sense of urgency because of the recent developments which have led, I am informed, to the appointment of a Committee which will report to your Government on the issue of imposing a ban on the slaughter of cows throughout India.

Indira Gandhi was a passionate ecologist herself but she was also a politician. She must have been in two minds but Haksar appears to have clinched the issue. A month later on 7 November 1967, the US ambassador to India Chester Bowles chided Ripley:

> At my request, my deputy Mr. Greene found an opportunity to sound out Mrs. Gandhi's right-hand man, P.N. Haksar about your letter. Haksar readily confirmed that it had been received ... and as much said that he thought it better to leave the complexities of the cow problem to the Government of India. Mr. Greene asked whether the Prime Minister had replied to your letter and was told that she had not; we infer that she probably will not ...

The committee was to keep meeting for 12 years but never produced a report or gave its recommendations. It was finally disbanded in 1979 by Indira Gandhi's successor Morarji Desai.

ॐ

In the final years of Nehru, on 23 June 1962 a Congress Forum for Socialist Action (CFSA) had come into being initially with 17 members under the leadership of a senior Congressman and labour leader Gulzarilal Nanda.[2] It had the support of others like Krishna Menon and K.D. Malaviya and the blessings of the prime minister himself who had sent a message on 10 August 1962 to the inaugural issue of its quarterly journal *The Forum*:

> The Forum is meant to spread socialist ideas and outlook among our people. More specifically, it is meant to help the study of various aspects of socialism in order to give an intellectual background to our people's thinking. This is welcome because there is great deal of vagueness in our thinking.

As long as Nehru was alive, the CFSA was active arranging symposia in different parts of the country, bring out the quarterly publication and printing booklets for party workers. But, thereafter, it became dormant and seemed to lose its influence. In 1966 and early-1967, even Indira Gandhi did not seem too terribly enthusiastic about the CFSA.

The electoral debacle of the Congress in the 1967 elections galvanized thinking about revival of the CFSA. A group of Congressmen met in April 1967 for this purpose. Soon the circle expanded and got new membership with the likes of Chandra Shekhar and Mohan Dharia now joining forces with younger men and women of the Congress, like K.V. Raghunatha Reddy, K.R. Ganesh, Nandini Satpathy, Shashi Bhushan, Chandrajit Yadav and others. The All India Congress Committee (AICC) was meeting in New Delhi on 23–25 June 1967. Two days before the conclave began, PNH told the prime minister:

> In the few weeks I have been here and in light of experience of the currents and cross-currents within the Congress Party I feel strongly that the draft resolution must reiterate the basic framework of our policies. I feel that we should do so even if the reiteration amounts to saying the obvious ... I cannot, of course, set myself to judge the mood within the Congress Party and my assessment, such as it is, is purely inferential. I do, however, believe that recalling and re-stating certain basic principles is necessary at the present time.

It is for this reason that I had attempted a longish draft on some of the major issues of our policy. I have tried to tread warily on the West Asian crisis. The position stated is the minimum which we should uphold.

This would be the pattern over the next five-and-a-half years. Between June 1967 and January 1973, no resolution on political, economic and foreign policy matters would be passed in any convention or meeting of the Congress party that did not have Haksar's imprimatur. And, of course, Indira Gandhi's speeches at these meetings were his handiwork.

A 10-point economic programme was adopted by the AICC at its June 1967 convention held in New Delhi. These included:

1. Social control of the banking institutions.
2. Nationalization of general insurance.
3. Progressive introduction of State Trading in import and export trade.
4. State Trading in foodgrains.
5. Expansion of cooperatives in processing and manufacturing industries.
6. Effective steps to curb monopolies and concentration of economic power in light of monopolies commission report.
7. Provision of minimum needs to the people.
8. Restrictions on une.   d increments in urban land values.
9. A plan for rural works programme and quicker implementation of land reforms.
10. Removal of privileges, incongruous to the concept of democracy, enjoyed by ex-rulers.

Those mainly behind these 10 points appear to have been Chandra Shekhar and Mohan Dharia with the backing of the home minister, Y.B. Chavan. While Haksar may not have contributed directly, he was to use these 10 points to devastating effect two years later when Indira Gandhi confronted her own party's bosses on ideological grounds.

As later events were to show, Haksar was not in complete agreement with some of these demands—the nationalization of import and export trade, for instance, as also the nationalization of wholesale trade in foodgrains. In later years, he would distinguish between those belonging to the 'left' and those belonging to what he called the 'mindless left'. The evidence suggests that while he had great sympathy for the CFSA, he considered some its members belonging to the latter category. One of Indira Gandhi's early biographers, Dom Moraes—who had full access to her while writing his book—was to say:[3]

> A grave gentle man, P.N. Haksar, then Mrs. Gandhi's Private Secretary and the best adviser she has ever had, kept the young Turks from exercising too positive an influence on her.

This AICC session of June 1967 had heralded the return of the CFSA. The CFSA now came into its own. Its growing clout was visible in subsequent sessions of the AICC—at Jabalpur during October 1967, at Hyderabad in January 1968 and at New Delhi in June 1968. Right through 1967 and 1968, both Indira Gandhi and Haksar were cautious in responding to the demands of the CFSA. For instance, while the members of the CFSA kept demanding nationalization of banks, the prime minister and her secretary stayed true to the script of 'social control'. They were quiet on the demand for the abolition of privy purses and princely privileges, as well. She, however, always expressed herself in support of the 10-point economic programme. At Jabalpur he had her saying:

> There were no 'ifs' and 'buts' in implementing the Ten-Point Programme and the Government is committed to implement it in toto. Strategy and timing can be decided by the Government.

And that is exactly how it proved to be. The CFSA kept up the pressure in Parliament, in party forums and in the public discourse. The prime minister and her aide only took note of what was being said, the prime minister spoke of her support to the demands but nothing much actually happened all of 1967 and 1968. The CFSA was very critical of the finance minister, Morarji Desai but the prime minister maintained a staunch silence—her silence being seen as a tacit approval of these criticisms.

The 1967 elections had seen fractured mandates in quite a few states. In Madhya Pradesh, a Congress government under the leadership of D.P. Mishra had been installed on 9 March 1967 but soon lost its majority because of defections. Haksar told the prime minister on 22 June 1967:

> I sincerely hope that if Shri D.P. Mishra feels that the dissolution of the Madhya Pradesh Vidhan Sabha is necessary, he would be allowed to tender such an advice to the Governor. *To my mind, nothing is more destructive of the elementary decencies of political life than to put even the slightest premium on floor-crossing. This simply must stop.* The only way to stop it is to assert the democratic right of the leader of a party, acknowledged in every country, to advise the Head of the State about dissolution. Without firmly establishing this principle, the kerb-trading which goes on will never stop. One understands conscientious objection. One understands that some people have certain political principles and for that reason, they cannot vote for a given party's policies. But in our country, crossing of the floor does not appear to be governed by any higher principle than seeking of office. [italics mine]

Haksar's advice was ignored and Mishra resigned seven days later to be replaced by Govind Narayan Singh who became chief minister of a non-Congress coalition. Indeed the period 1967–1971 was the worst in regard to political stability and adherence to some 'elementary decencies of political life' as PNH put it. 'Horse-trading'—that is, the shifting of political allegiances—was at a premium during this period.

D.P. Mishra was a close political adviser of Indira Gandhi during the late-1960s. Dubbed her 'Chanakya', he was to write in his memoirs decades later:[4]

> Despite my aversion to Communists … I respected Haksar for his utter loyalty to Mrs. Gandhi and at the same time his refusal to participate in anything illegal or unethical even for her sake.

For much of 1967 and 1968, Haksar focused heavily on science and technology issues. For instance, he moved quickly to organize a round-table with scientists and technologists, both from within government agencies and outside. He wrote to some 75 leading scientists and technologists on 1 September 1967, saying:

> ... Science, technology and scientific method appear to provide a means of transforming our society into a modern one ... We now have the experience of 20 years at our disposal. In the light of that experience, we have to consider the adequacy of the various measures adopted and of institutions set up to promote science, technology and the scientific temper in the country. We have also to assess the extent to which the slogan of "self-reliance" in the field of technology can be made meaningful and effective. Allied to this is the question of the extent and limits within which foreign collaboration is to be sought and encouraged ... Quite clearly, science and technology would be meaningless unless they begin to fertilise and feed our industry ... In order that the discussion may be fruitful, it is essential to bear in mind that one cannot obviously march forward all along the front. If this assumption is correct, then clearly one has to determine some order of priorities ...

The conclave was for two full days—7 and 8 September 1967. The prime minister inaugurated the proceedings and sat through some part of it with Haksar being present all the time. The big names of Indian science then—Vikram Sarabhai, S. Bhagavantam, D.S. Kothari and some others took part. But the gathering was significant for introducing a whole new generation of science and technology leaders like Homi Sethna, Raja Ramanna, Satish Dhawan, M.G.K. Menon, Yash Pal, S. Varadarajan, B.D. Nag Chowdhury, M.S. Swaminathan and V. Ramalingaswami who were to become the stars in the years to come.

A year later, on 12 November 1968, Haksar prepared and sent the prime minister an elaborate 10-page note entitled 'Organisational Framework for Development of Electronics in India'. That very day she was meeting with scientists and technologists to discuss what India should be doing to promote electronics. This note was to form the agenda for the interaction. It suggested the establishment of a fully empowered Electronics Development Board deriving its authority from an Act of Parliament similar to the 'Electronic Industry Promotion Act' in Japan, and in the same manner as the Atomic Energy Commission in India itself was written into the Atomic Energy Act of 1948.

Haksar recognized that the private sector would have a large role to play in the production of electronics hardware. He drew inspiration mainly from the Japanese experience which had 'not liberalized the import of either capital or technology in electronic computing machines' and which 'behind this protective wall … is making a determined bid to develop an R&D [Research and Development], manufacturing and marketing base'. He envisaged that given proper organization, incentive and support, 'India could well have certain advantages in the field of development of electronics which Japan may begin losing once its labour costs go high'.

It would take a little over two years for a final decision to be taken. There would be an extended debate on how India should organize itself for the electronics era and Haksar would clinch the issue on 1 December 1970 with another note to the prime minister which strongly endorsed the idea of establishing an Electronics Commission along the lines of the Atomic Energy Commission:

> My own approach is that Government should find a person who will be able, in its judgment to deliver the goods. Having found such a person, the organizational structure should be built around him. We should give him complete confidence and complete responsibility so that he is accountable for successes and failures. From this point of view, Government could do no better than to entrust the entire responsibility to Prof. M.G.K. Menon and let him have his way.
>
> There is another point which requires consideration, namely, the headquarters of the Commission. I feel that the headquarters must be in Delhi from a practical point of view. However, Prof. Menon would be free to move, at his discretion, between Delhi and Bombay. This is necessary since Prof. Menon insists on maintaining his connections with the TIFR [Tata Institute of Fundamental Research] of which he is Director. His point of view is that any live scientist tends to deteriorate very fast if he cuts off his moorings with scientific effort …

The Electronics Commission would come into being in January 1971.

Haksar's first visit to his ancestral land would take place in June 1968. But he and Sheikh Abdullah had been part of the Indian delegation to the UN in early-1948. One of his colleagues in the prime minister's Secretariat was Sushital Banerjee, who had served in Jammu and Kashmir and it is evident that he and PNH would spend much time discussing the affairs of that state. After one such conversation, on 14 September 1967, Haksar told Indira Gandhi:

> ... We had a certain vision that bound Jammu and Kashmir to the rest of India. That vision has dimmed. Precisely because of that, we have to renew our common faith ... I hope P.M. will speak to Shri Sadiq [Chief Minister of Jammu and Kashmir], so that he feels the depth of her anguish at the state of affairs prevailing there.
>
> P.M. will have to also share with Shri Sadiq her ideas about the future of Sheikh Abdullah. It is a difficult question, but we have to face it and Shri Sadiq and his colleagues have to face it too ...
>
> The process of so-called disillusionment through which some of our friends in Kashmir are going through may be understandable, but not justifiable. After all, one does not jettison one's convictions about right and wrong merely because one comes up against difficulties. If the concept of secularism is right and valid, then those who believe in it must fight for it, whatever the consequences and difficulties. The behaviour of Kashmiri Pandits does not provide adequate justification for disillusionment and disenchantment ...

Over the next few years, his involvement with Kashmir's affairs would grow. On 15 November 1968, he sent another note to Indira Gandhi, suggesting that the widely respected Gandhian leader Jayaprakash Narayan be encouraged to meet with Sheikh Abdullah and get his ideas for settling the J&K issue once and for all. He added that the 'question of arresting Sheikh Saheb which appeared at one stage to loom so large in the Home Ministry ought to be allowed to recede'. Nothing came of this initiative but four years later Haksar would have far greater success in opening a structured dialogue with Sheikh Abdullah.

In the first week of July 1968 the Indian government was informed by the Soviet government that a Pakistani delegation led by the chief of its army staff was in the USSR to negotiate supply of military equipment by the Soviet Union to Pakistan. Haksar promptly got Indira Gandhi to reply to Soviet premier, Alexei Kosygin, on 6 July 1968, registering India's strong objections to the Soviet move. Exactly a week later, he put down his views at some length in view of the fact that the news was out in the media and Parliament was agitated over the matter writing:

> ... *I have no doubt that the Soviet decision is erroneous and misguided. We should convey to them both our feelings and our assessment. However, relations between India and the USSR are many-sided and complex. We have, therefore, to carefully strike a balance-sheet of debits and credits.* The recent decision is heavily on the debit side. Nevertheless the overall situation remains favourable to us at the present time both in the economic and military fields ...
>
> However, when a Party like the Jan Sangh or the Swatantra uses the Soviet decision to supply some military hardware to Pakistan as an occasion for a frontal assault both on our foreign policy and on our relations with the USSR, we need to resist this with all energy and nerve ...
>
> The broad tactics of warding off the attack of Jan Sangh and Swatantra and others are to remind them that international relations are an amalgam of complex and even contrary factors. Look at our relations with the United States. We have friendly relations with that country. We engage in mutually beneficial relationship in the economic and political fields ... but the fact remains that between 1954 and 1965, the United States pursued certain policies which ran contrary to our interests ... Nobody with any sense of responsibility ... suggested or would have been right in suggesting, that we make an assault on Indo-U.S. relations, or that we turn those relations into one of hostility ... [italics mine]

Meanwhile, her political adversary and a future prime minister of India himself had written to Indira Gandhi on 11 July 1968, attacking the Indian government for its cowardice with regard to the Soviet decision. Haksar prepared a reply to Atal Bihari Vajpayee and told the current prime minister on 15 July 1968:

... I would submit that, at this stage, P.M. ... should give Shri Vajpayee some benefit of doubt and leave a line of retreat for him. I hope that as a result of this, he would respond.

When he does see P.M., he has to be told that howsoever painful for us the Soviet decisions are, we must not allow our emotions to cloud our national interest. Although we are bound not to disclose the quantum and nature of Soviet defence equipment we have been receiving in sizeable quantities, Shri Vajpayee ought to know that we, for the time being, depend heavily on Soviet sources of supply. As P.M. is aware, only recently the Soviets have authorized dispatch of large quantities of tanks to us. If Shri Vajpayee is at all responsive to our national interest, he should appreciate these inescapable facts of life ...

On Haksar's advice, Indira Gandhi wrote to Vajpayee inviting him to confer with her so that 'I could explain to you the situation arising out of the contemplated Soviet decision'. Just as the arms issue appeared to be getting under control, another issue regarding the USSR erupted in Parliament. On 23 July 1968, PNH told Indira Gandhi:

I place below a draft of Note Verbale which the Ministry of External Affairs has prepared for handing over to the Soviet Embassy in New Delhi. As P.M, would kindly notice, it is couched in the form of a "protest note". I have doubts about the wisdom of adopting this course.

... It may well be that these maps in which our boundaries are shown in a manner which we regard as inaccurate, also contain boundaries between the Soviet Union and China. These boundaries may well be favourable to the Soviet Union.

They could not possibly correct their maps in one respect, without at the same time, correcting them in another respect. This is, of course, pure speculation, but it does point to the necessity of studying the problem with certain amount of care and depth. There is also the tragic history of the protest note to China which, step by step led us into positions from which we could not resile. Protest notes, therefore, should be addressed only as a matter of last resort ...

The Ministry of External Affairs had said:

110

The Government of India hereby register their protest against the wrong delineation in Soviet publications of India's boundary with China in a manner prejudicial to India's territorial integrity and sovereignty and request that the mistake be rectified immediately.

Haksar changed this to:

The Government of India once again draw the attention of the Government of the U.S.S.R. to the delineation in Soviet publications of India's boundary with China in a manner prejudicial to India's territorial integrity and sovereignty and request that the errors be rectified.

Indira Gandhi agreed with PNH the same day saying:

I agree with Secretary. Our intention is certainly not to pick a quarrel but to express the feelings of our people.

Separately, she sent him a hand-written note saying that Swaran Singh, the defence minister had told her that the United States Information Service had sent the offending Soviet maps to MPs belonging to Jan Sangh and Swatantra Party. She posed a question: 'Does this mere act of distribution not constitute "interference" in our internal affairs?' Haksar's reply is not available but undoubtedly he would have agreed with Indira Gandhi.

It is remarkable, given what happened in July 1968, how Indo-Soviet relations were to be completely transformed in the next 18 months.

Foreign policy consumed much of Haksar's time in 1967 and 1968. Apart from the United Nations, Indira Gandhi visited as many as 22 countries in the 12 months beginning September 1967. Each of these visits demanded considerable preparation and it was but natural that the bulk of the burden fell on him, not just because he was her secretary but also because of his Foreign Service background. In August 1968 their diplomatic skills would be put to some test in Parliament when Indira Gandhi came under some attack for not unequivocally condemning the Soviet invasion of Czechoslovakia. Haksar had drafted her carefully worded statement of 21 August 1968 that had ended thus:

I am sure I reflect the opinion of the House when I express the hope that the forces which have entered Czechoslovakia will be withdrawn at the earliest possible time and the Czech people will be able to determine their future, according to their own wishes and interests, and that whatever mutual problems there may be between Czechoslovakia and its allies, will be settled peacefully. *The right of nations to live peacefully and without outside interference should not be denied in the name of religion or ideology.* [italics mine]

The statement had not satisfied many of the Opposition leaders including some who belonged to socialist parties. In his briefing notes for her interventions in Parliament, Haksar did avoid an explicit condemnation but put in language that supported the 'wishes and aspirations of the people of Czechoslovakia'. One explanation for this could well be given the state of Indo-Soviet relations then with the arms to Pakistan and maps issue agitating Parliament, he did not want to further embitter ties with the USSR.

We shall see later that Haksar was to play a decisive role in nudging Indira Gandhi to nationalize banks in 1969 and abolish privy purses and princely privileges in 1970. But as he started out in 1967, he was, in fact, quite cautious in his approach. On privy purses, he said this to the prime minister on 2 August 1967 on a query from her when she had received some representations from her socialist colleagues:

> This is not the first time that the question of privy purses and privileges has been raised. It has cropped up from time to time and has been considered by the Congress Party ...
>
> The AICC resolution on the privy purses and privileges calls upon the Government to "examine" the question.
>
> This the Government is doing. After this examination is over, Government will consider it and take decisions. The Home Minister has been dealing with this matter in Parliament on behalf of the Government.
>
> Until and unless a definitive stage is reached, it will not be appropriate for me to say anything more.

A young Indira Nehru in the lap of her mother Kamala,
as seen by Haksar probably in 1920.

This was the Haksar (seated right) who would have seen Indira Nehru probably in 1920. Others in picture are parents, elder sister and younger brother.

The public meeting of Mahatma Gandhi in Allahabad on
1 February 1931 that Haksar attended.

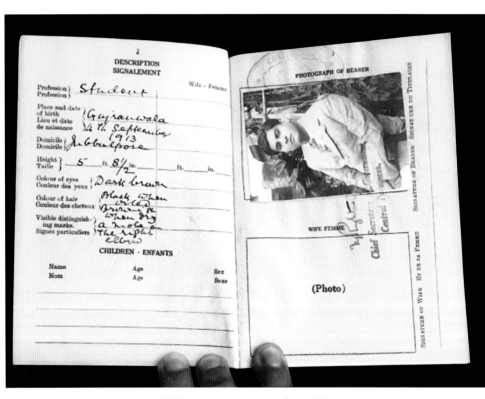

Haksar's passport, October 1935.

To dear
Kamala and
urmilla
with Babu Bhai's
fondes love
London
March 1937.

The photo Haksar (centre) sent in March 1937 from London to his second cousins, Kamla and Urmila Sapru. He married Urmila 15 years later.

James Klugmann (top row, centre of window), with Pieter Keuneman and Haksar to his left (in that order), World Student Assembly organized by Comintern, Paris, August 1939.

INDIAN STUDENTS CONFERENCE LONDON 1939.

Haksar (standing with overcoat on left arm) with Indian students, London, 1939. Standing right behind him is Mohan Kumaramangalam. Seated Himmat Sinh (third from left), Renu Roy later Renu Chakravarthy (fourth from left), Rajani Palme Dutt (sixth from left), Rajni Patel (extreme right). At the very rear on the right with cigarette dangling is most probably K.T. Chandy.

Haksar (centre) with V.K. Krishna Menon and D.N. Chatterjee entering the Foreign and Commonwealth Office, London, circa 1949.

Haksar's marriage to Urmila Sapru, Bombay, August 1952. Also seen are mother (sitting), elder sister (standing) and brother-in-law (standing left).

Nehru at the Conference of Indian Ambassadors and High Commissioners in Western Europe and North America, Burgenstock, Switzerland, May 1953. Nehru seated centre and Haksar standing second from right.

Haksar (left) with Lt Gen. K.S. Thimayya, Panmunjom, Demilitarized Zone, Korea, late-1953.

Haksar with Krishna Menon, New Delhi, probably 1958.

Haksar and wife with Nehru on the eve of departure to Nigeria, March 1960.

Nehru and Indira Gandhi, president of Nigeria and his wife, Haksar,
Lagos, September 1962.

Homi Bhabha with Haksar and Mrs Haksar, Vienna, September 1964.

Haksar flanked by Prime Minister Harold Wilson (left) and Lord Mountbatten (right), condolence meeting for late Lal Bahadur Shastri, London, mid-January 1966.

Sometime later, in response to a note prepared by the Home Ministry, Haksar told the prime minister on 23 October 1967:

> I have read through these notes on the question of privy purses and privileges of former rulers of Indian states ... After examining the legal, moral and historical aspects of the case, the Home Ministry has worked out what it calls as "transitional allowances" to be paid in lieu of privy purses. The total cost of this would be of the order of Rs 63 crores, payments to be spread over a period of 20 years.
>
> As regards privileges ... the recommendations are to abolish all the privileges which fall into the category of being "ostentatious". The ceremonial privileges are also sought to be curtailed. As far as those privileges which confer economic benefits, the Home Ministry's note recommends continuous exemption in respect of Central taxes, but recommends abolition of most others.
>
> The question for consideration is in what precise way Government should implement its decision. The Home Ministry's note argues against "executive decision". It suggests constitutional amendment. *However, before reaching this stage, it is essential that the Government should go through the process of negotiations. The constitutional amendment should embody the results of these negotiations unless the princes prove to be totally intransigent in which case Government may decide to the make the constitutional amendment required.* [italics mine]

On 4 December 1967, he recommended to an unsure prime minister that she honour a long-standing invitation from Indian Merchants' Chamber, Bombay to speak at its Diamond Jubilee:

> ... I have for a long time the need for clearly enunciating some of the principles which inform and guide Govt. policy in the matter of economic development in the private sector. If Shri Jamshedji Tata had been alive, I am sure there would have been no difficulty in finding with him a common language ... I thought the Diamond Jubilee celebrations of the Indian Merchants Chamber might provide a good opportunity for P.M. to begin a fresh dialogue with our business community ... It might also provide an occasion to pay tribute to the great pioneers of Indian industry.

Three days later, he sent her a reworked draft speech saying:

113

In the draft I have prepared I have endeavoured to get away from the controversies of the past. *We have a private sector in agriculture ad industry. We have a public sector too. Both have to bear the test of efficiency and profitability.* An atmosphere has to be generated in our country for a national consensus. The dividing line should be between those who would zealously safeguard our sovereignty and independence and those who would sacrifice it in the name of collaboration, profit or ideology. [italics mine]

Haksar was to be an unabashed champion of the public sector till his death. But his vision of the public sector was different from many others of his ideological fraternity who believed that the public sector could, in the name of social obligations, keep making financial losses. He would tell Indira Gandhi on 5 January 1968:

Our public sector enterprises are extremely diversified, extending from iron and steel to fertilisers, chemicals, petroleum industry, petrochemicals, aircraft, railway coaches, etc. We are all agreed that each one of these enterprises should run efficiently and producer profit.

His views on nationalization of banks too were initially guarded as he was feeling his way around and did not want to disturb the status quo dramatically. In response to a Cabinet note that had come from the Ministry of Finance, he told the prime minister on 12 December:

I have no comments to offer on the measures proposed to be taken to make "social control" of our banking system effective. On paper, the various powers which Government is assuming to control the composition of the Board of Directors and to have a say in the appointment of Chairmen of Commercial Banks, appear to provide the necessary mechanism for "control". However, much would depend on the persons appointed and how effectively they work for achieving the broader objectives which "social control" implies. My own feeling is that nothing much would change, but one has to go through the whole process of implementing these measures before reaching any conclusion.

The only new institutional device invented is that of the National Credit Council. The functions assigned to the Council belong properly to the Reserve Bank of India. However, it has been argued that it would be an advantage to have a forum where the relative claims of credit of different sectors could be discussed and priorities determined. Let us hope that this would work.

The CFSA had been asking to conduct an investigation into the Birla group. But Haksar was to advocate caution in a note sent to the prime minister on 16 December 1967:

> Item 2 raises the question, namely whether a Commission of Inquiry should be set up to go into the allegations against the Birla group of companies ...
>
> *To single out the Birla group of companies for a Commission of Inquiry would be justified only if it could be clearly established that this particular group has been systematically engaging themselves in malpractices and in defying the laws.* The question is: is there such a prima facie case? It is not clear to me why the Government could not fortify itself by the advice of the Attorney General. All the relevant material so far collected can be placed before him and he might be asked to give an advice. [italics mine]

In another note to the prime minister of 15 December 1967, he demonstrated his pragmatism yet again:

> PM has asked me to state my reactions to the Cabinet paper on Textile Companies (Acquisition of Undertakings) Bill, 1967 which is to be discussed at the Cabinet meeting this afternoon. My first reaction is a violent one. I think it is quite fantastic for public money to be utilized for propping up decaying, rotten mills. Private enterprise prides itself on efficiency. Here, we have a sorry spectacle of it. Why should Government at all get mixed up in running these mills? Why should public money be wasted?
>
> ... PM would also kindly notice that somewhere in the horizon, there is the question of setting up a Textile Corporation. I should have thought that the priorities would be to set up such a Corporation and for that Corporation to manage the mills which the Government might, in its wisdom, think of taking over. I think the two things need to be coordinated. Merely taking over the mills and running them by Government departments will not serve any purpose.

❧

Within a few months of his joining, Haksar had an opportunity of demonstrating how he would deal with matters concerning the bureaucracy. Sometime in November 1967, some MPs protested to the prime minister about the selection of two young IAS officers for a four-month course at the International Monetary Fund (IMF) in Washington DC. One of the officers was J. Murli, who was the son of S. Jagannathan, himself an ICS officer still in service. The selection board had comprised top civil servants. Because of the media controversy, Jagannathan persuaded his son to withdraw his name. PNH told the prime minister on 15 November 1967:

> There were as many as 14 candidates … I do not know much of this young officer but I have heard reports of his being a brilliant young man. Should he suffer because of his father? … I understand that one of the disappointed candidates is Shri V.K.Dikshit [son of Indira Gandhi's close political adviser Uma Shankar Dikshit]. He is B.A. (Hons) (History—3rd division) and M.A. (History—2nd division) as against J. Murli who is M.A. (Cantab) in Physics and B.A. (Hons) 1st Class and had, I understand, very high position in the I.A.S. examination. J. Murli has a brilliant scholastic record. Is it contended that sons of Secretaries should be subjected to special disabilities …
>
> I do not easily get worked up about injustices but the case of Shri Murli has affected my conscience … I have no doubt that friends and relations of some disappointed candidates have taken upon themselves an entirely unconscionable, illegitimate and reprehensible role in trying to assassinate the character of a young officer.
>
> As P.M. is aware I do not belong to the Indian Civil Service. Indeed I belong to none of the Service trade unions, *but I recognize that civil servants need to have an assurance that the Head of Government would protect them when they are innocent.* [italics mine]

Haksar would adhere to this policy for the time he had the authority and influence. He was to encourage youngsters and also bring in outsiders into the administrative system. He would be devastating but scrupulously fair in his assessment of people. In an overwhelming majority of the cases, the prime minister would go with what he recommended.

∞

Zakir Husain took over as India's third president exactly a week after Haksar joined Indira Gandhi. K. Subba Rao had been persuaded by the Opposition parties to resign three months *before* his retirement date as chief justice of the Supreme Court to contest against Husain. This, in some ways, began the process of embitterment of relations between the judiciary and Indira Gandhi. But there was nothing public about the embitterment as yet.

In later years, Haksar would be critical of the judiciary and he would have his reasons for being so. Even so, in the initial few years, he was not for confrontation and was a model of rectitude when it came to the judiciary. He advised the prime minister on 18 March 1968:

> Although I have recorded P.M.'s approval to the appointment of Sarvashri S. Ganesan and K.S. Palaniswami as Additional Judges of the Madras High Court for a period of two years, I still feel it is necessary that the Home Minister should speak over the telephone to the Chief Minister of Madras and tell him that while we respect his judgment, duly supported by the Governor, as against the judgment of the Chief Justice of Madras, we are bound to point out that the Chief Justice of India has supported the Chief Justice of Madras …

The controversy had been over the candidature of S. Rangarajan who had been supported by the judicial heavyweights but who had been rejected by the political leaders. Examining his records, Haksar had, earlier on 6 March 1968, told the prime minister that:

> … If we are to proceed on the basis of Shri Rangarajan's record, it is, by no means an unblemished one. However, I feel most reluctant to advise P.M. that a Chief Justice of India and the Chief Justice of a High Court should be easily over-ruled …

But his views would begin to change. A year-and-a-half later on 29 August 1969, he would tell the prime minister:

> PM has raised several questions about the selection and appointment of Judges of our High Courts. These matters have been troubling me for a long time. I had, in fact, mentioned to P.M. the extreme anxiety I have about the character and composition of the Supreme Court which is the

final Court of Appeal in India. I have thought a great deal of what we could do, more specially of the Supreme Court. One of the things I had in mind was that P.M. might establish a personal contact with the Chief Justice of India, whoever he might be, not with a view to "influencing him" but rather to share with him P.M.'s anxieties about the role of the judiciary in a changing society …

As far as Judges of the High Court are concerned, the situation is really hopeless. Under our Constitution, the Judges of the High Courts are appointed by the President after consultation with the Government of India, the Governor of the State who naturally acts on the advice of its Chief Minister and the Chief Justice of the High Court concerned. These appointments are made either from the members of the subordinate judiciary of the State concerned or from the Bar in the State. It is a hopeless task trying to find out the character and antecedents of persons whose names come up for a more or less routine approval. My own view is that if the Chief Justice of India could somehow be persuaded to see matters in proper light, he might be the instrument for bringing about some change in the character and temper of the judiciary …

After 1970, Haksar's views on judicial appointments were to undergo a complete reversal after the Supreme Court verdicts on bank nationalization and abolition of privy purses and princely privileges.

On 17 June 1967, China exploded its hydrogen bomb. Four days later, Defence Minister Swaran Singh gave a statement in Parliament saying that India's policy continued to be one of 'steadfastly adhering to the policy of developing nuclear energy for peaceful purposes', but also added, 'the effect of this policy on our security is also kept under constant review'. The statement was the result of long hours PNH had spent discussing India's nuclear posture with Indira Gandhi.

Meanwhile, international discussions had commenced on finalizing 'The Treaty on the Non-Proliferation of Nuclear Weapons,' commonly known as the Non-Proliferation Treaty (NPT). India's position was that before worrying about other countries going nuclear, the five nuclear powers should take steps to reduce their large nuclear arsenal, if not totally eliminate them immediately. On 20 April 1968, Haksar got Indira Gandhi's approval for 'Instructions to India's Representative to U.N. on Non-Proliferation Treaty'. His detailed note started thus:

> In defining our attitude to the Non-Proliferation Treaty, we have to apply the criteria we have been consistently applying in judging political events in terms of our interests. During the last twenty years, we have had occasions to define our attitude on a number of occasions, e.g, the Japanese Peace Treaty which we did not sign.

He then went to say:

> While we recognize that the Treaty is based on coincidence of interest between USSR and USA, we nevertheless believe that it will not lead to what we all desire, namely some tangible steps towards disarmament, both nuclear and conventional ...
>
> We cannot fail to notice that out of the five nuclear weapon powers, two will not be signatories to it. This might not have mattered but for the fact that one of the non-signatories is our neighbour, namely China, who is full of hostile intentions towards our country ...
>
> Having regard to the stockpiles which were there in 1963 and which have further increased ... we are entitled to ask: How does the Treaty alter these facts? The answer lies in the negative. By not signing the Treaty, India would symbolize a protest against this state of affairs in the world. It has very little to do about keeping the so-called options open, though, no doubt, *as a sovereign State, we have as much right to possess nuclear weapons as anybody else. However, we recognize that this is neither necessary nor desirable. At the same time, we are anxious that there should be no impediment put in our way in developing our nuclear energy programme for peaceful purposes.* [italics mine]

He then identified specific instructions to be sent to the Indian delegation in the United Nations to participate in the discussions in the General Assembly. Among these were: India should avoid a polemical tone against the nuclear powers even while stating its position; India should neither overplay nor underplay the Chinese nuclear threat even while expressing

India's concerns; India should avoid mention of Pakistan; India should
support proposals for disarmament, stoppage of further production of
nuclear weapons, cut-off of fissionable material for weapon purposes
and unhampered nuclear development for peaceful purposes. The
instructions were also that India should not spearhead any move for delay
or postponement of the conclusion of the Treaty.

Two years later, on 23 July 1970, the prime minister was to call a
meeting of her senior ministers to discuss a paper prepared by Vikram
Sarabhai, chairman of the Atomic Energy Commission and his colleagues
called 'Atomic Energy and Space Research, a Profile for the Decade
1970-80'. The draft record of discussions in the Internal Affairs Committee
of the Cabinet prepared four days later by B. Sivaraman, cabinet secretary
says:

> Discussion was held on the policy to be adopted about the atom bomb
> and the suggestion of the Department of Atomic Energy in their Paper
> was approved.
>
> Discussion was suggested on the paper "Atomic Energy and Space
> Research, A Profile for the Decade 1970-80" circulated at the meeting.
> Ministers expressed the view that it was not possible to digest the details
> of the paper in the short time available. Discussion was, therefore, held
> on certain broad principles. The following observations were made:
>
> (a) Normally, construction of a power plant based on atomic energy is
> considered from the economics of the unit in the grid. As a purely
> power project, justification will have to be given for the various units
> suggested.
>
> (b) *If we have to keep our options open about utilization of atomic power
> [that is, make the bomb], we may have to produce a certain amount
> of enriched fuel. For* this purpose, a certain minimum amount of
> power generation and fast breeder technique will be necessary. It will
> be a political decision that atomic power plants of this order will have
> to be installed, even if they may not qualify on the power economics.
>
> (c) It has been suggested that future atomic power plants should be of
> the order of 500 megawatts. It was considered that there need not
> be any firm decision on this ...

(d) It was agreed that in our situation, there has to be economic use of the enriched fuel that will be produced in the system. This has to be in peaceful uses of the atomic energy ...

... The aspect of Satellite promotion was initiated by mention of the defence use of satellites for gathering information. This subject was not pursued. [italics mine]

Clearly by 1970, Haksar would have convinced Indira Gandhi that India may have to, sooner or later, go nuclear and also have a military dimension to its space programme. His private exhortations were unequivocal, even though in public Indira Gandhi's posture was one of calculated strategic ambiguity.

On 1 October 1968, India's external intelligence agency called R&AW (Research and Analysis Wing) came into being. It was carved out of the Intelligence Bureau (IB) but was soon to acquire its distinctive identity. Two people were responsible for its creation—Haksar and R.N. Kao, a police officer who had been working in the IB. Kao was well aware of IB's failures in the run-up to the war with China in 1962 and with Pakistan in 1965. The design of the agency was the product of the conversations between these two who were to remain extraordinarily close till Haksar's death in 1998. On 2 February 1969, Haksar asked the prime minister to record the following minute in a file to be sent to the cabinet secretary:

The functioning and operation of a Foreign Intelligence Operation is an extremely sensitive and delicate matter. I am convinced that unless the Head of the Organisation is allowed the necessary power and autonomy to function as an Additional Secretary under the overall supervision of the Cabinet Secretary himself, the Organisation will run into great many difficulties. The Head of the Research and Analysis Wing having been appointed as Additional Secretary, it is in the interests of security and efficiency of work that he should function as such with all the powers, including financial powers normally exercised by Additional Secretaries and that the Organisation should be treated as an integral part of the Cabinet Secretariat. I see no objections to secretarial designations being given to officers of the

Research and Analysis Wing where it is necessary to do so. For dealing with matters relating to the Organisation's administration, establishment and finances, a separate Administrative Cell should be created in the Cabinet Secretariat. However, it should work under the Additional Secretary and should examine establishment and financial proposals made by the Research and Analysis Wing in consultations with its concerned officers. Where necessary, it should make its recommendations to the Cabinet Secretary through the Additional Secretary. [italics mine]

Even before it could take-off, R&AW had fallen victim to a bureaucratic tussle. Kao had objected strenuously to his playing second fiddle to some generalists and that too to officers much junior to him in the administrative hierarchy. He had been outraged and took his complaint to Haksar who immediately saw the point that 'no Intelligence Organisation can function in this fashion' and that Kao had to have full powers and independence from the usual bureaucratic scrutiny. Indira Gandhi fully backed PNH and Kao got what he wanted. It was to have its year of glory much sooner than expected in 1971.

What about the other intelligence agency—the IB? There are only two substantial notes relating to it in the PNH archives. The first relates to the publication of a book called *The Chinese Betrayal* by B.N. Mullik who had been the director of IB between 1954 and 1963. The book had come out in 1971 and the Ministry of Home Affairs had taken great umbrage at it saying that the author had violated the Official Secrets Act. This, the Ministry argued, was a fit case for prosecution. But on 1 September 1971, Haksar would advise the prime minister:

> It does not require any great astuteness to come to the conclusion that Shri Mullik has wantonly trespassed upon the Official Secrets Act. The easiest thing to do therefore is to register a case ... But I think that such a course would cause endless embarrassment all-round ...
>
> While Shri Mullik has been engaged in his great creative task of writing the book, he was enjoying various facilities afforded to him by the Intelligence Bureau. He occupied a house rented by the IB; he had the use of the telephone; and I have no doubt that he had free access to historical material without which he could not have written the book.

The question is: who provided him all this assistance and for what purpose? If Shri Mullik is driven to the wall, he is bound to bring all this out. And the Government would look a little ridiculous unless one is quite clear in one's mind that one would prosecute everyone, including the present DIB [director, Intelligence Bureau]; the former Joint Director Shri A.K. Dave and perhaps many others.

The prime minister accepted Haksar's line of reasoning and just allowed the matter to fade away. Incidentally, PNH himself would probably be guilty of violating the Official Secrets Act by retaining with him copies of numerous 'secret' and 'top secret' documents and classified correspondence that form the backbone of this book itself.

The second IB-related note in the Haksar archives is the one he would write to Indira Gandhi on 19 June 1972 on policy concerning posting officers in that agency:

... I [have] gathered the impression that I.B. at its higher levels of responsibility tends to be a highly in-bred organization. People tend to spend long years doing the same sort of thing. As a result distortions appear. I first became aware of it when Shri A.K. Dave resisted his transfer from the Bureau to the Police Academy in Mount Abu. And, indeed, he preferred to resign than go on this transfer. I should have thought that to train young policemen was an exciting job. However, Shri Dave did not look at it that way. He had grown in an environment and he did not wish to leave it. This led me to consider why and wherefore of it.

It appears that the first head of the Intelligence Bureau, Shri B.N. Mullik, had great passion for studying what was then fashionable "international communism". He took a great deal of personal interest in it. A little later he put Shri A.K. Dave in charge of it and for a long period—I believe nearly 10 years—Shri A.K. Dave steeped himself with the problems of international communism. Now every intelligent person knows that all these studies of so-called international communism are not worth the paper on which they are written.

... Shri K.N. Prasad has remained in the Bureau for now ten years without any change whatsoever. I rather suspect that Shri K.N. Prasad might develop the same kind of syndrome as Shri A.K. Dave did and I do not think that this would be good either for Shri K.N. Prasad or for the Bureau. I have, therefore, come to the conclusion that he should have a change and after a spell of service in a field post, he might be brought back to the Bureau somewhat refreshed. [italics mine]

H.Y. Sharada Prasad was Indira Gandhi's speechwriter from the day she became prime minister on 24 January 1966 till the day she was assassinated on 31 October 1984. But as long as he was in the prime minister's Secretariat, Haksar contributed very heavily to her speeches and, on many occasions, they were really joint ventures between him and Sharada Prasad. In the first 18 months of Haksar's tenure, Indira Gandhi delivered 75 major speeches, in India and abroad. Without exaggeration, each of these bore Haksar's distinctive imprint. It is only after Haksar quit around mid-Janury 1973 that Sharada Prasad became the supreme speech writer. Their partnership was to be captured very well in a note that Sharada Prasad was to send Indira Gandhi on 30 August 1970:

> Some points are submitted for PM's speech at the AICC Seminar on Foreign Policy. The ideas are Secretary's [PNH] with me acting as Rapporteur.

And when there were multiple drafts available to Indira Gandhi, Haksar's prevailed. For instance, in 1971, it would be decided to bring out the *Selected Works of Jawaharlal Nehru* and the question occupying the prime minister's mind was that of the Preface to go in the volume. Both Padmaja Naidu and Sharada Prasad were to prepare drafts. Clearly, the prime minister was not happy and she would ask PNH for his version which was to be sent on 7 May 1971:

> … Whatever may be the ultimate content of the Preface, I, at any rate have no doubt whatsoever that it should breathe an atmosphere of calm, academic detachment … I feel the kind of preface that Miss Padmaja Naidu recommends and what Shri Sharada Prasad has written may not be appropriate …

Indira Gandhi was to go with PNH's tribute to Nehru as her Preface which adorns each of the 91 volumes of the *Selected Works of Jawaharlal Nehru* that have been published so far with perhaps another 10 yet to come. The Preface is a masterly summary of Nehru's thinking and life:

> That imperialism was a curse which should be lifted from the brows of men, that poverty was incompatible with civilization, that nationalism should be poised on a sense of international community, and that it was not sufficient to brood on these things when action was urgent and compelling—these were the principles which inspired and lent drive to Jawaharlal's activities in the years of India's struggle for freedom and made him not only an intense nationalist but one of the leading figures of humanism ...
>
> No particular ideological doctrine could claim Jawaharlal for its own ... Never religious in the routine sense, yet the culture of his own land meant a great deal to him. Never a rigid Marxist, yet he was deeply influenced by that theory and was particularly impressed by what he saw in the Soviet Union on his first visit there in 1927 ... He himself was a socialist with an abhorrence for regimentation and a democrat who was anxious to reconcile his faith in civil liberty with the necessity of mitigating economic and social wretchedness ...
>
> So the story of Jawaharlal is that of a man who evolved, who grew in storm and stress till he became the representative figure of much that was noble in his time ...

This could very well be a portrait of Haksar himself, a Nehruvian to the core but not unmindful of what he considered mistakes made by India's first prime minister which he would point out to Indira Gandhi, as we shall see later.

Indira Gandhi's most famous speech was probably the one she delivered on 14 June 1972 at the first UN Conference on the Human Environment at Stockholm. In the Haksar archives there is a draft of that speech sent by him to her and Sharada Prasad with this note dated 9 June 1972:

> I place below a somewhat enlarged and revised draft of a speech to be made at the UN Conference on Environment at Stockholm.

That historic speech delivered five days later was about 75 per cent identical to this draft. Some themes did get added later but it would be fair to call this a Haksar–Sharada Prasad undertaking with the prime minister, of course, making her contributions as well.[5]

In the initial years Indira Gandhi dreaded Parliament. She went through it as a chore but was clearly tongue-tied most of the time. On 6 June 1967, one of her acerbic critics, the socialist M.P. Madhu Limaye had gone to the extent of describing her as a 'dumb doll'. Haksar would carefully write out whatever she had to say in Parliament whether they be short statements, 'spontaneous interventions' or long speeches. In 1967, 1968 and 1969, he would even go to the extent of drafting Indira Gandhi's written answers to questions asked in Parliament. One notable example of this is provided by what happened in response to a question raised by one of Indira Gandhi's bête noires in the Rajya Sabha, Raj Narain, on 21 December 1968. Narain had asked whether 'it is a fact that 24 boxes were received from Italy a week before the marriage of her son, Shri Rajiv', and went on to make wild allegations. The prime minister's Secretariat had put up an answer but that was to be redone by Haksar and sent to Indira Gandhi on 17 December 1968 saying:

> I do not think "Shrimati Sonia" is a correct description. At that time, her maiden name was Sonia Maino and there is no reason why it should not be stated.

The answer given by Indira Gandhi read:

> No boxes were received from Italy or elsewhere a week before the marriage.
>   One suit case left by Miss Sonia Maino at the time of her departure for India, was received in January as unaccompanied baggage …

Sonia Maino, of course, had become Sonia Gandhi on 25 February 1968.

In the initial years, Indira Gandhi was quite reluctant to accept too many public engagements, particularly if they related to economic issues. This could be perhaps because she may have been unsure of herself. A note that Haksar was to send her on 4 February 1970 is revealing in this regard and also shows how he communicated with her:

> P.M. has often chided me for recommending acceptance by her of invitations to preside over inaugural function of organizations like FICCI, Associated Chambers of Commerce and All India Manufacturers Organisation. However, I now find that P.M. is addressing the Lions Club in Calcutta. I would respectfully submit that of all the organisations, Lions Club should have been avoided, more especially in a city like Calcutta.

The prime minister somewhat sheepishly agreed with her secretary but went ahead nevertheless.

On 1 December 1968, Sanjay Gandhi applied to the Ministry of Industrial Development for a 'letter of intent' to manufacture a small car. There were some 15 Indian and foreign companies, as well as some other 'entrepreneurs' like Sanjay Gandhi who had also done so. Right from the very beginning Haksar had voiced his strong objections to the prime minister about her son dabbling in such a venture.[6] He had also told his friend from the London days that the son should not be staying with her in the prime minister's residence and continue to carry on his business activities from there, particularly in association with persons who Haksar considered were less-than-desirable.

PNH's objections were actually even more fundamental. He questioned the wisdom of scarce resources being diverted to the manufacture of passenger cars. He preferred to see an expansion of capacity to manufacture scooters and that too in the public sector. Decades later, on 15 March 1995, Haksar was to recall this issue in a letter to Abid Hussain who had sent him a report of India's transport policy prepared by the Asian Institute of Road Transport. He wrote:

> ... Way back in 1967-68, I fought and lost a battle for having a mass rapid transport system in the capital city of Delhi instead of going in for the small car project ...

Haksar had not only lost the battle but made a deadly enemy who would soon prove to be his nemesis. He had made his views known to the prime minister in clear and categorical terms. An uneasy truce prevailed. That was to end on 30 September 1970 when Sanjay Gandhi was finally given the letter of intent to manufacture 50,000 small cars every year without any foreign collaboration and without imported raw materials, components and machinery. Another letter of intent was given to another individual in Madras for making 25,000 such cars annually. My own reckoning is that this was the beginning of Haksar's estrangement from Indira Gandhi. The final break, however, would happen some 27 months later.

The Take-off Years (1969–1970)

INTERNAL

P.M. often chides me for recommending acceptance by her of invitation to preside over the inaugural function of organisationslike, FICCI, Associated Chambers of Commerce and All India Manufacturers Organisation. However, I now find that P.M. is addressing the Lions Club in Calcutta. I would respectfully submit that of all the organisations, Lions Club should have been avoided,more especially in a city like Calcutta.

I agree. Shri Siddhartha
Ray included it . I

(P.N. Haksar)
4. 2. 1970.

P.M. am so rushed that
I am not able to scrutinize
the programmes.

4.2.

Secy. to P. M.
No. 878/70
Date 4/2

250

Exchange between Haksar and Indira Gandhi, 4 February 1970.

SOMETIME IN EARLY-MARCH 1969, TWO OF INDIA'S BEST KNOWN economists, K.N. Raj and B.S. Minhas had prepared a note making out a case for taxation of relatively large incomes and assets in agriculture. They argued for a wealth tax on agricultural land with the revenues being earmarked for schemes of development benefitting the poorer sections of the population in rural areas. Such schemes, Raj and Minhas suggested,

129

could cover works providing employment to rural labour and mid-day meals to children attending schools. Both economists were close to Haksar who would consult them very often on contentious issues. On 6 March 1969, the Cabinet had a discussion on proposals for the forthcoming budget and after the meeting was over, Haksar expressed his frustration to the prime minister:

> … I should like to earnestly plead with P.M. that no quarter should be given to the faint hearts who spoke against the tax on fertilisers and against a possible wealth tax on agricultural land. The latter is in the nature of a trial balloon. The Central Government has been urging upon the State Governments to tax the farmers. The State Governments have been dragging their feet … If the State Governments do not have the political courage, the Central Government can say it is prepared to raise the tax and give it to them. The choice is theirs. The proposal for such a tax will also rescue the image of the Congress as a party tied to the apron-strings of the big landlords and big industrialists … *The poor would not go on voting for the Congress if it did not succeed in preserving its image of appearing to be concerned with poor farmers and landless labourers.*
>
> As for the tax on fertilizer, there is just no escape from it. It was an amazing spectacle to see those who opposed the tax on fertilizer were, only the other day, advocating in the name of socialism transference of credit from public financial institutions to public sector. Opposition to tax on fertiliser and concern for the public sector present a picture either of political innocence, combined with economic ignorance, or just playing politics for the fun of it. [italics mine]

This was to be one area where Haksar did not get his way. For a man with sharp political instincts, somehow he failed to see that what he was advocating was, no doubt, sound finance and economics but dangerous politics. It's not surprising hence that Indira Gandhi disagreed with him.

☙

A decision had been taken some years earlier when M.C. Chagla was education minister that a second university would be set up in the nation's capital. Chagla was keen that the university be named after India's first prime minister but Nehru himself had shot down the idea.[7] Subsequently, the proposal went into cold storage and got revived after Haksar came on the scene in 1967. By that time Nehru had passed away and the way was cleared for naming the university after him. But the issue of appointing the first vice chancellor was proving tricky. The position was first offered in June 1968 to the great astrophysicist S. Chandrasekhar who was then at the University of Chicago but he refused.[8] He was to later win the Nobel Prize in 1983. Then P.B. Gajendragadkar, the retired chief justice of India, was approached in November 1968 but he too declined. Then the prime minister suggested the name of G. Parthasarathi, the journalist-turned-diplomat for that position but that was not acceptable to V.K.R.V. Rao, the then education minister. On 24 March 1969, Haksar sent a note to the prime minister:

Shri G. Parthasarathi is understandably exercised about his future. He telephoned to me this morning and said that … it would be a good thing if some decision could be taken at an early date.

I understand from P.M. that the Minister of Education had said that he would prefer to have a man of academic distinction as the Vice Chancellor of the Nehru University and that he had in mind either Prof. [M.N.] Srinivas or Prof. P.N. Dhar. I spoke to both of them … Both Prof. Srinivas and Prof. Dhar confirmed that their existing commitments were such that they would not be in a position to resile from them and accept the Vice Chancellorship …

Dr. S. Gopal who came to see me, reported that Dr. V.K.R.V. Rao had spoken to him at great length … and he [Rao] felt that the Nehru University should have an academic person of distinction to be the Vice Chancellor. I told Dr. Gopal that while I agreed with the Minister of Education … our efforts to get Prof. Srinivas or Prof. P.N. Dhar or Dr. Satish Dhawan had not succeeded. Earlier Dr. K.N. Raj had also turned down the offer. I said my understanding was that academicians felt that at this stage of setting up of the university one required a person who would have to do lot of leg work and negotiate with a variety of institutions and departments of Government … I also told Dr. Gopal that he should go and speak to Dr. V.K.R.V. Rao about this and try to persuade him to accept the idea of appointing Shri G. Parthasarathi. Accordingly,

Dr. Gopal spoke to Dr. V.K.R.V. Rao yesterday. I understand that Dr. V.K.R.V. Rao was unrelenting in his attitude. However, he said that if P.M. were to give a directive, he would naturally agree …

If P.M. feels reluctant to speak to Dr. V.K.R.V. Rao and as a result the proposal to appoint Shri G. Parthasarathi as the Vice Chancellor does not materialize, we still have to consider something appropriate for Shri Parthasarathi. He found the chairmanship of the Policy Planning Division [in the Ministry of External Affairs] unacceptable … Shri [C.] Subramaniam once asked me if the Division could not be located in the Prime Minister's Secretariat. I told him that if the Policy Planning is to relate exclusively to foreign affairs, it could not be located in the Prime Minister's Secretariat … *If P.M. agrees with this, then it is for consideration whether the only way in which commitment to Shri G. Parthasarathi could be fulfilled would not be by appointing him as Secretary to P.M. … I shall gladly give way to him.* [italics mine]

Indira Gandhi was clearly irritated when she received this note. She noted in her hand with reference to the last two lines:

Secretary evidently enjoys writing these notes. He may like to write such things but I am not amused. The suggestion at the end cannot be taken seriously nor is it amusing.

But she spoke to V.K.R.V. Rao the very next day along the lines Haksar had suggested and Parthasarathi was soon appointed as the first vice chancellor of Jawaharlal Nehru University (JNU) and PNH continued to be her secretary.

1969 was the year Indira Gandhi aided, abetted and guided by Haksar truly changed the course of Indian political history. The internecine conflict within the Congress party was continuing and was to reach its peak at the Faridabad session of the AICC in April 1969. The session started with acrimonious debate on economic policy and attacks on the finance minister, Morarji Desai, who was himself chairing the proceedings of the panel on economic policy. The CFSA was in full cry and there were sharp exchanges between some of its members like Chandra Shekhar, Mohan Dharia and

Bhagwat Jha Azad on the one side and Morarji Desai on the other. But the final trigger was the speech of the Congress President S. Nijalingappa on 27 April 1969. Nijalingappa paid ritual obeisance to the 10-point programme but then went on to strongly criticize the very idea of a public sector.

This speech was seen by the CFSA as an attack on not just the prime minister but on the very fundamentals of Congress ideology itself. Haksar had equipped Indira Gandhi with adequate arsenal to counter-attack. His briefing notes were full of points of defence of the public sector, on the need for expanding public investment in industry, on the need for industrial licensing for the private sector and the on the imperative of self-reliance in science and technology. These had all come under assault in Nijalingappa's speech.

The AICC was to meet again in Bangalore in mid-July 1969. Meanwhile, just before that session, a brainchild of Haksar hit the headlines. On 31 August 1967, he had got Indira Gandhi to agree to set up what was initially called the Expert Committee on Industrial Licensing but later came to be known as the Industrial Licensing Policy Inquiry Committee. It was meant to find out 'whether the large industrial houses have, in fact, secured undue advantage over other applicants in the matter of issue of such licenses, and if they have received a disproportionately large share of such licenses, whether there was sufficient justification for this'.

The establishment of this committee was Haksar's response to a persistent criticism being made by the CFSA that the industrial licensing system had resulted in growth of monopolies and in increased concentration of economic power. Professor M.S. Thacker was made its chairman and Mohan Kumaramangalam and H.K. Paranjpe its members. Thacker was a former member of the Planning Commission and Paranjpe was a well-known economist.

The Committee soon got into serious trouble with the chairman at odds with the two members. Thacker himself landed into a huge controversy when news leaked that he had accepted the directorship of the-then privately owned Bank of India. There was a storm in the Parliament and he was forced to resign on 22 April 1968. Twelve days later, Subimal Dutt took over as chairman and his meticulous biographer notes that:

Surprised that he had been chosen, Dutt saw Haksar rather than the Prime Minister behind the decision. Being received by his two colleagues with some initial reserve, he soon found himself fully accepted and the task highly interesting.

Dutt was then the vigilance commissioner of West Bengal. Haksar had worked with him in the Ministry of External Affairs between 1955 and 1960. He was non-ideological but clearly PNH saw him as someone with the highest integrity. The Dutt Committee, as it has come to be known, was damning in its conclusion. In its report[9] it pointed that

> The licensing system worked in such a way so as to provide a disproportionate share in the new licensed capacity to a few concerns belonging to the large industrial sector. The maximum benefit of all this was to a few larger houses ...

This was not partial but total vindication of what the CFSA, and its prominent members like Chandra Shekhar had been claiming all along. Indeed, all through 1968, Chandra Shekhar made the Birlas the particular target of his attack, directly alleging collusion between that family group and Morarji Desai himself. Indira Gandhi had been silent during these attacks, never revealing her own mind on way or the other.

Haksar is known for his contributions to the emergence of Bangladesh in 1971. He has also played a crucial role in India's policy towards Sikkim that finally led to that kingdom's integration into the Indian Union in April 1975. He negotiated far-reaching agreements with Pakistan in 1972 and 1973. He opened doors to China in 1987. But early on he had thought of Nepal as well. On 1 May 1969, he told the prime minister:

> ... My own views for what they might be worth are set out below:
>
> (a) So long as the King lasts and symbolizes the state in Nepal, our inter-State relations should be correct. We should not do anything overtly to invite the charge of interference in the domestic affairs of Nepal.
>
> (b) We should devise ways and means of establishing clandestine contacts

with those segments of society in Nepal who are friendly to India ...

(c) In every dealing with Nepal we should insist on reciprocity.

(d) ... We must not talk down to the Nepalese but talk to them with firmness but with courtesy.

(e) While I agree that we should apply pressure to make the King feel that he cannot take us for granted, such pressure should be applied selectively ... The action has to be subtle and graduated and varied from time to time.

(f) We should try and probe what the American, British and Soviet intentions are and see to what extent they share our concern at the way the King is opening the country to Chinese penetration and influence.

These principles continue to have relevance for the way India should handle Nepal. Actually, Haksar had known King Mahendra. The Indian government had sent him twice to Cannes in the 1960s where the King was recuperating from a serious illness. His mandate was to get the King to transfer greater responsibilities to his heir, Prince Birendra. What he was now cautioning Indira Gandhi against was a movement from one extreme to another in dealing with a neighbour which, though culturally, historically and geographically bound to India, was fiercely independent.

On 6 May 1969, Indira Gandhi met the visiting Soviet prime minister, Alexei Kosygin, in New Delhi. Haksar's brief for her was significant for what it had to say about the Indo-Soviet Treaty that was to be signed in August 1971:

> ... As far as the suggestion of signing a Treaty between India and the Soviet Union is concerned, she [Indira Gandhi] has already made it known to the Soviet Government that her response was positive and constructive. Such a document should not appear to be a exercise in expediency but it should be a declaration of high principles. Nevertheless the signing of such a Treaty, apart from its importance in the further development of relations between our two countries, will have global significance, and

therefore, will attract global attention. We have to be prepared to meet these reactions on the international level and she should also be in a position to carry the Parliament and the country with her in achieving this objective. It is against this background that it would be important to discuss all the details and also essential preliminaries before we arrive at the actual stage of signing the Treaty. It was our feeling that discussions on these details should proceed in Moscow, away from prying eyes ... She had therefore authorized her Ambassador to carry on these discussions in Moscow.

India's ambassador to the USSR, D.P. Dhar, took forward the Kosygin visit but soon expressed his frustration at the brief he had received on the Treaty—that of 'continue to talk but no finality'. Haksar shared Dhar's frustration and told the prime minister on 31 May 1969:

... The Ambassador has done tight-rope walking with great finesse. However, he will soon topple over, unless he is steadied by some clear instructions as to how he should proceed and the extent to which he can respond concretely and constructively.

... Diplomacy deals with problems at a given time and a given place. The Soviet anxiety, which is so manifest at present, may change overnight. We have, therefore, to calculate our self-interest and not proceed on the assumption that time is on our side and that we can dilly-dally at our pleasure. The assumption is that India is of such vital importance to the Soviet Union that we can sit back and relax and do stone-walling. It would be a tragic mistake to work on this assumption ...

Diplomacy ... is a function of power operating in a concrete place and time. Ideological considerations are meant for the neophytes. Situated as we are in South Asia, with our entire Northern borders covered by China and USSR, we have to live with this geographical configuration. America can give us little comfort in such a situation.

I understand that a letter has been written to our Ambassador that he is not to enter into any commitment; that he is not to respond, but merely to listen and to report. If I had received such instructions as an Ambassador, I would have simply refused to carry on the job, for no Ambassador should be put in a position and asked to negotiate and yet be hamstrung in every way ... [italics mine]

It is clear that in mid-1969, Indira Gandhi was deeply ambivalent about the Indo-Soviet Treaty knowing as she did that it would further antagonize her party bosses who, in any case, were convinced that she was extra-friendly with the USSR. It is also possible that she nourished a hope that relations with the USA would improve. 1971 would change her mind completely.

༄

July 1969, however, was to see a transformed Indira Gandhi. She sounded the bugle through her historic 'Note on Economic Policy and Programme' that was circulated among delegates of the AICC at Bangalore on 9 July 1969. Quite a few people contributed with ideas. But the pivot was Haksar who gave shape, structure and substance with the help of some of his colleagues in the prime minister's Secretariat.[10] Whatever was given to Indira Gandhi by way of suggestions ended up on his desk and his task was to put it all together as a cohesive package. This historic note that was to change the nature of the Indian political economy began in Haksar's words thus:

> The time has come to restate our economic policy and set the direction in which we have to move to achieve our social goal. This has become all the more necessary in view of doubts that have been raised with regard to our intentions and our willingness to take the hard and difficult steps which are necessary. In respect of many of the items some steps have already been taken but what is important is to intensify our efforts and keep the social goal all along in the forefront.

The note ended by saying:

> These are just some stray thoughts rather hurriedly dictated.

Hence, this has come to be known as the 'stray thoughts note'. It went much further than the 1967 10-point economic programme of the CFSA. For instance, in the backdrop of the Naxalbari rebellion and the view gaining ground that the Green Revolution could well become a Red one, the stray thoughts note laid elaborate stress on land reforms and review of agricultural wages. It said:

Land reform is no less important. If we do not act urgently, grave political and economic problems will arise.

It went on to give suggestions to 'improve the lot of the tenant and agricultural labour' and called for 'rigourous and effective enforcement of the existing laws' to reduce 'some of the tensions in the countryside'. The final paragraph called for a review of agricultural wages and for measures to enable 'landless labourers to participate in the fruits of the green revolution'.

In keeping with the recommendations of the Dutt Committee, the stray thoughts note called for the expeditious appointment of 'Monopolies Commission manned by persons of integrity'. In line with something Haksar would fight for throughout his tenure with Indira Gandhi but did not exactly succeed, the note also suggested that 'public sector projects should be given more autonomy and manned by young competent persons committed to the project'.

On 9 July 1969, while the stray thoughts note was being circulated at the Congress conclave in Bangalore, he sent Indira Gandhi a note to prepare her for the tumultuous days ahead. Haksar wrote:

I feel that P.M. should show a sensitive understanding of the feelings, emotions, anxieties and thinking behind the economic programme elaborated by the so-called Young Turks. There is an evidence of sincerity of purpose ... The basic feature of our society is that there are millions upon millions of people who are dispossessed. In these conditions, the competitiveness of market economy, the struggle to get the good things of life in education, health, jobs becomes very intensely acute. And when one sees the contrast between the dire poverty of the millions and the riches of the few, the conflict becomes even more evident. If these things are allowed to continue, the society will be rent asunder.

I feel that P.M. should reiterate her faith in a socialist society alone being able to solve the problems of our country. For this purpose, it is necessary not merely to implement certain programmes like nationalization of banks, etc. but it is equally necessary to educate people politically; and above all the Congress cadres need to be educated ... *While PM should express, in a forthright manner, her deep commitment to socialism, she should, at the same time, express anxiety about producing bureaucratic State capitalism in the name of nationalization.* Therefore, a realistic approach to the problem of our time would consist in devoting next two to three years in improving the efficiency, the organization of our existing public sector enterprises, carrying out a vast educational programme in favour of socialism, building up new cadres to manage our new public sector enterprises ... In the meantime, a great deal could be done to improve the social control of banks by ensuring that the larger percentage of deposits is made available for the purposes of public sector development ... [italics mine]

Here was a prime minister's counselor giving her the courage of his convictions in an unequivocal manner. Haksar's ideology comes through clearly. But what also is very interesting is that on 9 July 1969, he was still thinking and talking in terms of 'social control' of banks. Within 10 days however, banks were to be nationalized. Those would be 'The Ten Days That Shook India'.

ॐ

It was on bank nationalization that Indira Gandhi and Haksar were to first change their stance and show their cards. So far they had gone along with Morarji Desai and had supported 'social control of banks', even though that had been considered an eyewash by Chandra Shekhar and rest of the CFSA. But now Indira Gandhi's stray thoughts note had her saying:

There is a strong feeling in the country regarding nationalization of banks. We had taken a decision at an earlier AICC but perhaps we may review it. Either we can consider the nationalization of the top five or six banks or issue directions that the resources of the banks should be reserved to a larger extent for public purposes.

The president of India, Dr Zakir Husain, had died on 3 May 1969 and Vice President V.V. Giri had become interim president. Almost immediately manoeuvring for filling the top constitutional post started and it was clear that there was a Prime Minister's Group and a Congress President's Group. As the Bangalore session of the AICC began, it appeared that the Nijalingappa group had decided to nominate N. Sanjiva Reddy as the official Congress candidate which was not to Indira Gandhi's liking.

The decision was formally announced on 12 July 1969 but it had not been an unanimous decision in the Congress Parliamentary Board with four voting for Sanjiva Reddy and two against him. The majority decision was widely seen as a snub to the prime minister, especially since Nijalingappa announced the name without going through the motions of consulting her. But while clearly showing her displeasure and distress, Indira Gandhi went along with the choice and filed one set of nomination papers on Reddy's behalf. A day after Sanjiva Reddy's candidature was announced, the acting president, V.V. Giri, decided to enter the contest as well. It is improbable that he would have done it without Indira Gandhi's knowledge although she denied it strenuously.

Things moved speedily thereafter. She went into a huddle with her close aides, including Haksar, who saw Nijalingappa's announcement and Sanjiva Reddy's anointment as a direct assault on her authority. So far she had treated Morarji Desai with respect, at least outwardly, and had been careful not to run him down in public. On 16 July 1969, she relieved him of the Finance Ministry and, at Haksar's suggestion, took it over herself. She asked Desai to continue as deputy prime minister but he refused and quit. Clearly, she saw him as a major obstacle in the implementation of the ideas contained in the stray thoughts note. But at the same time not wishing to defy the party bosses, she also announced her support to Sanjiva Reddy as the Congress's presidential candidate.

Morarji Desai's ouster needs a little explanation. Indira Gandhi's real ire was directed at her home minister, Y.B. Chavan, who she felt, had played a double game—pretending to be with her on the presidential candidate but actually going along with Nijalingappa and company when it came to the crunch in the Congress Parliamentary Board. Had she had her way, she would have made Chavan pay for this 'betrayal'. But instead Morarji Desai was eased out, becoming in some way collateral damage in the whole episode. In all probability, Haksar would have cautioned her against doing anything to Chavan because of his strong 'leftist' credentials and image. After all, since 1967 Chavan had been advocating abolition of privy purses and bank nationalization at a time when Indira Gandhi and PNH themselves had been cautious. When Haksar was getting Indira Gandhi to talk of an ideological battle within the party if she was to remove Chavan, it would appear totally incongruous. Hence, the relatively softer option of getting rid of Morarji Desai was exercised.

Chavan would survive till June 1970 when he would be, to his annoyance, shifted to become finance minister with Indian Gandhi taking over the Home Ministry which she would handle for almost three years. She would be criticized for two decisions she took while effecting this change: she delinked the Central Bureau of Investigation (CBI) from the Home Ministry and the Enforcement Directorate from the Finance Ministry and had them transferred to the Cabinet Secretariat which meant that she had direct control. There is no evidence available in the Haksar archives on whether he supported or opposed the move. But it would be fair to say that had he opposed it, she may not have gone ahead with it.

As later as 9 July 1969, Haksar was not entirely convinced that banks had to be nationalized right away. Then three days later came the assault on Indira Gandhi's authority with the announcement of Sanjiva Reddy as the Congress's presidential candidate. Subsequently, Morarji Desai's resignation was secured after four days. My guess is that between 12 July 1969 and 15 July 1969, Haksar and Indira Gandhi must have confabulated and decided to shed their caution on bank nationalization. On 16 July 1969, she asked PNH to meet with K.N. Raj, one of India's most distinguished economists and find out his views on bank nationalization. Another eminent economist, P.N. Dhar, was also present when PNH and Raj met. Dhar was to later write that Raj strongly favoured nationalization but felt it would take at least six months to carry it out.[11]

But just three days later, on 19 July 1969, 14 banks were indeed nationalized, making one of Indira Gandhi's 'stray thoughts' an immediate reality. This account is from the memoirs of D.N. Ghosh[12], who was then the official concerned in the banking division of the Ministry of Finance and who was to later become the chairman of the State Bank of India (SBI). It was the night of 17 July 1969 and Ghosh recalls being summoned to Haksar's residence:

I saw that Haksar was browsing through a mass of papers, among which I could spot the Reserve Bank publication, Statistical Tables Relating to Banks in India. He was trying to figure out how many banks accounted for 80 per cent to 85 per cent of the total resources of the system. Off the cuff, I said the number could be 10 to 12 banks.

Just then, the Union Minister of State for Company Affairs, K.V. Raghunatha Reddy, strolled in and stood listening to our discussion. He piped up that it was a golden political opportunity to nationalize all banks and that we should go ahead with the bold decision. Haksar waived his suggestion politely and requested him to keep his impetuous radicalism to himself. Haksar wanted to be left alone till he himself had been fully briefed on a subject that was entirely foreign to him. I then asked him if the Prime Minister had made up her mind on nationalizing the banks. 'Not yet', he replied. 'We are to discuss this tomorrow morning'. He was not sure if it would be possible to sort out all the legal conundrums involved and have the ordinance [for nationalization] ready by 19 July which was a Saturday. The date was crucial for two reasons. [Acting] President V.V. Giri was due to demit office on the forenoon of 20 July and the Lok Sabha would begin its monsoon session on 21 July.

The choice of Ghosh by Haksar to be the 'keeper of secrets' as far as bank nationalization was concerned reveals much of how PNH operated. A. Bakshi, who was then deputy governor of the RBI, had worked with Haksar in London in the early-1950s. They were ideologically also similar and were exceedingly close personal friends. Thanks to Haksar, Bakshi would join the soon-to-be-created department of banking in the Ministry of Finance and later become the comptroller and auditor general (C&AG) of India in 1972.[13] It was Bakshi who had given the seal of approval to Ghosh and had joined the duo late that night of 17 July 1969 for confabulations.

The next day, Ghosh writes, the prime minister herself summoned him in the morning. She wanted to be convinced that the legislative draft for nationalization of banks could actually be prepared in less than 24 hours. When she was told that such a draft had, in fact, existed from the end of 1963 when nationalization of five banks had first been considered, she appeared to relax and swore Ghosh to absolute secrecy saying that in case of any hitch he should apprise PNH. For the next few hours, Haksar, Bakshi, Ghosh and a few others who had been specially commandeered for this purpose, like R.K. Seshadri (an RBI official) and Niren De (attorney general) slogged to prepare the ordinance—which was an executive order that would have to be ratified by Parliament later.

At 8.30 pm on the night of 19 July 1969, Indira Gandhi addressed the nation on radio and announced the nationalization of banks. This was one speech of hers which had not been written or even worked upon by Haksar. Right down to the last comma and full stop, it was I.G. Patel's draft. It was indeed ironic because not only was he one of Morarji Desai's favourites, but he himself was at that time a votary of social control. In his memoirs,[14] Patel takes some pride—and rightly so—in the authorship of this landmark speech of Indira Gandhi:

> I drafted the Cabinet paper and the speech for Mrs. Gandhi ... Not a word I wrote was changed by Haksar or Mrs. Gandhi next morning ...

Incidentally, in the same memoirs he recalls Haksar in this fashion:

> ... What was not in doubt is that Haksar managed to concentrate enormous powers in the PM's Secretariat and that his intellect contributed much to Mrs. Gandhi' tactics and strategies. He was accepted as Mrs. Gandhi's alter ego, and by most as Mrs Gandhi's tutor, mentor and sole confidant ... He may have been all that is rumoured. But he was very able, and in my experience mostly fair and judicious and patriotic. I also found no particular ideological obsession with him ... He may have been drawn to leftists as friends and companions. But he understood the compulsions of the times and was too shrewd not to understand the weaknesses of individual leftists as well as rightists and was ready for practical compromises. If he disliked the Americans under Nixon and Kissinger, he had much reason to ...

I.G. Patel was generally considered a non-ideological, market-friendly (in today's language) economist and, therefore, not instinctively in PNH's orbit. But on 9 September 1969, Haksar asked Indira Gandhi to send this note to the cabinet secretary:

If I recall correctly, a proposal was made last year that Dr. I.G. Patel should become a full-fledged Secretary. I felt at that time that it was perhaps a little too early to do this. Dr. Patel has now been Special Secretary for some time and I feel he deserves to be made Secretary of the Department of Economic Affairs. The Cabinet Secretary may take necessary steps.

Three years later, on 6 July 1972, Haksar was to plead Patel's case once again when a proposal had come to the prime minister that the economist leave government for a while and go as the number two man at the United Nations Development Programme (UNDP) in New York. There was some bureaucratic resistance but PNH would have none of it:

> ... Dr. I.G. Patel is 47 years old. He has, therefore 11 more years of service left and if he is to serve India's interest in UNDP, he should have a stake in coming back; otherwise like most Indians, his loyalty to UNDP, which would be a euphemism for self-interest, might be at the expense of India's self-interest. Every self-respecting Government sends its high officers to U.N. Agencies on secondment and not for permanent absorption ...

IG, as he was popularly known, went to UNDP and in 1977 was made governor of the Reserve Bank of India by Indira Gandhi's successor Morarji Desai. He was later to be P.V. Narasimha Rao's first choice as finance minister in 1991, and only when he had declined was the job offered to Dr Manmohan Singh.

Haksar was also responsible for what he himself called 'a somewhat unorthodox' appointment in the RBI to get nationalization of banks achieve its socio-economic objectives. The RBI Governor L.K. Jha wanted a bureaucrat, failing which a banker. PNH was not terribly enthused by Jha's names and got Indira Gandhi's approval to appoint a 39-year-old industrial economist called R.K. Hazari as a deputy governor in place of Bakshi. Hazari had shot into fame in the late-1960s as the author of a deeply researched study on the functioning of the industrial licensing system in actual practice. Hazari was young by RBI standards but commanded great respect. He would go on to spend six years at the RBI.

Haksar fought quite a battle with the bureaucracy and succeeded in establishing a Department of Banking in the Ministry of Finance to take forward the objectives of bank nationalization. He would also get the prime minister to over-rule L.K. Jha, I.G. Patel and others and make Bakshi in charge of the new department. Ghosh himself was a key part of it and he recalled to me:[15]

> While he [PNH] took it upon himself to see that the department of banking, the new entity established after nationalization, is manned by competent individuals, he never interfered with its functioning. I would also assert that in no decision on central banking, commercial banking and allied matters he had brought to bear any personal influence.

Ghosh also remembers that some four years after bank nationalization, he and Haksar were travelling by train to Calcutta and he asked him whether he believed the decision taken in July 1969 with such great speed and secrecy was the right one. PNH replied promptly: 'Of course, I have always believed so. We would have in any case taken that step, sooner or later. Timing was dictated by political necessity.'

While all this drama was taking place in the Congress party and Indian politics was being given a whole new orientation by the nationalization of banks, President Richard Nixon came to New Delhi on a flying visit. A day before Indira Gandhi met him on 31 July 1969, Haksar sent her a briefing note:

> PM might recall that at the time of her visit to Washington on early 1966, I had submitted to her for her consideration that there was an urgent need for frank exchange of views on Indo-American relations on a stable footing. In order to do this, it was essential, as befits two friendly countries having many things in common, to be extremely frank with each other.
>
> So far as we are concerned, nothing has bedeviled Indo-American relations more than the unfortunate and tragic policies pursued by the United States vis-à-vis Pakistan ... The second factor ... is a feeling in India that in her desire to fight Soviet or Chinese ideological and power influences, U.S. was prepared to support regimes which do not even possess any democratic pretence and that tended to support extreme right-wing elements ...

There is widespread questioning [in the USA] about India's viability and, of course, much alarmed head-shaking about our so-called socialistic tendencies. This is spread, to a very large extent, by our own industrialists visiting Washington and New York. However, one can proceed on the assumption that Nixon and his top advisers are sophisticated enough for us to try and persuade them that not only are we politically stable and economically progressing, but that the methods we are following to move even further on political consolidation and economic development are the right methods for us … [italics mine]

In view of events that were to take place less than two years later in the sub-continent, what Haksar had to say on Pakistan is of particular relevance:

… The sad fact is that the ruling hierarchy in Pakistan—a nation that has yet to find its identity—finds tension with India vital, not only to their attempts to maintain national unity but even more to ward off democracy and, above all, to keep themselves in power. And now, since they are finding it difficult to keep East Pakistan in their orbit, they have tried to blow out of all proportions the so-called Ganges Water Dispute … It is to be hoped that the United States will continue to avoid entanglement in Indo-Pak affairs and above all, will not repeat the mistake committed by them when they began supply of arms.

He urged Indira Gandhi to be specific in her meetings with President Nixon and not engage herself in general global surveys which was being suggested to her by the Ministry of External Affairs and others. He ended his note by urging her 'to breathe confidence in the strength and destiny of our nation and spend time telling President Nixon the basic problems and urges of the people of India'. She did precisely this in her two sessions with the American president.

The very next day, on 1 August 1969, Haksar met Henry Kissinger for the very first time. They would have much to do with each other in 1971 with Haksar clearly emerging the winner in their confrontation. But for now, their encounter was placid and even-keeled, often good-humoured. The US record of the meeting had this to say:[16]

Mr. Haksar opened the conversation by expressing Prime Minister Gandhi's deep concern that Indo-US relations be put on a stable basis. He stated that this had been her goal ever since her first visit to Washington as Prime Minister in 1966. He asked whether Mr. Kissinger felt there were any outstanding differences in the bilateral relationship at this point. Mr Kissinger replied seriously that he could not think of one. Then he added with a smile, "None now that you are giving US less public advice on how to conduct our policy in Vietnam ...

When the Indians urged US not to renew military sales to Pakistan, Mr. Kissinger asked them whether India had an interest in driving Pakistan into the hands of Communist China. Mr. Haksar responded that the question was sort of like asking someone when he had stopped beating his wife. With all respect, he felt it was the wrong question. Obviously Pakistan would get its military equipment wherever it had to, but it had no interest in becoming totally dependent on China ...

Mr. Haksar reiterated the need not to equate India and Pakistan. He even intimated that some Americans wanted a weak India and then argued that a strong India would help some of the Southeast Asian nations. He thought Indonesia would welcome this. Mr. Kissinger assured Mr. Haksar "categorically" that the U.S. had no interest in a weak India—"Not that (with a smile) a strong India will be any joy to deal with".

The polls to elect the fifth president of India were to be held on 17 August 1969. As things stood, it was anybody's guess who would win, although Sanjiva Reddy appeared to have the edge given that Indira Gandhi had come out in his support. But three days before the poll, she sprang yet another surprise and called for 'conscience voting' opening the doors for Congress MPs to defy the party whip to vote for Sanjiva Reddy. This is exactly what happened and on 20 August 1969, Giri was declared the winner by a slim margin. The party fissures were now completely in the open.

Efforts were then mounted for bringing about reconciliation but by the end of October it had become clear that the breach was total. Then ensured a war of letters between the two sides with Indira Gandhi's missiles being crafted and drafted by Haksar based on conversations with her. The sequence was as follows:

28 October 1969	S Nijalingappa writes to Indira Gandhi
2 November 1969	S. Nijalingappa writes to Indira Gandhi
3 November 1969	S. Nijalingappa releases letter of 28 October 1969.
3 November 1969	Indira Gandhi replies to S. Nijalingappa's letter of 28 October 1969
4 November 1969	Indira Gandhi replies to S. Nijalingappa's letter of 2 November 1969
8 November 1969	Indira Gandhi writes to all Congress MPs

PNH's note to Indira Gandhi of 31 October 1969 was typical of how things happened then:

> P.M. had asked me to look at the draft reply to Shri Nijalingappa's letter prepared by Shri Subramaniam. With great respect, I should like to say that it plays into the hands of Shri Nijalingappa by failing to define issues and merely engaging in a point-counterpoint debate; and thus bringing P.M. down to the same level as that of Shri Nijalingappa. I would submit this is not the kind of reply which P.M. should send.
>
> Shri Nijalingappa's letter broadly deals with four major issues ... I think the draft reply must begin by stating these main issues and before P.M. sets out very briefly and succinctly her point of view on each of these issues, P.M. should briefly correct the grosser mis-statements of facts in the letter and correct inaccuracies ...
>
> PM should then end the letter by asking stating something along the following lines:
>
> (a) It is no use pretending that everything is all right with our Party and that we can solve all our problems and discharge our responsibilities ... by mechanical repetition of slogans like 'unity', 'discipline', etc.
> (b) We have to recognize that our Party in recent years has suffered serious setbacks and has ceased to evoke the kind of massive response from our people ... and that we have to make a ... critical analysis of its causes.
> (c) If the Congress is to become a dynamic, live organization capable of securing once again the decisive allegiance of our people, a new life has to be breathed into it.
> (d) PM recognizes that a democratic Party like the Congress in a country of our size must always include a great variety of ideas and attitudes.

> Nevertheless the predominant image at all levels of its functioning
> must be that of a Party ... working single-mindedly for transforming
> this beautiful country of ours into a united, secular, socialist state
> ...

Naturally, PNH's drafts prevailed. What he had done is convert a clash
of personalities and battle of egos and gap in generations to a conflict of
principles and ideologies. He had sufficient ammunition with the stray
thoughts note and the nationalization of banks which had already happened.
The letters were sent late at night and reached the media before the recipient
had time to read and digest their text and sub-text. It was actually a
non-contest. Nijalingappa was outflanked. Sharada Prasad had a vantage
position in the prime minister's Secretariat. He admired Nijalingappa the
state leader, but wrote many years later that 'he was badly out of his depth
as a national one'. He went on to say of this period of Indian politics:[17]

> Through her brilliant generalship, Indira Gandhi outmanoeuvred the
> Syndicate at every turn. The battlefield itself changed from one day to
> another ... One day it was about bank nationalisation, the next day it
> was about Privy Purses ... The Syndicate's blunder, as Kamaraj confessed
> later to a leading journalist, was to think that Indira Gandhi would
> not see through their game that in wanting to install Sanjiva Reddy in
> Rashtrapati Bhavan they were planning her eventual removal.

Indira Gandhi deserves full credit for her brilliant generalship as Sharada
Prasad describes it. But the essence of brilliant generalship is to choose,
trust and empower aides as well, who will plan and execute the strategy of
behalf of the general. This is exactly what Haksar did. His archives are full
of notes and drafts that became Indira Gandhi's missives to Nijalingappa
that changed the direction of Indian politics. His opening lines for Indira
Gandhi's letter to all her party colleagues summed up the letter war that
was raging between her and Nijalingappa. Indira Gandhi sent this letter
on 8 November 1969 but its authorship becomes clear from two notes of
Haksar to her. The first was on 5 November 1969 and reads:

> P.M. had directed that I should prepare a draft of a letter to members
> of the AICC. I have prepared one. It is placed below. I had shown it to
> Dr. K.S. Shelvankar who has helped in editing it ...

The very next day, he told the prime minister:

> Yesterday I had submitted to P.M. a draft of a letter to be addressed to
> the members of the AICC. It represented a great effort on my part to
> calmly and objectively analyse in depth the real source of tensions and
> conflicts in the Congress Party. However, I have felt that the kind of
> analysis contained in the draft may not correspond to the level of political
> understanding of an average Congressman. I have prepared another draft
> which is dripping with words. P.M. may kindly like to glance through it …
>
> … A letter to AICC members has to be distinguished from any
> speech one might make at the session of the AICC. That would be the
> occasion for presenting a programme of action.

The draft 'dripping with words' as PNH called it became Indira Gandhi's
letter and began thus, pithily capturing the essence of what was at stake
as PNH saw it:

> There is a crisis in the Congress and in the nation. It is not a crisis
> which has come about all of a sudden. It has been building over a long
> time. What we witness today is not a mere clash of personalities and
> certainly not a fight for power. It is not as simple as a conflict between
> the parliamentary and organizational wings. It is a conflict between two
> outlooks and attitudes in regard to the objectives of the Congress and
> the methods in which the Congress itself should function.
>
> It is a conflict between those who are for socialism, for change and
> for the fullest internal democracy and debate in the organization on the
> one hand, and those who are for status quo, for conformism and for less
> than full discussion inside the Congress …
>
> I do not want a split in our great national organization. But I want
> unity which is a unity of principles and on methods of work. To speak
> of socialism and secularism, to vote for them in meetings but to have
> public image of association with those who are opposed to secularism
> and socialism is no service to the nation …

As Sharada Prasad writes:[18]

> … the tactical error committed by Nijalingappa by appealing to the Jan
> Sangh and Swatantra Party to support Sanjiva Reddy [placed] in Indira
> Gandhi's hands a weapon she could use with telling deftness.

Clearly the weapon was placed not just in Indira Gandhi's hands but also in Haksar's. He had convinced Indira Gandhi to battle it out because as he told her, 'what is involved is nothing new but the continuation of the unresolved conflict between the Party organization and the parliamentary wing'. He had invoked no less a person than Nehru himself to tell her on 28 August 1969, before the confrontation with Nijalingappa gathered momentum that:

> ... on several occasions Nehru consistently held that the Party organization could not expect the Prime Minister and his Government to be directly responsible to the Party executive. The Prime Minister or Chief Minister, he noted, "is the archstone which forms the basis of democratic structure. Once he is chosen he must have the full discretion left to him. If he does not command the confidence of the legislature, he must go". Nehru considered it wholly unjustified to expect the Prime Minister only so long as the Party executive permitted him to remain in office. To do so, he argued, would reduce parliamentary democracy to a "mockery".

The establishment of the Congress party, Haksar contended, was 'glibly mouthing the slogan of discipline' but 'the essence and substance of the matter was something else'. And that something else was a conflict that Indira Gandhi's father had himself faced and resolved and which Haksar wanted her to do likewise.

A very good example of the type of advice Haksar was giving Indira Gandhi during the crisis days of mid-1969 is revealed by the note he sent her on 30 August 1969. The prime minister's political colleagues were trying to convince her to call a meeting of Congress legislators from all the states so that she could establish direct contact with them. He was not impressed and told her that 'the following aspects need to be carefully considered and weighed':

(1) Is P.M. to call a meeting over the heads of Chief Ministers and without consulting them and getting their approval?
(2) Has the possibility of Gujarat M.L.A.s turning up in strength and creating a pandemonium been considered?...

(3) I presume the Home Minister [Y.B. Chavan] has been consulted, at least in his capacity as a person who still appears to have sway over Maharashtra M.L.A.s.

(4) What precisely will be the agenda for this meeting? What concrete decisions will flow from such a meeting or are intended to flow from such a meeting?

(5) Having regard to the tempo of political development, would it not be better at this stage that P.M. meets Congress M.L.As and P.C.C. members as part of her forthcoming tour programme?

Haksar ended by expressing his concern, stating 'such ideas are already in the Bazaar with various bright-eyed persons claiming to be its parents'. The prime minister got second thoughts and met the Congress legislators in their respective states when she went there—exactly as he had recommended.

Sanjay Gandhi's obsession with producing a small car continued to bother PNH all through 1969. Actually, Haksar's objection was to the idea of the small car itself. He made this abundantly clear to the prime minister on 16 September 1969:

> The Ministry of Industrial Development's passion for the small car mystifies me a great deal. I personally feel that the Ministry has put itself on completely wrong tracks in chasing the so-called small car project. Why should Government tie up considerable resources which, according to my estimates, could be no less than Rs 40 crores in manufacturing cars even if it were to cost Rs 12,000 as claimed the Ministry of Industrial Development on the basis of the Renault proposal? I do not think that the social and political climate which Government wishes to create at present is consistent with Government's interests in the manufacture of cars. Government will earn some popularity and indeed gratitude of the public at large if it were to do two things: Firstly, improve in a decisive manner the public transport so that ordinary citizens could travel in comfort. The second best thing it could do is make available to messengers, stenographers, clerks, section officers and others a really cheap scooter ...

A month later the Cabinet was to consider licensing of additional capacity for the manufacture of scooters. Haksar told the prime minister 15 October 1969:

> I should like to submit to P.M., with all the emphasis at my command, that under no circumstances must Government entertain the proposal for licensing of additional capacity for the manufacture of scooters in the private sector. If we were to do so, we shall be committing the same folly as was done in the case of licensing three separate manufacturing units for motor cars ... I should like to submit that scooter ... is one consumer item that should be taken into the public sector. We should license a large capacity. Further, I should like to add that we must not rush to having a collaboration agreement ... If Government were to set a challenge to Indian engineers, mechanical, electrical, design and automobile, they are fully capable of developing an indigenous design for a motor car or a scooter.

Thus, in June 1972 Scooters India was incorporated as a public sector scooter manufacturing company near Lucknow. But contrary to what Haksar had recommended, this company got the entire plant and machinery as well as design and documentation from Innocenti, an Italian company which also picked up a 20 per cent share in the new company. The scooter brand was called 'Lambretta'. But within a few years, it became painfully evident that it would never fulfill the expectations with which it was established.

By today's standards or even by the yardstick of the 1980s, these views of Haksar could certainly be considered antediluvian. His views on priority to public transport were and continue to be unexceptionable. His views on encouraging Indian designers too were commendable. But his opposition to the manufacture of a small car, by later day standards, was certainly to be proved comprehensively wrong, as was his opposition to expansion of scooter manufacturing in the private sector.

The cross that Haksar has to bear is that he did nothing really to free India from the license-quota-permit raj when he was in a position to do so. On the contrary he did not seem to think that there was anything fundamentally faulty with this system. It is extraordinary that he would see nothing wrong in writing this letter on 18 December 1970 to B.D. Pande, secretary, Department of Industrial Development:

> S.K. Sikka Personal Assistant to the Prime Minister, bought a Vespa scooter in June last year out of Government quota. Unfortunately, the scooter was stolen on the 2nd December, 1970. I understand the police authorities have given their final report saying that they have not been able to trace the scooter and have closed the investigation. There is thus no hope of recovering the scooter.
>
> Sikka is living in Lajpat Nagar which is nine kilometres away from the Secretariat and he has to conform to abnormal office hours ... He is also required to attend office on Sundays and official holidays. It is thus essential that he should possess a conveyance to enable him to discharge his duties in an uninterrupted manner. I shall, therefore, be glad if you will be good enough to have a Vespa scooter allotted to him immediately.
>
> A formal application in the usual form is enclosed.

But his obsession with the public sector was not always misplaced. He played a pivotal role in the establishment of the Indian Petrochemicals Corporation (IPCL) in March 1969 which turned to be a highly successful and pioneering venture. Between 1968 and 1972, PNH would spend a great amount of time on reshaping and restructuring ONGC. He persuaded Indira Gandhi to set up a committee under the chairmanship of K.D. Malaviya to review its functioning and got one of India's most distinguished oil technologists, M.S. Pathak, to be the committee's driving force. Haksar had earlier overcome objections and got a 43-year-old Pathak appointed as chairman and managing director of a fledgling Engineers India.[19] It was almost entirely at PNH's insistence that ONGC was given the responsibility for exploring and drilling for oil in offshore Bombay High after a Soviet team had earlier established its hydrocarbon-bearing potential.[20] Oil was to be struck in February 1974 and commercial production was to commence two years later. This was a turning point for India's energy economy.

Right through his tenure in the prime minister's Secretariat and later in the Planning Commission, Haksar agonized over the special development challenges in India's two most populous states—Uttar Pradesh and Bihar. He never let go of an opportunity of imploring the prime minister to put her personal weight behind land reforms, especially in Bihar. Indira Gandhi was going to that state in mid-September 1969 and on 10 September 1969 Haksar exhorted her:

> P.M. has written to the Chief Ministers inviting their attention to this problem [land reforms]. I feel that an atmosphere has to be created for tackling this problem ... PM may wish to do this during her forthcoming visit to Bihar where the problem of small farmers, share-croppers and landless labourers is particularly acute and has become more so in contrast to the success of farmers who have profited by the green revolution ...

Mindful of political realities and the nature of the Congress party itself in that state, he told the prime minister to say that she was not demanding any radical overhaul of the existing structure, but that she expected the better-off farmers not to thwart the implementation of existing laws for the protection of tenants, small and marginal farmers and landless labourers. It was a curious position for a bold thinker like Haksar to advocate. He was wanting the prime minister to appeal to the altruistic instincts of the powerful and say that it was in their self-interest to ameliorate the living and working conditions of the rural poor.

The prime minister did heed his advice when she spoke but it was to have no effect whatsoever. Even Haksar's asking the prime minister to persuade the state government to resume the process of registration of tenants and completion of land records that had been stopped in 1964, which she did, had no effect. It was a communist regime in neighbouring West Bengal which was to do so over a decade later and earn kudos for its Operation Barga.

Indira Gandhi would be expelled from the Congress party by its bosses on 12 November 1969. She must have had an inkling that something like this was in the offing for Haksar sent her a note two days before her expulsion:

P.M. had enquired the other day about the position of the Prime Minister under our Constitution who may be the leader of a party which may not have an overall majority. I had submitted to P.M.—and I thought I should set it down in writing—that our Constitution makes no reference to political parties at all. Article 74 merely provides for there being a Council of Ministers to aid and advise the President. The only provision is that this Council of Ministers shall be collectively responsible to the House of the People. So long as the Council of Ministers, including the Prime Minister, enjoys the confidence of the House and is not voted out by a motion of no confidence, it is perfectly legal, constitutional and moral for the Prime Minister to continue as Prime Minister enjoying the confidence of the House even though the Prime Minister may not be the leader of the majority party in Parliament. This is the position as I see it. However, P.M. may wish to have this matter examined by our legal pandits.

Soon thereafter, Indira Gandhi's government was reduced to a minority in the Lok Sabha and she had to depend on the Left parties and the DMK to cross the half-way mark needed for survival. This she was able to do easily with her socio-economic programme and this co-habitation would last for slightly over a year. In March 1971, she would storm back to power on her own with a thundering majority.

On 15 November 1969, Indira Gandhi sat down for an unusual interview. It was for a small circulation but high-brow publication called *The Citizen* which was bringing out a special number on the public sector. The publication was run by a three-member group of trustees, the chairman of which was Jayaprakash Narayan, who would become her nemesis five years later. Interviewing the prime minister was P.N. Dhar, who was then director of the Institute of Economic Growth in New Delhi. The interview that appeared in the publication's issue of 24 January 1970 is most interesting on two counts. First, P.N. Dhar himself would join the prime minister's Secretariat a year later and would subsequently take over from PNH. Second, the answers to most of the questions put by Dhar were prepared by Haksar.

In his answers, PNH expounded on the economic philosophy that Indira Gandhi stood for. He spoke of the mixed economy being a viable concept and a means to attain a socialist society and said that the most suitable areas for public sector investments are those where the social returns are the highest. He advocated detaching the process of decision-making in respect of public investments from unwarranted and costly political interference through, for instance, an autonomous development bank. He accepted that public enterprises must make profits and should have pricing and limited investment autonomy. In an answer that would not have endeared him to his leftist circle, Haksar stated that the agitational approach of labour ran counter to the very concept of the public sector.

Haksar tried to implement many of his ideas on the public sector when he was in a position to do so. Unfortunately, he was unable to do much about eliminating bureaucratic and political interference in the running of public sector enterprises. He also took issue with the trade unions who he felt were being irresponsible and handicapping the functioning of public sector companies. On 12 June 1972, he would write to Mohan Kumaramangalam, the minister of steel and mines:

> I was dining with the Czech Ambassador the other day. After a great deal, of hesitation he sought my permission to raise with me a matter to which, he said, he attached the highest importance and which had been causing him great worry. He said that Czech reputation had been seriously undermined by the functioning of their foundry forge plant which is part of the HEC complex ... A very small section of the artisan class numbering 1400 decided to go on strike on the pretext that they would not abide by the prescribed rules that provide that promotions will be made only if they passed certain tests. What worried the Ambassador was the total indifference of the State Government of Bihar to these 1400 holding the entire HEC to ransom ... I am passing on this information for what it is worth to you because I must confess the picture painted by the Ambassador looked to be pretty dismal and that if we do not do anything and merely sit back and relax, HEC, which is one of our finest national assets, will continue to run down to the detriment of all of us.

Sadly, Heavy Engineering Corporation (HEC) which was started in Ranchi with high hopes and expectations soon became a millstone around the government's neck and neither Haksar nor Kumaramangalam could do much about it. In any case, a year later both of them were gone and those who came after them never shared their excitement for HEC.

ᑫ

Indira Gandhi turned 52 on 19 November 1969. She was greeted throughout the day including by Haksar who also sent her a note somewhat irritated by her appointments.

> I was surprised to see that Prime Minister agreed to see Mrs Taya Zinkin. I do not know how this appointment was arranged but Mrs Zinkin is a most vicious person whom has carried on anti-Indian campaign over the years. In all her books she has reviled J.L.N. [Jawaharlal Nehru]. I know that both Mrs Zinkin and her husband are great friends of the ICS fraternity. But that is no reason why they should have so ready an access to Prime Minister.
>
> I was also distressed to learn that Mrs Fischer gained entry to see P.M. today. Earlier in the day, the Soviet Ambassador had telephoned me to say that he had received a birthday message of greetings from Brezhnev, Podgorny and Kosygin which he wanted to deliver to P.M. I asked him if he could deliver it to me so that I could convey it to P.M. He readily agreed and said that he would not like to trouble P.M. at a time when she was very busy. A little later Mrs Fischer telephoned and said that she would like to deliver a message to Prime Minister. I told her that P.M. was busy but that she could deliver the message either to me or to Shri Seshan [prime minister's personal secretary].
>
> I am not troubled about my own amour-propre which is always open to an outrage as part of professional hazard, but I do feel that some semblance of orderliness should normally obtain in matters affecting access of diplomats to Prime Minister. P.M., may wish to give suitable directions.

A chastised prime minister complied with what her secretary had demanded and issued the necessary directions.

∾

After the Congress had formally split in mid-November 1969, Indira Gandhi called a meeting of the All India Congress Committee on 22 November 1969 in New Delhi. It was meant to be a show of strength and demonstrate that the bulk of the party remained with the prime minister. Haksar was asked to prepare her speech for the occasion which he sent the previous day with this note:

> The speech is in three parts. The first part deals with an analysis of the current conflict in the Congress; the second part deals with the definition of democracy and socialism under concrete Indian conditions of today. I feel that some such elaboration of the concept of socialism is essential and unless this is done, we are likely to be swept off our feet by the ideologues both on the Right and on the Left. The last part of the speech is mere exhortation.
>
> I also feel that P.M. should give a call to all those who left the Congress to return to the fold and also for a rallying together and consolidation of democratic socialist forces in India ...

Some of the important themes he had incorporated into her speech were: '...economic growth and socialism have to proceed concurrently, rather than sequentially; equality should be defined as equitable distribution of income-earning opportunities rather than of existing incomes; socialism does not necessarily mean controls and bureaucratic power; a reduction in controls is likely to lead to higher output, lesser corruption and release of administrative personnel from negative tasks and also shrink the swollen black-markets and reduce the sources of black incomes.' These are themes associated with a pragmatic socialist not a doctrinaire ideologue, as Haksar is sometimes portrayed to be. He went one step further and had Indira Gandhi say something that continues to have significance for the country even though he formulated it in the context of the need for the Congress party to retain its socialist credentials:

... We cannot practice superstition and worship science; we cannot practice communalism and preach secularism; we cannot incite regional and linguistic passions and claim to be the foremost protagonists of the concept of Indian citizenship; we cannot promote egalitarian concepts of socialism and remain tied to hierarchy of caste and class.

A month later the Congress's plenary session was held in Bombay in late-December 1969. As usual, Indira Gandhi's speeches as well as the main resolutions had gone through Haksar and reflected his draftsmanship heavily. Typical was this note from him to the prime minister on 23 December 1969:

P.M. gave me, some time ago, the draft of a resolution on foreign policy and I felt it was most inadequate. I have attempted to prepare a new draft which is placed below for P.M's consideration.

This was also the time when a third person from Haksar's London circle of the late-1930s came into prominence in the Congress party. This was Rajni Patel, who organized the plenary and later got a large group of professionals and intellectuals to declare their allegiance to Indira Gandhi. Haksar wrote to the prime minister the same day, that is on 23 December 1969:

In the paper placed below, I have set out some points for P.M's consideration for her speech at the meeting in Bombay organized by Shri Rajni Patel and others.

In that speech, Indira Gandhi said:

... The intermingling of the intellectual and political life and its cross-fertilisation is a necessary pre-condition for our survival and progress. For too long the intelligentsia has lived a cloistered life. For too long the political life has remained impoverished by lack of contact with the intelligentsia. No country can afford this divorce. And a country like ours engaged in deep and fundamental processes of transformation of every facet of its life can never hope to consummate its social, political, economic and cultural revolution without an organic interconnection between the political and the intellectual effort ...

In our country the intellectual effort remains weak and anemic ...

One looks in vain for that mighty unrelenting intellectual onslaught against spurious doctrines, social efforts that bedevil our efforts to fly aloft the banner of secularism, of democracy and of socialism ... Only an informed, alert intelligentsia can put an end to this debasement of our political life.

Just the previous year, the murderous Cultural Revolution had been launched in China where the intelligentsia was being crucified. Here, in India, a prime minister was exhorting this class to 'reflect the agony and ecstasy of our national endeavor' and fight for upholding and propagating 'all the traditions of humanism from Buddha to Gandhi and Nehru'.

ॐ

Indira Gandhi would get importuned by Muslim organizations that not enough is being done to protect and promote the Urdu language. Before the year ended, she received a manifesto called *Urdu ki Maang* that was also endorsed by many Indian writers. She asked Haskar for his views which he gave on 28 December 1969:

> I love Urdu. It is a beautiful language. Its poetry and prose have a quality of its own. Hindus and Muslims have both contributed to the growth of its literature. If it is to survive, it must receive official recognition, patronage and encouragement ...
>
> ... I may be mistaken, but Urdu is now tending to be exclusively the language of Muslims ... I am wondering whether Urdu ki Maang has not become indissolubly linked with the protection of the cultural rights of Muslims in India.
>
> Frankly I have never understood the logic of linking up the rights of Muslim minorities in India with the protection of Urdu language. The Muslims of Bengal retain their religion by speaking Bengali. In Kerala and Tamil Nadu although they may be speaking some sort of pidgin Urdu, they are quite content to learn Tamil and Malayalam. Only the Muslims of the Indo-Gangetic Plain have a problem; but doesn't this reflect an atavism? ... What I fear is that protection to Urdu will merely postpone the day of emergence of the Muslims of Indo-Gangetic plain from their sulking tents.

The central point made in the document entitled "Urdu ki Maang" is that it is an error to think that Urdu is a language of the Muslims ... My own guess is that if we took a census of the *post-independence* generation, it may well be found that Urdu has in fact become the language of the Muslims and that too, of those living in the Indo-Gangetic Plain excluding Bengal.

Haksar's advice to Indira Gandhi was that 'the future of Urdu needs to be discussed in somewhat greater depth and in an atmosphere of academic detachment'. But in his note he made a curious statement that 'if Hindi is our national language and is going to be our national language and must become the national language, why should a Muslim feel a sense of loss of his religion if the new generation were to learn Hindi?'. The factual position was and continues to be that Hindi is, strictly speaking, not India's national language but it is the language of the state as far as the central government is concerned.

Jawaharal Nehru had started a tradition of a prime minister inaugurating the annual session of the Indian Science Congress in the first week of January of the year. Haksar would be the main author of Indira Gandhi's addresses to this forum till 1973. In the 1970 speech he had Indira Gandhi highlight two areas of scientific research which would acquire increased importance in the years ahead. The first was the area of earth sciences, such as geology, geo-physics, meteorology, paleontology, hydrology, geo-chemistry which 'is basic to the investigation, discovery and estimation of our natural resources'. These earth sciences, she said, 'are an excellent example of how basic research can be related to objective-oriented research and can be undertaken to the economic advantage of the country and the scientific advantage of the research community'. The second area was the biological, ecological and health sciences which, Indira Gandhi pointed out, can 'contribute to social and economic benefit of our nation' adding that the 'conservation and utilization of our natural plant and animal resources will be an important and primary scientific task'.

Haksar's view of science and society had been profoundly influenced by J.D.Bernal, the eminent British physicist who was a Marxist.[21] In the speech he had prepared for Indira Gandhi Haksar also stressed that the 'scientific community is a republic, not an oligarchy ... Unless the scientific community is critical and conscious of its responsibility in withstanding the pressures of tradition and hierarchy it cannot forge a community that is republican in character.' He went on to delineate the characteristics of this republic of science:

> It is that every rational voice has a right to be heard and has the right to influence decisions. However, once decisions are made all members of the community have the obligation to work together ... The real tests are whether the scientific community is dynamic and forward looking; whether every scientist no matter how young or how low in the hierarchy can present his views and feel that he is a partner, a team-mate; whether the community is self-critical and corrects itself or tends to gloss over its errors and mismanagements ...

By this Haksarian yardstick, India's republic of science is still a mirage, although there is a very large scientific and technological community with many accomplishments to its credit.

A few months later at his behest, a National Conference on Electronics was being organized, perhaps for the first time in Bombay from 24 March to 28 March 1970. Of particular interest to Haksar was what India should be doing in the area of computers. It was at his suggestion that a Working Group on Computers had been set up in late-1969 to suggest a 'framework of policy within which computers—both the hardware and software—should develop in our country'. On 20 March 1970, he informed the prime minister that the conference would be discussing both manufacturing and R&D. At that time, the public sector company Bharat Electronics (BEL) was proposing to enter into acollaboration with a UK company ICL and PNH briefed in the prime minister thus:

> It is quite extraordinary that two non-technical persons, namely the Secretary, Ministry of Defence and the Secretary, Ministry of Defence Production [both ICS officers] should set themselves up to make a decision on this matter.

There are 130 computers in India a large fraction of which are IBM. The rest are ICL and come from other countries. These various computers are not compatible with each other. The result is that our maintenance costs are very high. It is of utmost importance that we should develop an adequate computer policy which will take into account compatibility, proper maintenance service, building up of our computer maintenance repair and spare part manufacture capabilities which should be planned in such a manner to provide a viable computer manufacture in India ...

Haksar's frustration with IBM which he had expressed to Indira Gandhi the previous year in May 1969 was that 'IBM simply refuses to take Indian equity. I also know that they have no plan to manufacture anything, but merely to assemble computers which have become obsolete in the United States.'

The AICC was having its convention in Bombay in early-January 1970. There was added interest on this session because it was the very first to be held after the Congress had split two months earlier. It met again in early-June 1970. On both occasions Indira Gandhi called on Haksar to help prepare the resolutions to be adopted. She would give him the drafts prepared by her political colleagues to work on. On one such draft on the communal situation, he told the prime minister on 1 June 1970:

I must confess to a feeling of deep disappointment after reading the draft of the communal situation. It totally lacks touch with reality. There is no attempt to analyse the basic factors of communalism and seeks refuge in the old, old ways of thinking that communalism can be fought merely buy uttering some Shlokas.

It is not for me to draft Resolutions for a political party which should be able to have within its fold persons who can give meaning and substance to these Resolutions. However, I have attempted a brief draft and I feel strongly that something along these lines needs to be said.

Needless to say, Haksar's draft won the day. There was also a note on nationalization of banks and its impact that he had got Dr Hazari to prepare which also got circulated at the June 1970 session. And, of course, she depended on him for her own speeches as this note from him of 10 June 1970 shows:

> P.M. had said that a statement should be prepared for her use at the forthcoming A.I.C.C. Session. I have drafted one. P.M. may like to indicate its inadequacies.

As it turned out, her final speech was almost the exact one that Haksar had sent her.

Every year, the Government of India announces Republic Day Awards a day before 26 January. These are hugely sought after. Haksar refrained for making any recommendations on his own and, in fact, he was to refuse the award himself in January 1973. He would scrutinize the lists that would come for the prime minister's approval and make comments on them. One of the few recommendations he would make during his tenure was on 8 January 1970 and this is what he told the prime minister:

> ... There is one name which has been weighing on my conscience. Viewed from any point of view, the most creative, the most original and the most outstanding writer in Hindi is Yashpal. He does not fit into the establishment but anyone who has read his books over a period of last 30 years or more recognizes in him as the most creative person, the most uncompromising critic of our social and political scene and a person who devoted his youth in the national movement and the terrorist movement and later on contributed a great deal by his writings. In his novel which was published in two parts, entitled *"Sacch Aur Jhoot"*, I believe there is some implied criticism of Jawaharlal Nehru. I believe this has built up some sort of prejudice against him. In fitness of things, P.M. should include him in her list despite the criticism. *I yield to no one in my devotion to the life and work of Jawaharlal Nehru. However, if I were to write of the period I served under him, there will be many occasions when I shall have to make a critical assessment of some of the things he did or failed to do.* To leave a man like Yashpal from the list of award winners is doing grave

injustice to those of us who are concerned with the giving of the awards
or of suggesting suitable names for such awards. [italics mine]

Yashpal received the Padma Bhushan in 1970. Haksar's note reveals that
he was well read in Hindi literature as well. It also shows that while was
a Nehruvian to the core, he was more than prepared to recognize the
intellectual value of those who were critical of Nehru.

PNH was instinctively allergic to the American ruling establishment. But
this was only in part due to his naturally 'leftist background' and his past
political associations. The USA gave him cause to get peeved. This was
to reach its peak in 1971 with the way President Nixon and his advisor,
Henry Kissinger, handled the Bangladesh issue. There were earlier episodes
as well. On 12 February 1970, Haksar sent the prime minister a strongly-
worded note:

> Item 6 on the agenda of the Cabinet today is a curious one. It brings
> confirmation of the theory widely held that after Panditji's death and
> during the period of Shastriji, we allowed a certain amount of flabbiness
> to creep into our system of governance and let Americans loose in our
> country ...
>
> It has been stated in the Cabinet note that there is, apparently, a
> body called an American Committee for the History of South Asian
> Art. It is located in Chicago and is part of the University of Chicago.
> This body decided to set up an Academy in Varanasi without taking
> anybody's permission.
>
> What is the idea of the Academy? It is to advance knowledge
> and understanding of the art of South Asia. A question might be
> asked: amongst whom do they wish to advance the knowledge and
> understanding of art? Is it amongst Indians, or amongst Americans? If it
> is amongst Indians, the next question is: are there any Indian institutions
> which could have the instrument of this laudable purpose? Why should
> a separate Academy, which is merely an arm of a foreign Academy, be
> set up in India? ... *Apparently, we, as a nation have lost all sense of self-
> confidence ...*

I am also troubled about the reckless way in which PL-480 funds are used for one purpose or another and we are confronted each time with a fait accompli.

To sum up: I have nothing against Americans who have an insatiable thirst for knowledge to study South Asian Art, but such a centre for study should be located in the United States … The Russian can do the same in their own country. *But if we in India want to study South Asian Art, we should do it ourselves and set up an Academy for it and pay for it* … [italics mine]

This note would be characteristic of what and how Haksar would tell the prime minister. He would always be devastatingly frank, both on men and matters. On this particular issue, he could be accused of only one thing—of being, perhaps, excessively nationalistic and being suspicious of foreign intent. But those were different times with both the Americans and the Soviets doing their best to spread their tentacles in this country, particularly in the academic community. What Haksar was clearly highlighting is that India as a once colonized nation, should have acted with greater confidence keeping in mind its own self-interest.

On 12 February 1970, the ne minister was to meet leaders of the Opposition parties to discuss the fall-out of the Supreme Court judgment that had been delivered annulling the law that had nationalized banks the previous year. Haksar briefed her on what she could expect and how she should respond:

Broadly speaking, there will be two views expressed:

(1) That Government should bow to the Supreme Court decision and agree to restore the status quo ante. It will be further argued that bank nationalisation has not produced any visible gains and that the entire thing was really motivated by political considerations.

(2) The second group of arguments would be that the Supreme Court has posed a challenge to Government and Government should meet it by nationalizing all the banks, including the foreign banks,

Both points of view would have to be resisted ...

As against the attack on bank nationalization itself, P.M. may wish to summarise the position since banks were nationalized. The achievements are significant considering during all this period nationalized banks were surrounded by uncertainties created by a litigation ... Bank nationalization has served a most useful economic and social purpose and there is no reason to go back on it.

... The philosophy behind nationalization of 14 banks was for Government to acquire a commanding height in our credit institutions and we were quite content to leave marginal smaller amount of credit available through the smaller banks through their own devices. We do not wish to take management responsibility for a large number of small banks and also pay them compensation. Similarly we do not wish to pay compensation which will involve a large outgo of foreign exchange which will be incurred in the event of nationalization of foreign banks. There is also the case that just as foreign banks operate in India, so do Indian banks operate abroad. There has to be some reciprocity in this respect. Therefore, the broad approach of Government at the time of nationalization of banks, which was well thought out, still stands. *We shall neither be swayed by those who attack us from the Right for giving up nationalization nor from the Left who would impose upon public exchequer a very large burden involving payment of compensation without any significant corresponding advantage accruing to the community as a whole.* [italics mine]

But that the government was under international pressure was evident when the minister-counsellor of the US Embassy, Galen Stone, met Haksar on 12 February 1970 itself, 40 minutes before the prime minister's meeting the Opposition leaders. The next day Haksar briefed the prime minister about Stone's visit:

[Stone] said that he had been instructed to make a representation to the Government of India at the level of the Prime Minister about the adverse consequences which might flow, should the Government of India decide to nationalize foreign banks. He then read out a long aide- memoire which, he said, he wanted to leave with me. He then went on to say that he had been advised that such a demarche from the United States Government might help the Government of India and particularly the

Prime Minister, in withstanding pressures that seemed to be developing for nationalization of foreign banks. I told him that if the motive of the United States Government was to assist in the manner Mr. Galen Stone had suggested, the step he was taking was perhaps not quite appropriate … The Government of India's policies were well-defined at the time of nationalization of the 14 banks and they were not accustomed to changing their policies merely because of certain pressure here and there. *I then told him that he should really take back the note and not leave it with me, so that if anyone said that the United States Government had made representations, I would say that no such representation was received.* [italics mine]

❧

In early-March 1970, Indira Gandhi was faced with a hugely ticklish problem. She had approved the award of the Padma Shri to a film director of great talent, Ritwick Ghatak, which had been announced on 25 January 1970. But, thereafter, slanderous statements made by Ghatak on Mahatma Gandhi came to light and he was pilloried both in the media and in Parliament. In light of this raging controversy, the Home Ministry decided to cancel the award and sent the file for the prime minister's approval. Haksar observed on the file on 2 March 1970:

… Human history is full of examples of artists of genius living in destitution and penury, because they cannot compromise their art with the vulgarity of public taste of their time. And Shri Ritwick Ghatak is one such artist. From all accounts, he lives in utter poverty and his family is needy and hapless.

As often happens, life inflicts a heavy roll and Shri Ghatak alternates between moments of sanity and long periods of insanity. During one such spell, he uttered some words in the privacy of his house. These were blasphemous words and I would not like to repeat them, but these were words uttered when the man was not in possession of his senses … Even apart from this can anyone say that Mr. Ghatak's words have diminished in any way the stature of the person against whom he used the atrocious language? If one spits at the sun, the spit comes back to him. The sun shines brightly and so do the names of Gandhiji and Jawaharlal Nehru.

Why then are we so worked up? …

 If a man says something which he knoweth not, God forgives him, but man, his creature, cannot.

The next day Haksar met L.P. Singh, the home secretary who had recommended the cancellation of the award to Ghatak. Haksar showed Singh a signed statement by the film director that the 'shockingly indecorous language used by him against Mahatma Gandhi was done when he was mentally ill'. He also brought to Singh's attention that 'a number of persons of some standing have testified to Shri Ghatak's great creative talent as a film director and have taken a liberal view of his trespasses'. Singh agreed with his Allahabad University contemporary and got his minister to say in the Lok Sabha on 6 March 1972 that 'After carefully weighing that statement [signed statement of Ghatak] and its genuineness, government have come to the conclusion that the father of the nation, Mahatma Gandhi, would have himself forgiven Shri Ghatak his trespasses and recognized his creative talent embodied in his work of art'.

Two key appointments were to be made in the prime minister's Secretariat in 1970. For some time, Haksar had been feeling that he was spending far too much time on matters relating to science and technology which, important as they were, were also getting more demanding and complex. There was not only the nuclear energy establishment but India was also embarking on a full-fledged space programme. Discussions were also going on to bring India into the age of electronics. Two vast scientific agencies—the Council of Scientific and Industrial Research (CSIR) and the Indian Council of Agricultural Research (ICAR) presented numerous administrative and organizational problems.

 Thus, it was that in June 1970 Haksar inducted a 30-year-old scientist who had studied radio astronomy at Cambridge and had been working in the Atomic Energy Commission in Bombay into the prime minister's Secretariat. It did not hurt that the young man so designated was also the son of his close friend G. Parthasarathi, who was then vice chancellor of the JNU. 'GP' as he was popularly called, was, in turn, the son of N. Gopalaswami Ayyangar with whom Haksar had himself worked with Ayyangar as part of India's delegation to the UN in the early months of 1948.

Haksar's philosophy of working in the prime minister's Secretariat is best described by Ashok Parthasarathi in his memoirs of his tenure there.[22] Haksar had passed an internal order stating that 'Shri Ashok Parthasarathi has joined the Secretariat as Special Assistant for Science and Technology. He will normally put up papers directly to PM. On important matters he will put up papers through me.' When Ashok Parthasarathi asked Haksar for some guidelines regarding what constituted 'important matters', Haksar replied:

> That is entirely for you to decide. You have to make the judgment ... You should use the phrase PM desires to any entity outside the Prime Minister's Secretariat only under one of the following three circumstances: PM has sent you a note asking you to do something, PM has spoken to you to do so, or, in exceptional circumstances, I have asked you to do so. Under all other circumstances, including where you want some information from a ministry or agency when advising to do something, you should make clear that your request is being made at your level.

In fact, Haksar would lay down strict ground rules for his colleagues: 'The Prime Minister's Secretariat should be seen to be not existing, only the PM exists.' That is perhaps one reason why in all the years he worked with Indira Gandhi it is very difficult to find photographs of the two together.

Other than science and technology, Haksar had been telling Indira Gandhi for quite some time that the prime minister's Secretariat needed somebody with specialized expertise in economics. Thus, it was that on 24 September 1970, Haksar he wrote to Dr V.K.R.V Rao who was chairman of the Board of Governors of the Institute of Economic Growth (IEG), New Delhi:

> A post of Adviser has been lying vacant for a long time in the Prime Minister's Secretariat. We have been anxiously looking for a suitable person and we feel that Shri P.N.Dhar, Director of the Institute of

Economic Growth will answer to our needs. Since you are the Chairman of the Board of Governors of the Institute, P.M. said that I should request you to let me know if you would be prepared to let us have his services for a period of 2 to 3 years on a contract basis. I am not sure if Shri Dhar would agree to come, but obviously, even if he were to, he could not possibly do so unless you could release him.

Dhar not only came on board two months later but stayed on for some six-and-a-half years. He had known Indira Gandhi since 1965 and Haksar since 1966. He was in touch with them on economic issues and on matters relating to his home state since he continued to have deep roots in the Kashmir Valley. In his memoirs of his years with Indira Gandhi Dhar writes:[23]

> ... Indira Gandhi had no ideological fixations in economic matters... It was therefore no surprise to me that, knowing my views on several issues which did not tally with those of some of her favourite advisers [read: Haksar], she wanted me to join her office. In fact, I got the clear impression that was because of my being something of a Doubting Thomas that she wanted me around. What was really surprising was that Haksar too wanted me on her staff, despite his views that economists have no political sense, and despite some of his progressive friends complaining against my being a reactionary ... Haksar did not tell me at that stage that I was expected to succeed him nine months later when he retired ...

That he had actually welcomed Dhar's appointment and had already thought of him as his successor shows that there was a strong streak of pragmatism in Haksar. Unlike other progressives in his circle he was not dogmatic when it came to people who had a different point of view, provided he was convinced about their intellectual integrity.

There was a third appointment Haksar orchestrated in July 1970 and this was that of the nuclear physicist B.D. Nag Chowdhury as scientific adviser to defence minister with the explicit objective—known only to the two of them and Indira Gandhi, of course—of building long-range ballistic missile capability. That nuclear weapons were very much on Haksar's mind is revealed by the fact in mid-December 1970 he conveyed to Admiral Nadkarni, chief of Naval Staff that 'the Prime Minister has cleared the Indian Navy to look into the feasibility of having nuclear propulsion for marine purposes...'

A small but highly significant change made by Haksar in Nag Chowdhury's appointment terms was to give him the status of secretary to the government so that he reported to the minister directly and had vastly greater decision-making authority. Nag Chowdhury who had been brought from Calcutta to the Planning Commission by Haksar in 1967 was to be intimately involved with India's 1974 nuclear test. Nag Chowdhury had been a student of the eminent Indian astrophysicist Meghnad Saha who had been Haksar's teacher in Allahabad University during 1931–1933. He laid the foundations for India's missile programme and after the successful nuclear test of 1974, Haksar placed Nag Chowdhury as the second vice chancellor of JNU as G. Parthasarathi's successor.

∾

Haksar and Indira Gandhi would differ, for instance, on appointments. On 24 December 1969, for instance, Haksar had sent a note to the prime minister:

> It seems that there is a clear division of labour. The Cabinet Secretary and the Minister of External Affairs are charged with the responsibility of creating problems while I am burdened with the responsibility of finding solutions.
>
> I have endeavoured, with varying degrees of success, not to deliberately or with malice towards anyone to tread on anyone's toes or to hurt anyone's amour propre. But I find it extremely difficult to express myself with restraint when I find that I am supposed to constantly display restraint and responsibility and even be mindful of what is best in the interests of Government, while senior officers like the Cabinet Secretary and Foreign Secretary show scant regard for it ...
>
> In my view, it has been a major tragedy of India that we have treated economic diplomacy totally divorced from political diplomacy and it is

about time that one called the bluff about the virtues of our economic diplomats.

Regretfully I know far too much about the manoeuvrings and alignments which exist in Delhi to be taken in by the plea about the inadequacies of Shri B.R. Patel ...

Two days later, Indira Gandhi responded:

The question is not so much of Shri Patel's competence which is not in doubt. It is his integrity or his reputation which may not be all that in demand for that particular job.

Haksar would not let it go and on 1 January 1970 responded to the prime minister's response:

I noted the way I did because it was being argued that Shri P will not be able to handle the job. I do not know what is meant by his "reputation".

As it turned out, on Haksar's insistence, Patel was to be appointed India's ambassador to the European Economic Community (EEC), as it used to be known then, in April 1970.

On sensitive appointments, Haksar was a stickler for propriety. He would make his recommendations strongly, no doubt, but would also advise the prime minister not to sign blindly on what he had said. On one such case, he had sent up a file to the prime minister on 16 September 1969, writing:

Before she records the minute [being suggested by Haksar], PM may informally consult her senior colleagues, including the HM [home minister].

Likewise, on 6 January 1970, he told the prime minister who, was also the finance minister then:

I had submitted a note this morning to P.M. seeking her approval to Shri S. Jagannathan's appointment as Governor of the Reserve Bank of India and to sending him a telegram. While I feel that Shri Jagannathan would still be the best person to have as Governor of the Reserve Bank, it might be appropriate if P.M. were to send for the Finance Secretary as well as Dr. I.G. Patel and ask them what their suggestions are ... This would be the proper thing to do, so that Secretaries of the Ministry of Finance have a feeling of being at least invited to express their views.

But he could be merciless as well, as this noting of 21 March 1970 reveals:

> ... I am amazed at the total sense of irresponsibility of the Department of Defence Production. They have stated that there as many as five young design engineers in the HAL [Hindustan Aeronautics Limited] with most impressive track records whom are apparently not yet fit to take over from Dr. Ghatage, but who would by sheer flux of time mature. *We know that young Indian scientists and technologists are flying out to United States and other countries and are occupying high positions of responsibility but we in India are stifling them and suffocating them* ... P.M. may kindly consider turning down the proposal made by the Department of Defence Production in the following terms:
>
>> I regret I cannot accept the proposal for re-employment of Dr. Ghatage. No reasons have been given why one of the younger men listed by the Department of Defence Production cannot take over now. From the particulars of their records all of them have impressive qualifications and experience. It is quite extraordinary that *while young Indian scientists and engineers are occupying positions of responsibility in the United States and other countries, we find it difficult to give them that responsibility in our own country.* [italics mine]
>
> ... It is high time that P.M. takes a meeting for examining in depth the problems of the aeronautics industry.

Haksar would time and again take personal interest in the development of the aeronautics industry in India—in large part influenced by his friend Satish Dhawan, then director of the Indian Institute of Science, Bangalore and who, two years later would become the chairman of the newly formed Space Commission. But while Dhawan would lay the foundations of India's enormously successful space programme, the aeronautics industry never took hold in the country, unlike, for instance like it did in Brazil.

❧

Haksar had been part of the Kashmiri Pandit network in central India and particularly in Allahabad in the 1940s. He had dealt with Kashmir-related issues in the United Nations in early-1948 and got to know Sheikh Abdullah well. But he had never been to the state. In the prime minister's Secretariat he allowed Sushital Banerjee to deal with matters concerning J&K because of his great familiarity with people and the ground situation in that sensitive state. It was only in June 1968 that Haksar had made his first visit to Srinagar for a meeting of the National Integration Council. He struck up an instant rapport with Chief Minister G.M. Sadiq—perhaps their communist backgrounds helped in this. After this visit, Haksar started getting himself involved more closely with issues relating to Kashmir and, on 31 December 1970, sent this note to the prime minister showing how, even though an administrator, was very sensitive to political considerations and activity:

> I have no comments to make on the proposed plan of action. However, like everything the Home Ministry does, it is intensely bureaucratic. I won't blame them for it, because the political side of the question is, presumably, left to the politicians.
>
> I, for my part, would like Sadiq Sahib together with Mir Qasim, either jointly or severally, to be making a public statement on or about the 4th and 5th of January in Srinagar or in some part of the Valley. In the course of that statement, the leaders of the Plebiscite Front and, in particular, Sheikh Abdullah and Afzal Beg by name, should be challenged to state publicly their position on the question of their unquestioned allegiance to the Constitution of India. They should be asked to be brave enough and courageous enough to publicly state that they are working for severance of the constitutional and other ties of Jammu and Kashmir with India. They cannot be allowed to use the freedom and liberty given to them to arrange for secession of a part of India. Such a statement should be made in a challenging and combative spirit. This statement should be picked up by some of our political leaders outside Jammu and Kashmir and the leaders of the Plebiscite Front must be questioned. Their failure to respond to such challenge or their equivocations would provide the political atmosphere and political justification for what might follow; but without taking into account the political dimensions of the problem and

merely to proceed in the manner suggested is, to my mind, not he best way if doing things ...

On 30 April 1970, a political hot potato was handed over to Haksar. That day, the Committee on Public Undertakings (COPU) of Parliament submitted its 66th report which covered the award of contracts awarded by a state-owned enterprise in the early-1960s for laying oil pipelines in the eastern part of the country. The COPU indicted senior officials for favouring an American design engineering company Bechtel, and wanted action taken against the erring officers. The report created a stir with many members of the Parliament, cutting across party lines demanding action from the government. The media, particularly the tabloid *Blitz*, joined in the chorus demanding action against the 'errant' officials—prominent among whom was P.R. Nayak, an ICS officer who had been managing director of Indian Refineries Ltd when the controversial pipeline contracts had been awarded. Nayak subsequently became secretary, Ministry of Petroleum and Chemicals and in February 1969 he was shifted as secretary, Ministry of Works and Housing.

Bowing to political pressure, in August 1970 a one-man commission of inquiry was set up to investigate the matter further. This was headed by J.N. Takru, a retired judge of the Allahabad High Court. The COPU had listed several acts of commission and omission committed by Nayak and others. The Ministry of Petroleum and Chemicals thereafter had framed charges against Nayak. These charges were referred to Takru to advise the Government if there was a prima facie case established in respect of these charges.

Nayak was retiring in November 1970. Since he wanted time to respond to Takru's queries, he was given an extension till the end of March 1971. After giving a hearing to Nayak and after scrutinizing various documents, Takru gave his findings in early-1971 that almost all the charges were prima facie established and referred the matter for departmental action against Nayak. On 20 March 1971, Haksar would give the prime minister the background to the case and 'pose the issues for consideration in the following terms':

(1) Should the officer with a good record of service face odium of suspension pending enquiry into serious charges against him?

OR

(2) Should Government face the odium of granting extension of service to a senior officer facing serious charges?

In the light of the past history of the case, the Report of the Parliamentary Committee and references thereto in Parliament in subsequent discussions and the Report of Justice Takru, the image of the Government would suffer if they opt for the second of the two alternatives which I have set out above. I deeply regret having to reach this conclusion but I cannot escape it.

Nayak was suspended from service three days before his extended tenure was to end on 25 March 1971. He appealed and lost in the Delhi High Court. He then approached the Supreme Court, which in December 1971, by a 4–2 majority, quashed Nayak's suspension order. Was an innocent man and an upright officer unjustifiably fixed? In his autobiography[24] put together by his son and grand-daughter, Nayak had this to say about Indira Gandhi:

From January 1966 to June 1967, she governed as I would expect the Prime Minister of a country to, more or less along the lines of her father. But after the 1967 elections due to a sense of insecurity, and not getting a clear majority in the Lok Sabha, her government seemed to falter … and she gathered around her a set of advisors and assistants of "curious background" and "strange values" …

If it was Haksar Nayak was alluding to, surely his background was anything but 'curious' and his values anything but 'strange'. But the autobiography does go on to say:

Mrs. Gandhi took as her principal Chief of Staff one gentleman who had a sense of self-importance. He and Ajja [Nayak] did not like each other, as Ajja often stood up and argued for what he thought was right and would not pay "respects".

Haksar may well have had an air of self-importance as Nayak suggests but he always listened to officers with views different than his own. He stood up for many ICS officers who were not on his ideological wavelength. No doubt, Haksar had stoutly opposed the involvement of the American company Tenneco in the development of the oil reserves in the Gulf of Cambay which Nayak was enthusiastic about. On 10 April 1968, Haksar had told the prime minister:

> Item 3 on the agenda for the Cabinet meeting tomorrow is on the subject of offshore drilling for the exploration of oil in the Gulf of Cambay. I am truly amazed at the persistence with which the Ministry of Petroleum & Chemicals is pursuing this project. When it was first considered, I viewed it with a certain amount of sympathy. However, the more I have studied the state of our oil industry, the more I am amazed why we should be so desperately anxious to give away concessions for oil exploration in the deep seas to a foreign oil company. This conviction of mine has been reinforced by the Report of the Soviet oil experts who recently visited our country at our invitation ... We have knowledge and experience of drilling. Why can't we put these resources to utmost use and augment our oil reserves before we give concessions to a foreign oil company? This is a simple question ...

Haksar was for ONGC while the minister of Petroleum, Asoka Mehta and Nayak were for Tenneco. But these were purely professional disagreements. Haksar's references to Nayak himself in the notes to the prime minister do not reflect any bias against him. In fact, in late-1970 but before Takru gave his report, Haksar brought Nayak's name to Indira Gandhi's attention as a possible cabinet secretary but also told her that since there were others with a longer tenure in service left, Nayak's case was weak.

On 1 May 1970, the prime minister received a cable from India's charge d' affaires in China, Brajesh Mishra, who was to occupy Haksar's position when Atal Bihari Vajpayee was prime minister during 1998–2004. The cable which had been copied to the foreign minister as well read:

At this evening's May Day celebrations all Heads of Missions were invited to sit at the Tie An Men rostrum to watch the fire-works. MAO arrived late at 9pm. Half an hour later MAO accompanied by LIN PIAO CHOU EN LAI and three other members of the Standing Committee of the Politburo as also SIHANOUK and PENN NOUTH went around the nostrum shaking hands with all Heads of Missions and their wives. The surprise of the evening was his longish (for him) conversation with Soviet Charge d' Affaires and the number 2 man in the Soviet delegation to the Sino-Soviet talks and a shorter one with me.

MAO said to me: "We cannot keep on quarrelling like this. We should try and be friends again. India is a great country. Indian people are good people. We will be friends again some day". I replied: "We are ready to do it today". Then MAO said: "Please convey my message of best wishes and greetings to your President and your Prime Minister". I assured him that it most certainly be done and then congratulated him on China's success in launching an earth satellite. MAO then moved on to shake hands with others.

In any thing connected with Chinese leaders it is difficult to say whether it was premeditated or not. My judgment is that MAO was fully briefed before arriving on the rostrum. In any case expression as above of friendship by MAO himself should be given the most weighty consideration ...

After a discussion in New Delhi in which Haksar's views prevailed, Mishra was sent a message from the foreign minister on 6 May 1970, the text of which was PNH's.

Your telegram ... of May 1. We do not wish to under-estimate the significance of MAO's words. However, we have to assess the significance of the relations between our two countries in the immediate future. Further probing will have to be done. Opportunity for this may present itself when you call on the Director of the Asia Department on May 8.

In the course of your conversations, you might say that you were personally touched by Chairman MAO's references to India and by his message of greetings to the Prime Minister and President; that you had conveyed these to New Delhi; New Delhi has asked you to reciprocate these sentiments and to say that India too sincerely believes that two great countries like ours cannot keep on quarrelling; that we should try and be friends again; that Prime Minister has, on all occasions, stated that the doors of friendship are always open; that we too believe that China and the Chinese people are great people, full of creative energy and that we should try and work for restoring friendship. You may then recall the words used by Pandit JAWAHARLAL NEHRU in one of his letters to CHOU EN-LAI in which, even in the midst of the crisis then prevailing, he had given expression to the hope that if that crisis could be got over, the relations between India and China would not only become normal, but might even be bettered. You might then ask: question, however, is what steps could be taken to fulfill hope expressed by Chairman MAO which we share, that "we will be friends again some day"?

You could say that you are leaving for India and that you would like to have precise guidance in interpreting the precise significance of Chairman MAO'S observations ...

If the atmosphere surrounding your talks ... gives you an opportunity you should raise the question of the extremely hostile, false and tendentious propaganda from China against our country ... There is a contradiction between our mutual desire to improve relations and such hostile propaganda. You might ask: How can such a contradiction be resolved?

Our feeling is that whereas China would not be indifferent to normalizing our relations to the extent of exchange of Ambassadors, there will be no let up in their propaganda against us. We would like to test the validity of this assessment ... [italics mine]

Mishra was asked to meet his counterpart and 'keep the ball rolling'. He reported back on 8 May 1970:

I called on the Chinese Foreign Office today and was received by YANG KUNG SU ...

YANG himself referred to MAO's conversation with me on May Day and added that for them MAO's word represented the basic principle guiding the relations between the two countries. When I talked of concrete action from both sides to improve relations he tried to maintain that it was for the Government of India to take concrete action. However towards the end he said: "Mr. Mishra said just now that both sides should

181

take concrete action. Our great leader, Chairman MAO, has talked to you personally; that, I think, is the greatest concrete action on our side and it is the principle guiding the relations between China and India. Mr. MISHRA has heard personally what Chairman MAO said and we want to know what reaction the Government of India has after listening to Chairman MAO and what concrete action the India side will take". We went back and forth a little on the question of concrete action and finally I said: "I take note of what you have said. And I hope you will also take note and consider what I have said, that concrete action must be taken on both sides". YANG replied, "then, let both sides consider".

The event described in Mishra's dispatch of 1 May 1970 has become part of diplomatic history and has come to be known as 'Mao's Smile'. In an oral history interview published in 2000, Mishra suggested that India did not take full advantage of Mao's gesture and should have followed it up immediately. Mishra always believed that while Indira Gandhi was willing, Haksar was amongst the few who prevented her from reciprocating Mao's gesture and creating a new opening with China. The evidence available shows that Haksar was extremely worried by China's continuing support to rebels fighting the Indian state in the Northeast region. He was also peeved with the barrage of invective against India in the Chinese media which obviously had official sanction. How tense the bilateral relationship was during that period can be seen from the fact that between June 1967 and April 1970 India handed over to China 22 strongly worded notes that protested China's actions in regard to this country.

There is a sequel to this exchange between Haksar and Mishra of May 1970. Indira Gandhi was to send down a note to Haksar on 6 November 1972 in which she asked:

There is a telegram from Mishra in Peking (CCB No. 13231 dated 31.10.72). While we should not get over-enthusiastic perhaps the time has come for us to take some initiative. What should this be?

Haksar's immediate response to this query from the prime minister is not available but many years later on 3 April 1992, he was to write to J.N. Dixit, then foreign secretary, in which, among other things, he recalled:

He [Mishra] came to India and, as is customary with him, stressed and strenuously urged that we take the initiative in sending India's Ambassador to Peking. I said that this was desirable and that since we were the first to withdraw our Ambassador, it would be appropriate if we were to send back our Ambassador. *However, I wanted to be quite certain that the Chinese would reciprocate. Somehow Mishra had not taken kindly to this suggestion of mine. I had then told Indira Gandhi that without such an assurance of reciprocity a unilateral action on our part will raise controversy in Parliament which could only be silenced if we were to say that a decision was taken by both the governments to have Ambassadors.* After Mishra's departure, [from China on transfer] Lakhan Malhotra was going to China. He would, I am sure, recall my telling him that his task was to have an agreement reached about the mutual exchange of Ambassadors between our two countries with India sending its Ambassador first. This was ultimately agreed upon. [italics mine]

Full diplomatic relations between India and China were to be restored in May 1976 after a gap of 14 years when K.R. Narayanan was sent as India's ambassador to that country.

On 7 June 1970, Haksar submitted to the prime minister a 'set of proposals involving a thoroughgoing reshuffle of the Cabinet portfolios'. He recommended that Indira Gandhi give up the finance portfolio which she had held since July 1969 and hand it over to Y.B. Chavan. Seventeen days later, she did precisely that. But contrary to Haksar's suggestion that Swaran Singh be made home minister in place of Chavan, she decided to keep that portfolio to herself. His suggestion that she take over external affairs was rejected and instead Swaran Singh was given charge of that ministry but Haksar's recommendation that Jagjivan Ram be made defence minister was accepted. He made numerous other suggestions—the most notable of which was that either P.B. Gajendragadkar, the retired chief justice of India or K.N. Raj, the distinguished economist be inducted as education minister. That was, however, not to happen.

One suggestion of Haksar was that Nandini Satpathy, an ex-communist, who was then deputy minister under the prime minister be elevated as minister of state. This elicited a slip of paper from the prime minister:

> Nandini will be very upset if she has only Atomic Energy. Can she not have some small part of Home [Ministry] as well? Could NS [Nandini Satpathy] not do Union Territories?

Haksar's response on that scribble was straight-forward.

> I am afraid not. Besides, this small allocation would be ridiculous.

This is how Haksar would communicate with his boss—and the best part was that the boss would take it showing the chemistry that existed between them—at least till early-1973.

Indira Gandhi would get a large number of representations from all sorts of people and organizations. In early-December 1970, a delegation of villagers from Uttar Pradesh had met her and handed over a representation which she passed on to Haksar, observing 'This is most distressing. How can one deal with it? They say that the DM [district magistrate] is involved. Can B.B. Lal help?' Uttar Pradesh was then under President's Rule and B.B.Lal was one of the advisers to the governor. Haksar's response shows his sharp political instincts. He replied to the prime minister on 14 December 1970:

> If the facts narrated are even partially true, this is a God-sent opportunity for the State Congress to champion the cause of the Sevagram Krantikari Parishad. It should not be beyond the realm of possibility for the State Congress Secretary or the General Secretary of the A.I.C.C., Shri Bahuguna or any other person who is active in the affairs of U.P. Congress to proceed to the Tehsil in question, meet the representatives of Sevagram Krantikari Parishad and if the facts stated by them are true, then lead the agitation in support of the demands made by the Parishad and in "exposing" what the representatives have said to be "the modus operandi of village officials". *I hope P.M. will forgive me if I were to say that the Congress Party has been so long in power that it has forgotten the most elementary principles of politics, namely, to help the people fighting*

injustices. In such a situation what can poor B.B. Lal do or advise. *There is hardly any point in writing to the Home Minister of the State Govt. And even if one were to write to him, it is not likely to produce any result unless this is backed up by political effort at the local level.* [italics mine]

He noted on the margin the names of two prominent Congressmen of that time who were avowed socialists—Chandrajit Yadav and K.N. Singh—who could be asked to take interest in the matter.

Fourteen banks had been taken over by the Government of India in July 1969. Not unexpectedly, that decision had been challenged in the Supreme Court whose judgment came on 10 February 1970. This was to mark a watershed in the relationship between the prime minister and the judiciary. Actually, the Supreme Court had upheld the acquisition of the 14 major banks and had also upheld the legislative competence of Parliament to do so. However, the verdict had invalidated the principles and methods provided in the nationalization law to determine the amount of compensation to be paid to the affected shareholders. But these provisions could not be separated from the main law which had, therefore, itself been struck down. Subsequently, the compensation formula was reworked and the new legislation with this formula became law on 31 March 1970.

The second blow to the government–judiciary relationship in the initial years of Indira Gandhi's tenure was delivered on 15 December 1970. This was the day when the Supreme Court struck down a presidential order ending privy purses and privileges for the ex-princes who had integrated their domains into the Indian Union following Independence in August 1947. The presidential order had been necessitated because the bill giving effect to the abolition of privy purses and princely privileges had been passed in the Lok Sabha but fell short of the required majority in the Rajya Sabha by a bare one-third of one vote. On 5 September 1970, Haksar had recommended to the prime minister this route:

The President has the unquestioned power to de-recognise the Rulers. During the debate in Parliament, it was even urged by some members that Government should have resorted to this power instead of bringing a Constitution Amendment Bill.

While Government would have preferred that the exercise of Presidential powers to de-recognise the Rulers should await the adoption of the Constitution Amendment Bill, it is regretted that this has not been found possible through lack of a fraction of a vote in the Rajya Sabha.

However, Government is fortified in the belief that there is widespread support in the country for putting an end to an outmoded and antiquated system which permitted the enjoyment of privileges and privy purses by a small section of our people without any corresponding social obligation on their part.

During the course of the debate in Parliament, even many of those who opposed the Constitution Amendment Bill expressed themselves in favour of the abolition of privileges and privy purses.

As it is Government's declared policy to abolish these privileges and privy purses and also put an end to the very concept of Rulership, Government feels that they would be justified in de-recognising the Rulers and thereby terminate their privy purses and privileges with immediate effect ...

On 25 December 1970, Indira Gandhi put a series of questions to Haksar to answer:

1. In what precise manner the Lok Sabha is to be dissolved?
2. What happens to the residences occupied by M.Ps. after dissolution?
3. Should Prime Minister tender her resignation and should there be a Caretaker Government?

Haksar replied to these queries the same day and sent the prime minister a note:

In the event of P.M. seeking a dissolution of Parliament and President acting upon it, I submit the following action be taken.

PM should immediately call a Press Conference. At that Press Conference, P.M. should issue a statement, of which a draft is attached. This statement should be cyclostyled and should be handed over to the members of the Press and , thereafter, P.M. may invite questions.

P.M. should also broadcast to the Nation for not more than two minutes. The object of broadcasting should be to inform the people of India about the dissolution of Parliament. A draft for the broadcast needs to be prepared very carefully. I have prepared one such draft which is attached.

Thereafter, on the morning of 27 December 1970, Mohan Kumaramangalam sent this handwritten note to Haksar:

Dear Parameshwar:
Yesterday Siddharth [Shankar Ray], CS [C. Subramaniam] and I made a redraft of my original draft. Here is a copy. The marked copy is with CS who will hand it over to the PM. I myself am meeting the PM at 1230 pm. I shall look you up after seeing her.
Yours,
Mohan

This was the quartet—C. Subramaniam, Siddhartha Shankar Ray, Mohan Kumaramangalam and Haksar—that had convinced Indira Gandhi to go for mid-term polls in early-1971. The statement that got issued finally plus the radio broadcast that got made bore the imprint of the four. Indira Gandhi had added the peroration in the broadcast at the end: 'We are on the right road, we shall reach our cherished goal.' That night she went on radio to announce to the nation that elections to the Lok Sabha due in 1972 were being advanced by a year and would be held in early-1971.

That very day before the broadcast Haksar sent the prime minister a draft to be sent to the president of India:

Dear Rashtrapatiji:
The Council of Minister at its meeting held on Sunday, the 27th December, 1970 at 6 p.m. decided that I should recommend to you that the Fourth Lok Sabha may be dissolved w.e.f _____
With kind regards,

Haksar had deliberately kept the date of dissolution blank. Indira Gandhi was to add in her hand 'with immediate effect'. We don't know whether 'with immediate effect' had been discussed earlier by her with her core group. My sense is that if it had, Haksar would have said so in his draft.

Haksar was perhaps also responsible for a new feature of the 1971 elections: For the first time, elections to Parliament got delinked from elections to state legislatures. This was clearly because he and the CFSA felt that this would enable Indira Gandhi to build support for her personally and for her agenda of social transformation which was unveiled in the party's manifesto put together by him.

The Glory Years (1971–1972)

Indira Gandhi with President Nixon, White House, 4 November 1971.
Haksar is standing fully visible behind the lady in a saree.

INDIRA GANDHI WAS PREPARING FOR HER UPCOMING ELECTION CAMPAIGN
when she received this note from Haksar five days into the new year, on
5 January 1971:

> P.M. may kindly see the report placed below prepared by the Research
> & Analysis Wing (R&AW). I have long been feeling a sense of
> uneasiness about the intentions of Pakistan in future. The recent
> political developments in Pakistan have added to my anxieties. With the
> overwhelming victory of East Pakistan wing [Sheikh Mujibur Rahman],
> the solution of internal problems of Pakistan have become infinitely more
> difficult. Consequently, the temptation to seek solution to these problems

189

by external adventures has become very great. *I think that the time has come when our Armed Forces need to make a very realistic assessment both of Pakistan's capability and our response.* I have a feeling that there are many weak spots in our defence capabilities. These need to be remedied without loss of time. I know how busy P.M. is. And yet, I venture to suggest that P.M. should call in all the three Chiefs of Staff, Defence Secretary and the Defence Minister and share with them her anxieties and ask them to urgently prepare their own assessment and make recommendations of what the requirements of each of the Services are so that we can feel a sense of security. I suggest that such a meeting should be held quietly and without any publicity… [italics mine]

Just as Haksar was worrying about Pakistan based on his meetings with Kao, Ritwick Ghatak cropped up again. The eccentric Bengali film-maker had made a film on Lenin but it had run into controversy. On 6 January 1971, a day after sharing his worries about Pakistan with the prime minister, he told her:

In matters of this sort one is apt to be carried away by somewhat exaggerated notions that our society, such as it is, would be seriously deflected from its course of evolution by a film on the life of Lenin as produced by Shri Ritwick Ghatak. Generations of people all over the world have seen far more inflammatory films by Eisenstein, Pudovkin, Rossellini and others, These films, at any rate, were shown on a mass scale. And nothing very much really happened. Even if the film is certified as it is, hardly any cinema would show it on a commercial basis. *I myself saw the film and I cannot say with any sense of realism that Ritwick Ghatak's film on Lenin will bring the revolution even fraction of a second earlier. However, I am rather more oppressed by the poverty of Shri Ghatak who has staked up a little money with the help of some hapless financier and they are both desperately trying to sell this film to the Soviet Union. It would be great fun exporting Indian Lenin to the Soviet Union! I hope the Soviet society survives the depredations.* It is really quite comic that so many hours of official time should have been wasted in considering the solemn question whether the film should or should not be released. I feel that we can well afford to let the film go giving it a "A" certificate [Adults only]. [italics mine]

After dictating the note Haksar realized that he may have been carried away by his liberalism and suggested to the prime minister that she may agree to having the film certified 'for adults only' subject to deletion 'only of that portion of the commentary on land grab sequence'. The prime minister agreed!

Thereafter, the prime minister plunged into her campaign in right earnest. Haksar was fully involved in the campaign at every step—writing substantial parts of the manifesto, suggesting possible candidates and getting feedback from his band of political and non-political friends in different states. People approached him with suggestions which he duly passed on to Indira Gandhi, and some even met him to offer themselves as candidates. One such person was a distinguished army man who had done India proud in the 1965 war with Pakistan. Haksar informed Indira Gandhi on 16 January 1971:

> General Harbaksh Singh called on me today at 1230pm. He said that he had been approached by the Akali Party to stand from the Sangrur Parliamentary Constituency. He said that he belongs to this area. He further said that there are hundreds of thousands of people, especially amongst ex-servicemen, who are just fed up with the low level of Akali politics. He will have nothing to do with them. In fact, Punjab needs to be rescued from the Jathedars. They have no morals, no scruples and no ideology of any sort. He would, therefore, be glad to place his services at the disposal of the Prime Minister and would like to give a fight ...
>
> *Generally speaking, I take a dim view of soldiers, sailors and airmen entering politics. I must say that I was agreeably impressed by the earnestness and sincerity of General Harbaksh Singh. May be, he is an exception.* [italics mine]

The next day, Indira Gandhi asked Haksar to speak to the president of the Congress Party in Punjab, Giani Zail Singh, about the general but it is obvious that his candidature went nowhere. On 30 January 1971, Haksar reported to the prime minister:

> General Harbaksh Singh telephoned to me this morning to say how depressed he felt the way the Congress Party was dealing with him. He said that P.M. can make enquiry from any independent sources to discover

what wide support he enjoys in Sangrur Parliamentary constituency. He said he is anxious to give a fight to the Akalis. He added that he had heard that he was accused of flirting with the Akalis. This, according to him was a strange allegation when one knows that Giani Zail Singh and Sardar Swaran Singh were themselves carrying on with the Akalis ... And now Sardar Swaran Singh tells him that he cannot get Sangrur because the need for adjustments with CPI has arisen. The General said that he had nothing against the CPI but there is no chance for that Party to win from Sangrur ...

I cannot say that General Harbaksh Singh is being unreasonable. In fact, the method of handling some of these people could certainly be greatly improved ...

As it turned out, the general did not contest.[25] Surjit Singh Barnala of the Akali Dal won this seat and many years later would become the chief minister of Punjab and later the governor of Tamil Nadu.

That Haksar was intimately associated with the distribution of Congress tickets for the 1971 elections is evidenced by a note that he would send on 4 February 1971 to the prime minister when it had almost been decided to leave the New Delhi seat to the CPI in preference to Mukul Banerjee, an active Congresswoman:[26]

As per P.M.'s directions, I dutifully saw Mukul [Banerjee] and Bavani [her husband] and when I finished hearing what they had to say, I did not have the heart to suggest to Mukul that she might accept an assignment. Such an offer would have been, rightly, construed as adding insult to injury. They remain and will remain, loyal, devoted workers, but obviously P.M. has to find a solution to their problem. To put it simply, their problem is that they have neither a position in the Party organization nor a position in public life. They have no money and live under conditions of destitution. *A political party or leader which fails to look after such people will have to do a lot of accounting. In many matters I exercise self-restraint but the way things are happening it is becoming increasingly difficult for me to bottle myself up.* It is a particularly bad day for me. I have had the misfortune to hear another story from Goa ... *If P.M. has got the impression that a crook and criminal like Bandodkar should be encouraged and Sequeira and Kakodkar sacrificed, I feel that there is hardly any point in carrying on.*

192

Even ordinary courtesies and decencies are not being shown. Kakodkar was called to Delhi and he is being made to cool his heels here. *One does not do such things even to one's enemies, let alone to one's friends. And I feel that having allowed certified enemies to enter the gate, the time has come to cry a halt.* [italics mine]

Mukul Baneree finally did get the Congress ticket for New Delhi and won handsomely. But from this note it is clear that Haksar was getting increasingly frustrated and was even thinking of quitting as we shall see very soon.

❧

On 18 January 1971, Haksar sent Indira Gandhi a note the significance would be revealed much later. He wrote:

I have received a programme drawn up for P.M. to tour her own constituency on the 1st February, 1971. I find that helicopter is being used twice. P.M. has to consider this carefully. Also whether this was done in 1967. Use of helicopter which West Bengal is advising in the interest of security, is one thing. Its use in going to inaccessible places is also understandable. Whether similar justification exists for its use by P.M. in her own constituency, requires, I submit, careful consideration.

Some months later after the election results were declared and she had won handsomely in a landslide, her opponent Raj Narain would petition the Allahabad High Court that Indira Gandhi was guilty of a series of electoral malpractices, including the use of government helicopters for her campaign. I will be discussing that case a little later. Suffice it to say for the moment that she was held 'not guilty' by the judge of the charge of misusing helicopters because she had confined it to specific areas on security considerations as advised by Haksar. As it is, she would be held guilty on two counts. There may well have been a third count had she not heeded Haksar's advice on the use of helicopters in her own constituency of Rae Bareili in Uttar Pradesh.

❧

The election campaign was in full swing and Indira Gandhi had returned to New Delhi to take part in the Republic Day celebrations on 26 January 1971. Just the previous day, Haksar delivered a bombshell of sorts to her:

I was born on 4th of September 1913. I, therefore, reach the age of superannuation on 4th of September 1971.

Under Fundamental Rule 86, it is provided that leave at the credit of a Government servant in his leave account shall lapse on the date of compulsory retirement provided that if in sufficient time before that date he has formally applied for leave due as preparatory to retirement and been refused it, or ascertain in writing from the sanctioning authority that such leave, if applied for, would not be granted—in either case the ground for refusal being the requirements of public service, then the Government servant may be granted, after the date of retirement, the amount of leave so refused subject to a maximum of six months.

My leave account standing as on 31st December, 1970 shows that I have the following amount of leave due to me:-

(i) Earned leave—-180 days
(ii) Half Pay leave—-440 days

In accordance with the provisions of Fundamental Rule 86, I therefore apply for leave preparatory to retirement for the entire amount of leave due to me with effect from 1st of February 1971. [italics mine]

Haksar was clearly telling the prime minister that he wanted to leave. She sat on Haksar's note and a few days later, on 2 February 1971, sent him an extraordinary note of her own:

You know that I am neither morbid nor superstitious but I do think that one should be prepared. The thought of something happening to me has haunted me—not so much now, as during the last tour—and I am genuinely worried about the children. I have nothing to leave them except very few shares which I am told are hardly worth anything. There is some little jewelry, which I had divided into two parts for the two prospective daughters-in-law. Then there are some household goods, carpets, pictures, etc. It is for the boys to decide. I personally would like everything to be as evenly divided as possible, except that Rajiv has a job but Sanjay doesn't and is also involved in an expensive venture. He is so much like I was at his age—rough edges and all—that my heart aches for the suffering he may have to bear. The problem is where they will live and how ... I can only hope and trust for the best. But I should like the boys and some to feel that they are not quite alone, that they do have some one to lean on.

This was a most unusual Indira Gandhi—emotional and baring her soul out to her aide. Was she telling him that she still needed him and that he should not press his resignation? Whatever it was, events soon overtook both of them when on 30 January 1971, an Indian Airlines plane flying from Srinagar to Jammu was hijacked to Lahore and destroyed there. India immediately suspended flights of Pakistani civil and military aircraft over Indian territory. Indira Gandhi issued two statements in quick succession, both drafted by Haksar. From Calcutta, on 6 February 1971, she appealed to 'all political parties in the country not to use this incident for narrow political ends', and ended by saying 'I should like to warn all elements, inside the country or outside, that we stand united in the defence of our national honour and interests and shall not allow them to be threatened or jeopardized under any circumstances'. The same day, Haksar sent her a message:

> A message has come from Islamabad saying that Pakistan Government has sent a note requesting mutual talks and consultation for overcoming difficulties that have arisen and saying that India should not have acted unilaterally in cancelling civilian and military overflights. This I interpret as a good sign. We have said that we are considering this request made by Pakistan, but in the meantime Government of India's decision in respect of overflights remains, expressing the hope that Pakistan would create a better atmosphere for mutual negotiations by paying compensation for the loss and damage suffered by India.

But the message also carried some political advice for a prime minister on her election campaign:

> I would submit that the main theme for P.M.'s talks with the business and industrial community in Calcutta should be on 'politics of growth with stability' to which Government is committed and the Congress Party is

committed. Stability cannot be reached on the basis of grand alliances or on the basis of extreme left. The path which the Congress Party led by the Prime Minister is treading is the only path on which one could have some assurance that stability could be reached and growth ensured ...

On 18 February 1971, the Soviet ambassador called on Haksar at his own instance. Right through 1971 this diplomat Nikolai Pegov would meet Haksar very often both formally and informally. Haksar recorded of that early-February 1971 meeting:

> The Ambassador handed over to me in extreme confidence, a Photostat copy of a letter written by the Ambassador of Pakistan in Moscow to Chairman Kosygin. I place below a copy of it. The Soviet Ambassador said that Chairman Kosygin had not yet replied to this letter and wondered if there was anything which Government of India would like Chairman Kosygin to do. I asked him what he had in mind. He replied by saying that perhaps some meeting could be arranged at an appropriate level in Moscow between the two sides [India and Pakistan] and with Soviet presence. He said, for instance, that the Ambassadors of the two countries could meet. I told him that the issues involved were fairly simple and straightforward. An Indian aircraft on Pakistani territory was wantonly destroyed and the Pakistani authorities looked on; the President of the ICAO [International Civil Aviation Organisation] had recommended to Pakistan that the aircraft, together with the passengers, mail, etc., should be allowed to continue their journey and that the hijackers must be prosecuted. Pakistan has to set right the wrong done. Once this was achieved, the proper atmosphere would be created for restoring confidence without which restoration of air flights over the territories of the two countries concerned could not be resumed. The Ambassador did not argue against my line of reasoning.

The Pakistan Government's complaint to the Soviet Union and asking for its mediation had fallen on deaf years. On the contrary, India was shown a copy of the Pakistani letter and allowed to put forward its arguments to strengthen the Soviet case for non-involvement. A week later, Haksar sent a telegram to D.P. Dhar, India's ambassador in Moscow, identifying specific military equipment which were urgently required by India 'based on a review (a) of our deficiencies and (b) of substantial accretion to Pakistan's offensive capabilities'. The list included tanks with matching ammunition with spares, armoured personnel carriers, guns, ammunition, bomber aircraft, surface-to-air guided weapon, low-looking radar and aircraft for India's aircraft carrier. It was a long wish list and Haksar ended the telegram by telling Dhar that:

> Pakistan has acquired qualitatively a new dimension in its capability in the air in terms of quality of aircrafts, their range, their numbers etc. We have no, repeat no, other source of supply than to rely upon Soviet readiness to understand and respond to our needs.

Simultaneously, Haksar handed over a detailed aide memoire to Pegov giving full details of what exactly the Indian armed forces exactly wanted from the USSR.

Clearly, military contingency plans were being drawn up even as the country was preparing to go to the polls. On 2 March 1971, Haksar secured Indira Gandhi's approval to set up a five-member committee chaired by the cabinet secretary and including himself to 'immediately examine the issue of giving help to Bangladesh and give their assessments to the PM'. The entire exercise was to be coordinated by Kao. The issue was to be examined from the following angles—the language being clearly that of Haksar's:

(a) What would be the implications, internal as well as external, of India giving recognition to an independent Bangladesh?

(b) If India gives aid to Bangladesh what would be the various implications under the heads given below. These may be considered under two sets of circumstances viz., with and without formal recognition of Bangladesh:-

Implications to be examined

(a) Political-both internal and external implications should be considered.

(b) Economic-the implications of economic aid should be examined with reference to India's foreign trade, the possible trans-border trade into Bangladesh and all other relevant factors including an estimate of the cost likely to be entailed in giving such aid.

Note: The requirements of Bangladesh include the following:

(i) Arms and ammunition (including LMGs, MMGs and Mortars).

(ii) Food supplies amounting to 3 million tonnes of food stuffs.

(iii) Medicines.

(iv) Communication and Signals equipment.

(v) Transport for quick movement inside India around the borders of Bangladesh. The transport includes a small passenger aircraft plus a helicopter.

(vi) A radio transmitter with facilities for Bangladesh broadcasts.

(c) Military—This assessment should include the question whether West Pakistan would retaliate against India particularly in Kashmir. Also whether there would be any military reaction on the part of China as a close ally of Pakistan.

This was Haksar at his analytical, meticulous best. What is interesting is that he had got the government thinking on 2 March 1971 itself. The background to this was clearly a 25-page note that had been sent to him by Kao on 14 January 1971, of which the main points were:

(a) the impressive increase in Pakistan's armed might since her confrontation with India in 1965; and

(b) the possibility of a combination of circumstances leading to a situation in which Pakistan might be tempted to start fomenting violent agitation, sabotage, etc. in the J&K State followed by extensive infiltration.

On 9 March 1971, Haksar informed the prime minister:

... P.M. may kindly recall that when she last visited the Operations Room, the Chiefs of Staff had given assessment of the relative position of India vis-à-vis Pakistan in terms of men and material. It was found that we were deficient in a number of respects. Subsequently, I had arranged a series of meetings to precisely estimate our requirements, taking into account the augmentation of the material strength of Pakistan's armed forces through a variety of sources, including the United States of America. As a result of this exercise the Defence Secretary wrote to me suggesting that the matter should be taken up between India and the Soviet Union at the highest possible level. It was also suggested that P.M. write to Chairman Kosygin. I had some hesitation in straightaway committing P.M. to making a demand without some assurance it would be met ... It was then decided that I should send for the Soviet Ambassador which I did. I told him of our urgent requirements ... I then informally handed over to the Soviet Ambassador an aide memoire. The Soviet Ambassador promised to convey our requirements to the Soviet Union at the highest possible level ...

I should perhaps also inform P.M. that we have had two meetings up to date with the Soviet Ambassador and his experts. The first meeting was devoted to identifying the various difficulties which our Air Force is experiencing in getting more spare parts and other essential supplies. The second meeting, which took place this morning, was devoted to an examination of the various requirements of our Navy consisting largely of spare parts, oil and lubricants for vessels we have purchased from the Soviet Union. These meetings have been extremely useful in resolving many difficulties and streamlining procedures, etc.

Indira Gandhi secured a spectacular mandate in the elections. She was sworn in as prime minister a third time on 18 March 1971. Before that, Haksar was very heavily involved in the selection of ministers. On 14 March 1971, he told her:

> *The selection of Members of the Council of Ministers must mirror the political upheaval which is taking place in the country.* People will scrutinize minutely the composition of the Cabinet. P.M.'s accountability will be total and absolute. It is for P.M. to carefully consider how she should wish to discharge her responsibilities.
>
> *Whatever be the composition of the Council of Ministers, it is, in my submission essential to impress upon the Ministers that hereafter their performance will be judged. They will have to show results and would be accountable for their failures ...* The Ministers, in their turn, must activate the Civil Service and make them accountable to the Ministers ...
>
> Since Parliament will have a very large number of Congress MPs and since only a fraction of them can be used up in the Council of Ministers,

it is essential energies of the remaining back-benchers are utilized for some purpose. I feel that P.M. should personally select Congress MPs and associate a group of them with each Ministry ... I would also submit that every Member of Parliament of the Congress Party should be made to contribute compulsorily to the Party funds ... [italics mine]

Three days later, after submitting various names for inclusion and exclusion as ministers, Haksar advised the prime minister:

... Once P.M. has decided to drop certain members who were in the outgoing Council of Ministers, it is, I submit, necessary for P.M. to personally send for each one of them and speak to them. Older men ... should be thanked and put in good humour and asked to available for their counsel ... Those who are young and have been dropped, should be enabled to entertain the hope that after a period of work in the House [Parliament], in the Party organisations , they can entertain the hope of returning to Government ...

While I understand the political necessity for a balanced Council of Ministers reflecting the aspirations of the various regions and also reflecting the interests of the vast majority of the electorate who constitute the Scheduled Caste and Backward Classes, it is difficult to conceive a Council of Ministers which is an arithmetic sum of all castes and creeds of India. Indeed, those who have contemplated the contemporary election results with a certain amount of depth, *have all come to the conclusion that the class-line has dominated the caste-line ... It seems to me, and I say so with utmost respect, that the level of political thinking of Congress functionaries appears to be more backward than the thinking of the electorate.* [italics mine]

Some of his suggestions were accepted—for instance, the dropping of Dinesh Singh. But a number of his suggestions—for instance, the dropping of Jagjivan Ram, Fakhruddin Ali Ahmed and Karan Singh— were not accepted. Three names he suggested for inclusion—Mohan Kumaramangalam, K.V. Raghunatha Reddy and K.R. Ganesh—were, in fact, included and all got plum assignments. Kumaramangalam became minister of steel and mines while the other two became junior ministers for company affairs and finance respectively.

Later in the year, in October 1971, Nurul Hasan, an eminent historian with as strong a link to the CPI as PNH, was inducted into the council of ministers and given charge of education and culture. Haksar would undoubtedly have had a role in this. Nurul Hasan was to set up the Indian Council of Historical Research (ICHR) in early-1972. At its creation, Haksar got Indira Gandhi to send this message:

> ... I hope that the Council will encourage an objective and scientific research into the various aspects of the history of our country. It is essential that our people should know the influences which have moulded them over thousands of years so that they are better able to face the problems of change without loss of their moorings.
>
> Our historians have a great part to play in giving to our people a vision. That vision can only be sustained if the study of our history is freed from shackles of artificially created framework. History of our country is sought to be identified far too much with political or cultural conflicts. It seems to be very little concerned with the people themselves, with the changes in society, with the processes of culture. *Sometimes mere chauvinism and blind acceptance of the past passes off as a re-interpretation of history.*
>
> *Pseudo-history needs to be subjected to rigours of scientific approach. Historical analysis must take into account the whole complex of interactions between the economic, political, intellectual and technological factors.* [italics mine]

Within a few days of taking over, Indira Gandhi faced a crisis of epic proportions on India's eastern border with Pakistan. From the midnight of 25 March 1971, a brutal crackdown by the Pakistani army began in what was then East Pakistan. This created an enormous humanitarian crisis leading to millions of refugees fleeing to India. It also led to huge pressure on Indira Gandhi to intervene militarily. This story of 1971 that culminated in India's victory in the war with Pakistan and the emergence of a sovereign Bangladesh has been told brilliantly in two books—one by the noted historian Srinath Raghavan[27] and the other by the political scientist

Gary Bass.[28] Both have made extensive use of Haksar's archives and have highlighted the pivotal role he played all through 1971, orchestrating and managing India's response to the crisis in East Pakistan.

Sheikh Mujibur Rahman was arrested in Dacca on the midnight of 24 March 1971, and flown to West Pakistan. On 26 March 1971, Indira Gandhi, fully briefed by Haksar with extensive talking points, met with leaders of all Opposition parties. Haksar had urged her to be firm and say that India's response to what was happening in East Pakistan should not become a subject matter of public debate as 'such a debate would defeat the purpose of giving such comfort as we can to democratic forces in Pakistan as a whole'. He asked her to emphasize that while India's sympathy towards the people of Bangladesh was natural, India, as a state had to walk warily because Pakistan was a sovereign member of the United Nations, and 'outside interference in events internal to Pakistan would not earn us either understanding or goodwill internationally'. From his own personal knowledge he mentioned the Biafra secessionist movement in Nigeria which had fizzled out because of lack of international support. There were other factors weighing on Haksar's mind while briefing the prime minister— the impact of what India might say or do on its own consistent position on Kashmir and to what extent would Sheikh Mujibur Rahman and his colleagues be able to establish their legitimacy in the eyes of the world.

In short, Haksar was advising the prime minister that the Government of India must move with a great deal of circumspection and 'not allow our feelings to get the better of us'. Evidently, she was in full agreement with this line for she followed Haksar's script largely at the meeting with Opposition leaders. But the Fifth Lok Sabha, which was then in its opening session, was agitated and already voices were being raised for some decisive 'intervention' by India. To cool passions, Indira Gandhi moved a resolution in Parliament on 31 March 1971, drafted by Haksar, promising 'whole hearted sympathy and support for the people of East Bengal'.

That very day, she received a letter from former Cabinet Minister Triguna Sen on behalf of the Bengali residents of Delhi, which lamented that 'we are not standing by our brothers and sisters of Bangladesh the way we should and the policy of our Government is not yet clear and firm enough to meet the demands of the hour'. Haksar was incensed with this letter and told the prime minister sometime later on 31 March 1971 itself:

> When I read a letter of the kind written by Dr Sen, I am reduced to a state of despair and dark foreboding about our country. Here is a man who is a trained engineer, has been Vice-Chancellor of a University and has occupied the position of a Cabinet Minister. I should have thought that during the three years that he had been Cabinet Minister, he should have understood some elementary principles on which Governments are run in the world and international relations conducted. I should have also thought that he would have the sensitiveness to see that what is happening in East Pakistan is a matter of national concern and that Bengalis, as Bengalis, especially those who claim to be Indians, have no special responsibility, any more than Tamilians should have a say in fashioning our relations with Ceylon or with Malaysia, or Gujaratis should have a say in how we conduct our relations with East Africa. It is really quite preposterous how these eminent worthies think loosely and appear to wear their emotions on their sleeves ...
>
> I would beg of P.M. to send for Dr. Sen and request him to behave with greater maturity than he has shown in the letter ...

Two days later, Ashok Mitra, then chief economic adviser in the Ministry of Finance, received a call in his office from a professor of the Delhi School of Economics. The professor was calling from Mitra's residence asking him to come home immediately to meet two close friends of his who were facing some problems. The professor who called would win the Nobel Prize in Economics 27 years later—Amartya Sen. The two friends of his were Anisur Rahman and Rehman Sobhan, then rising stars amongst Pakistani economists. The two—both Bengalis—had fled Dacca and somehow managed to reach New Delhi. Mitra too was well known to them, and so they took refuge in his residence under assumed names. What was to happen next is best recounted in Mitra's own words:[29]

> ... On the evening of the day Anis and Rahman took shelter in my house [2 April 1971], I took them to Haksar's residence ... This bit of history is not known to any outsiders. It was from that evening that India's secret but activist role in the Bangladesh War of Liberation got going. Haksar

could establish links with the Awami League Leadership with these friends
of ours doing the bridge-building ...

Mitra exaggerates slightly since Haksar had already started the ball rolling
on Bangladesh on 2 March 1971. But Mitra is right that Anisur Rahman
and Rehman Sobhan may well have been the first people who had escaped
from Dacca to meet Haksar. Sobhan himself has written that Haksar's
reactions suggested that the encounters that he and Rahman had with
him 'was his [Haksar's] first such exposure to these events [the crackdown
by the Pakistani army and the launch of the genocide soon thereafter]'.
On 3 April 1971, fully briefed by Sobhan and Rahman, Haksar met with
Tajuddin Ahmad, the top Awami League leader and Amirul Islam, when
they called on Indira Gandhi. Exactly a fortnight later, on 17 April 1971,
Sobhan writes that 'Tajuddin Ahmad was sworn in as the Prime Minister
of an independent Bangladesh "at a mango grove near Kushtia ... which
is now known as Mujibnagar'.[30]

Tajuddin Ahmad met Indira Gandhi again on the night of 6 May 1971.
Before the meeting she sent Haksar a handwritten note:

> Re this evening's meeting. If you think Sardar [Swaran Singh] etc should
> be called, by all means do so. You should anyhow be there.
>
> However, Sardar is a little doubtful about our policy re. B. Desh.
> This should be kept in mind.

On his part, Haksar sent a note to the prime minister:

> P.M. might begin by telling our friends that G.O.C.-in-C Eastern
> Command has had conversations with Shri T [Tajuddin Ahmad]. Her
> understanding is that Gen. Arora has explained to him our assessment
> of the present situation and directions in which we should move forward
> from here onwards. Obviously, it is essential for us to feel that the
> Government of Bangladesh not only shares our assessment but agrees
> wholly and without reservations with the plan of action ...
>
> The second point to be raised is about the role which the Government
> of Bangladesh wish to assign to variety of other political elements inside
> Bangladesh. It appears that there are, for instance Members of the
> Communist Party of Bangladesh. There are also Members of the National

Awami Party led by Wali Khan. There may be others. P.M. might ask Shri T how the Government of Bangladesh visualizes the precise role which these elements would play in the total struggle for national liberation.

P.M might wish to inform Shri T of all the sustained efforts which the Government of Pakistan is now making the various Governments in the word that a situation of normalcy is about to be restored; and that as soon as this situation is achieved, President Yahya Khan will resume negotiations; that his expectation is that a sizeable number of the elected representatives of the Awami League will cooperate ... P.M. might enquire how realistic is this assessment of President Yahya Khan ... and what effect it would have on the resistance movement inside Bangladesh.

On 7 May 1971, Indira Gandhi had a second meeting with Opposition leaders. Haksar now informed her that:

We are now at the commencement of the second phase of the struggle in Bangladesh. This would require consolidation and centralization of political direction from the Bangladesh Government. A common strategy of warfare over a comparatively prolonged period will have to be evolved. The main characteristics of this would be guerilla tactics with the object of keeping the West Pakistan army continuously off their balance and to gradually bleed them.

If the struggle could be sustained over a period of time of 6 to 8 months it is not unreasonable to expect that sheer burden on Pakistan of carrying on this struggle will become, sooner or later, unbearable.

Haksar proved prescient. As it turned out, in slightly over seven months time Pakistan would give up. He also advised Indira Gandhi to stress that the best that the Government of India could do at this stage was 'wait and watch' for the situation to develop. His assessment was that the Government of Bangladesh had yet to acquire legitimacy both within its own territory as well as internationally. On the all-important issue of recognition of Bangladesh, which was the clamour in Parliament, he asked the prime minister to say that such recognition at that point of time will not be very productive and it raises 'false hopes that recognition would be followed by direct intervention of the Armed Forces of India to sustain and support such a Government'. A number of political leaders, strategic experts and others were advocating military action by India. In this background, Haksar wanted Indira Gandhi to be categorical in stating that :

> We cannot, at the present stage, contemplate armed intervention at all. It would not be the right thing to do. It will evoke hostile reactions all over the world and all the sympathy and support which the Bangladesh [government] has been able to evoke in the world will be drowned in the Indo-Pak conflict. The main thing, therefor, is not a formal recognition, but to do whatever lies within our power to sustain the struggle.

D.P. Dhar was a key player in the events of 1971, first from Moscow and later from New Delhi. He had unparalleled access to the Soviet leadership and, of course, to Indira Gandhi and Haksar as well. He had great influence on how Soviet thinking on Bangladesh evolved from one of extreme caution in early-1971 to one of full support to India's position by the middle of the year. But 'DP', as he was popularly called, was desperate to leave Moscow and be in New Delhi where all the action was. He wrote to Haksar on 12 May 1971 on his discussions with Soviet leaders including Prime Minister Kosygin and ended that letter thus:

> … Finally where do you intend to place me? If I have to be in the Prime Minister's outfit, I shall have to synchronise exit [from Moscow] with yours.
>
> … Many people have talked to me with grave concern about the prospect of your quitting the present assignment—Krishna [Menon], Shashi Bhushan, Arunaji, Nahata, Nurul [Hasan] and others. I am happy to know from your letter that you still have an open mind on this issue. As I will be back by about the 20th of June, I would take the opportunity of discussing then some alternatives I have in view. In the meanwhile, I beg of you not to feel tempted or provoked to close any one of the available options.

On 14 May 1971, Haksar had the prime minister write to 39 world leaders, including the president of the USA, the prime minister of the UK, the chancellor of Germany, the prime minister of Japan, the president of France, among others. The letter focussed less on Pakistan's actions in 'East Bengal' but more on the 'gigantic problems which Pakistan's actions in East Bengal have created for India'. The letter estimated the number of refugees till then at about 3 million with 'about fifty thousand pouring in every day'. It spoke of the grave security risks India was facing as a result of this huge influx, and sought 'the advice of all friendly Governments on how they would wish us to deal with the problem'. It also expressed deep concern with the personal safety of Sheikh Mujibur Rahman and sought international assistance 'to impress upon the rulers of Pakistan that they owe a duty to their own citizens whom they have treated so callously and forced to seek refuge in a foreign country'. More such communications to over 30 other countries were to go over the next few days.

But Haksar had not forgotten D.P. Dhar's latest missive. He replied on 22 May 1971:

> ... As you will be here soon, I will let myself be dissected by you. As far as I am capable of knowing about myself, all that I can say at this stage is that I feel, physically and mentally, stretched beyond the breaking point. I feel that I just cannot carry on. Maybe my outlook and the way I look at things now will radically change after I have had a little rest and time to think. *My present assessment is that for the new phase that has begun I am not the man.* However, as I said, we can discuss till the cows come home. [italics mine]
>
> As for yourself, I devoutly hope that you are well. Proceeding on that assumption, I am just wondering whether if you would contemplate to continue being a "civil servant"; or would you wish to regain your freedom and return to politics? You might ask what I have in mind? I shall be precise: I want you to be the Chairman of the Policy Planning Committee of the Ministry of External Affairs and be, simultaneously, principal political liaison man for the Bangladesh Government. The alternative is, of course, to be a Member of the Rajya Sabha and be "available". Knowing as I do how our system works, what sounds theoretically attractive can be extremely unnerving in practice and also unproductive. All this is my brain child, but I have vaguely mentioned it to Tikki [T.N. Kaul] ...

DP would be appointed chairman of the Policy Planning Committee of the Ministry of External Affairs as identified for him by Haksar. He would also become India's interlocutor with the political leaders of Bangladesh. As far as Haksar was concerned, clearly by mid-1971 he had made up his mind to leave. The main reason could well have been the political ascendancy of Sanjay Gandhi. Indira Gandhi still depended heavily on Haksar but it would have been natural for equations to have changed subtly after her stupendous electoral victory that would have given her enormous self-confidence.

On that very day of 22 May 1971, when Haksar made DP the job offer, he wrote him another letter which was yet another demonstration of the special warmth that existed between the Soviet leadership on the one side and Indira Gandhi and Haksar on the other. The previous month, on 19 April 1971, Arshad Hussein a former foreign minister of Pakistan had been to Moscow as a special envoy of President Yahya Khan. He had met Kosygin a week later and presented Pakistan's case on the Bangladesh issue forcefully. This had been done very quietly. Haksar told DP:

> My dear Durga:
> I enclose a copy of a note setting out the conversation which recently took place in Moscow between Chairman Kosygin and Arshad Hussein. This is for your own personal information. The Soviet Ambassador has conveyed this is strictest confidence to Prime Minister.

There would be other instances in the coming months when Pegov, obviously acting on Kosygin's instructions, would share with Haksar top secret communications of Pakistan with Soviet leaders.

On 30 May 1971, Haksar met with a leading political figure of Bangladesh—Muyeedul Hasan. Hasan was to recall later[31] that he was at first reluctant to meet Haksar because he had heard that Haksar had taken 'a negative stand when some of our cabinet members pressed for recognition to Bangladesh during a meeting with Indira Gandhi in New Delhi hardly a week ago'. But Tajuddin Ahmad persuaded him, saying 'Haksar was the

I have talked to P.N.Haksar about my future
some time back and I didn't get anything concrete out
of it. He seems to be of a similar opinion as you are
"Plans won't work" before even knowing what they are.
As far as the exams coming are concerned, I would be
surprised if I don't get credits right through. That
would leave me with an "O.N.C." which I have already
told you is on the same level as the 2nd year of an
Indian University. I can continue afterwards (if I
should want to do so) anywhere in the world where an
English diploma is recognised. I know that to get an
H.N.C. (what you wrote about) would help if I wanted to
go straight into a job; but I don't want to. As far
as getting a base for experience and knowledge, to do
anything with direct relevance to one's job I would
have to study for at least another 2 to 3 years after
the H.N.C. I know what the H.N.C. course is and all
the help it would be in one's job is the certificate
that it carries.

As far as staying with Rolls Royce is concerned,
I am wasting my time here now and have been doing for
the last 4 or 5 months. I don't want to continue doing
so for 2 more years. It is a good week I do 4 hours work.
Usually I am just doing either my own work or college
work or just read. I don't really relish going on with
this for 2 more years. Besides I am not the only
apprentice that sits around doing virtually nothing,
most of them are in the same boat.

Extract from Sanjay Gandhi's letter to Indira Gandhi, 9 May 1967.

I enclose a list of names suggested for the Planning Commission. I have just had a talk with Pitambar Pant. I suggest that you may also do so. He suggests that the best combination in the circumstances might be to have Subramaniam as the Deputy Chairman and to persuade B.K.Nehru to join as a Member. B.K. will not like this much, but if he feels that it will give him the opportunity to become Deputy Chairman after a few years, he may agree. Do you think you could sound him on this on your own? This arrangement would certainly give a balance to the Commission.

2. Professor K.N.Raj should also be sounded whether he will join.

3. As you know, the only other name suggested for Deputy Chairmanship is that of Prof. D.R.Gadgil. Pitambar does not think he will accept. But I do not wish to sound him until we are sure of the other position.

----

4. What is the latest position regarding the Bennett Coleman case?

----

5. I believe there are some aspirants for the title of National Professor. So far we have kept this up to a certain standard. I hope that we are not intending to lower the standard. Apart from anything else, the existing National Professors will be irritated and may well express themselves.

----

6. K.D.Malaviya came to tell me that the Russians blame Tikki for the Svetlana affair. K.D.'s suggestion was that Tikki might be sent to Moscow on some excuse to explain the whole thing. I do not think any purpose will be served by his going, but I thought I would bring this to your notice.

14.5.1967

Secretary.

Indira Gandhi's note to Haksar on 14 May 1967, sending him Sanjay Gandhi's letter to her.

Shri Krishna Menon has just been to see me.

He is going abroad, first to Cairo for an Afro-Asian Solidarity Conference; next to Stockholm for the Peace Council; then to Tanganyika for a Conference on Apartheid. He says that U Thant is very anxious that he should attend this Conference.

This is the very first time since independence that he is going abroad as a private citizen. Knowing him you will understand his feelings. He wants help with regard to passport and other formalities and would like our Ambassadors informed.

What is the position with regard to his house? He is under the impression that ex-ambassadors are allowed special consideration. He gave me the example of Renu Chakravarty's husband. He was occupying the house when she was an M.P. and now that she has not been re-elected, he is still occupying the house as an Editor. Krishna Menon says that he is an ex-Ambassador and an Editor.

I think it would be a good thing if you see him and sort out this matter with him.

22.6.67

Secretary:

I saw Shri V.K. Krishna Menon at 8.15 A.M. today. I shall look after him so far as his passport and other formalities are concerned.

2. As regards his housing problem, this, I am afraid, is a little difficult. Ex-Ambassadors have no special privileges in the matter of housing unless they are Members of Parliament. Editors also do not enjoy any facility. There is a special pool for journalists, but I am sure, Shri Krishna Menon would not like to avail himself of the kind of accommodation which is offered under this pool arrangement.

3. I understand papers regarding Shri Krishna Menon's housing problem are being personally dealt with by the Minister (Shri Jagannath Rao). As far as I can see, the only way in which he can retain his house is to pay commercial rent which, I believe, will be something like Rs.1300/- per month.

4. P.M. need not trouble herself about these matters. I am only setting the facts out for her information.

(P.N. HAKSAR)
23.6.1967.

P.M. 23.6.

P.N. Haksar
23.6.67

Indira Gandhi and Haksar exchange on Krishna Menon, 16 June 1967.

Haksar with engineers involved in putting up India's first atomic power plant, Tarapur, October 1967. Haksar is seated with cigarette in mouth and next to him is Maheshwar Dayal, the project manager.

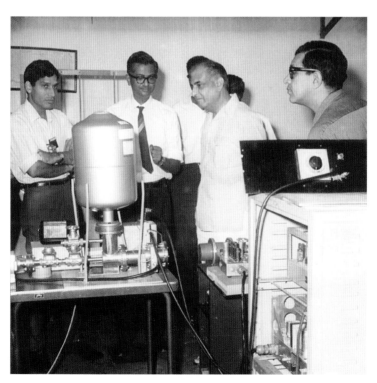

Haksar with Raja Ramanna on left (with tie) and Homi Sethna on right at the Bhabha Atomic Research Centre, Trombay, October 1967.

Indira Gandhi receiving Soviet premier Alexei Kosygin at New Delhi airport,
21 April 1969. Behind Indira Gandhi in black suit is Nikolai Pegov,
the Soviet ambassador in New Delhi who met Haksar every
other day in the crucial months of 1971.

STRICTLY
PERSONAL.

24.3.1971

Dear Sam,

Change & Adaptation are
Darwinian imperatives. And So
Dinosaurs became Lizards and
Survived. Perhaps, Esquires could
be shrug. Also, I am not I.C.S
only, poor IFS.

Please return this with your
Comments.

afg
Babboo.

196

From the desk of ....

COAS   PERSONAL.

Dear Babbu-

Sorry to lose breadth. You
will the stigma of the ICS: on the
strength of which you may claim
your pension or stealing or at
Rs 18/- be found stealing in Indian
currency — !!

"Shri P.N. Haksar" sounds
wonderful, but "Shri" (which is Indian)
does it sorrow go will
Secretary to the Prime Minister (which
is so English.) Likewise,
"Jurnail Manekshaw - Senapati"
would cause few comments, BUT
"Jurnail Manekshaw - Chief of the
Army Staff" would sound odd. You
agree? No- Yours ever 195
Sam. 25/3/71

Humorous exchange between Haksar and
General Sam Manekshaw, March 1971.

Re this evening's meeting.
If you think Sardar etc
should be called, by all
means do so. You should
anyhow be there.

However, Sardar is a
little doubtful about the
own policy re B. Desh. This
should be kept in mind.

246

Note by Indira Gandhi to Haksar, March/April 1971. 'Sardar' refers to
External Affairs Minister Sardar Singh, 'B Desh' refers to Bangladesh.

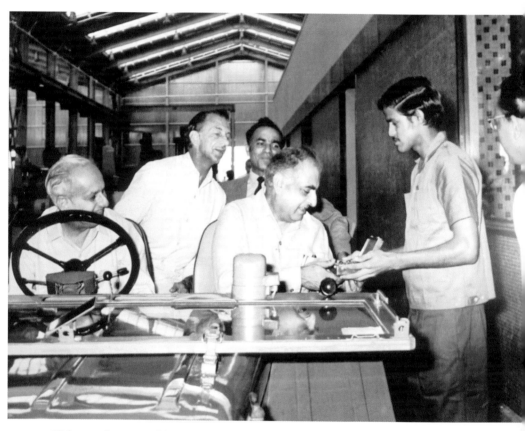

Haksar on his visit to Tata Engineering and Locomotive Company, Poona, June 1971. Managing Director Sumant Moolgaonkar is at the steering wheel and J.R.D. Tata (back seat) is craning his neck.

D.P. Dhar in conversation with General Sam Manekshaw at the Palam airport, New Delhi, 24 October 1971 as Indira Gandhi departs for Belgium, Austria, UK, USA, France and West Germany. Haksar joined her in Austria.

Opening session at Simla Summit, June 1972. From left: T.N. Kaul, D.P. Dhar, Haksar, P.N. Dhar. Facing D.P. Dhar, fourth from right is Aziz Ahmed.

Opening session between Indira Gandhi and President Bhutto, Simla, 1 July 1972. Swaran Singh and T.N. Kaul are on Indira Gandhi's right, D.P. Dhar, P.N. Haksar and P.N. Dhar are on her left in that order.

Officials meeting in Simla, 1 July 1972, Haksar flanked by T.N. Kaul (right) and S.K. Banerjee (left). Facing Haksar is Aziz Ahmed and Rafi Raza is on Ahmed's right.

Haksar and Rafi Raza shaking hands. Aziz Ahmed is next to Raza and
T.N. Kaul is next to Haksar.

Indira Gandhi and President Bhutto after signing the Simla Agreement, July 1972.
Haksar is behind Indira Gandhi.

Meeting of the Space Commission, probably New Delhi, mid-1973. Satish Dhawan is in the chair and to his right are M.G.K. Menon, Haksar and Brahm Prakash. Facing Haksar is the prime minister's secretary, P.N. Dhar.

I think the better way to proceed would
be to have a comprehensive list of those whom we
must invite on the first days. This will
facilitate the drawing up of ~~the~~ lists. I have
attempted three such lists for consideration.

A. President Tito   (2)
    Sheikh Mujibur Rahman (1)
    Mrs. Bandaranaike   (1)
    President Daud Khan   (1)
    Emperor Haile Selassie(1)
    House Party   (4) ? /10

B. President Allende   (1)
    Mr. Fidel Castro.   (1)
    Prince Sihanouk   (1)
    PRG RSVN   (2)

C. President Kaunda   (1)
    President Sadat   (1)
    General Ne Win   (2)
    President Nyerere   (1)

30.8.1973.

~~D.O.~~ Shri Haksar.

PS: According to Ministry of External Affairs
    King Mahendra is coming from heaven or
    wherever he is, specially to attend the
    Conference.

Some light-hearted comments by Indira Gandhi to Haksar, Algiers, August 1973.
King Mahendra of Nepal had died in 1972.

Haksar with Sheikh Mujibur Rahman, Dacca, August 1973. Next to Haksar is Foreign Secretary Kewal Singh and to the right of Bangladesh's prime minister is Kamal Hossain, his foreign minister.

Sudir Dar cartoon in *Hindustan Times* on Haksar and Aziz Ahmed negotiating, July–August 1973.

Indira Gandhi flanked by Aziz Ahmed (left) and Haksar, New Delhi, August 1973, after signing of agreement between India and Pakistan. Between Indira Gandhi and Haksar are P.N. Dhar and Foreign Secretary Kewal Singh.

M.G.K. Menon seeing one of the earliest television set 'Sanjay' assembled in India, Nagpur, May 1974. On his left is Dhanraj Acharya (in shirt). Haksar is behind Menon. Haksar and Acharya were CPI activists in Nagpur, 1942–1943.

Haksar being heard with rapt attention by three iconic academics, New Delhi, probably mid-1974. From left: C.R. Rao, then director of the Indian Statistical Institute, Sukhamoy Chakravarty, then member of the Planning Commission and T.N. Srinivasan, then professor at the Indian Statistical Institute.

Haksar alongside Indira Gandhi, 13 days after his family had been harassed and humiliated, New Delhi, July 1975.

Haksar in conversation with Indira Gandhi, meeting of the National Development Council, New Delhi, September 1976.

Haksar with Margaret Thatcher, then leader of the Opposition in the
UK House of Commons, New Delhi, September 1976.

Haksar with Robert McNamara, then president of World Bank, New Delhi, November 1976.

Haksar delivering the Feroze Gandhi Memorial Lecture, New Delhi, November 1976. Seated next is Union Education Minister Professor Nurul Hassan.

New Delhi.
30.4.77

My dear Babboo Bhai,

As discussed with you, enclosed is the draft of a note which you might wish to use as you think best. I have tried to include in it only the most important points, to avoid making it too long.

Yours ever

Ramji

Sri P.N. Haksar

Note from R.N. Kao to Haksar, April 1977.

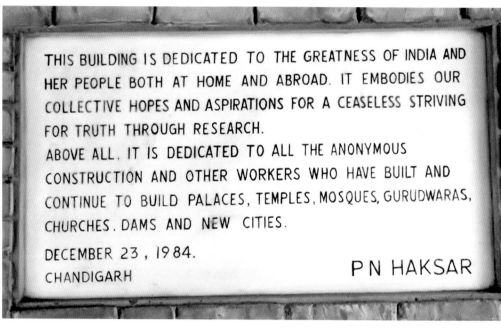

THIS BUILDING IS DEDICATED TO THE GREATNESS OF INDIA AND HER PEOPLE BOTH AT HOME AND ABROAD. IT EMBODIES OUR COLLECTIVE HOPES AND ASPIRATIONS FOR A CEASELESS STRIVING FOR TRUTH THROUGH RESEARCH.
ABOVE ALL. IT IS DEDICATED TO ALL THE ANONYMOUS CONSTRUCTION AND OTHER WORKERS WHO HAVE BUILT AND CONTINUE TO BUILD PALACES, TEMPLES, MOSQUES, GURUDWARAS, CHURCHES. DAMS AND NEW CITIES.

DECEMBER 23 , 1984.
CHANDIGARH

P N HAKSAR

Plaque at Haksar's insistence at the Centre for Research in Rural and Industrial Development (CRRID), Chandigarh, of which he was chairman during 1980–1998.

Haksar with Dr Manmohan Singh, then deputy chairman of the Planning
Commission, Chandigarh, October 1986.

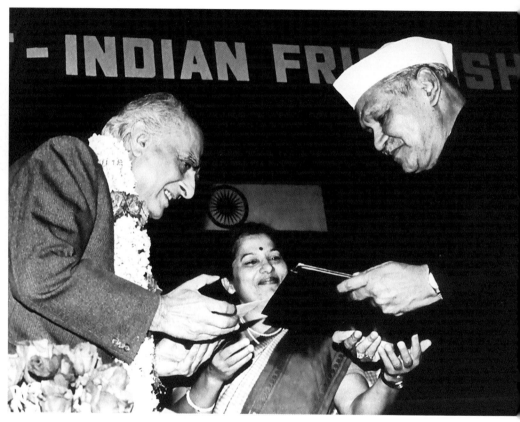

Haksar accepting the Soviet Land Nehru Award for 1987 from Vice President of India Shankar Dayal Sharma, New Delhi, November 1988.

Haksar flanked by noted space scientist Yash Pal (left) and eminent astrophysicist Jayant Narlikar, after delivering the foundation day speech at the Inter-University Centre for Astronomy and Astrophysics, Poona, December 1990.

Haksar with eminent historian S. Gopal (white hair) and H.Y. Sharada Prasad, on the occasion of his 80th birthday, New Delhi, September 1993. Next to Sharada Prasad is J.C. Kapur (standing), R.C. Dutt (in suit) and Gopi Arora (seated second from left).

Haksar (extreme right) with Dr Manmohan Singh, Chandigarh, March 1997.

Last public appearance of Haksar, eight months before his demise. Next to him is Vice President of India Krishan Kant, who had been a Young Turk in the 1960s and worked closely with Haksar to give Indira Gandhi's policies a decided 'left' orientation.

key person needed to be convinced before any proposition had a reasonable chance of progressing further'. Hasan writes of his second meeting with Haksar on 1 June 1971:

> He wanted to know more details about the prospect of floating a multiparty front and the ground work required to be done in this connection, and said that he would remain interested to know about its progress. Second he said that someone on behalf of the Bangladesh Prime Minister should try and set up direct contact with the Soviet Ambassador [in India] or a senior embassy official and should maintain regular contact with them to exchange views. He said nothing about the prospective security cooperation agreement with the Soviet Union, nor did he dispel our perception about China's possible collusion with Pakistan to derail the liberation war. But by showing interest in promoting a liberation front, to suit Soviet Union's ideological taste, and by advising that regular contacts be started with Soviet embassy officials in India, he gave me an impression that our views were worth considering.

Haksar was firmly convinced that no military operation by India would work in the absence of insurrection from the inside in East Pakistan. It was this that led to him and Kao to get Indira Gandhi's approval sometime possibly in early-1971 to support the training and arming of 'freedom fighters' in order to create the conditions that could pave the way for Indian military intervention, *if needed at all.* This military intervention was to be the last, extreme resort after all diplomatic and political means had exhausted themselves.

But by mid-June 1971 it would appear that Haksar had begun to believe that it was only a matter of time before Bangladesh came into being. He wrote on 29 June 1971 to Natwar Singh, India's ambassador to Poland:

> I have your letter of June 25, 1971 about Shri Mohan Kumaramangalam's visit to Poland and Rumania. He will certainly carry a letter of introduction from Prime Minister. A visit to Rumania is essential irrespective of the treatment we might receive there.
>
> I was delighted to learn of the response of school children and others in Poland to human suffering. I should want you to probe in depth Polish Government's position on Bangladesh. *The central point of my enquiry*

is to know if they have reached the stage of accepting the inevitability of Bangladesh, or whether they still think that the Humpty Dumpty could be put back on the wall again. [italics mine]

∾

Henry Kissinger was in India on 6 and 7 July 1971. Haksar and he first met on the evening of 6 July 1971 and had a 90-minute conversation. When Kissinger referred to India's support to the guerilla movement in East Pakistan, Haksar replied:

> ... As you are aware, prior to the events of March 25,1971 there were a large number of East Pakistani Bengalis who has received military training and formed part of military and para-military organisations ... Our estimate is that these people who had military training and had arms and equipment deserted en bloc. They numbered some 40,000 to 50,000 people ... According to our information, they put up desperate but heroic resistance to the onslaught of the West Pakistan army. Even if one assumes that three-fourths of them died there still remain 10,000 to 12,000 of these people inside Bangladesh. They provide the hard core of the *Mukti Fouj* [liberation army]. Many foreign correspondents who have recently been to East Bengal at the invitation of the Pakistan government have testified to the fact that these people are active there. So far as we are concerned we have given no arms ... Of course, our frontier is such that even with the best will in the world we could not possibly seal it at every point and it is not impossible for these people to go in and out ... We have bent over backward to ensure that despite many provocations given to us day after day by the regular Pakistan army, neither our Border Security Force nor our Army respond to such provocations ...

In response to Kissinger's raising the possibility of a conflict between India and Pakistan, Haksar replied:

> We in India are not seeking the conflict. In fact, we wish to avoid conflict. We want a peaceful solution. Prime Minister has written to President Nixon and Heads of other friendly Governments seeking their advice on how to solve this problem. Everyone has testified to the restraint we have shown ...

When Kissinger asked Haksar whether any changes had taken place in bilateral ties in recent months, Haksar replied alluding to the CIA undoubtedly:

> ... It seemed to me that some old habits persist. After all United States was a big Power having a large Mission. It also inevitably had Intelligence Agencies operating. I can imagine that when they first began their operations in India way back in 1947 during the cold war period and found the Government of India and Mr. Nehru seemingly unsympathetic to the United States' cold war aspirations, Intelligence Agencies must have established contacts with those elements in India which were opposed to the Government and Mr. Nehru. In human affairs, there is a tendency for things to continue unless positively checked. These continue at lower levels even when higher levels are clear about things.

The previous year, on 27 October 1970, Indira Gandhi and Haksar had met with US secretary state, William Rogers, and his colleague Joseph Sisco at the United Nations in New York. The meeting had been somewhat acrimonious as Rogers himself was to reveal to Kissinger the next day taking pride in the fact that he had let Indira Gandhi 'have it' and that he had 'put her in her place'. Indira Gandhi had minced no words in telling Rogers what she thought of Nixon's decision to sell arms to Pakistan which 'would be used only against India'. She was also critical of the CIA's activities in India which Rogers had strongly refuted. Referring to that uncomfortable meeting, Haksar continued his conversation with Kissinger:

> Kissinger ... I had a report of what took place in New York when Prime Minister was last there.
>
> PNH: Yes, that was quite extraordinary. Mr. Rogers apparently forgot for a moment that he was the principal diplomat of the United States and he even forgot that he was addressing not only a Prime Minister, but a gracious lady. I also felt that perhaps Mr. Sisco could have spoken less loudly. In any case, the matter raised by the Prime Minister was important.

There is one more vignette in the PNH–Kissinger conversation that bears mention. The Bangladesh issue has dominated all histories of 1971 and it is often forgotten that in April–May 1971, India had, in response to Prime

Minister Sirimavo Bandaranaike's request, extended military assistance to
Sri Lanka. The island republic was witnessing an armed insurrection by
an extreme left-wing group—JVP—that was getting help from China
and North Korea. Prompt intervention by India had helped Bandaranaike
crush the rebellion. She would write to Indira Gandhi on 25 May 1971
thanking India for its non-combat but crucial assistance. Haksar referred
to this episode and told Kissinger:

> ... As I said, if we can get over the past and also work together in solving
> the most critical situation created by the events in East Pakistan, then we
> can calmly look forward to a long period of stable, friendly relations with
> the United States. And if the problem of South Vietnam is resolved, and
> we have in South and Southeast Asia States which are truly sovereign,
> indeed as sovereign as Ceylon. I, for my part, see no difficulty in entering
> with these States into arrangements which will ensure the security and
> sovereignty of these States and their neutralization. I said that you may
> not have regarded it as of any great significance India's recent response
> to the request of the Government of Ceylon to send our troops and our
> Navy. It signifies the extent to which India can play a part in safeguarding
> the security and territorial integrity of friendly sovereign states in this
> part of the world.
>
> Kissinger: Yes, we were most impressed by India's response to the situation
> in Ceylon and felt most heartened.

Haksar and Kissinger met again on 7 July 1971 at a private lunch hosted
by Vikram Sarabhai. This time Haksar did not speak much. The American
record of that meeting had this to say about his interventions.[32]

> Concerning Pakistan, Dr. Sarabhai and Mr. Haksar agreed that it was
> in India's interest to see this country stronger. In response to Mr. Lord's
> question, Mr. Haksar confirmed that he meant East Pakistan as well as
> West Pakistan ... He said that Pakistan was overly Punjabi-oriented ...
> and needed some form of democratization or the tensions there could spill
> over and make trouble for India. India too has its problems but was able
> to diffuse them. Dr. Sarabhai was very unlikely to attack India. Mr. Haksar
> was less categorical, noting the hotheads among the younger generation
> which had been brought upon hostility towards India ... Mr. Haksar

noted that pressures against India from outsiders had always come across the northwest frontier and that it would be a very dangerous situation, for example, if Ceylon fell under malevolent influence ...

Later that very day, Kissinger met with Indira Gandhi. Haksar was present and the record of conversation prepared by a Kissinger aide has the following:[33]

> ... The Prime Minister then turned to Mr. Haksar and said that she had found the news alarming that the West Pakistanis were talking about errors in the past census ... There was a brief exchange on the political nature of a census, beginning with Mr. Haksar's comment that a census can produce political problems ...
>
> Dr. Kissinger told the Prime Minister ... [that] Mr. McNamara's judgment in the World Bank is that [economic] pressures [on Pakistan] would begin to mount in September. Mr. Haksar said that India's assessment is that Pakistan can last beyond that. Economies like Pakistan's have a remarkable capacity to retrench and to go on well beyond the time when Western economic experts feel they should have collapsed ... Dr. Kissinger asked if it is true that Pakistan can survive economic shortages for a substantial period under present conditions, what can the US do? What is the point of cutting off economic assistance?
>
> Mr. Haksar stated that ... there is no diminution yet in the flow of economic assistance to Pakistan. Then, if the Pakistanis can anticipate new commitments through the consortium in September, there has not been present in this situation a concern in the Pakistani government that it will lose outside support. Dr. Kissinger said that Pakistan, as of the present, cannot anticipate new aid commitments in September ...
>
> Mr. Haksar said that there is unrest among the Karachi commercial/industrial community ... Dr. Kissinger, still probing the question of what effect the cut-off of assistance would have, said the limited number of arms now being shipped to Pakistan makes almost no difference in the military balance. What, therefore, is the actual effect of cutting off assistance?
>
> *Mr. Haksar replied that it is important to make clear that future aid is dependent on well-timed political developments ... He felt that the act of cutting off assistance, while it might not have an economic impact forcing*

Pakistan to take certain political steps, could have the effect of forcing President Yahya and others in Pakistan to face up to the costs of their present policies. This would be the purpose of cutting assistance... [italics mine]

Of course, the US did nothing of the sort that Haksar was asking for in order to force Yahya Khan to arrive at a political settlement with Sheikh Mujibur Rahman. It is clear that while military preparations had begun and the freedom-fighters were being given assistance, Indira Gandhi's priority and that of Haksar was *not* for a military intervention.

The PNH–Kissinger conversation is fascinating both for its sweep as well as its depth. Both appeared to acknowledge the intellectual capabilities of the other. Some months later in January 1972, a former prime minister of France, Pierre Mendes France was to meet Haksar in New Delhi and write a book,[34] in which he compared Haksar and Kissinger by observing:

> ... I am confronted with Mr. Haksar's temperament of philosopher or sociologist who refers sometimes to J-J Rousseau, sometimes to Clausewitz, to demonstrate India' genuine right and the certainty of success at the end. His approach to problems is obviously conditioned by a set of unwavering convictions and certainties. While I listen to him argue having an impressive luxury of vast knowledge and reading, I cannot restrain myself from comparing him to another very influential counselor of another head of government. Between Mr. Haksar and Mr. Kissinger, the resemblance is not only psychological, but almost physical. Mr. Haksar is larger and exudes a kind of power which is not palpable in Kissinger, but they have the same kind of gravity; both are obviously hard-working individuals, men who have poured over files and have given them much thought, formed convictions and doctrines and who fight tirelessly to shape the policy of their country accordingly.

Mendes France's comparison of Kissinger and Haksar would reach the latter some months later and Haksar was to write to his friend Dwarka Chatterjee, India's ambassador in Paris on 22 August 1972:

> I believe that Mendes France wrote something silly about me. Do you know anything about it? Could I have his magnum opus? Quite frankly, I was rather disappointed meeting him and the disappointment was greater

214

because from a distance, I had a romantic admiration for this great man who tried, howsoever unsuccessfully to get the French to drink milk rather than wine. And I thought at that time that a man who could do this must be truly heroic. His wife appeared to me to be more down to earth than the great man himself. *But then it has been my life's misfortune to not being able to find a man whom I could admire and love with total abandonment. The only person who came near was Paul Robeson.*[35] *But then he was utterly childlike a person with no pretensions of moving history.*[36] [italics mine]

What did the two antagonists of 1971—Haksar and Kissinger—think of each other? Forty-seven years later, Kissinger recalled:[37]

I had a high opinion of him ... He struck me as very intelligent and purposeful. He was clearly suspicious of America but wanted a practical relationship ... I remember that during that disastrous visit of your Prime Minister with Nixon he and I tried to salvage things. He was more constructive than his boss.

Kissinger's aide Sam Hoskinson was more forthcoming:[38]

First, it is important to recall the historical context. During the period in question, Washington tended to view New Delhi through the Cold War prism of US-Soviet relations. In retrospect, this may have colored our impressions of controversial players such as Haksar.

Generally speaking Haksar was viewed at the White House/NSC, and to a considerable degree by the State Department, as an important player but negative influence on Prime Minister Gandhi as far as American interests were concerned. At best he was regarded as essentially anti-American, at worst as a controlled KGB agent of influence. A seemingly arrogant personality did not help either. And all this within the context of a White House that was inclined to think the worst about India anyway ...

Haksar, while an admirer of Kissinger's intellectual prowess, felt that he lacked moral fibre and sensitivity to democratic processes. The two never struck a rapport with each other. A quarter of a century later, in November 1986, Haksar was to meet Anatoly Dobrynin, then a foreign policy adviser to Mikhail Gorbachev. Dobrynin had been Soviet ambassador in Washington between 1962 and 1986. His opening words to Haksar were:

"I am very glad to meet the man who outwitted Henry Kissinger." Haksar replied in his most avuncular tone: "Am I expected to be flattered?" He and Dobrynin became good friends.[39]

✑

On 15 July 1971, V.V. Giri, then president of India, wrote to Indira Gandhi what must be considered a truly unusual letter:

> Although it may look somewhat out of the way, I feel that I should mention of the outstanding and meritorious service that Haksar has rendered during the last few crucial years that the country has faced. I have found in him an officer of transparent honesty, steadfast loyalty, coupled with an abundance of intelligence and courage. He has, of course, been much closer to you than to me but yet I have felt that Government could ill-afford to lose his services at this juncture. It is in this context, coming to know of his retirement within a few weeks, that I have thought of writing to you and have no hesitation in stating that the overall interests of the Government amply justify his retention in some appropriate way. He could continue to be of great use to you as well as of valuable assistance to me. I thought I would mention this for what it is worth and leave it to you to decide as he is primarily working on your side.

It is more than clear that Haksar had played a role in swinging Indira Gandhi's mind in favour of V.V. Giri during the 1969 presidential elections at a time when she had come out openly in favour of Sanjiva Reddy. Some years later Haksar was to become chairman of the Giri Institute of Development Studies in Lucknow and also of National Labour Institute (NLI) near New Delhi that was to be renamed in 1995 as the V.V. Giri National Labour Institute, in recognition of Giri's contributions to the labour movement in India.

✑

That very day, 15 July 1971, Jayaprakash Narayan who had taken up the Bangladesh cause in right earnest wrote to Foreign Secretary T.N. Kaul that leaders of Bangladesh he had been in touch with were unhappy with

Haksar and he himself was worried about Haksar's approach. JP had met with Indira Gandhi and Haksar three days earlier to brief them about his discussions with members of the Bangladesh 'Cabinet', including Nazrul Islam (acting president), Tajuddin Ahmad (prime minister), Khandakar Moshtaque Ahmad (foreign minister) and others. JP wrote:

> There is only one more point about which I wish to write here, which I must say I am doing with a certain amount of hesitation. But as I have come to know you quite intimately over the past few months I hope there will be no mis-understanding. I would have written to Mr. Haksar directly, but I do not know him well enough to do that. This is about Mr. Haksar's attitude to the Bangladesh leaders. I may be mistaken but I got the impression that he is annoyed with them. I am saying this because I noticed a certain amount of asperity in his tone when he reacted to some of the things I reported at our meeting. For instance, when I said that Mr. Tajuddin Ahmad had said that while the pro-Peking groups, except for the Maulana Bhashani group, had their differences, they were agreed on one thing: the slogan-'Indira-Mujib are stooges of imperialism'. Mr. Haksar reacted in a rather annoyed tone saying that he had found no evidence at all of that. That rather surprised me, the state of our military and civil intelligence being what it is. He spoke in the same tone again when he said that it was not a question of our being not in good time to suggest to them to hold a conference of their legislators, but the fact the idea instead of occurring to them had to be suggested by us. Maybe I am reading too much into Mr. Haksar's tone. But I have been troubled by that ...

Many things were at work here. Haksar was certainly wanting the Awami League leaders to 'broadbase' their movement so that it could be seen that the creation of an independent Bangladesh was not the demand of just one political party but reflected popular sentiment. He certainly wanted all left-oriented forces including the Communists to be part of this broad-based movement. He also seemed to have some misgivings about the authority and sanction under which the Bangladesh government had been installed, worried as he was that this might lead to a war with Pakistan—which he wanted to avoid at all costs. There was also some irritation with J.P.

himself because Haksar felt that the government was being presssurized into action by him on matters like the early recognition of an independent Bangladesh.

∿

On 4 August 1971, Kao communicated a message that he had received from P.N. Kaul, then India's deputy high commissioner in London. It had been transmitted through top-secret R&AW channels. The message read:

> Zabludowicz cut short holiday to see me this afternoon at my request. He warmed up as I gave him your greetings and message to expedite deliveries. In reply, he asked me to convey his best regards and wishes to Prime Minister and all those who are engaged in handling big problems. He said he was impressed by you because you had faith in him. He promised as before he will do what is possible and will not disappoint you. Situation not easy this time because he has to seek your releases from Israeli army. He has spoken to Israeli Minister of Finance and Industry and is hopeful of airlifting ammunition and mortars in September. He expects to send 3 instructors also with the first lot.

Haksar was deeply mindful of what he believed to be grave injustices done to the Palestinian people. Yet at a time of grave crisis for India he reached out to one of his friends, a Polish-Finn-Israeli named Shlomo Zabludowicz, who was in the armaments business. The well-connected Zabludowicz must have intervened for on 23 August 1971, he was to get a letter from no less a person than the prime minister of Israel, Golda Meir, a close personal friend of his. The letter available in the original Hebrew with the English translation in the Haksar archives reads:

> While you were in Israel during the month of July I asked you to be so kind and find a way to comply with the Indian request. I knew then that the subject was difficult and complicated, but I believed that you knew how to arrange that. Just as you know how to help and find solutions in the past to difficult problems.
>
> I am very glad when I was informed that you succeeded to find the solution and that this time as in the past you arranged their request and the help will continue.

I asked you to inform the Prime Minister Mrs. Indira Gandhi, that we believe she will know how to appreciate our help at a time when they were in difficulties in the past and our complying with their approach now.

I thank you wholeheartedly and wish you and your family good health.

With appreciation and thanks,

Actually, this was not the first time that Zabludowicz had helped India. Through his Liechtenstein-based company, Etablissments Salgad, he had supplied ammunition to India in October 1962 at the time of the war with China and in late-1965 during the war with Pakistan. On 30 November 1965, as deputy high commissioner in London, Haksar had written to Zabludowicz saying, among other things:

> … You are undoubtedly aware of our sincere and earnest desire to develop further our relationship to mutual advantage. Having regard to our present situation, it will go a long way towards further consolidation of our relations if in this particular instance the incidence of shipment cost is kept at its lowest.

In 1969, when in connection with the supply of Israeli ammunition some questions had been raised in India on Zabludowicz's connections, Haksar had told the prime minister on 24 October 1969 that:

> … in terms of equity, good conscience and political considerations, we should allow the performance of contract to take place and so long the ammunition supplied is of right specifications, we should not look to the source whence it has come. There is no reason to believe that if the 1965 contrsact could be executed with utmost secrecy, why the present contract should not be similarly executed.

Military supplies from Israel were to be justified in Haksar's mind on grounds of supreme national interest. Yet this was the same person who had also advised Indira Gandhi that he was not in favour of Parliament paying homage to Levi Eshkol, the Israeli prime minister who had passed away on 26 February 1969. Haksar had argued that such homage being demanded by some political parties would needlessly antagonise India's

Arab allies and that Eshkol had done nothing extraordinary to deserve such a tribute. I wonder what Haksar would have done had he known then what was to be become public much later—that Eshkol as prime minister had intervened to overcome some opposition and ensure military supplies to India during the India–Pakistan war of August–September 1965.[40] As for Golda Meir, she had opposed the arms supply in 1965 but thanks to Zabludowicz she changed her stance six years later. The genocide by the Pakistani army and the huge humanitarian crisis that India had to confront also played a role in shaping her response. It also bears mention that from 1968 itself R&AW had established contacts with the Israeli intelligence agency Mossad through a channel in Geneva.

After Kissinger's surprise China trip of 9 July 1971 from Pakistan, there was now an obviously a transformed geo-political situation confronting India. Haksar had told Kissinger when they had met three days earlier:

> … As I said, we want, and we would like, to avoid a conflict. However, if one is forced upon us, I can understand your fears about China reacting in a particular way, that is, in a way that is detrimental to us. However, in such a situation, it is not unreasonable for us to expect and to hope that United States would take a sympathetic attitude towards our country. Viewed in this context, I am a little puzzled by your saying that if we get involved in a conflict [with Pakistan] which is not of our choosing and the Chinese intervene in one way or another, United States, instead of assisting us, would feel some sort of discomfiture.

Haksar, T.N. Kaul and D.P. Dhar moved with alacrity to convince a now more-than-willing Indira Gandhi that the time for an Indo-Soviet pact had finally arrived. Dhar was asked to meet Kosygin to convey Indira Gandhi's readiness to sign the treaty at the earliest. This meeting took place in Moscow on 5 August 1971 and four days later the India–USSR Treaty of Peace, Friendship and Cooperation was signed between Sardar Swaran Singh, India's external affairs minister and his Soviet counterpart Andrei Gromyko in New Delhi.

In point of fact, the wheels for formalizing the bilateral agreement had been set rolling much earlier. The idea for such a treaty had first been mooted sometime in February–March 1968 by Marshal Andrei Grechko, the Soviet defence minister, at about the time the USSR was contemplating selling arms to Pakistan. The Indo-Soviet treaty had actually been all but finalized by end-1970 itself, thanks to the untiring efforts of Dhar. He had called Grechko's offer in early-1968 as 'guilt complex on the part of the Soviets' as they had been taken aback by the strong reaction of Indira Gandhi, Haksar and others to the Soviet arms offer to Pakistan.

Alexei Kosygin, the Soviet premier, had left it to Indira Gandhi to decide on the exact timing for signature by both sides. She, however, was not sure about the reactions such a treaty would evoke both within India and in Western capitals. She certainly wanted Soviet military hardware, particularly aircraft bombers but on the treaty itself she was careful not to make an irreversible commitment.

On 23 March 1971, Dhar had called on Kosygin in Moscow and there is no mention of the treaty in the official record of that meeting. But on 5 June 1971 in his farewell meeting with Marshal Grechko, Dhar had raised the issue of the treaty. Even so Dhar, echoing Indira Gandhi's concerns, was himself ambivalent as his letter to T.N. Kaul of the same day reveals. He ended by confessing:

> … Once again I would like to mention here that I am not sure whether the conclusion of a treaty in the form in which it was discussed in 1969 would satisfy the needs of the present situation. Perhaps, an exchange of letters which would set out the same objectives as were contained in the treaty would be an equally good substitute for the treaty at the present juncture. Or, again we could think of a secret document which could emerge as a result of the joint consultations between the General Staffs of the two countries or as a result of consultations which could be held on a purely political basis.

On 15 June 1971, T.N. Kaul, the foreign secretary, sent Haksar a copy of the draft of the Indo-Soviet Treaty. Haksar made some changes here and there but more importantly responded negatively to Kaul's suggestion that 'if it is considered desirable we could offer a similar Treaty to USA and some of our neighbouring countries like Afghanistan…'. Haksar remarked 'I have doubts about this'.

However, while the text was almost final, it had not yet been decided to sign the Treaty. This ambivalence ended once and for all with Kissinger's China gambit. The original Soviet idea even till early-August 1971 was to have the two heads of government sign the treaty in Moscow with the two foreign ministers only initialing it in New Delhi. Ultimately, however, it was signed by the two foreign ministers in New Delhi. Not only that but Andrei Gromyko, the Soviet foreign minister, was prevailed upon not to visit Pakistan on his way back after the treaty had been signed on 9 August 1971. A note from Haksar to Indira Gandhi on 10 August 1971 said it all. Gromyko was meeting Indira Gandhi at 11:15 am that day and Haksar had, in his brief, written:

> Re: Mr. Gromyko's visit to Pakistan, I had informed FM [foreign minister] yesterday on behalf of PM that he might tell quite firmly Mr. Gromyko that the reaction in India of such a visit to Pakistan would not be favourable and might, in fact, dilute the effect of the Treaty. FM told me that this had been duly conveyed and that Mr. Gromyko has accepted the advice. PM need not raise this matter unless Mr. Gromyko does it himself.

On 12 August 1971, that is three days after the Indo-Soviet treaty had been signed, Indira Gandhi sent a slip to Haksar that read:

> Should we not indicate to Mishra [Brajesh Mishra, then India's *charge d' affairs* in China] that the Indo-Soviet Treaty does not preclude a similar Treaty with China?

Haksar's response was uncharacteristically delayed by a week but he was stunningly forthright saying:

> I would respectfully submit that a Treaty of the kind we have just concluded with the Soviet Union reflects, in time and space, a particular

coincidence of interest. In all the Chanceries of the world the Treaty has been interpreted in this light and I believe rightly so. For us now to go round saying to all and sundry that we are prepared to sign a similar Treaty would appear either unrealistic, or if I may so, something lacking in seriousness ... I think we have to be quite clear in our mind as to which countries might sign such a Treaty and then we should quietly work for it and not publicly state, day in and day out, that the Treaty with the Soviet Union is so routine that we are ready to sign it with everyone ... As for signing a Treaty with the Chinese, even a talk about it would not bring about a Treaty with China and it would certainly attenuate greatly the effect of the Treaty which we have signed with the Soviet Union.

Haksar had his reasons. On 3 August 1971, Swaran Singh informed the Parliament that India was willing to normalize relations with China 'provided there was a response from the other side'. On 25 August 1971, it was officially confirmed that Indira Gandhi had written to the Chinese Premier Chou En-lai the previous month, a few days after Kissinger's visit to China. This letter was mostly about developments in Bangladesh and along the lines of similar communications that had been sent to other world leaders in different continents. But it also contained an expression of India's readiness to have a dialogue at any level with China on bilateral issues. The hitch was that there had been no response from China. On 1 September 1971, Brajesh Mishra was called for consultations and he once again pleaded for exchange of ambassadors. But Haksar advocated caution saying that he was not sure whether the Chinese leadership was really serious. The fact that Chou En-lai had not yet replied to Indira Gandhi's offer was cited by him as proof of China's lack of seriousness. As it turned out, about four months later, on 11 December 1971, Indira Gandhi wrote again to Chou En-lai in the midst of the Indo-Pak War explaining the background to the conflict and suggesting that the Chinese use their leverage with Pakistan to bring about an end to hostilities. She ended that letter by saying:

We seek friendly relations with all our neighbours and we seek China's friendship too. In my last letter I had indicated our readiness to discuss the problems of mutual interest.

223

There was to be no reply to this letter too. Given this Chinese silence, Haksar was justified to temper Mishra's enthusiasm in 1970 and 1971. It has been suggested that Haksar may not have wanted to antagonize the Soviets at this critical juncture by making the first moves vis-à-vis China. That may have been in the back of his mind but the evidence suggests that more than the Soviet factor it was China's lack of response to Indira Gandhi's letters and continuing attacks on India in Chinese official media that led him to advice Indira Gandhi not to go along with Mishra at that point of time.

Haksar was to turn 58—the normal retirement age for civil servants then— on 4 September 1971. He had decided to leave. On 2 September 1971, he sent Indira Gandhi a note on arrangements to be made in view of his of impending departure:

> The post of Secretary to Prime Minister has become so institutionalized that I feel that [it] is necessary that until such time as P.M. is able to appoint a new Secretary arrangement should be made for someone to occupy the post so that he could receive all the telegrams which are addressed to the Secretary, attend all the meetings of which Secretary is a member. I am, therefore, wondering if P.M. would agree to send the following minute to the Cabinet Secretary:
>
>> On retirement from Foreign Service, Shri P.N. Haksar is proceeding on leave preparatory to retirement. I have not yet thought of precise arrangements to be made for his replacement. It is possible that he might agree to return and occupy the post of Secretary to the Prime Minister on the basis of re-employment. Until this is done, it is necessary for some one to carry on the duties and responsibilities of the Secretary. Shri P.N. Dhar, who is the next senior officer in the Prime Minister's Secretariat, should officiate as Secretary to the Prime Minister until further orders. I should like the Cabinet Secretary to process this matter.

The next day Haksar proceeded on two months leave preparatory to retirement. But before leaving he sent her another note—perhaps, the very last of this innings—on 3 September 1971:

> ... A careful choice needs to be made of the candidate for the Rajya Sabha from Bombay. That city is dominated, in many ways by Gujarati industrial, commercial and trading community. Hitherto this community sought to solve its problems either through Shri S.K. Patil or through Shri Babubhai Chinai. If we could find a Gujarati Congressman of proven integrity and dedication to the principles for which P.M. is committed, it would be possible to undermine the influence of both Shri Patil and Shri Chinai. There are two candidates who could provide an alternative focus of attention for the Gujarati community in Bombay. They are Shri Rajni Patel and Dr. M.R. Vyas. My own preference, based on knowledge of both these persons over a period of 35 years, would be for Dr. M.R. Vyas because Rajni's connections and personal life, at the moment, are not of the kind which one would wish to see. Also, his connections with the Congress Party as such are of very recent origin. Dr. Vyas, on the other hand, is of the Congress and had grown with the Congress ... He is an extremely stable person with a clear head and utmost integrity. He used to be with us in the student movement in England.

One of Haksar's greatest qualities was that he could be clinically objective of his closest circle.[41] As it turned out, M.R. Vyas was made a Rajya Sabha member in 1972 and had a six-year term. In this note, Haksar also advised Indira Gandhi that she should have an emergency declared because of the extreme threat India faced on its western and eastern borders. He wanted her to make a public appeal as well. As it turned out, she did not agree but such an external emergency was to be declared three months later.

Haksar and his wife left New Delhi on 5 September 1971 for Geneva, Paris, London, Moscow and Warsaw. Vikram Sarabhai joined him in Geneva and the two spent 10 days together attending a conference on the peaceful uses of nuclear energy. On 17 September 1971, while in Paris he was handed over a letter addressed to him from Moni Malhoutra, a deputy secretary in the prime minister's Secretariat who had written to him obviously at the behest of Indira Gandhi. Malhoutra wanted to know whether Haksar would join the prime minister on her forthcoming visit to important Western capitals to explain India's position on the refugee crisis. Haksar replied:

> Being a Hegelian, I recognize the great wisdom of his aphorism that "freedom consists in recognizing necessity". Therefore the answer to the question put you is in the affirmative. I will gladly join PM's party in Vienna and will be available thereafter during her visit to U.K., USA, France and Germany. I shall have a little problem with Urmila, but we shall try and solve it to our mutual satisfaction.

He also told Malhoutra that he would still like to be on leave till 3 December 1971, and thereafter 'I would be ready for "re-employment"', expressing his hate for that term nevertheless. He laid down some terms and conditions for his rejoining duty with effect from the afternoon of 4 December 1971. In response to another of Malhoutra's queries, he suggested the composition of the prime minister's delegation to the Western capitals and gave some ideas for her speech at Chatham House in London. Indira Gandhi was scheduled to visit Moscow in a few days time and Haksar would not be there with her but he told Malhoutra:

> I hope P.M.'s visit to USSR has been prepared with thoroughness and that the joint communiqué to be signed in Moscow will represent tangible gains to us especially in the field of direct Soviet assistance for the refugees. I hope too that some suitable formulation could be agreed upon between USSR and India which will mark an advance on that portion of the joint communiqué which we signed during Gromyko's visit which dealt with the Soviet position on Bangla Desh [sic] as part of Pakistan.

A few days later, on 29 September 1971, Haksar sent Indira Gandhi a long message from London bemoaning 'the state of chaos which prevails in postings and transfers abroad' and 'how no one in Delhi apparently knows the requirements of a particular post or has the knowledge in depth of the persons posted'. He also suggested that since 'temperamental stability, sobriety and a rounded personality were needed for being India's High Commissioner in London', T.N. Kaul be considered for appointment after his retirement as India's permanent representative to the United Nations in New York where 'Tikki would feel at home and be in his natural surroundings', and not for the London assignment. As it turned out, Haksar was asked by Indira Gandhi to convince a reluctant Kaul to become India's ambassador in Washington after his retirement as foreign secretary in November 1972.

Indira Gandhi went to Moscow on 27–29 September 1971 accompanied by Foreign Secretary T.N. Kaul and others. On 9 October 1971, P.N. Dhar wrote to Haksar:

I have been meaning to write to you all these days. If I have not done so it is only partially for lack of time. Your parting words "Please leave me undisturbed" were a constant deterrent.

The job you have entrusted me with is one for a Trimurti with all the extra limbs that adorn our gods and goddesses. I simply cannot get over my childlike wonder about how you did it. And yet, I understand, what I do is only a fraction of what you did. Let me now allow myself to slip into things which will remind you of your "kindred points of Heaven and Earth".

PM needs a good medical check up. Dr. Mathur feels that the best place for a check up will be Vienna. Instead of writing to the Ambassador I thought it more advisable to write to you about it so that you may be able to fix it with the Ambassador on a personal basis and in a confidential manner ...

This letter of Dhar's unfortunately finds no mention in his memoirs. That the prime minister's Secretariat was suffering during Haksar's absence will be further revealed by another letter from Moni Malhoutra to Haksar on 12 October 1971. Haksar was in Moscow at that time. Malhoutra wrote:

Herewith the briefs and PM's programme. Sanction for your journey from Warsaw to Vienna will be cabled direct to Warsaw.

After further consultations, may I put the following suggestions re your telex message?

(a) It would not be appropriate to call you PPS [principal private secretary] and Dhar Saheb Secretary. This will mean basically, that PND [P.N. Dhar] will be Head of Office and thus militate against putting you just below Cabinet Secretary in the Warrant of Precedence. A better solution would be to call you Principal Secretary to PM. This will help in terms of the Warrant. PND can be described as Secretary or Special Secretary or Adviser ...

An air of crisis seems to be building up here and there is much speculation among the diplomatic community whether PM will be able to go at all on this foreign tour. I need hardly say how greatly you are being missed ...

I hope you are refreshed: turbulence and hard decisions obviously lie ahead ...

To Malhoutra, therefore, goes the credit for coming up with the designation 'Principal Secretary to Prime Minister', a position which every prime minister after Indira Gandhi has filled. As it turned out, technically still on leave preparatory to retirement, Haksar joined Indira Gandhi in Vienna on 27 October 1991 and went with her onward to London, New York, Washington, Bonn and Paris. While in Vienna, Haksar ensured that Indira Gandhi sent a message of greetings to Chinese premier Chou En-lai on China's re-admission into the United Nations, something that India had been advocating for well over two decades. After his visit to Moscow and Leningrad, Haksar had come to Warsaw where he stayed with the Indian Ambassador Natwar Singh, who recalls arranging for Haksar's meeting with the Polish prime minister. This is what leads me to believe that there was more to it than just a holiday before retirement in Haksar's visits to Geneva, Paris, London, Moscow and Warsaw between 5 September and 25 October 1971. There was definitely some super secret diplomacy going on regarding Bangladesh.

Indira Gandhi and Haksar were in Washington on 4 November 1971 for the all-important meeting with President Nixon and Henry Kissinger which took place at 10:30 am in the Oval Office of the White House with only the four of them present. The record of that historic meeting reveals Indira Gandhi at her combative and courageous best. She did all the talking with Nixon. The only time Haksar intervened was when President Nixon suggested some disengagement by Indian forces back from the border to lessen tensions. Haksar, the record of the meeting[42] says:

... noted the difficulties for India by the displacement [that is, disengagement] of Indian forces...

The next morning—5 November 1971—Nixon and Kissinger met again with Indira Gandhi and Haksar at the White House. Indira Gandhi inquired about the situation in Southeast Asia and the Middle East and Haksar asked Nixon about the US's relations with China. This was certainly a more cordial meeting than the one on the previous day.

On 6 November 1971, Indira Gandhi and PNH met with US Secretary of State William Rogers to continue from where they had left off with Nixon and Kissinger. Part of the conversation went thus:

Rogers: Would not an unilateral withdrawal be useful?

PNH: Withdrawal can be misleading. We have had memories in Kutch and Rajasthan. In what way can it be more harmful if Yahya Khan negotiated with Awami League?...

Rogers: We can act only as a catalyst. Yahya Khan is desperately looking for a political solution.

PNH: The practical difficulty is that we cannot say Yahya Khan wants a political settlement. Hitherto all his actions are not consistent with a political settlement. He wanted to finish this job in a week's time. When he failed he blamed India and called Mujibur Rahman a traitor ... Then he removed Tikka Khan but that did not improve matters ... The British talked to Gandhi and Nehru, Sapru and Jayakar, but Yahya Khan is not willing to talk to with Mujibur Rahman ...

Rogers: What is your conclusion? ...

PNH: I am not scoring a point. We have a common diagnosis and should seek common remedy. We have 9 million refugees and an increasing influx. Where is the light at the end of the tunnel, I asked Kissinger. This is our common concern.

Rogers: No one sees the light at the end of the tunnel ... We, by and large, agree with you. We all agree and so does Yahya Khan that there has to be a political solution ... War would be tragic for India ... but we cannot force Yahya Khan to deal with Mujibur Rahman whom he regards a traitor.

PNH: So he regards all the Bangladesh leaders. Churchill said worse things about Gandhi.

William Rogers got not only an assessment of how India viewed Yahya Khan but also got a quick mini-lecture on sub-continental history. Haksar was also at his sarcastic best when, referring to a briefing held the previous day, he told Rogers, 'Your Ambassador in Pakistan made a valiant effort for Pakistan'.

Pakistan attacked India on the evening of 3 December 1971. Indira Gandhi was then in Calcutta, Defence Minister Jagjivan Ram was in Patna and Finance Minister Y.B. Chavan was in Bombay. She rushed back to the capital that very night, giving instructions for Cabinet meetings to be called on her return and for Haksar to be present as well. He was asked to prepare the text of her midnight broadcast to the nation. A state of emergency under Article 352 of the Constitution was also declared that very night—the second time this was done, the first being on 26 October 1962 at the time of the war with China. Orders appointing Haksar as principal secretary to the prime minister were issued on the morning of 4 December 1971 when India was at war with Pakistan.

On 6 December 1971, Indira Gandhi formally announced India's recognition of Gana Prajatantri Bangladesh. Her caution and that of Haksar can be gauged from the fact that a sovereign, independent Peoples Republic of Bangladesh with Sheikh Mujibur Rahman as its head had been first proclaimed on 26 March 1971, and a request for India's recognition of it had first been made on 24 April 1971. It had taken almost eight months for India to grant formal recognition.

On 11 December 1971 when the war was in full swing Haksar sent a telegram marked 'Personal' to India's ambassador to the USA, L.K. Jha that read thus:

... We have no territorial claims or ambitions as far as Bangladesh is concerned. If we had any, we would not have accorded recognition to that Government. The act of recognition means self-imposed restraint on our part against making any claims whatsoever.

We have no claims against the territory of West Pakistan. However, this does not mean that Pakistanis can continue to savagely attack our forces and occupy our territory and that we should, in advance, declare to them that they can do all this and we shall sit with our hands tied and surrender meekly to their attacks.

As far as Azad Kashmir, the [US] State Department ought to know that for a period of 24 years India has consistently maintained that this territory legally belongs to us. Pakistan, on the other hand, has not only seized this territory, but continues to advance claims on our state of Jammu and Kashmir. And yet we have in the past said that we will not alter the status quo by force ...

The next day, on 12 December 1971, Indira Gandhi wrote a letter to President Nixon that must be amongst the most eloquent diplomatic history. The letter was quintessential Haksar in its sweep of history and politics. It began this way:

... I am setting aside all pride, prejudice and passion and trying, as calmly as I can, to analyse once again the origins of the tragedy that is being enacted.

It ended with this dignified admonition:

Be that as it may, it is my earnest and sincere hope that with all the knowledge and deep understnding of human affairs you, as President of the United States and re   ing the will, the aspirations and idealism of the great American people, will at least let me know where precisely we have gone wrong before your representatives or spokesman deal with us with such harshness of language.

On 13 December 1971, Haksar alerted the prime minister and the Army Chief General Sam Manekshaw:

According to the Assistant Secretary-General of the U.N. in Dacca, Bihari and U.P. Muslims and probably other "collaborators" have been concentrated in one area in the city of Dacca and have been armed to the teeth. All of them are animated by animal fear of being massacred and will, therefore, give a fight. It might, therefore, be useful to allay their fears. This has to be done both by our Army, by the Mukti Bahini and by the Bangladesh Government. Urgent consideration may be given to this.

The same day he wrote along similar lines to his colleague R.C. Dutt, secretary, Ministry of Information and Broadcasting:

> In his report to the U.N. Secretary General U Thant, UNEPRO Administrator Paul Marc Henry has reported that a very large number of U.P. and Bihar Muslims and others have been concentrated in a particular area in the city of Dacca. All of them are gripped by an animal fear of being massacred by Mukti Bahini or by Indian Armed Forces. They have been armed to the teeth and would naturally fight for their lives. He has stated that All India Radio has been feeding their fear by threats of reprisals. I do not know if this is a fact. Quite obviously, such threats are self-defeating. We should, on the contrary, say that Indian Armed Forces will not resort to the barbarism of Pakistan Armed Forces [and] that everybody who peacefully surrenders will be treated with respect and his life safeguarded. You might also say that Major General Farman Ali, under instructions of President Yahya Khan had offered to transfer power to the elected representatives of Bangladesh but that President Yahya Khan displaying total insensitiveness to the suffering of the people, has withdrawn the offer. Therefore, responsibility for continuing unnecessary bloodshed rests squarely on the military junta in Rawalpindi who enjoying safety and comfort of Islamabad are showing callous disregard for the suffering of the people in Bangladesh and in Dacca.

Haksar followed this up with a note to the prime minister a few hours later:

> I do not know whether P.M. has mentioned to the Chief of Army Staff at this morning's meeting that the complex political factors dominating our Western front with Pakistan require extreme care on our part. All the reports received yesterday from Washington, London and Moscow point to the fact that the United States are likely to react to any development on that front which might give them an impression that we are seeking some territorial gains in West Pakistan, including Azad Kashmir and that it is our intention to transfer our forces from the Eastern theatre to the Western theatre to carry war deep into the territory of West Pakistan.

Clearly much was happening on 13 December 1971, since on that very day the Soviet First Deputy Foreign Minister Vasily Kuznetsov met Haksar. He had been sent by the Soviet leadership to find out Indian thinking on the war. Kuznetsov conveyed to Haksar that the Soviet Union did not want India to enlarge the conflict on the Western front because that would provoke the Americans. He also wanted India to enable the Soviet Union to say something in the UN Security Council that would not be altogether negative in character and that would help convey the keenness of India to restore peace in the sub-continent. Kuznetsov handed over a set of proposals from the Soviet side and Haksar handed over a set of proposals on behalf of India. Haksar informed Indira Gandhi of this meeting and ended his note by saying:

> Since I have taken in hand in setting down these proposals, naturally my own feeling is that no harm would be done if we were to tell the Soviet Union that proposals along these lines and in the sequence set out would not be rejected by us and we shall give them our consideration. I feel that we should also advise them that if these proposals are to see the light of the day, it might be desirable for some country other than the Soviet Union or Poland to take the initiative. This would enable the Soviet Union to be free to resist amendments which would not be acceptable to us or even use veto if the proposals take a shape which is unacceptable to us.

Right through the crisis Soviet envoys had unfettered and quick access to Haksar. That Indira Gandhi commanded great credibility with the top Soviet leadership is obvious from the fact that on 6 August 1971, Pegov had handed over to Haksar a copy of an 'extremely confidential' letter that President Yahya Khan had written to Soviet Prime Minister Kosygin. Eight days later, Haksar had with him, courtesy the Soviets, a copy of a letter the Government of Pakistan had written to the-then Chairman of the UN Security Council, namely the Italian Permanent Representative at the UN.

It is clear from the manner in which Haksar dealt with Kuznetsov that his paramount objective was to have the USSR completely on India's side at the UN, more so since both USA and China were hostile to India. To put it simply, he was finding ways of using the USSR to India's strategic and political advantage. Of course, he did this with the full backing and involvement of the prime minister. On 14 December 1971, he cabled Dhar who was then in Moscow:

We have told KUZNETSOV that the threatening postures of the United States signified by the movement of their Navy and similar postures by the Chinese are having opposite effect on the people and Government of India. Far from fraying our nerves it is promoting greater determination. We have suggested to KUZNETSOV that it may be worthwhile for Soviet Union to make a public announcement carrying the seal of the highest authorities in the Soviet Union that involvement or interference by third countries in the affairs of the sub-continent cannot but aggravate the situation in every way. It is for the Soviet Union to find appropriate words. A mere Tass statement would not do. What we want is reiteration through highest level possible of what in fact the Soviet Union said right at the beginning of the debate in the Security Council warning against intervention. The only extra thing which needs to be said is not merely warning against such intervention but the consequences of such an intervention.

Please reassure Chairman KOSYGIN that we have no, repeat no, territorial ambitions anywhere in East Pakistan or in West Pakistan. Our recognition of Bangladesh is a guarantee against territorial ambitions in the East and our position in the West is purely defensive. [italics mine]

Indira Gandhi was at pains all through December 1971 to make clear that India had no ambitions whatsoever to dismember Pakistan. She called a meeting of the Political Affairs Committee of the Cabinet on 14 December 1971, two days before Pakistan accepted defeat, to get the approval of her colleagues to her viewpoint. The note for the Committee was prepared by Haksar. He submitted six principles for its consideration and in view of their historical significance are being reproduced in full:

1. Peaceful transfer of power in Bangladesh (East Pakistan) to the genuinely elected representatives of the people headed by Sheikh Mujibur Rahman who should be immediately released.
2. Immediately on commencement of the process of the transference of power, there shall be cessation of military actions in all areas and a cease-fire for 72 hours initially.
3. With immediate commencement of the initial period of the cease-fire, Pakistani armed forces shall begin withdrawal to designated places in

Bangladesh (East Pakistan) for the purpose of evacuation from the Eastern theatre of war.

4. Similarly, all West Pakistan civil personnel and other persons wishing to return to West Pakistan as well as East Pakistani civil personnel and other persons in West Pakistan wishing to return to Bangladesh (East Pakistan) shall be allowed to return under U.N. supervision.

5. As soon as the withdrawal of Pakistani forces and their grouping for that purpose had commenced within a period of 72 hours, the cease-fire shall become permanent. Indian forces shall withdraw from Bangladesh (East Pakistan). However, the commencement of such withdrawal of Indian Armed Forces will take place with the consent of the newly established authorities set up as a result of transference of power to the genuinely elected representatives of the people headed by Sheikh Mujibur Rahman.

6. Recognising the principle that territorial gains made by the application of force shall not be retained by any party to a conflict, Governments of India and Pakistan through their appropriate representatives of the respective armed forces shall immediately commence negotiations in the Western theatre of the war as soon as possible.

I suspect that these broad principles and the sequence had been discussed by Haksar with Kuznetsov the previous day—if not the exact language then at least the broad spirit and thrust. That very day, on 14 December 1971, Haksar wrote to Defence Secretary K.B. Lall:

> … All the reports we have received yesterday from Washington, London, Moscow and sources close to China point to the fact that the United States and China have only one dominant interest, namely to preserve the integrity of West Pakistan. Anything that we may do or say which gives the impression that we have serious intentions, expressed through military actions or dispositions and propaganda that we wish to detach parts of West Pakistan as well as that of Azad Kashmir would create a new situation.

Haksar sent a copy of this letter to R.C. Dutt for his 'information and guidance', and added the following instruction:

> It appears that PIB [Press Information Bureau] had prepared some material calculated to stimulate Sindhi irredentism in West Pakistan.

The PIB Release was picked up by the PTI [Press Trust of India]. Such a publicity within our country has to be stopped forthwith and all PIB releases fanning Sindhi, Baluchi or Pathan irredentism must be withdrawn.

On the evening of 15 December 1971, at 18:00 hrs, Haksar called in the US Deputy Chief of Mission in New Delhi Galen Stone and handed over to him the response of General Manekshaw to the proposals for a ceasefire made by General A.A.K. Niazi who was in charge of the Pakistani army in Bangladesh.[43] Niazi's proposals had been communicated to India at 14:30 hrs the same day through US Embassy in New Delhi. The Indian reply—drafted by Haksar and Manekshaw—was tough and uncompromising. It called for an immediate cease-fire and surrender of Pakistani troops. Haksar drew Stone's pointed attention to the fact that India had ceased air attacks from 17:00 hrs of 15 December 1971 itself. But the written Indian reply made clear that if Pakistan did not agree to India's terms, India would resume its offensive at 09:00 hrs the next morning. The die was cast with the Pakistani army surrendering in Dacca by the evening of 16 December 1971. The next day, India declared a unilateral ceasefire everywhere on the Western front effective from 20:00 hrs Indian Standard time on 17 December 1971. Yahya Khan followed suit.

Significantly, a couple of months later, 1 on April 1972, Haksar was to tell the prime minister:

> P.M. may kindly forgive me, but I would submit that it is not right for us even to remotely suggest that we had cease-fire on the western front because China and the U.S. would not have allowed us to take over West Pakistan. This is precisely what China and U.S. are saying. They are pretending to be the saviours of Pakistan. The real reason why we called the cease-fire was that:
>
> (a) Continuation of conflict would not have produced a decisive military victory; and
>
> (b) That even in the event of a victory, it was quite unthinkable for us to enter Pakistan as occupying power. If we had allowed ourselves to be carried away by our emotion and carried out the war, we would have been in complete mess with our garrisons in Lahore, Rawalpindi,

Islamabad, Peshawar, Karachi, Hyderabad, etc. Even to think of it is nightmarish, because we have no political base, specially in Punjab, on which to restructure West Pakistan. In Bangladesh, we had political allies. In West Pakistan we had none, except, marginally speaking, people in Baluchistan and Frontier Province.

A day after the cease-fire, Haksar was thinking about the next phase of India's involvement in Bangladesh and told the prime minister on 18 December 1971:

I submit to P.M. the imperative need for sending Shri D.P. Dhar to Dacca ... He can be called a Special Representative of the Government of India. It should be made clear that he is going there for a period of two to three months ... I cannot find suitable words to emphasise that unless Shri D.P. Dhar is dispatched to Dacca post haste, we may win the war but we will lose the future of our relationship with that country. Bangladesh at present is, politically speaking, a primordial slime. Out of this chaos, cosmos has to be created ... Shri D. P. Dhar should go tomorrow and Shri Tajuddin Ahmad and as many of his colleagues as possible should install themselves in Dacca the day-after. The Chief of Army Staff feels Dacca would be safe enough for such installation. But to install Tajuddin and Company without Shri D.P. Dhar is to launch a ship without an anchor, a rudder and a compass.

As suggested by Haksar, the 'anchor, rudder and a compass' in the person of D.P. Dhar went to Dacca on 19 December 1971 as a special envoy. Eight days later, Haksar cabled Dhar in Dacca:

I am sure you are aware of a new kind of propaganda being built up against us as well as against Bangladesh centering around massacre and other atrocities being perpetrated in Bangladesh. One or two ghoulish pictures have been shown widely on television networks in America and elsewhere. We and the Bangladesh Government have to bend over backward to ensure that our fair name is not besmirched by interested parties. It would also be a good thing if some representative of Bangladesh, who is intelligent and perceptive, would handle the foreign press correspondents now in Dacca ...

I presume Ramji [Kao] has conveyed to you certain thoughts as they occurred to me. A broad framework of policy has to be evolved with the consultation of the Bangladesh Government on the question of (a) the functioning if the Foreign Consulates in Dacca, and (b) operations of international as well as private relief agencies ...

Our thoughts and good wishes are with you in this most difficult assignment. Your photograph with Nazrul Islam published in newspapers here today was reassuring.

A month later into the new year, Haksar would persuade his old boss Subimal Dutt to become India's first high commissioner to Bangladesh. There were other names being suggested but Haksar backed Dutt all the way. Indira Gandhi and Sheikh Mujibur Rahman would first meet in Calcutta on 8 February 1972 and on 19 March 1972, the two prime ministers would sign the bilateral Treaty of Friendship, Cooperation and Peace in Dacca. Haksar himself would make two visits to Dacca—in July and August 1972—to further cement bilateral ties.

The story of 1971 would not be complete without a reference to an extraordinary conversation between the Indian ambassador in the USA, L.K. Jha and Henry Kissinger at San Clemente, President Nixon's home in California. This meeting took place on 25 August 1971 and Kissinger's record of that meeting dictated five days later is a sad reflection on Jha who had been Haksar's predecessor in the prime minister's Secretariat and who later became governor of the RBI and of Jammu and Kashmir before being reincarnated as Indira Gandhi's economic 'wise man' in 1981 and as a Rajya Sabha MP in 1986. Kissinger recorded:[44]

> Dr. Kissinger said he did not really know what India wanted. If India wanted to become an extension of Soviet foreign policy, then inevitably the American interest in India was bound to decline ...
>
> Ambassador Jha replied that the situation in India was very difficult. First of all, Madame Gandhi was not pro-Soviet. She had for a long time resisted the proposal—that had first been thought up by Dinesh Singh, the former foreign minister—of this treaty of friendship. (In fact, Jha said

on a personal basis, he wouldn't be a bit surprised if Dinesh Singh actually received pay from the communists). At the same time he also thought that Kaul and Haksar were very much under the Soviet influence. In short, for both these reasons Madame Gandhi was under great pressure ...

That might be so, Dr. Kissinger said but the problem is how she would carry out the policy. Dr. Kissinger could tell her that from our selfish point of view it did not hurt us to have India pursue such a pro-Soviet line in relation to our China policy nor should the Ambassador have any illusions that it was possible to stir up any basic American public support on the Bengal issue ...

The Ambassador repeated that Haksar and Kaul were the real obstacles in India and that in the Foreign Office there were many pro-Soviet elements ...

This is truly an amazing record. Jha's own detailed seven-page record of that meeting and dictated two days later begins thus:

I had a conversation lasting nearly three hours with Dr. Kissinger at San Clemente White House on the 25th of August. When we began talking, at Kissinger's suggestion, I agreed that the conversation should be off-the-record, in the sense that nothing which is said would be quoted in any formal talks and that we should speak with candour rather than with the courtesies and reserves of a diplomatic dialogue.

Obviously Jha's record makes no mention of his remarks on Haksar and others but it does have his stout defence of the Indo-Soviet Treaty. One of Jha's colleagues in the Embassy who later became foreign secretary in 1982, M.K. Rasgotra, has written in his memoirs[45] that upon his return from San Clemente:

[Jha] told me that he had a good talk with Kissinger during which the latter had spoken critically of Foreign Minister Dinesh Singh [he had ceased to be Foreign Minister in 1969] for having thought up and proposed the [Indo-Soviet] treaty and said that Prime Minister's two main advisers, P.N. Haksar and T.N Kaul (foreign secretary) were pro-Russia and it was under their pressure that she had given the go-ahead for signing the treaty.

If Kissinger's record is even partially accurate then it is a damning indictment of L.K. Jha, one of India's most distinguished civil servants. If Jha's record is accurate, then Kissinger is exposed at his mendacious worst. Shankar Bajpai feels that the Roshomon effect[46]—when the same event is given contradictory interpretations by different individuals involved—may well be at work here.

Haksar's own relationship with Jha was cordial and proper, but not particularly close. In March 1970, when the question of a successor to Jha as governor of the RBI was being discussed, Haksar had recommended the name of S. Jagannathan, another ICS officer with considerable experience in finance. After agreeing to his name, Indira Gandhi had, based on what some MPs had told her, asked Haksar 'whether there was anything against Shri Jagannathan'. Haksar had then told the prime minister on 8 March 1970:

> ... It is incumbent on the person [who complained about Jagannathan's appointment to Indira Gandhi] not to make vague allegations, but to come forward with all the facts ... It is a bit cowardly to indulge in uttering half-truths.
>
> There were all kinds of unkind things said against the present Governor of the Reserve Bank [Jha], but I don't think these things were ever held against him.

Jagannathan was appointed and went on to have a noteworthy five-year tenure at the Reserve Bank of India.

Field Marshall Sam Manekshaw is an authentic Indian hero and he did much to deserve that exalted status. He has bequeathed to us the story that Indira Gandhi and her advisors were keen on an early military operation, and that he put his foot down asking for more time. The *documentary* evidence does not lend any support to the claims made by Manekshaw. At no time did Indira Gandhi or Haksar betray any impatience for war—not in their public statements or actions and in Haksar's case not in his internal notings either. And this even though many influential Opposition leaders and public figures like Jayaprakash Narayan were clamouring for it—and so were some strategic experts like K. Subrahmanyam, who wrote a detailed paper making the case for an early intervention and had it circulated at the top echelons of the government.

Manekshaw's view, which has become the stuff of military legend, has been conclusively refuted, on the basis of primary, archival material by Srinath Raghavan and by an eminent diplomat-scholar Chandrashekhar Dasgupta. Raghavan writes:[47]

> ... Contrary to the assertions of Manekshaw and his military colleagues, the prime minister did not contemplate such an intervention in the early stages of the crisis.

Dasgupta is more cutting. He writes:[48]

> One of the most popular anecdotes of the 1971 war is Field Marshal Manekshaw's tale of how he restrained an impatient Indira Gandhi from ordering an unprepared Indian army to march into East Pakistan in April. The Field Marshal's prowess as a raconteur fully matched his military skills but exceeded his grasp of the political and diplomatic dimensions of the grand strategy shaped by Indira Gandhi and her advisors. The prime minister had no intention of going to war in April since India's political aims could not have been achieved at that stage simply through a successful military operation.

Dasgupta's meticulous marshaling of archival evidence points unambiguously to just one conclusion: that, more than anyone else, it was Haksar who masterminded what Dasgupta calls 'the framework of a grand strategy integrating the military, diplomatic and domestic actions required to speed up the liberation of Bangladesh'.

Haksar and Manekshaw enjoyed each other's company. On 22 March 1971, Manekshaw sent a note to Haksar marking it to him as P.N. Haksar, Esq. ICS. Two days later drawing a circle around ICS, Haksar sent a 'Strictly Personal' chit to the general:

> Dear Sam:
> Change and adaptation are Darwinian imperatives. And so dinosaurs become lizards and survived. Perhaps Esquires could be Shris. Also I am not ICS, only poor IFS.
> Please return this with your comments.

The next day, Manekshaw responded:

> Dear Babbu:
> Sorry to have branded you with the stigma of the ICS on the strength of which you may claim your pension in sterling or at Rs 18 per pound sterling in Indian currency!!!
>
> Shri P.N. Haksar sounds wonderful but "Shri" (which is Indian) doesn't somehow go with "Secretary to Prime Minister" (which is so English). Likewise "Jurnail Manekshaw—Senpatti" would cause few comments, but "Jurnail Manekshaw-Chief of Army Staff" would sound odd. You agree? No—

That was the last bit of light-hearted banter between them for a long time for that very night the army crackdown in Dacca and other places in East Pakistan began.

∽

India had experienced both triumph and tragedy in a matter of a few days in December 1971. On 16 December 1971, Pakistan surrendered and India had won the war convincingly and comprehensively. But a few days later on 25 December 1971, the 52-year-old Vikram Sarabhai died suddenly. He was the chairman of the Atomic Energy Commission and was also laying the foundations of India's space programme. A decision had already been taken by Indira Gandhi when Sarabhai was alive, at Haksar's prodding, that the dual responsibility had to end soon and that the space programme needed full-time attention. Had he lived, there is little doubt that Sarabhai would have opted to run the space programme since, as Haksar was to recall to Satish Dhawan many years later: 'Vikram was always looking towards the sky.'

Both the nuclear and space programmes now needed leaders. Haksar then made what must be perhaps his most inspired appointment during his entire time at the prime minister's side. He picked Satish Dhawan, then director of the Indian Institute of Science, Bangalore to take charge of the space effort. Dhawan was a distinguished aeronautical engineer who had completed his doctorate at the prestigious California Institute of Technology (Caltech) and come back to India in the early-1950s.[49] Haksar not only respected Dhawan as a technologist but there was also 'ideological congruence' between the two as the latter's daughter told me. Dhawan's sister and her husband Satish Loomba were very active in the CPI with which Haksar had close affinity.[50] Dhawan himself was active in the World Federation of Scientific Workers in the 1950s when it was headed by Nobel Laureate Frédéric Joliot-Curie who was a communist. The Federation was well-known for being a leftist network.

The only problem was that Dhawan was on a sabbatical at his alma mater. Hence, Haksar got Indira Gandhi to send him a personal letter which was cabled to L.K. Jha, India's ambassador to the USA for onward transmission to Dhawan in California. The cable of 7 January 1972 read:

> Dear Dr. Dhawan:
> Vikram's sudden and tragic death has deprived our entire space research programme of leadership. You are aware of the heavy investment we have made in it. The ten-year profile of the development of space shows the extent of our commitment. We cannot afford to allow the entire organization to crumble. I should like you to accept the stewardship of our space organization which I am proposing to separate from the Atomic Energy Commission. It will be for you to structure this new organization. Please let me know urgently when I may expect you to return and what arrangements you would like us to make for the interim period. I hope you will respond to an emergency situation in a sensitive area of national importance.

How could anyone say 'no' to such a letter from the prime minister herself? Dhawan conveyed to her his acceptance but also let his terms be known: that he would continue as director of the Indian Institute of Science in Bangalore and that the Space Commission should be headquartered in that city. Both these conditions were accepted with alacrity by Haksar and the rest is history.

In the interim Haksar got Indira Gandhi to appoint M.G.K. Menon as the chairman of the Indian Space Research Organisation (ISRO). Menon was then chairman of the Electronics Commission and Haksar had the prime minister write to him on 12 January 1972:

My Principal Secretary, Shri P.N. Haksar, has reported to me the conversation which he had with you this morning about the interim arrangements to be made to look after the work of the Indian Space Research Organisation. I am glad that despite your heavy commitments, you have agreed to become the Chairman of ISRO pending return of Dr. Satish Dhawan who will be the Head of the Space Organisation. Dr. Dhawan would like to discuss the ultimate structure of this Organisation when he returns.

I have long felt that there has to be some linkage between our Space Programme and defence needs. It might be a good thing if you and Dr. B.D. Nag Chaudhuri were to discuss in a preliminary way how best this could be achieved. [italics mine]

This letter is important because it reveals that both the prime minister and Haksar were not unaware of the military implications of what India was about to embark upon under Satish Dhawan's stewardship. India's space programme—unlike that of the USA, USSR, France and China—did not emerge from the military. It was to start out as an enterprise to fulfill developmental needs like communications, weather forecasting and natural resource mapping. In fact, Dhawan himself was particularly allergic to any military dimension or involvement. But clearly Haksar knew that down the road there would have to be a strategic content as well.

The broad vision of India's highly successful space programme was Sarabhai's but the detailed architecture was that of Dhawan. He was scheduled to meet Indira Gandhi on 25 May 1972 at 4 pm to formally convey acceptance of her offer. Before that meeting Haksar sent the prime minister the following note:

Dr. Satish Dhawan is an extremely sensitive human being. Hitherto, he has led a relatively cloistered life devoting himself wholly to the pursuit of his own scientific specialty in the field of aerodynamics. I know that he had many doubts and hesitations in accepting the responsibility of heading our Space Organisation. And if he were to opt out of it, we literally have no one at present even as a second best choice. It is therefore, of importance for P.M. to express in her own way her appreciation of the high sense of duty which has led Dr. Dhawan to respond to P.M.'s call on him. *It is equally necessary to say that Dr. Dhawan will continue to receive her personal support in sorting out any problems he may run up against any administrative and other fields and that Dr. Dhawan should not hesitate in coming to P.M. and that he always have direct access.* [italics mine]

In suggesting Satish Dhawan's name and backing him in this manner, Haksar possibly did the greatest service to the nation. Dhawan first became secretary, Department of Space and chairman of the Space Commission. On 12 June 1972, Haksar communicated to him that the prime minister had approved the following composition of the Space Commission:

1. Shri P.N. Haksar, Principal Secretary to the Prime Minister— Member
2. Dr I.G. Patel—Member (Finance)
3. Prof. M.G.K. Menon—Member
4. Dr. Brahm Prakash, Director, Space Technology Centre—Member

Dhawan had specifically asked for Haksar to be a member and Haksar had told the prime minister two days earlier:

Although this will add to my burden, I did not have the heart to say no to him if only to help him to settle in.

Haksar and Dhawan were to remain close till the end of Haksar's life. For the nuclear programme, Haksar pushed for Homi Sethna to take over from Sarabhai. There was initially some doubt on Sarabhai's successor because J.R.D. Tata, in his capacity as member of the Atomic Energy Commission, had written to Haksar on 5 January 1972 pointing to Sethna's 'lack of intangible quality of leadership' and suggesting that M.G.K. Menon, then director of the Tata Institute of Fundamental Research (TIFR) would be the right choice. Tata's views were made known to the prime minister but at Haksar's insistence Sethna was selected. When Sethna was appointed chairman of the Atomic Energy Commission of India, it was natural that Raja Ramanna takes over as the director of what came to be called the Bhabha Atomic Research Centre (BARC) in early-1967. Years later, Haksar would recall that much of his time would be spent bridging the differences between Sethna and Ramanna—both strong-willed individuals.

Haksar made one more everlasting contribution to Indian science in March–April 1972. M.S. Swaminathan had been selected to succeed B.P. Pal as the director-general of the Indian Council for Agricultural Research (ICAR). He was the obvious choice given his contributions to launching the Green Revolution in India in the late-1960s. But there was sting in his appointment which was to be as director-general ICAR and ex officio additional secretary in the Ministry of Agriculture which was Pal's designation. What he then did is best described by Swaminathan himself:[51]

> When I was selected as DG, ICAR he [Haksar] asked me to wait for a few days. Inspite of opposition, he got a Department of Agricultural Research and Education created with the DG concurrently serving as Secretary to Government. I was thus the first DG who was also Secretary to the Government of India in the newly created Department of Agricultural Research and Education. Shri Haksar played an important part in getting a special stamp on the wheat revolution issued in 1968 with the approval of the Prime Minister.
>
> His contributions to strengthening the relationship with Nepal are also praiseworthy. He ensured that Nepal and India work together, particularly in the Tarai region which led to initiating and sustaining the wheat revolution ... There are many occasions when I had the good fortune of witnessing the way in which he guided the Prime Minister along the right lines. I had his full support when I went to Vietnam after the unification of Vietnam in establishing a Rice Research Institute for the Mekong Delta.
>
> His role in shaping Indira Gandhi's policy on building up grain stocks was considerable. He insisted that India should maintain a substantial grain reserve, so that we can have an independent foreign policy.

PNH's approach to scientific enterprise is also revealed what he had done the previous year for the Raman Research Institute (RRI), started by C.V. Raman, who had received the Nobel Prize in physics in 1930. Raman had passed away on 21 November 1970. A few months later, on 31 July 1971 when he was immersed in the Bangladesh issue, Haksar had sent a note to Indira Gandhi:

... Dr. V. Radhakrishnan is the son of late Professor C.V. Raman. I have referred to his paternity only by way of identification. Dr. Radhakrishnan is personally most allergic to being identified as son of his distinguished father. In point of fact, he left this country for Australia only to escape being submerged in the dominant personality of his father. I am glad he did this. He has now blossomed forth as one of the world's leading astrophysicists. Although he has agreed to become Director of the Raman Research Institute, he is still extremely sensitive and apprehensive. His main concern is to assure himself that he will receive blessing and support from Government for his ideas on how the Raman Research Institute should develop.

I place below a paper he has prepared. I submit that PM should give him encouragement and express the hope that he will develop his proposal and that P.M., on her part, will give support. The amounts involved are pitifully small, but if Dr. Radhakrishnan comes and takes up his residence, we will have in Raman Research Institute one of the finest institutions of scientific eminence from world standards.

And so it has turned out to be.

Elections to a number of state assemblies were to be held in early-1972. PNH had played a major role in finalizing the Congress party's manifesto for the 1971 national polls and he was to play a similar role now. He informed Indira Gandhi on 13 January 1972:

I am returning to P.M. the folder containing the Election Manifesto 1972, which has apparently been approved by some appropriate organ of the Congress Party. An alternative redraft is submitted. The election manifesto 1972 should be printed with election manifesto 1971. The two together will constitute the programme, policies and pledges of the Party. Purely presentationally, it would be most confusing if bits and portions of 1971 manifesto are bodily incorporated in 1972 manifesto. The result would be that the 1971 manifesto which was a self-contained document will lose its own identity without acquiring another identity. By taking out portions of 1971 manifesto and incorporating it 1972 manifesto, the

Party might be accused of resiling from portions of 1971 manifesto—an impression which, I am sure, it is not intended to convey.

Haksar's views prevailed and the Congress continued its winning streak, winning over two-thirds of the seats. Indira Gandhi had now really not just the Central government, but all states barring one at her command. Haksar's advice to her to become the symbol of socialism and relate to the needs of the poor and deprived sections of society coupled with her own instincts and campaigning style had catapulted Indira Gandhi into a dominating position—from where the journey could only be downward as subsequent events were to show.

Haksar had acquired a reputation of being soft on the USSR and its Warsaw Pact allies. On 23 January 1972, Labour Minister R.K. Khadilkar told him that there was wide consternation among the 'progressive' circles about Haksar's standing in the way of the recognition by India of the German Democratic Republic (GDR). Haksar told Khadikar that he was greatly flattered that he should be credited with the 'power of veto over Government decisions' and reiterated his stance to the prime minister the next day:

> I am not against recognition of GDR. Question of timing, however, remains of vital importance. And the only appropriate time for recognition would be after the ratification of the Soviet-German accord and the Agreements in respect of Berlin.
>
> In granting recognition to GDR, we have naturally to ask ourselves how best our own interests are served. It is, I believe, in our interest that while we improve and enlarge the area of friendship with GDR, we should not correspondingly diminish the area of friendship with FRG [Federal Republic of Germany] ...
>
> We have also an interest in not unduly upsetting the West German Government headed by Chancellor Brandt. After a long travail in Europe, a social democratic Government has come to power in West Germany. Prior to the emergence of Nazis in Germany, *Communist attitude towards the social democrats was that they were "social fascists" ... Brandt should*

not be treated with that kind of political immaturity which Communists generally tend to show in their oversimplified labeling of political realities.

... One cannot overlook the fact that Chancellor Brandt has the courage to engage in new Ostpolitik despite a very slender majority ... During the Bangladesh crisis and the war, Chancellor Brandt showed understanding of our position. Unlike Japan and the United States, Germany did not cut off aid. Are we to overlook all these things? ...

... *I would submit that we should certainly do so* [recognize GDR] *if we are determined to sacrifice our national interests for the sake of enjoying mere emotional effervescence.* [italics mine]

Like Nye Bevan, Willy Brandt was one of Haksar's favourite political figures. The fact is that since 1969 there had been huge pressure on Indira Gandhi from various quarters—both from within her own party and from her allies—to get India to formally recognize East Germany. In August 1970 an Indian consulate had opened in East Berlin. But on full diplomatic ties she had deferred to Haksar's strong views that had become stronger after Indira Gandhi and he had met with Chancellor Brandt in Bonn in November 1971. Nobody could accuse Haksar of being a communist after reading this note. Later in the year, on 2 September 1972, saying that full recognition anytime after October 1972 would be fine, Haksar again told the prime minister that she should inform Chancellor Brandt that India proposed to recognize the GDR from a particular date and that 'our recognition will be without prejudice to the desire of the German people for unity, should they wish to achieve it peacefully and by means of bilateral negotiations'. India and GDR decided to exchange ambassadors on 8 October 1972 and the desire of the German people that Haksar alluded to was to become a reality 18 years later.

Incidentally, it was not just on GDR that Haksar's 'progressive credentials' came to be suspect. Even on North Vietnam he resisted full diplomatic recognition, saying that the consular relations India had established in 1969 were adequate. When the proposal came in June 1970 from the foreign minister to establish a consulate in East Berlin, it was accompanied by a proposal to exchange ambassadors between North Vietnam and India which Haksar had stoutly resisted. Haksar had told the prime minister on 13 June 1970:

If we are to consider these very important matters strictly in terms of their own merits rather than as an exercise in domestic politics to show that one is more progressive than the other, then it is of vital importance that the [Congress] *Party should take up positions on this question.* If, for instance, we wish to go ahead with exchange of embassies between GDR and ourselves as well as between Hanoi and ourselves, then the hands of the Government would need to be strengthened by Party taking up a position which is left of the Government. *Nothing is more persuasive in international relations than for a Government to plead the pressure of political opinion in the governing party.*

I thought I should invite P.M.'s attention to this because I have not seen any resolution on foreign policy for the forthcoming session of the AICC which appears to be concerned exclusively with domestic problems. I am afraid this neglect of foreign policy, especially in extremely complex and difficult situations now developing, is most undesirable. [italics mine]

Indira Gandhi had read what Haksar had to say and, not surprisingly, had asked him to draft the foreign policy resolution for that June 1970 session of the AICC.

Both Nixon and Kissinger believed firmly that India had every intention of marching into West Pakistan after securing victory on the eastern front on 16 December 1971. They would hold on tenaciously to this opinion. They also took pride in the fact that it was the dispatch of the US Seventh Fleet to the Bay of Bengal that sent the right signals to India not to escalate the war on the western front. L.K. Jha, India's ambassador to the USA, wrote to Haksar on 17 February 1972, saying his information was that Nixon and Kissinger had based their conclusions on a CIA report. Jha's letter read:

My dear Babbu,
I have now been able to get some reliable information about the alleged Cabinet source for the US intelligence report indicating India's intention of dismembering Pakistan and destroying its military potential.

There were quite a number of intelligence reports coming into Washington from New Delhi at that time. One of them said that Prime

Minister mentioned to her Cabinet colleagues that once Bangladesh had been liberated, the Indian army would attack Pakistan in full strength and settle the problem once for all. Equally, there were further intelligence reports which gave a contrary view and indicated that once liberation of Bangladesh had been complete, we would not wish to prolong the fighting with Pakistan.

It is the practice that these individual reports are then digested into one single assessment and submitted to higher levels. In the summary which was made of the incoming reports, the particular one of which so much is being made was not given place of pride but referred to on the second page of the summary ... The reason why it is being played up is to find support and justification for the policy which the President has pursued. The report does not provide the rationale of the policy, though it is being used as a method of rationalizing the policy.

Haksar showed this letter to Indira Gandhi who noted in her hand on 2 March 1972:

Perhaps it is not necessary but we should nevertheless inform LK that at NO time have I ever made such a statement. Besides such a discussion had not taken place at any Cab[inet] Meeting.

Consequently, Haksar replied to Jha the next day:

... While it is interesting to learn about the vagaries of the C.I.A, I should like you to know that at no time Prime Minister ever made a statement even remotely resembling what the C.I.A. agents have reported. You should also know that there was no occasion for the Cabinet to discuss the question. The only time when this matter was discussed was on the evening of 16th December, first in the Political Affairs Committee of the Cabinet and later on in the Cabinet as well as with leaders of the Opposition. At these discussions, no one suggested that we might continue the war. *The C.I.A. having led President Kennedy up the garden path has done it again.* [italics mine]

Sheikh Mujibur Rahman was making his first foreign visit to Calcutta after becoming prime minister of the new sovereign country of Bangladesh. This was from 6–8 February 1972 and Indira Gandhi was going to receive him. Haksar sent her a briefing note that very day:

> …At present Sheikh Sahab, the bulk of MPs and the bureaucracy constitute a pattern of power structure which is to the right of the Centre. The logical development of such a power structure will lead it inevitably to reliance on US, UK and the West. And if Bangladesh begins its economic development on the basis of Western aid, it will slide imperceptibly into a position of estrangement, if not hostility towards us. China might then aid and abet this hostility and thus restore the second front against us …
>
> However, there are important countervailing forces against such a development. For the next year or so, at any rate, an open alignment with US and/or China will not be popular; the youth and students are radical enough to prevent the right of the centre political structure to assert itself … We have to build on this …
>
> We should also get Sheikh Sahib to define the broad framework of foreign and defence policies. Obviously we desire perpetual peace and amity with Bangladesh. We can formulate this desire in a solemn manner in a Treaty …
>
> We are thus on the eve of a long journey together to the end of the night or, hopefully, to the beginning of a dawn. We should remove all the factors which might impede this journey. The most negative factor would be the continuance of the armed forces in Bangladesh … Withdrawal of [Indian] armed forces is a matter of very high priority. A time and date should be fixed now …
>
> Finally, we have to take into account the method and style of Sheikh Mujibur's functioning … He is desperately anxious to establish a working relationship with PM. A hot line has been established. But this may not be enough. It would be necessary for PM to select an emissary who could go to Dacca and follow up any point which might be raised through the Hot Line … PM might suggest to Sheikh Mujib, in response to his desire to maintain personal contacts with PM, that on her part *PM would be prepared to send from time to time a personal emissary enjoying full confidence. She might then select an emissary who could be either the*

Principal Secretary to the PM or Shri D.P. Dhar and leave the choice to him
[Sheikh]. Better still both might be used to maintain a balance with change
and continuity. [italics mine]

This is exactly what Indira Gandhi did. She would use both Haksar and D.P.
Dhar as her special emissaries to Bangladesh over the next year-and-a-half.
On 19 March 1972, the formal accord that Haksar had mentioned was to
become a reality when Indira Gandhi and Sheikh Mujibur Rahman signed
the 'Treaty of Peace, Friendship and Cooperation' in Dacca during her visit
there. But that trip had not been without its hiccups because Haksar felt
that the Ministry of Irrigation and Power was not being sensitive enough
on the water resources issue vis-à-vis Bangladesh. Haksar wanted India to
take 'a more positive and constructive approach on issues relating to the
Farakka Barrage in West Bengal and flood control and regional development
of Ganga-Brahmaputra-Meghna Basin'.

In early-September 1972, Sheikh Mujibur Rahman sent word to
Indira Gandhi that he would like to discuss a number of issues with her,
including the political situation prevailing in Pakistan and the question of
Bangladesh's admission to the United Nations. Haksar's response to this
on 13 September 1972, the day the Bangladesh prime minister was to be
in New Delhi on his way back to Dacca from Geneva, was:

> One should have a clear assessment of alternatives to Mr. Bhutto which
> might be of advantage to us and to Bangladesh. This in turn requires
> an assessment of the situation in Punjab, Baluchistan, Sind and Frontier
> Provinces. Tactically speaking, we should never give an opportunity
> to Bhutto to raise the bogey of Indian interference; that he should be
> allowed to stew in his own juice and that unless one can clearly see an
> alternative political framework in Pakistan, headed by someone more
> acceptable than President Bhutto, we should not unduly rock President
> Bhutto's boat if the only result would be to bring back the army rule,
> added Chinese interference, American reinforcement of the armed
> strength military regime of Pakistan and the consequent confrontation
> with India. Bangladesh can be relaxed about this being far away from the
> scene but we have common frontiers with Pakistan which Bangladesh
> has not. Excessive hopes that Baluchis, Pathan and Sindhis by themselves

would be able to successfully carry out a revolution might be dangerous. The heart of the matter lies which way Punjab moves. *One should also bear in mind that the Western Powers and even perhaps the Soviet Union have a vested interest in maintaining the integrity of what is left of Pakistan …*

As for the implication of the Chinese veto against Bangladesh's admission to the UN … Bangladesh has to face a moment of truth. They had unusual hopes of befriending China … We are of course not taken aback by the Chinese action which is consistent with their desire to continue to fish in the troubled waters of the sub-continent and to prevent these waters becoming calm. [italics mine]

Haksar also advised Indira Gandhi to tell her Bangladeshi counterpart that under no circumstances should the trial of prisoners of war (POWs) accused of war crimes be staged before the debate in the U.N. General Assembly on the admission of Bangladesh was completed.

As for the forthcoming debate in the General Assembly, we have to be extremely careful that it is not diverted into a discussion on the question of return of prisoners of war or passing of a resolution recommending admission of Bangladesh to U.N. with the proviso that Bangladesh and India should agree to the return of the POWs unconditionally …

Indira Gandhi and Haksar met Sheikh Mujibur Rahman that afternoon and these points were put across to him by her.

Nani Palkhivala had led the legal fight in the Supreme Court against two signature decisions of Indira Gandhi—nationalization of banks in 1969 and abolition of privy purses in 1970. In both cases, Palkhivala had won. But he and Haksar continued to be good friends. In fact, sometime in 1968, Palkhivala had been offered the post of attorney general of India and he had accepted. But, by his own admission,[52] after having said yes, Palkhivala, backed out and Niren De had been appointed

On 4 April 1972, Haksar told Indira Gandhi that she should let Palkhivala call on her saying:

I do not know if P.M. has ever met him or knows him. I should, therefore, like to lay bare a little bit of his anatomy. When I was called to the Bar, I started devilling for a leading counsel in England. He had his chambers in Lincoln's Inn. Next to his chambers was the chamber of one Mr. Bowen who was a very distinguished chancery lawyer specialising in mining matters. I came to know Mr. Bowen and he told me that he was brought up in extreme poverty by his father being a miner; how he had to struggle hard and make good. Having made good, he became an arch conservative. Shri Palkhivala's background is similar to Mr. Bowen's. He was brought up in extreme poverty and his conservatism is similar to that of Mr. Bowen. However, there is a slight difference. Shri Palkhivala is still young and is not very confirmed in his ideas and attitudes. Indeed, on several matters, he has some useful ideas. He has interesting things to say how the litigation centering around taxation could be reduced. In fact, he might be flattered if P.M. were to say that she understood that Shri Palkhivala has some interesting suggestions about how the mounting arrears of tax cases could be reduced by an alternative machinery for dealing with them... He is extremely knowledgeable about taxation matters and knows all there is to know how tax can be avoided and how, in fact, it is being avoided.

The idea of joint sector is quite acceptable to him. Unfortunately, Government have [sic] not done any thinking on this. If Shri Palkhivala has his ideas on how he would like the joint sector to run, he might be flattered if P.M. were to ask him to acquaint Government of his own conception of working of the joint sector.

Today's public–private partnerships are nothing but the 'joint sector' of the 1970s which Haksar championed. On 25 March 1972, he got Indira Gandhi to float the idea in her address to the Federation of Indian Chambers of Commerce and Industry (FICCI) in New Delhi. She defined the joint sector as one in which the 'managerial ability of the private sector was harnessed with support from public financial institutions'. The other thing about the Palkhivala note is that it shows how Haksar was always getting people from diverse backgrounds and different viewpoints to see the prime minister. He never functioned as her gate-keeper but more as a facilitator as far as people meeting her was concerned.

On his part, Palkhivala would continue to torment Indira Gandhi's government, particularly in a landmark case in the Supreme Court whose verdict on 24 April 1973 severely circumscribed the power of Parliament to amend the Constitution. But when she ran into legal problems with the Allahabad High Court verdict of 12 June 1975 against her on charges of electoral malpractices, Indira Gandhi's first instinct would be to turn to Palkhivala. He would appear for her in the Supreme Court on 23 June 1975, win her partial relief but was to later withdraw. When the harassment of Haksar's family by the tax authorities started during the Emergency in July–August 1975, the only intervention Haksar was to make was to get his wife to meet Palkhivala who, as it turned out, quite strangely refused to appear for them.

Haksar was uncompromisingly secular to the core. In 1972, he could not speak publicly but made his views forcefully clear when the issue of declaring Aligarh Muslim University as a minority institution erupted and began to engage the prime minister's attention. Legislation to declare the university a minority institution came to the Cabinet for approval. Haksar used this opportunity on 26 May 1972 to tell the prime minister:

> The central—in fact the only—issue raised by the proposed Bill on the Aligarh Muslim University is a very simple one: is the Government of India going to create a precedent by setting up a Central University for a minority community? If the answer is in the affirmative, the question would arise whether such an Act would be in consonance with the letter and spirit of our Constitution. The further question would be that if an educational institution wholly maintained out of State funds is to be established for a religious minority, namely the Muslims, why should it not maintain similar educational institutions out of State funds for other minorities, be they linguistic, religious or ethnic? And if the Aligarh Muslim University is to be wholly maintained out of State funds for the benefit of Muslims, why should not Banaras Hindu University be wholly maintained for the benefit of the Hindus? Thus, the communal forces which are wittingly or unwittingly, fanning up the demand for the Aligarh

Muslim University retaining its Muslim character, are giving sustenance and support to the R.S.S. and the Jan Sangh to raise a similar demand vis-à-vis the Banaras Hindu University.

The foregoing considerations lead one to the only conclusion possible, namely that the Government of India cannot possibly treat the Aligarh Muslim University on any different footing than any other Central University. Of course, this would mean withstanding the pressure of those Muslim communal elements who are mounting up agitation. They have to be fought just as Hindu communal elements were fought the other day in the Banaras Hindu University. [italics mine]

Haksar's vies prevailed even though the prime minister was under pressure from many MPs and others to have Aligarh Muslim University declared as a minority institution. When it came to secularism, Haksar was uncompromisingly Nehruvian—that the State had no business promoting the interests of any one religious community and that communalism of all kinds need to be combated unapologetically.

A few months later the prime minister would tell Haksar about her anxiety on the agitation then being carried out against privately managed educational institutions in Kerala. The majority of these institutions were run by various societies of the Roman Catholic Church, the Syrian Christian Church and by other Christian denominations, the Nair Service Society, the Sree Narayana Guru Trust and the Muslim Educational Society. Thus, except for a few colleges most of these colleges were run by caste-based or religion-based organizations. A similar situation prevailed in secondary education as well. Haksar himself had received a telegram from the leading Malayalam newspaper *Malayala Manorama* asking for his intervention to quell the agitation. Haksar told the prime minister on 14 July 1972:

As in most parts of the country, private educational institutions have become a money-earning racket. Due to hunger for education, there has been a mass influx into the colleges which has resulted in deterioration in the quality of education and has enabled the private managements to literally fleece every family in the state. Admission to these privately-managed institutions as well as recruitment of staff is the subject-matter of gross abuse ...

There has been insistent demand from the teachers, educationists, students and all classes of society for a change in the educational pattern and for increasing State control over management ... There has been a big disparity in the fees collected by the Private Colleges and Government Colleges ...

... It will not be correct to say that the Government of Kerala acted precipitately when they issued an Ordinance on June 15, 1972 standardising the fees ... From all accounts, the Ordinance has had a widespread political impact. The Marxist Party has been forced to give its grudging support and some of the coalition partners of the present Government of Kerala, who regarded it as of doubtful utility, have now changed their attitude ... I understand that even within the Church, there are serious differences. The most interesting feature has been the wide support given to the Ordinance by Christian workers in Congress even at the risk of ex-communication.

The whole agitation has to be viewed not as one of minority rights, but purely as one of putting a stop to widespread mismanagement of privately-run educational institutions. It might be a good thing to speak to Church dignitaries pointing out to them that they are on a morally weak wicket in seeking to defend privately-managed institutions which are known to indulge in questionable practices in the field of education. [italics mine]

In June 1972, Indira Gandhi was to take a major new initiative on Kashmir, the roots of which can be traced back to Haksar's conversations with her. The fact that a summit meeting was going to be held with President Bhutto of Pakistan at the end of the month gave these conversations added meaning. On 2 June 1972, Haksar wrote to the prime minister:

... We have been lacking in subtlety in handling Sheikh Abdullah. A variety of vested interests have made the task of looking at Sheikh Abdullah, as he is, an extremely difficult one. Nevertheless it is imperative to make a fresh start and lead him by hand on the difficult and tortuous road whose ultimate destination is reconciliation ...

Even apart from the wider considerations of need for reconciliation, there is an imperative necessity of not keeping Sheikh Abdullah in our custody and thus having his skeleton in our cupboard when we talk to President Bhutto and tell him that Kashmir is ours with Sheikh Abdullah in our custody rather than a free man ... I mentioned all this to Shri D.P. Dhar several days ago and told him quite frankly that since the original sin of what was done in 1953 [Sheikh Abdullah's arrest and dismissal as chief minister] lay largely on him, he should ponder deeply over the problem of what to do with Sheikh Abdullah ... I believe that he subsequently spoke to P.M. and I was glad to learn from P.M. last night that the Chief Minister of Jammu and Kashmir feels that the Sheikh should immediately be released ...

But releasing Sheikh Abdullah is not enough. Before he returns to the Valley, P.M. must meet with Sheikh Saheb. The meeting is going to be painful, because P.M. will have to show extreme forbearance and listen to his long tale of woes; but PM should let him unburden himself and then say we must look to the future ... Given this, we can begin, step by step, the long journey towards reconciliation, that Sheikh Saheb should appoint someone and that P.M. would also appoint someone and two of them can quietly talk things over ...

If it is decided to release Sheikh Saheb in the next 24 hours, Dr. Bajaj of the All India Institute of Medical Sciences [Sheikh Abdullah's personal doctor] *should be instructed ... that he should advise Sheikh Abdullah to enter the All India Medical Institute for a thorough check-up ... that Sheikh Saheb should return to Kashmir after he has gone through the check-up, if he wishes to do so.* I think P.M. should meet Sheikh Abdullah on June 11, 1972 just on the eve of her departure [for Stockholm]. [italics mine]

Haksar's script was played out exactly as he had dictated, as the Sheikh himself was to recount in his autobiography many years later. The only addition to the script was that Haksar himself first went to the All India Institute of Medical Sciences to meet with Sheikh Abdullah and give him a bouquet and greetings on behalf of the prime minister. Sheikh Abdullah was released from prison on 5 June 1972. Ten days later, on 12 June 1972, Haksar wrote out another script for the prime minister:

... I submit PM should send for Shri G. Parthasarathi sometime today. This is because Shri Parthasarathi is sensitive about his own dignity and would prefer that the assignment which PM is about to give him is done so directly rather than through an intermediary like me ...

Shri G. Parthasarathi should be told that the proposed dialogue—and it should be a dialogue rather than "negotiations"—should be conducted quietly without any publicity. The object of this dialogue is to find the terms and conditions on which Sheikh Abdullah could participate in the political life of not only Kashmir but of India as a whole ...

The dialogue is not intended to upset the existing set-up in Kashmir but to look to the future ...

The question of autonomy should be discussed not in abstract but concretely in terms of genuine interest of the people of Kashmir ...

The dialogue should be a prolonged one. With this object in view, Shri Parthasarathi might call on Sheikh Abdullah when he is about to leave for Srinagar; thereafter he might get in touch with Mirza Afzal Beg who should be invited to Delhi. I would not recommend the dialogue to commence from Srinagar as this would cause undue publicity. If Delhi is too hot for Afzal Beg, some other quieter venue might be found ... [italics mine]

Thus would begin the 'dialogue' between the two emissaries of their respective sides—G. Parthasarathi and Mirza Afzal Beg which would last for slightly over two years. A few months later, on 26 July 1972, Haksar informed the prime minister:

A lot of time had elapsed since Shri G. Parthasarathi had conversations with Mirza Afzal Beg. I suggested to him that he might see him again and request him to come to New Delhi as it was not very desirable for Shri Parthasarathi to be constantly going to Srinagar. Accordingly, Shri Beg arrived in New Delhi. Shri Parthasarathi ... asked me to join ... which I did ...

In the course of the conversations I told Beg that Sheikh Saheb tended to make "instant" responses to questions put to him; consequently, the press reports tended to create impressions which were not desirable. I advised that people like Beg should dissuade Sheikh from making daily statements and that in whatever he has to say he must sustain a particular position; that to my mind his position should be that such differences as exist between us are those between brothers and sisters of India and should be settled by means of a dialogue. I said that it was important to establish the nexus between us as fellow citizens of India because for a variety of reasons an impression has gone around among the wide mass in India that both Beg and Sheikh had in the past allowed their basic loyalty to seek a solution within the framework of India to be doubted; for, after all, the audience of Sheikh Saheb did not consist merely of the people of the Valley but also of Jammu and naturally the rest of India … I did not feel any great resistance on the part of Beg to these ideas … He asked G.P. and I if we could give him an assurance which was not to be publicly repeated that we conceded the principle that relations between India and Jammu and Kashmir were based on the Instrument of Accession and that once this was conceded, we could then work out the basis of our present relationship. We naturally gave no such assurance and merely stated that the time for seeking such assurance or giving such assurance had not yet arrived and that we should for the next few months concentrate our energy and attention to restoration of trust and confidence which should be palpable to the people of India.

Beg and Parthasarathi would arrive at a final understanding on the night of 13 November 1974, paving the way for Sheikh Abdullah to return as chief minister of Jammu and Kashmir on 25 February 1975 after a gap of 22 years. Behind GP was Indira Gandhi and behind her was Haksar who had got the ball rolling in the first place in 1972 with his visit to the All India Institute of Medical Sciences to see the Sheikh.

While Haksar's manifold contributions to the emergence of Bangladesh are beyond dispute and are acknowledged handsomely in that country itself, his role in Simla thereafter has come under criticism especially in India. The Simla Summit began on 28 June 1972 and four days later the Simla Accord was signed under dramatic circumstances at well past midnight.

How did the Simla summit come about in the first place? On 31 January 1972, Pegov had called on Haksar 'at his own instance' to understand what India would do to counter Pakistan's efforts to activate the UN Security Council to mediate between India and Pakistan. Haksar spelt out India's approach and told the Soviet envoy in no uncertain terms that the Security Council should not allow itself to 'become merely the vehicle for Pakistan's propagandist efforts'. The record of this conversation prepared by Haksar for the prime minister the same day also went to say:

> The Ambassador enquired about the prospects of negotiations with President Bhutto. I said we were ready to engage in such negotiations. He said that in the conversations that Bhutto had with the Soviet Ambassador, he seemed anxious to have a dialogue with India. I asked him if the Soviet Ambassador in Islamabad had enquired how, where and with whom and when precisely would Bhutto be ready for these negotiations. The Soviet Ambassador asked me if he would have these questions put. I said he was certainly welcome to do so. In fact, these questions were so obvious that I thought that the Soviet Ambassador in Islamabad might have thought of them in the ordinary course.

It was obvious to Haksar that given Bhutto's aggressive lobbying at the United Nations India had to do something to wrest the initiative. On 12 February 1972, India formally informed the UN secretary general, through a letter drafted by Haksar, that it was ready to have *direct* talks with Pakistan at any time, at any level and without any preconditions. This communication from the prime minister went thus:

> India unilaterally offered to Pakistan a cease-fire on December 16, 1971. Upon its acceptance by Pakistan a cease-fire became effective from 2000 hrs Indian Standard Time on December 17, 1971. The Security Council Resolution No. 307 of December 21, 1971 took note of this. In all this India had been inspired by her consistent desire to contribute to the restoration of durable peace and stability.
>
> The Government of India are firmly convinced that lasting peace between India and Pakistan can and should be achieved as soon as possible in the interest of both countries and peoples. For this purpose the Government of India are prepared to have direct talks with the Government of Pakistan at any time, at any level and without any preconditions. The Government of India believes that this is the best way of serving the principles and purposes of the [UN] Charter. The Government of India hope that the Government of Pakistan will respond to this initiative in a positive and constructive manner ...

A few days later this letter was shared with members of the Security Council and on 17 February 1972, the Swiss ambassador in Islamabad handed a copy of it to the Government of Pakistan as well. That very day, the Ceylon High Commission delivered a message from President Bhutto that said '… I am ready to meet her [Indira Gandhi] with an open mind and without any preconditions whatsoever … I would be willing to come to New Delhi on any mutually convenient date'. On 2 March 1972, Haksar asked Indira Gandhi to send this note to the foreign minister, Swaran Singh:

> The exchanges which have taken place so far between Pakistan and ourselves through the Swiss and Soviet Embassies as well as the High Commission of Ceylon indicate a readiness on the part of President Bhutto to engage in direct negotiations with India. He has also conveyed to us through the Soviet Embassy the timing of the commencement of such negotiations … We have now to carefully prepare for such a meeting, the venue, the procedural questions such as the level of the initial meeting as well as the more substantive questions relating to the objectives we seek to achieve through the means of these direct negotiations …

On 20 March 1972, British Home Secretary Alec Douglas-Home sent a message to Indira Gandhi:

> I had a talk with President Bhutto this morning [in London]. He is very anxious to talk over with you the ways in which an entirely new relationship with India may be established … He is anxious that such a meeting should be convened quickly before the middle of next month … He would like the invitation to come from you …

Earlier Bhutto had met Kosygin in Moscow on 17 March 1972 and had received the message from the Soviets that he should open a dialogue with Indira Gandhi. This would have been known to Haksar, thanks to his contacts with Pegov. Douglas-Home's communication would lead Haksar to get Indira Gandhi to once again tell Swaran Singh on 25 March 1972:

> We discussed amongst ourselves the broad lines of approach to the forthcoming negotiations with Pakistan. We now have to evolve a more definitive position on a number of related questions. In his message, Sir

Alec Douglas-Home had suggested that I might extend an invitation to President Bhutto to visit India. There is also the question whether we should firmly adhere to our view that prior to a summit meeting, our Special Envoys should meet. What would we say if President Bhutto were to take the initiative and says that he wants to come to New Delhi? We should also have a clear picture of what we should do if negotiations take place at whatever level ...

Thereafter Haksar prepared an invitation from Indira Gandhi to Bhutto on 30 March 1972 that was handed over to the Swiss ambassador to be delivered to the Pakistani President:

It has always been my desire to have lasting peace between our two countries because of my firm belief that this would be to our mutual interest. I have tried to work towards this end ...

The tragic events and the sufferings of the last year would be mitigated to some extent if we could turn our backs on the past and, together, lay the foundations of an enduring peace between our two countries. This is the denouement we sincerely seek. The Government and the people of India are convinced that the pursuit of peace, cooperation and good neighbourliness are more worthwhile objectives than a confrontation which diverts our energies and resources from our war against poverty and backwardness ...

On February 14, 1972, the Government of India wrote formally to the Secretary-General of the United Nations suggesting direct talks between Pakistan and India without any pre-conditions. This was also conveyed to you through the Swiss Government. Since then I have a received a message through the courtesy of the Soviet government and one through Sir Alec Douglas-Home that you would like a meeting with me sometime in the first half of April 1972. I have also received a message through His Excellency M. Rene Keller [Swiss ambassador in Pakistan].

I agree that we should meet and in order to prepare the ground for such a meeting, I suggest that Special Emissaries who have our complete confidence and carry our full authority should meet to settle the modalities for the summit meeting and to delineate the subjects we should discuss ...

Haksar then asked Subimal Dutt, India'a ambassador in Dacca to 'acquaint Sheikh Mujibur Rahman immediately with the substance of the letter'. On 12 April, India received Bhutto's reply through the Swiss. Soon thereafter, D.P. Dhar was nominated as Indira Gandhi's special emissary and his counterpart in Pakistan was to be Aziz Ahmed. When Dhar went to Islamabad in April 1972 to do the preparatory work for the summit with Aziz Ahmed, Haksar sent him a message on 29 April 1972 through a top secret channel:

(1) We should not be anxious to publish the agreed items of the Agenda [for the summit] ...

(2) We should not show any anxiety to agree immediately on the implementation of any item of the Agenda except stoppage of hostile propaganda. Our idea is to give priority to an overall peace settlement including J&K ...

(3) If Aziz Ahmed's assertion that there is no pressure on Pakistan for return of Prisoners of War is true, then Pakistan need not give it such a priority ...

(4) ... It is only after the emissaries have agreed on the agenda and the priorities that the real summit to decide these matters can be held. A series of summits would not, in our opinion, be the best way to settle these matters ...

You should contradict any suggestion that summit meeting will be held in any third country as has been put out by the Pakistani press and radio and attributed to a member of the Indian Delegation.

Finally it was decided to have the summit in Simla between 28 June and 2 July 1972. On 30 May 1972, Haksar laid out a timetable for the prime minister to help her prepare for the summit:

I submitted to P.M. yesterday that it is necessary to go over the ground to be traversed in our negotiations with the President of Pakistan. For this purpose, a meeting should be called at P.M's earliest convenience ... After the various steps for negotiations have been identified and aims and objectives defined, a meeting of the Political Affairs Committee of the Cabinet should be called. At this meeting it is essential for P.M. to ask each member of it to express himself of his concept of the aims and objectives of our negotiations with Pakistan. *As these negotiations are of cardinal importance, it is not enough for members to keep their counsel to themselves, as is customary with them.* Later on, it might be necessary to call the Members of the Cabinet. At some stage ... it will be necessary to call in the Chiefs of Staff ... [italics mine]

Here was Haksar goading the prime minister to coax her senior-most colleagues (Jagjivan Ram, Y.B. Chavan, Swaran Singh and Fakhruddin Ali Ahmed) to speak out frankly. They were men of enormous political experience and sagacity but were careful of expressing their views—they would prefer to listen to the prime minister first before speaking.

One bit of preparation for the Simla Summit was actually quite hilarious. Foreign Secretary T.N. Kaul sent out instructions on 24 June 1972 that:

PM will stay at The Retreat along with some personal staff. The rest of PM's Secretariat and staff will stay in Punjab Bhawan (Dane's Folly). It should be referred to as Punjab Bhawan and not Dane's Folly.[53]

Before leaving for Simla, President Bhutto had addressed his nation on 27 June 1972. A day later, Haksar sent a detailed assessment of that speech to Indira Gandhi along with what he thought might be a structure of negotiations at Simla. He ended his analysis by saying:

The terrible legacy of the past has to be got over. And this can be got over if we are able today to enunciate the broad features of our future relationship in which the strongest element should be our firm resolve not to use force in settling our differences either as they exist, or might arise in future. Such a declaration accompanied by some concrete steps towards implementation of this resolve would put us on the new road to life of peace, amity and good neighbourliness. P.M. might then ask President Bhutto: how do we set about it?

Negotiations started on 28 June 1972 with D.P. Dhar chairing the Indian side and Aziz Ahmed heading the Pakistani team. They continued the next day when Haksar said that 'the UN Charter itself mentioned other peaceful means by which international disputes could be settled'. He went on, according to the official record of discussions, to make the following two points:

(a) that we should not allow ourselves to be influenced by the echoes of the past but come with new ideas and new approaches which can help us solve our problems ourselves, instead of either going to war or involving distant countries into our disputes.

(b) Indian politics has its own compulsions and complications. We consider it our business to manage our obscurantist and hard-core elements. We are similarly hopeful that you will be able to manage yours. But we cannot permit our individual internal compulsions to affect the settlement in favour of either party.

Haksar took over as head of the Indian delegation on 30 June 1972 since Dhar had, all of a sudden, suffered a heart attack and had to be evacuated to New Delhi. This was a second tragedy for Haksar personally in two days. As the Summit had got under way, Haksar had been informed that his close friend P.N. Kaul, then deputy high commissioner in London had suffered a heart attack and passed away. P.N. Kaul had been well-known to Indira Gandhi as well, and in her condolence message she recalled her long association with him including his acting as her interpreter during her 1953 visit to the USSR.

On 29 June 1972, India shared with Pakistan a 'Draft Treaty for Reconciliation, Good Neighbourliness and Durable Peace' and added a note saying that whatever was agreed to on the question of Jammu and Kashmir that was to be discussed separately would be included appropriately in the Treaty. The next day, Pakistan shared its draft of an 'Agreement on Bilateral Relations between the Government of India and the Government of Pakistan'. The same day—that is on 30 June 1972—the two sides resumed negotiations with Haksar now chairing the Indian side. The official record of discussions reads:

Principal Secretary [PNH] said that he had few observations to make. We had deliberately not called into witness the past history of our relations. Both sides had their own respective "mythologies". What was now required was to work for durable peace. Secondly, India believes that her own domestic compulsions would also have to be reckoned with in any consideration of the question of peace in the area. If we accept the Pakistani draft our people would feel that the sourest factor of our relations had not even been referred to and no hope or direction had been indicated as to how the problem could be resolved.

Mr. Ahmed stated ... why was it necessary to settle the Kashmir question today, especially when Pakistan did not enjoy equality in negotiations? Let us wait for a few months, perhaps a year.

Principal Secretary ... wondered whether there was any way of persuading Pakistan to accept that discussions were being conducted on one basis—that of equality ... We would like to remove the endless curse of conflicts on the question of Kashmir. There are differences in our positions ... While we believe that Jammu and Kashmir is part and parcel of India, as stated in our Constitution, President Bhutto keeps calling for a solution through self-determination. We frankly do not understand what this means ... We do not accept the concept of self-determination for integral parts of a country ... We would, however, like to find some solution. For this, Principal Secretary said, it would be useful to know the parameters within which Pakistan envisaged a solution to the question of Jammu & Kashmir. Pakistan should take us into confidence even if we do not come to any agreement ... Principal Secretary reiterated that for India the question of Kashmir was very important and if there was no understanding, a new situation would be created which would require serious consideration.

Indira Gandhi and Bhutto then met at 3.45 pm on 1 July 1972 accompanied by their top aides. In this meeting, Haksar remarked:

The officials have met and we have exchanged ideas. We feel that we are on the eve of a new kind of relationship. Discussions at our level could not produce results on the question of P.O.W.s. Mr. Aziz Ahmed had suggested that we have the Bangladesh Government's agreement on this subject in our pocket. That is not so. We are leaving some difficult questions behind, not because we have forgotten about them but for discussion at future meetings ... We are not using them as pressure points but there is need to discuss them further in order to solve them. Confidence would have grown by the time when we meet next; other obstacles would have been removed. There is agreement about good neighbourliness and to solve problems peacefully.

On the same day, that is on 1 July 1972 India handed over to Pakistan a draft called 'Agreement on Bilateral Relations between the Government of India and the Government of Pakistan'.[54] Two formulations in this draft had Jammu and Kashmir in mind. Para 1 (ii) said that:

... the countries will not use forces for the settlement of any differences between them and will resolve them exclusively (by peaceful means) through bilateral negotiations ...

Para 1 (iv) went to state that:

... the basic issues and cause of conflict which have bedeviled the relations between the two countries for the last 25 years shall be resolved bilaterally and by peaceful means.

This draft ended by saying:

Both Governments agree that their respective Heads will meet again at a mutually convenient time in the future that, in the meanwhile, the representatives of the two sides will meet to discuss further the modalities and arrangements for the establishment of durable peace and normalization of relations, including the question of Jammu & Kashmir, repatriation of prisoners of war and civilian internees, withdrawal of all armed forces to their respective territories and the resumption of diplomatic relations.

Pakistan, too, submitted a counter draft on 1 July 1972. The same day Haksar sent Indira Gandhi a note:

P.M. has with her the draft which the Pakistanis gave us yesterday. P.M. will kindly see that there is a reference there to a U.N. Resolution. P.M. may wish to see the text of that Resolution which I attach to this note. The Pakistanis might ask why we are objecting to a reference to this Resolution in their text. Our answer is that this Resolution does not, by any means, replace the [UN] Charter and cannot be deemed to be an amendment of the Charter. Consequently, reference to it has no greater sanctity than a reference to the Charter itself and that even in this Resolution, paragraph 6 strictly provides that the parties are free to use "other peaceful means of their choice". Since in the context of the Indo-Pakistani relations, we have not got anywhere by invoking the United Nations and in particular the Security Council, we have felt all along that if two of us cannot settle anything by mutual agreement , nothing can be settled by any other processes. I thought that P.M. should have this background just in case the matter is raised.

A day later in the morning of 2 July 1972, India handed over yet another draft agreement to Pakistan marked 'Final Indian Draft'. Para 4(ii) read:

In Jammu and Kashmir, the line of control resulting from the cease-fire of December 17, 1971 shall henceforth be respected by both sides, as a line of peace. Neither side shall seek to alter it unilaterally, irrespective of mutual differences and legal interpretations. Both sides further undertake to refrain from the threat or the use of force in violation of this line.

The concluding para 6 of this draft now read:

Both sides agree that their respective Heads will meet again at a mutually convenient time in the future that, in the meanwhile, the representatives of the two sides will meet to discuss further the modalities and arrangements for the establishment of durable peace and normalization of relations, including question of repatriation of prisoners of war and civilian internees, a final settlement of Jammu and Kashmir and the resumption of diplomatic relations.

This para 6 was to remain the final para 6 in the Simla Agreement that was soon to be signed. The officials of the two sides met again at 3.30 pm on 2 July 1972 but the meeting did not yield any agreement. Aziz Ahmed rejected the latest Indian draft of that very morning and suggested a Joint Communiqué instead. Haksar countered Ahmed's objections by saying that India was not asking Pakistan to give up her position on J&K, but India would certainly resist Pakistan's thrusting the U.N. Resolution down its throat. He also pointed out that India was offering to vacate Pakistani territory captured during the December 1971 conflict. While deeply regretting Pakistan's dismissal of the Indian draft, Haksar handed over a draft communiqué with Aziz Ahmed promising to share his version before the dinner that night.

The dinner took place and, thereafter Indira Gandhi and Bhutto had a one-on-one conversation. It looked all was lost but miraculously at 40 minutes past midnight the two leaders signed the Simla Agreement. How different was this final agreement from the Indian draft of the morning of 2 July 1972? Para 6 was identical. The change that India agreed to was in Para 4(ii) of its draft of 1 July 1972 which now read:

> In Jammu and Kashmir, the line of control resulting from the cease-fire of December 17, 1971, shall be respected by both sides *without prejudice to the recognized position of either side*. Neither side shall seek to alter it unilaterally, irrespective of mutual differences and legal interpretations. Both sides further undertake to refrain from the threat or the use of force in violation of this Line. [italics mine]

The italicized portion was indeed a concession to Bhutto in order to bring Pakistan on board.

The Accord has been both hailed and attacked. Interestingly this is true not just in India but in Pakistan as well. Conceivably Indira Gandhi and Haksar did not want Pakistan to leave as an embittered foe hell-bent on taking revenge for being humiliated so comprehensively. Whether he got her around to his point of view or whether she was determined to have an agreement of her own volition is impossible to know. Dhar has written that she may have been mindful of what the Soviet position was: that Bhutto should not leave Simla empty handed.[55] Sharada Prasad has written:

> I vividly remember a particular meeting of the Political Affairs Committee [of the Cabinet] at which Indira Gandhi met with uncomfortable, non-committal silence from her colleagues when she mentioned her proposal about releasing prisoners of war and returning territory. She then asked Haksar to set forth the reasons for the proposal. This he did, taking almost three-quarters of an hour. It was a masterly exposition, notable for its incisiveness and grasp of political realities and psychological insights. When he had done, Indira Gandhi posed the question again, and one

by one, Jagjivan Ram, Y.B. Chavan, Swaran Singh and Fakhruddin Ali Ahmed indicated their assent.

On his return from Simla, Haksar must have briefed the intrepid journalist A. Raghavan of the *Blitz* for that tabloid carried a detailed account of what had transpired at Simla. *Blitz*'s publisher R.K. Karanjia and Haksar were close personal friends so much so that Karanjia's wife Aileen would complain to Haksar about her husband's colourful personal life. Raghavan himself had been a member of the CPI. His article called 'Five Days That Changed History' appeared in publication's 5 July 1972 issue. It carried snippets that are not there in the official records. Writing of what happened on 1 July 1972, Raghavan wrote:

> About 7 p.m. Pakistan officials return to the negotiating table. The Indian delegation, headed by Haksar, presents a revised version. Expressions like "no-war pact" and "treaty" have been shunned. "No-war pact" has been replaced by "renunciation of force" and "treaty" by "agreement". This, for the first time, offers the withdrawal of Indian troops and the vacation of Pakistani territory occupied on either side of the international frontier during the December war. Pakistan should do the same. As for Jammu and Kashmir, says the new draft, the line of control resulting from the cease-fire on December 17 shall be respected by both sides.
>
> Aziz Ahmed explodes. Calls the document "a step back". He says the international position of Jammu and Kashmir is not mentioned. Nor is the role of the UN mentioned. No solution offered to the issue of prisoners of war and so on and so forth ...
>
> *Haksar tells the Pak delegation leader that the pull-out is a major concession made by the Prime Minister in consultation with her Cabinet colleagues. If he rejects such a concession, WELL THEY CAN WIND UP.*
>
> Thereupon, Aziz Ahmed offers to withdraw his angry remarks. Haksar says there is no need for amends. The negotiating table in the Himachal Secretariat is not the United Nations where everything goes on record, he concludes.
>
> Similar exchanges take place on other matters ... P.N. Dhar, a member of the Indian delegation and a distinguished economist ... analyses incisively the Pakistan budget and concludes that 9 per cent of

Pakistan's national income is spent on its defence, while India spends only 3.6 per cent. Ahmed and his aides enter the caveat: Defence expenditure at home [in Pakistan] is the concern of technical experts, meaning military experts. Haksar would not let go such juicy bone of contention. He quotes the adage that war is too serious a business to be left to the generals, and adds that in India civilians are in command ...

Rafi Raza gives an account of the industrial and technical backwardness of Pakistan ... He pleads for exchanges in science and technology. Progress is barred by other types of "old sticks" like Mullahs and Sardars. *Haksar jumps in and avers that he has a vested interest in Indo-Pak cooperation in science and technology. India has its own Mullahs—both Muslim and Hindu. He hopes that the process of modernization in Pakistan will enlighten the co-religionists in India.* [italics mine]

Thereafter, Haksar prepared the resolution passed by the Congress Working Committee (CWC) hailing the Simla Agreement. But the Cabinet had also to formally approve it to secure its ratification. On 11 July 1972, in a communication to the foreign secretary who was preparing the note for the Cabinet, Haksar asked him to make the following points:

(i) The Simla Agreement, which is annexed to this note, was signed by the Prime Minister of India with the approval of the Political Affairs Committee of the Cabinet and is now submitted for the approval of the Cabinet.

(ii) The important features of the Agreement are:

(a) That for the first time in 25 years, Pakistan has jettisoned all references to the United Nations Security Council Resolution on Kashmir.

(b) That contrary to her earlier position, Pakistan had given up its insistent demand for a self-executing machinery to deal with the question of Kashmir, e.g., mediation, arbitration, judicial settlement, etc.

(c) That Pakistan had agreed to the doctrine of non-use of force in settlement of bilateral disputes. That paragraphs 1 (ii) and 1 (iv) of the Agreement, when read in the context of Pakistan's consistent stand all these years is, in all material particulars a 'No War Pact' which Pakistan all these years resisted;

(d) That despite strenuous efforts to retain the cease-fire line in Kashmir as it obtained in 1949 and subjected to U.N. supervision, Pakistan has now agreed in paragraph 4 (ii) to accept the cease-fire line as on December 17, 1971 and has further agreed not to alter it unilaterally or by use of force; and

(e) That Pakistan did not succeed in basing its case for withdrawal of the armed forces as well as the question of the release of prisoners of war on the Security Council Resolution.

But Haksar did not forget the 'small things of life' in his pre-occupations with drafting the CWC Resolution and Cabinet note on Simla. On 12 July 1972, he wrote to K.N. Channa, chief secretary of Himachal Pradesh:

> One of your officers, Shri A.S. Jaswal, left an indelible impression on my mind of quiet efficiency combined with a tremendous sense of devotion and dedication to duty. I and my colleagues, who stayed at "Hem Kunj" in Simla, often made demands on him in the midst of all the hectic activities in which we were all engaged and we found him always responding without a trace of being harassed. I thought I should write to you about him, and I shall be glad if you will convey my deep sense of appreciation to him.

It is gestures like this that would characterize his entire life and make him what he was: shorn of all the power and the glory, a deeply compassionate and caring human being.

The same day, on 12 July 1972, Haksar was asked by the prime minister to speak to the minister of state of home affairs, K.C. Pant, on a sensitive issue which had been hanging fire for the past few months—that of the fate of Hindus who were Pakistani citizens who had crossed the border in Gujarat and Rajasthan because of the 1971 war and had stayed back in India. After the meeting, Haksar told the prime minister:

> Shri K.C. Pant says that "an immediate decision has, indeed, become necessary". I asked myself: Decision on what? I gathered the impression that we are being ... pressurised into accepting the proposition that Hindus living in Pakistan are our responsibility. In the whole history of Indo–Pakistan relations, this psychology has proved disastrous and

in my view the Nehru-Liaquat Agreement was one such major disaster where Pakistanis acquired a locus standi in safeguarding the interests of Muslims in India and we acquired a similar interest in being the guardians of Hindus in Pakistan. Thus, we became, unwittingly, the victims of the two-nation theory, even when we denounced it from house-tops ...

I am afraid this matter requires political handling. The Congress workers of Gujarat and Rajasthan should be mobilized ... [The refugees] should be told that there is no reason why they should leave their hearths and homes and be wandering nomads in India. We should also get in touch with the Pakistanis ... and request them to look after their nationals belonging to the minority community ... *If we start ab initio by conceding that we have to absorb them automatically just because they happen to be Hindus, we shall be committing the gravest error. Of course, if the Congress Party in Gujarat and Rajasthan is totally paralysed and if the sentiment that Hindus all over the world are a special responsibility of India, then there is no problem. The more we have them, the merrier we shall all be.* [italics mine]

This was the arch secular-nationalist in Haksar speaking. Amongst the hundreds of notes he would have sent to the prime minister during his tenure, this must rank as being among the most brutally honest and that went against the grain of conventional thinking. He even took Nehru to task for the 1950 agreement with the Pakistani Prime Minister Liaquat Ali Khan, but in this he was a bit unfair since he seemed to overlook the immediate background against which that accord had become necessary. Sardar Patel too had defended that agreement.

On 15 July 1972, in response to a request from the prime minister, he sent a note to Chandrajit Yadav, general secretary of the Congress party in connection with a pamphlet it was proposing to publish on the Simla Agreement to counter its critics, mainly the Jan Sangh. Haksar wrote:

(i)   ... I set out below some of the main points which need to be made in any article dealing with the Simla summit:

(ii) The agreement signed on July 2, 1972 at Simla between Prime Minister of India and President of Pakistan has been welcomed all over the world. In our own country too it has been widely welcomed. Naturally, amongst some sections doubts have been expressed about it. This is understandable considering the history of our past relations with Pakistan ... These doubts expressed in some quarters however are of a different category and kind from the jingoistic and immature postures of the super-patriots of the Jan Sangh who are like the twin brothers of their Pakistani counterparts who think that confrontation, conflict and mouthing slogans are a substitute for a sober, finely balanced statecraft ...

(iii)   In order to understand the true meaning and significance of Simla agreement, it is not enough merely to look at the words of the agreement. One must see the totality of facts and circumstances. The first most important fact to be remembered is that Pakistan with which India was negotiating at Simla was totally different from Pakistan of Ayub Khan with which India negotiated the Tashkent agreement ... The most populous part of it has seceded from it and established itself as a sovereign, independent State which is today recognized by more than 82 sovereign States. Within the residue of Pakistan, democratic forces had emerged for the first time in the last 25 years ...

(iv)   Historians now say that if those who sat around the table at Versailles to conclude a peace with Germany defeated during the First World War had acted with wisdom and not imposed upon Germany humiliating terms of peace, not only rise of Nazism would have been avoided but also the seeds of the Second World war would not have been sown ... *[If] India behaved with immaturity and appeared internationally as a country dictating terms to a vanquished country, we would have played into the hands of those interested in fomenting discord in the sub-continent ...*

(v)   Simla agreement is entirely and exclusively a bilateral agreement. And unlike the Tashkent agreement, the Simla agreement has been subject to debate and discussion in Pakistan and a solemn ratification by a democratically elected Parliament of Pakistan.

(vi)   ... The Simla agreement is based on the assumption of common interests of the people of India and the people of Pakistan in peace, democracy, economic development and social progress. [italics mine]

There is a lot of retrospective angst on the Simla Accord, especially in view of the acrimonious and tense bilateral relationship that has existed between India and Pakistan since the mid-1980s. In my view, this is what has given that agreement a bad name in India. But admittedly not all of Indira Gandhi's opponents were critical. C. Rajagopalachari (Rajaji), had been 'delighted' with the Simla agreement calling it the 'Pact of Good Hope.'[56] Rajaji had gone further and asked for an early second summit for resolving the unsettled issues. Jayaprakash Narayan, had issued a long statement and said that 'every Indian desirous of peace in the subcontinent must give it hearty support'.

The revisionism on the Simla Accord simply does not take into account the full facts. There were definite limits on what India could accomplish after the military victory on the eastern front on 16 December 1971. Haksar was painfully aware of these constraints. India could not keep over 90,000 prisoners of war forever, nor could it hold on to West Pakistani territory in perpetuity. And we should not forget the pluses from Simla—the Cease Fire Line being replaced by the Line of Control and the Pakistani commitment to bilateralism. In some ways, the 'mediation' by the USSR at Tashkent in 1966 had undergone 'remediation' at Simla so as to make the Kashmir issue a matter to be settled between India and Pakistan themselves without outside intervention.

India gained immeasurably in terms of international support when in 1999, during the Kargil war, Prime Minister Atal Bihari Vajpayee decided that India would not escalate the war with Pakistan beyond this Line of Control agreed to at Simla. There has been criticism of Haksar that he did not insist that this Line of Control become the international border but even well-meaning critics of Haksar's stance at Simla like Shankar Bajpai, the distinguished diplomat, concede that to expect that would happen at Simla was totally unrealistic.

Criticism of the Simla Agreement fails to take into account what Bhutto himself wanted and what he ended up getting. Here is how another participant at Simla, T.N. Kaul, described it much later:[57]

He [Bhutto] wanted India not only to vacate all West Pakistan territory occupied during the war, but also the immediate return of 90,000

Pakistani prisoners of war. He was reluctant to give up the use of force (as at Tashkent) or to accept the actual line of control in Jammu and Kashmir, which gave back to India about 400 sq. miles more of her own territory than the old ceasefire line. He also wanted to bring in the UN machinery under Article 33 of the Charter—of arbitration, mediation, etc. to settle bilateral disputes. And what is more he did not want to mention Kashmir at all. He also wanted immediate restoration of diplomatic relations with India but would not recognize Bangladesh.

There was certainly one option available to Haksar—to advise Indira Gandhi not to sign any agreement unless the line of control became an international border. Would that have been acceptable to large sections of political opinion in India, especially since for decades the public discourse was based on the assertion that Pakistan was in illegal occupation of one-third of the erstwhile princely state of Jammu and Kashmir and that the entire state was an inalienable part of India? Further, would even India's allies like the USSR been comfortable with President Bhutto returning to Pakistan from Simla without any agreement? The answers to both these questions have to be a resounding 'no'.

How did Haksar come across to the other side at Simla? Abdul Sattar, the noted Pakistani diplomat who was at Simla and later wrote one of the classic books on Pakistan's foreign policy was to recall much later:[58]

P.N. Haksar, secretary general in the Indian prime minister's office became the leader of the Indian official delegation at the conference after D.P. Dhar was taken ill. Without a peer in knowledge and erudition, he was also blessed with lucidity of expression to match the clarity of his thought. He seemed to relish saying: 'Only the Devil knows what is in your mind; I can only go by the words you use'. But the chuckle at his own wisecrack instantly reassured everyone that he meant no offence. No one could doubt his desire for a positive outcome of negotiations ...

Haksar himself did not write or say much publicly about what had happened in Simla. But, in 1984, while speaking at a seminar he looked back momentarily and allowed himself to say this:[59]

While I had no great illusion about the durability of the Bhutto regime, the Simla Agreement was in the nature of an investment in the future and was, in my view at any rate, an attempt to make an impact upon the wide mass of people of Pakistan that India, in a moment of victory, would act as a long-term friend of the people of Pakistan and not as an enemy.

Alas, his hopes were belied. But that he was a realist is borne out by what he went on to say at that same seminar:

In the course of our discussions, a great deal was said about Pakistan's nuclear probability. I have little doubt that they are developing such capabilities. The logic of development of these capabilities will produce, in time, nuclear weapons. In such an event, no government in India could fail to respond to Pakistan's nuclear threat in the military field ...

India and Pakistan were to get overtly nuclear 14 years later.

On their return from Simla, the prime minister would obviously have asked Haksar to give thought to a Cabinet reshuffle she wanted get done for he sent her an 11-page note on 10 July 1972:

I find it extremely difficult to engage in the exercise of Cabinet reshuffle. My awareness of what needs to be done and what can, in fact, be done makes the exercise even more meaningless. And when I find that the calibre of human beings available is hopelessly inadequate for the tasks which confront our country. I feel utterly distraught and distracted. The situation becomes unbearable when the handful of people who are of some calibre have to be subjected to the scrutiny of caste, religion and region. However, I am duty bound to obey P.M.'s directions.

... I have been urging for some considerable time that Shri C. Subramaniam should now accept the biggest challenge of his career, namely to put our industrial growth on its right path. He acquired such reputation as he possesses for what he did to our agriculture; and if he can something really imaginative for industrial growth, he may well be regarded as one of our great Ministers ... In order to add to the empire of Shri C. Subramaniam assuming that he accepts the challenge of industrial development, P.M. might wish to agree that he may continue to retain with him the Department of Science and Technology …

… It has been suggested that Shri D.P. Dhar might take over Industrial Development. I am afraid, we shall be putting once again a square peg in a round hole. Industrial Development is not his cup of tea. He will be excellent as Deputy Chairman of the Planning Commission and Minister of Planning …

Another ailing Ministry of the Government is the Ministry of Railways. Everything is wrong about this Ministry. The Railway Board is a run-down organization. The entire railway system is groaning under the weight of inefficient management in the largest of our public sector undertakings. The appointment of Shri Gulzarilal Nanda was a disaster and the present Minister is almost the proverbial last straw on the camel's back. I submit for P.M.'s consideration T.A Pai as Railway Minister … [italics mine]

Each of these three appointments was accepted by the prime minister and they were sworn-in on 23 July 1972. In addition, Haksar had posed a question in his note and answered it himself:

Are there any, relatively speaking, Cabinet Ministers of lesser weight but of proven incompetence compounded by lack of integrity? The most outstanding person in this regard is Shri Moinul Haque Choudhury. He is occupying what I regard as, perhaps the most important Ministry of the Government of India [Industrial Development].

Choudhury would be dropped from the Cabinet the night before the swearing-in ceremony. There were many other changes that Haksar had suggested, some of which were accepted but many were rejected by Indira Gandhi. He ended the note by saying:

If P.M. is inclined to retain Shri Raj Bahadur and give him a trial before throwing him out, he might be made Minister in charge of Transport, Shipping and Communications. From his bio-data I find he was Deputy Minister of Communications 1951-56; Minister in the Ministry of Communications from December 1956 to April 1957; Minister of State in the Ministry of Transport and Communications from 1957 to 1962; Minister of Shipping in the Ministry of Transport and Communications from 1962 to 1963 and so on. *With all this background, if he does not make any impact on his combined charge of Shipping, Transport and Communications, he would deserve to be thrown out. I hope that P.M. will introduce a system of accountability hereafter, so that P.M. has a good idea of what progress each Minister is making in his respective field. This can easily be done.* [italics mine]

Haksar's assessments of Indira Gandhi's ministerial colleagues were brutal. But they were not born out of any prejudice or malice. It was cold-bloodedly clinical and strictly performance-based.

No sooner had he come back from Simla, the issue of appointment of High Court judges in different states pre-occupied Haksar. Every state presented problems and this note to the prime minister of 13 July 1972 on Uttar Pradesh was typical:

> I find from P.M.'s programme for this afternoon that she is meeting the Chief Minister of U.P. at 545 pm. I think that P.M. might take this opportunity to mention to him that the appointment of High Court Judges is a matter of highest political importance. Many of our problems get complicated by the fact that the higher judiciary in our country has over the years precipitously declined in ability, character and integrity. Consequently, it should be a matter of common concern of the Chief Minister of U.P. and Prime Minister, who belong to the same political party, share common ideals, desire social and economic progress in a particular direction, to have identity of approach and views on this vital matter. It is not fair for him to take umbrage if the Central Government at the level of the Prime Minister point out that the suggestions made for appointment need to be reconsidered …
>
> P.M. might also say that under the Constitution, the President appoints a High Court Judge after consultation with the Chief Justice of India and the Governor of the State. The word "consultation" cannot be construed to mean "concurrence". And if it is a question of amour proper of the State Government, it is a matter of amour proper of the Prime Minister and the President. The question of amour propre might

have been understandable if the argument had been between the Central Government and a Government like that of Tamil Nadu. But when the question of "prestige" is raised between the Chief Minister of U.P. and the Minister of Law & Justice in the Central Government, who was in effect speaking on behalf of the Prime Minister, we are reaching a situation of complete impasse.

It may well be that all my arguments are of no avail and the Chief Minister will continue pursuing the path of unwisdom. I personally have no great expectations that he would respond to an argument calling for qualities of wisdom, judgment, prudence, etc. But I thought that if P.M. cannot persuade him to relent, then the Government of India will have only two courses left open to it: (1) To totally surrender to the Chief Minister; or (2) to exercise its constitutional right to advise the President that a particular Judge may or not be appointed after due consultations have taken place. I am afraid in this respect, there is no other path except to make the Chief Minister see reason. [italics mine]

Haksar did indeed have problems with proposals that came from Tamil Nadu which, since 1967, was being ruled by the DMK. In this case, his advice to the prime minister was to avoid confrontation, But when proposals came from states that had Congress chief ministers (which meant all other states) and Haksar was uncomfortable with some names being suggested. He was particularly irked with Kamlapati Tripathi, the chief minister of Uttar Pradesh. Earlier, on 25 February 1972, he had told the prime minister that:

... the Department of Justice is content to function as a mere clearing house, without applying its own independent mind and judgment to the proposals emanating from the States ... It is disquieting that State authorities should come to contradictory assessments of individual District Judges within a few months. Important appointments to the Allahabad High Court have been treated somewhat like a game of skittles. Members of the higher judicial service considered suitable for appointment a few months ago are now considered unsuitable; and others considered unsuitable are now found to be eminently suitable.

1972 was the high noon of nationalization under Indira Gandhi. Haksar and Mohan Kumaramangalam were the prime movers. In May 1972, the first phase of coal nationalization began with the take-over of coking coal mines and the entire industry would come under government control a year later. In July 1972, the Steel Authority of India (SAIL) was established and the Indian Iron and Steel Company (IISCO) was nationalized. SAIL was meant to represent a new paradigm in the management of the public sector. The first chairman of SAIL was M.A. Wadud Khan, who was then chief executive of the Tata Oil Mills Company and had been a communist activist alongside Kumaramangalam in Bombay in the 1940s. In September 1972, the general insurance industry was nationalized. This was also the time when Haksar convinced Indira Gandhi that the time for taking over the foreign oil refineries had come. On 12 July 1972, Finance Minister Y.B. Chavan wrote to the prime minister:

> I understand from the Minister of Petroleum and Chemicals that you would like to have a note stating the views of the Ministry of Finance on the Petroleum and Chemicals Ministry's note on the oil companies, particularly with reference to the prospects of our getting rescheduling of debt payments and any adverse reaction that our action might cause in the United Kingdom and Holland since nationals of these countries also hold shares in Burmah-Shell.
>
> I am enclosing herewith a copy of the note of the Ministry of Finance on the various points regarding oil companies ...

Indira Gandhi passed Chavan's letter to Haksar who observed on it the next day and sent it 'in a sealed cover to be opened by PM':

> I am amazed at this. It is a verbatim reproduction of the points I had made in the FM [finance minister]'s house last Sunday and marks a complete departure from the earlier stance ...

The three-page note sent by Chavan said:

> Basically, the Ministry of Finance accepts the judgment of the Ministry of Petroleum and Chemicals that the nationalization of the refinery and marketing operations of the oil companies is inescapable and cannot be

postponed for long. This is mainly because it is going to be increasingly difficult for us to justify in Parliament and elsewhere the provision in the Refinery Agreements which gives the oil companies the right to import crude from their own sources ... It seems best to terminate our present relationship with the oil companies as soon and as amicably as possible.

The Ministry of Finance had been reluctant to support nationalization because it thought it could affect India's economic relationship with the USA (because of Esso and Caltex) and with the UK and Holland (because of Burmah-Shell). It was also worried that it would impact on on-going discussions on debt rescheduling and foreign aid.

Clearly, Haksar had taken it upon himself to convince Chavan and his colleagues in the Ministry of Finance that nationalization of the refineries and marketing operations was imperative and indeed immediately needed for a number of reasons. He was able to convince them that the compensation formula being proposed to compensate the shareholders who would be affected was more than reasonable.

But strangely, nationalization of the refineries got postponed probably due to the ongoing discussion with the World Bank on rescheduling of India's debt and the clout of the oil companies in their respective countries. However, a meeting taken by the prime minister on 18 September 1972 concluded that 'purely on economic and practical considerations, nationalization is the best alternative to adopt; only its appropriate timing has to be determined'. As things turned out, however, 74 per cent of Esso was acquired in 1974 and two years later the balance, when Burmah Shell and Caltex were also taken over fully at one go.

Haksar had one more radical idea relating to nationalization which he put across to Indira Gandhi earlier on 1 June 1972:

We are on the eve of large-scale industrialization of our country. The road may be long and hard, but we are on it. Urbanisation is the natural concomitant of industrialization and every growing urban aggregate presents many economic, social and civic problems. Cities require sewage, water supply, electric supply, roads, public transport, prevention of slums, slum clearance, housing, recreation facilities, parks, etc. If land were to become privately owned, the creation of each such facility becomes extremely difficult and expensive. *That is why urban land and the land which is likely to become urban needs to be nationalized so that the evils of speculation on land, fantastic increases in land values leading to very high costs of providing civic amenities, are avoided.* There should, therefore, be no private ownership of land in urban areas.

Once we decide to nationalize urban land and put a ceiling on the ownership of that land to 300, 400, 600, 800 or 1000 square yards, the use of that land could be controlled in future by town planning policies, tax policies, etc. Nationalising land and converting such existing land as lease hold will yield to Government an immediate return because the lease hold rights would be subject to the payment of ground rent which would be reviewed from time to time. As for the properties built on existing urban land converted into lease hold, we have to carefully consider what to do with such property ... [italics mine]

But Haksar's proposal soon ran into rough weather in the Congress party. It not only drew strong support but also attracted fierce opposition, especially from a number of chief ministers. Indira Gandhi set up a number of groups to examine the proposal and, finally, four years later the Parliament passed the Urban Land (Ceiling and Regulation) Act, 1976. This was to be on the statute books for slightly over two decades before being repealed in 1999.

Having said this, the evidence also shows that Haksar was not a mindless believer in nationalization. In May 1970, he had poured cold water on a proposal made by Charan Singh, the chief minister of Uttar Pradesh to nationalize sugar factories in that state, and in April 1973, he opposeed the nationalization of the wholesale trade in wheat.

Television had just come to India and amongst the first persons to appear on it on 19 September 1972 was Haksar. The fact that he had mentally prepared to leave the government by then would explain this departure from his usual penchant for anonymity. He was interviewed by the noted cartoonist Abu Abraham, Haksar's friend from the London years in the early-1950s. Haksar played a key role in Abraham's nomination to the Rajya Sabha in 1972. In the interview, Haksar confessed that the Indian administrative structure needed a change but that change should be 'within the broad framework of the democratic system'. He took satisfaction in the fact that during his tenure 'specialists such as technologists and scientists had been appointed as secretaries to the Union government'.

When Abraham suggested that Haksar's wielding of power and influence suggested a 'Kennedy style of government', Haksar recoiled and said that the analogy was dangerous. He compared his role more to the British prime minister's privy office, saying that the Indian system was not a presidential one like in the USA. Abraham got him to speak about his London days in the late-1930s and Haksar recalled that 'one had to be particularly insensitive to escape being a nationalist'. He admitted he had no particular hero but Gandhi, Nehru and Tagore had definitely inspired him.

A number of senior civil servants, including Cabinet Secretary T. Swaminathan were retiring in October–November 1972. On 30 September 1972, Haksar submitted another 11-page note to the prime minister containing proposals for key bureaucratic appointments:

> ... In my view, the best possible candidate [for the post of cabinet secretary] would be Shri B.D. Pande. In all these years, there is no whisper against his integrity. He is also known as an officer of considerable ability ... He has sufficiently wide experience embracing, finance, industry, life insurance, Planning Commission, etc. to be an effective Chairman of Committee of Secretaries ... He will retire in March 1975. He will thus have nearly three years as Cabinet Secretary which is just right.
>
> As P.M. is aware, Dr. I.G. Patel is going away to take up an appointment in the United Nations Development Programme as its Deputy Director ... The question is who should take his place [as secretary, Department of Economic Affairs] ... *We have now appointed a very distinguished, sober and practical economist of high academic distinction to be the Chief Economic Adviser. He is Dr. Manmohan Singh.* I feel that the combination of Dr. Manmohan Singh Chief Economic Adviser and Shri M.G. Kaul, who is Additional Secretary in the Department of Economic Affairs would be an excellent one. Shri M.G. Kaul has very good record

... and should be appointed Secretary, Department of Economic Affairs ... [In addition] a very bright and relatively young man I know in the Reserve Bank, of the name Narasimham might be brought to the Deptt. of Economic Affairs as Additional Secretary. [italics mine]

These and other suggestions made by Haksar were approved by the prime minister a few days later and the new appointments were announced. Dr Manmohan Singh's later career path is well-known. A few years later, M. Narasimham became governor of the Reserve Bank for a very short while, had distinguished tenures in international financial institutions and, in 1991, helped the newly appointed Finance Minister Dr Manmohan Singh prepare a roadmap for financial sector reforms.

A week later, on 7 October 1972, Haksar sent the prime minister a set of proposals relating to the appointment of governors:

P.M. has already made up her mind about appointing B.D. Jatti as Governor, U.P., and that the Chief Minister, who has been consulted, has agreed to this ... I would have myself preferred appointment of Muslim (Sunni) as Governor of U.P. Such an appointment would have had a calming effect. By tradition, the Governor of U.P. never had any political role, or even an advisory role to play. He has become a patron of art and culture. I believe that Raj Bhavan is a place where mushairas are held. I do not think Shri B.D. Jatti is familiar with U.P.'s culture and its traditions ... If my proposal in regard to U.P. commends itself, then I would suggest that Shri Jatti might be sent to Orissa.

I had submitted to P.M. that since the Congress Party in Parliament is so singularly lacking in talent, it is really heart-breaking not to use every single talented person who has been brought up within the Congress. I believe Shri Dev Kanta Barooah is one such person. He is being wasted as Governor when he could as well be brought into Government ...

I would submit that we should request Shri B.K. Nehru to continue as Governor of Assam till October/ November next year ... I have already submitted that Shri L.P. Singh might be considered as Governor of Assam ...

Regarding Jammu and Kashmir ... I submit that we inform Shri Bhagwan Sahay that he should be ready to leave in February 1973 [and] that I write to Shri L.K. Jha on behalf of P.M. enquiring from him if

Governorship of Jammu and Kashmir would be acceptable to him and asking him to leave Washington early in January 1973.

Each of these proposals was accepted by Indira Gandhi even though one of them—regarding B.D. Jatti, the Karnataka leader—involved reversing a decision she had already taken. Barooah was to be inducted into the Union Cabinet as minister of petroleum and chemicals. Haksar was a great admirer of the literary accomplishments of the Assamese leader and the fact that Barooah considered himself a staunch leftist did not hurt him as far as Haksar was concerned.

ॐ

While the Simla Agreement had been signed well past midnight on 2 July 1972, its implementation was proving contentious. General Manekshaw and his Pakistani counterpart, General Tikka Khan, had met in Lahore on 28 November 1972 but it had not been possible to reach any agreement on delineation of the line of control in Jammu and Kashmir as envisaged in paragraph 4 of the Simla Agreement. This would be the springboard for implementation of other provisions in the Agreement. Haksar was in touch with Aziz Ahmed on how best to break the deadlock and strongly reiterated India's commitment to accord which was, in his words, 'deep and abiding' and that he did not have to 'present our credentials of sincerity and consistency'. On 2 December 1972, Aziz Ahmed accused India of inflexibility to which he replied two days later:

> During our negotiations both in Simla and Delhi, we have endeavoured with utmost sincerity to take into account your difficulties and even domestic compulsions. It is, therefore, very unfair to attribute to us inflexibility.

Finally, 7 on December 1972, Haksar was able to report a breakthrough achieved in Lahore to the prime minister:

> Sam Manekshaw telephoned me at 7 pm. His mission has been successful. General Tikka Khan agreed to sign the communiqué we had in mind. The surveyors will meet again on the 9th, finalise the maps and

the Senior Army Commanders will meet on the 11th and make their recommendations to the respective Governments. It would then be for the Governments to signify their approval to the line of delineation. The withdrawals would then commence. Compared to the withdrawal of Pakistan from Thako Chak, we have really given away nothing. And, in fact, one could truthfully say that in consideration for Pakistani withdrawal from Thako Chak [which Aziz Ahmed had been resisting all along], all that Pakistan has got is rationalization of the line of control.

Four days later, an announcement was made simultaneously in New Delhi and Islamabad:

The line of control has been delineated in Jammu and Kashmir in accordance with the Simla Agreement of July 2, 1972 and that it has the approval of both Governments. Adjustments of ground positions will be carried out to conform to the line of control approved by both Governments within a period of 5 days from the date of this announcement.

Pakistan had agreed to give up its claims amounting to about one-and-a-half square miles in area and India agreed to vacate an area amounting to about 0.45 square miles situated along the line of control. The broad details of the line of control were no doubt finalized but the ambiguity inherent in them would, a decade later, lead to the dispute over the Siachen glacier which continues till this day.

As far as Manekshaw himself was concerned, there appeared to be a serious problem. He was scheduled to retire in April 1972. He was very keen on being the first Indian army officer to be appointed field marshal. From January 1972 onward his future was discussed by the prime minister with her senior Cabinet colleagues. But no agreement on what precisely was to be done without ruffling any feathers could be reached. Initially Haksar was of the view that, in view of the exceptional circumstances prevailing then, which included 'uncertainty on the intentions of both Pakistan and China and the need to absorb and internalize the lessons from the 1971 war', Manekshaw should be asked to continue for two years and there would be no objection to his being designated field marshal. He said so in a note to the prime minister on 30 January 1972 but also added that his becoming field marshal was likely to be misunderstood in India and would excite petty jealousies.

Consequently, Haksar advised the prime minister to meet with the general and request him not to press for 'this nomenclature of Field Marshal', and also 'not ask for any extra emoluments or pensionary benefits'. More than extension of service, Manekshaw was fixated on the field marshal designation and hence Haksar's advice to the prime minister went nowhere. On 23 March 1972, after consulting the defence secretary, Haksar sent another proposal to the prime minister suggesting that Manekshaw be appointed as chief of Defence Staff with the rank of field marshal and given a term of two years.

But this proposal was not accepted by the prime minister's senior-most political colleagues—Swaran Singh, Jagjivan Ram and Y.B. Chavan. More importantly, it was also opposed by Air Chief Marshal P.C. Lal, chief of the Indian Air Force as recounted by him 14 years later:[60]

> ... I was at Chabua near Dibrugarh on 24 March 1972, when a telephone call came through from Delhi. Mr. P.N. Haksar ... said that Government was considering the creation of the post of CDS [chief of defence staff] and appointing Manekshaw to it in recognition of the manner in which he had directed the Bangladesh war. My views were invited before a final decision was taken.
>
> My comments went to Haksar that evening. I drew attention to the fact that the three Service Chiefs had operated as equal partners in the Bangladesh war and that they had demonstrated their ability to work effectively together without having a Super Chief sitting over them. I could not accept the argument that a CDS was necessary to resolve disputes between the Services because he could be expected to be impartial in his judgment. This might be one way of sorting out inter-Service problems but such imposed solutions were unlikely to produce satisfactory results ... Indeed, I saw in the proposed arrangement a positive danger to frank and free discussions particularly if the CDS happened to be excessively assertive and intolerant of the ideas of others ... Service Chiefs should function as equals and sort out their inter-Service problems, both administrative and operational, amongst themselves.

With no agreement having been reached, on 1 April 1972, Manekshaw was then asked to continue beyond his retirement date 'at the pleasure of the President of India'. It was informally understood that this extended period would be six months from April onward. But since the implementation of the Simla agreement dragged on, Manekshaw was asked to keep going.

Meanwhile, in early-December 1972 the question of a successor to Air Marshal Lal, who was retiring in mid-July 1973, came up and Haksar supported the choice of Air Marshal Mehra. In a note arguing Mehra's case on 8 December 1972, Haksar observed, among other things, that:

> … Defence Minister might insinuate that Air Marshal Mehra is lacking in integrity. This would be a preposterous thing to say and such a private insinuation is not enough to overlook his claim. *At the time of the appointment of the present Chief of the Army Staff also various things were said against him bearing on his reliability and even on his integrity. P.M. then took a position that one cannot overlook his claim unless we have something tangible to base one's decision.* [italics mine]

As it turned out Lal was given a six month extension till 15 January 1973 when Mehra took over as head of the air force.

By this time, everybody had come around to the idea of making Manekshaw field marshal. But then the question arose whether it should be while he was still in service or after his final exit? Manekshaw wanted the former and Haksar while a few others the latter. But Haksar was persuaded by Manekshaw that the conferment of the higher rank should be while he was still in service. In addition, Manekshaw wanted the financial benefits associated with being a field marshal to continue in whatever job the government gave him after retirement. But Haksar was adamant that if Manekshaw became, for instance, a governor or an ambassador, he should get the salary and perquisites associated with those assignments. He told the prime minister in a note on 24 December 1972:

> General Manekshaw's insistence on receiving the emoluments and perquisites of the Field Marshal in his future employment in Government would be a disincentive for Government to give that employment, because these terms will be highly obtrusive in a democratic country like ours.

If General Manekshaw continues to insist on these terms, the best thing would be to inform him that Government proposes to appoint the new Chief of Army Staff with effect from January 25, 1973; that General Manekshaw might go ahead bidding farewell to his troops and we can all forget about honouring him by promoting him to the rank of Field Marshal, because he wishes to convert the honour, which the nation wishes to bestow on him, into hard cash.

On this, Haksar got his way and the general fell in line. He was promoted to the rank of field marshal on 1 January 1973 and retired quietly a fortnight later with a special pay and pension. Haksar had suggested a number of post-retirement assignments—governor of Andhra Pradesh, ambassador to Burma or member of the Planning Commission—but none of them fructified.

By early-December 1972, Haksar had decided to finally call it a day in a few weeks. But there were some critical issues that needed his attention. On 7 December 1972, he received a copy of a letter addressed to the minister of law & justice by Attorney General Niren De which reads thus:

> The basic argument on behalf of the Petitioners in the Constitutional cases now being heard by the Supreme Court has been that there are implied limitations to the amending power as provided for in Article 368 before the 24th Amendment, and that certain essential features of the Constitution, e.g, the core of fundamental rights, cannot be abridged and that, as such, the 24th Amendment is ultra vires or, in the alternative, the 24th Amendment should be read down. Some judges ... have made observations in Court which indicate that they may eventually take this line in their judgments and, as this line appears to be prima facie attractive as a sort of compromise, it will not be surprising if some other judges accept this line too. The danger of reading down the 24th Amendment is obvious.[61]
>
> I would like to have specific instructions from Government as to whether Government will, in the long run, accept reading down the 24th Amendment ...

Almost immediately, Haksar replied to De:

> I have just received your letter of December 7. I am giving you a purely
> personal reaction to the problem posed by you. The Minister of Justice
> will no doubt let you have Government's response.
>
> First of all, might it not be more appropriate for Government to
> have your advice whether the 24th Amendment should be read down? Do
> you think Parliament and Government would have gone to the length
> of enacting the amendments if there was ever any intention to willingly
> accept implied limitations? Perhaps, the arguments which are being
> advanced by Shri Palkhivala are succeeding in creating an atmosphere
> in which it is difficult to see that there are real problems to be solved for
> the social, economic and democratic evolution of our society.

The attorney general responded the next day thanking Haksar for his
prompt reply and reiterating his opinion that 'Article 368, as it stood
before the 24th Amendment, was not subject to any implied limitation'.
Four months later, the Supreme Court verdict on this case was pronounced
and it was to be hailed as being amongst the most significant judgments
ever. It held that Parliament's right to amend was not absolute and that
any amendment that violated what the majority opinion called the 'basic
structure' of the Constitution would be judged as being unconstitutional.
This has come to be known as the Kesavananda Bharati case. It would
trigger the supersession of three judges and the appointment of a judge
who had sided with the government view as chief justice of India. By then
Haksar was out of the seat of power and main players in the supersession
saga were Mohan Kumaramangalam and Law Minister H.R. Gokhale. But
it would be fair to say that Haksar would have supported the views and
moves of these two ministers. It is inconceivable that he was not aware
of the supersession. Kumaramangalam would have definitely discussed it
with Haksar.

ॐ

Haksar would get letters from all sorts of people asking his help for all sorts
of things. This happened when he was in office and also long after he had

quit. Sometime in mid-November 1972 he received one such letter from a Chunno Gurtu in Cuttack:

> My dear Parameshwar Bhai:
>
> Remember me? Years and years back when you were practicing at Allahabad Bar, you were staying at our house at 8 Katra Road. I am the youngest daughter of Late Pran Nath Agha. Now can you please place me? Then I was a mere chit of a girl studying in Class 9th ... Since a year I have been gathering up my courage to write to you ...
>
> Parameshwar Bhai, I need your help. It is regarding my second son Ajay Kumar Gurtoo. He is doing B.Com ... He earnestly wishes to join Tata Administrative Service ... I am fully aware that Tata administrative job is a highly coveted job and only those fortunate few who know Sir J.R.D. Tata can dream of getting an admission there as there are no open vacancies ... It is here where I want your most needed help. You are at the topmost. Your words carry power and have tremendous influence. I feel only you and you alone can make Ajay's dream come true ...

There was much more emotional stuff from a concerned and worried mother in the letter to which Haksar replied on 20 December 1972:

> I am sorry I took so long in replying to your letter. However, I remember you rather well. I also understand that you as a mother would wish to do the best for your son. But you have asked me to do something which I would not do even for my own children. I will not speak to J.R.D. Tata under any circumstances. In any case recruitment to Tata Administrative Service is done on a fairly systematic and scientific basis. They interview the candidates and take them on merit.
>
> The only concession I can make is that your son is free to quote me as a referee in his application. Even this I very rarely allow to be done, but your pleadings have softened me only to this extent. Please do not misunderstand, but I cannot depart from certain principles to which I always adhere without any exception ...

Indira Gandhi had been receiving representations from different quarters that India should also celebrate 16 December in some appropriate manner as Bangladesh was also celebrating that day as Victory Day. Haksar reacted strongly when he was told about it by P.N. Dhar and told the prime minister on 13 December 1972 in no uncertain terms:

> My own view is that we should let the day pass: Firstly, there is no obvious theme around which we can observe December 16; we cannot, for instance, celebrate it as "Liberation of Bangladesh Day"; nor can we celebrate it as "Victory over Pakistan Day", without appearing to be a juvenile nation given to glorifying way which all mature nations have given up doing. We have already done what was needed to be done on January 26 this year. We have given awards to all the heroes of the battle; we have lit five flames in memory of those who had fallen and I presume, on January 26, 1973, we shall have a little commemorative ceremony before the main parade. A country actively pursuing the path of reconciliation and peace in the sub-continent should, therefore, let December 16 pass.
>
> There is another ticklish question to be considered. Assuming that we observe December 16 as a first anniversary of December 16, 1971, is it intended that such annual observance should become part of another ritual to be observed hereafter, year after year. I rather suspect some patriotic people have worked themselves up to doing something. If the position has become non-negotiable and something needs to be done, then the House [Parliament] might stand up in silence for two minutes in memory of all those who had fallen on the clear understanding that this will not become an annual event.

Haksar's views did not prevail. The country does mark 16 December as Vijay Diwas (Victory Day). Twenty-seven years later, another government decided to mark 26 July as Kargil Vijay Diwas to mark India's victory over Pakistan in the Kargil war of 1999.

By mid-December 1972 Haksar had finally told the prime minister that he was quitting soon. Indira Gandhi made no special effort to hold him back—perhaps she knew Haksar had made up his mind but also perhaps she was not entirely unhappy that he was leaving. But she did write to him a most unusual 'Dear Haksar Saheb' letter on 25 December 1972 which reads thus:

> I have hesitated to write or to speak. Some things are too deep for words or it may be that I am not enough of a writer to find the right words. I have no new or better phrases in which to tell you what so many have been repeating—much to your annoyance—all these days and even months, whenever the question of your leaving us has arisen.
>
> *During a period which has spanned so many crises you have stood like a rock. Your wise guidance has been invaluable in helping us negotiate the obstacles and steer clear of the many pitfalls endangering our onward journey, and even our survival.*
>
> There is perhaps no dearth of worthy, intelligent, even sincere or conscientious persons. But the need is for something over and above that—as you yourself are well aware. These qualities can be useful only if they are combined with a depth of judgment which is based on long experience of men, especially in government, and affairs of India as well as the world; on an insight into trends and forces. *There can be no doubt that your retirement will greatly diminish the efficacy of the PM's Sectt and will be a great loss to me.* [italics mine]

Starting with the salutation itself, this letter says it all about the relationship the two had shared. But the letter also makes it abundantly clear that Haksar himself had wanted to exit from the prime minister's innermost circle for quite some time. He had first wanted to quit way back in January 1971 and then in May 1971. He had actually left in September 1971, but had been persuaded to return not on extension but to a new position especially created for him for which he got no salary. On 29 December 1972, he wrote to the prime minister:

> PM has very kindly agreed to let me retire as Principal Secretary to the Prime Minister and avail myself of whatever leave is due to me. That leave consists of two elements, viz leave of 36 days I have earned since I became Principal Secretary on December 6, 1971 plus the unexpired portion of the refused leave I had earned on retiring from the foreign service on September 4, 1971.
>
> Subject to PM's approval, I propose to proceed on leave of 36 days

earned by me as Principal Secretary with effect from January 15, 1973, join for a day on February 20 and proceed to avail of the unavailed refused leave of 87 days which stands to my credit. PM's formal approval is requested.

And very soon, on the last day of the year, he was back in 'Dear Induji' mode now that he was departing with his head held high:

The warmth and generosity of what you wrote in the letter of Christmas Day shall remain my most precious possession. What else can I say without banality and sentimentality? I am not ungrateful.

In a few hours the calendar will revolve and a new year will dawn. May courage never fail you in facing the fearful odds.

Please accept my heartfelt good wishes for every success and, if possible, some happiness in the service of our country.

It is conventional wisdom that Indira Gandhi shunted Haksar out of the prime minister's Secretariat and banished him to the Planning Commission. This assertion by all her biographers has no factual basis whatsoever. She did nothing of the sort. He had insisted on opting out on his own and he was to join the Planning Commission only two years later.

Why did this estrangement happen? What caused the rift between the two? Was it a case of familiarity breeding contempt, proximity creating distance? Sharada Prasad put it pithily and said it best.[62] He wrote that the reason why Indira Gandhi and Haksar, who were so close to each other for decades, drifted apart was because:

… there was growing friction between sovereign and chamberlain over the doings of the prince.

The allusion was unmistakably to Sanjay Gandhi, the young man with whom Haksar could never succeed in building even a semblance of a rapport. From perhaps December 1968 itself, Haksar had kept telling Indira Gandhi what he thought of Sanjay Gandhi's business ambitions. That was when Sanjay Gandhi had unveiled his Maruti car to the public. Haksar had consistently objected to the prime minister's son staying in the prime minister's residence, carrying out his business activities. In September–

October 1970 there must have been a second spat on Maruti between Indira Gandhi and Haksar because the 'letter of intent' for the manufacture of 50,000 'people's car' annually had been issued to Sanjay Gandhi.

Sanjay Gandhi had been given the usual six months time to convert the preliminary 'letter of intent' issued in September 1970 into an industrial licence. Without the papers going through Haksar in the prime minister's Secretariat as they should have, this conversion time was extended to 18 months and the condition of no import of raw material was relaxed. As it turned out, that conversion happened only in July 1974, and even thereafter, not one finished vehicle approved by the testing agency involved had actually been put on the road.

Sanjay Gandhi's political and economic views were diametrically opposite to those of Haksar. Sanjay Gandhi was, as he was to admit in an interview published in 1976, virulently anti-communist and felt that the type of socialism being espoused by Haksar was not in India's interests. Whether Sanjay Gandhi came to hold this position because of his friends or because of his own beliefs is impossible to figure out. But the fact remains that he and Haksar were poles apart, and even if Haksar had gone along with his Maruti venture, it was only a matter of time before Sanjay Gandhi would have come into conflict with Haksar.

Apart from the Sanjay Gandhi factor, there may well have been one more reason why Indira Gandhi may have allowed Haksar to go, albeit gracefully and voluntarily. After March 1971, Indira Gandhi was a hugely transformed figure having won a staggering mandate in the polls. After December 1971, her political stature had grown even further. She was now 'Durga' as her political opponent Atal Bihari Vajpayee hailed her[63] or the 'Empress of India' as the London magazine *The Economist* acclaimed her. She was at the zenith of her glory and Haksar would certainly have sensed that the equation between her and him was changing. He had emerged as a major figure in his own right with ministers and MPs kowtowing to him. The media too had begun to speak of his awesome powers and authority that he derived not just from the prime minister but also from the force of his own personality and accomplishments. No prime minister would like to be in the shadow of an aide or like the aide to acquire a larger than life personality on his own steam. The prime minister must have felt that she now could do without Haksar bombarding her with his long, often verbose notes and his advice which many times was unpalatable.

Notes

1. The UNEF was headed by Major General Inder Jit Rikhye of the Indian Army.
2. Awana (1988).
3. Moraes (1980).
4. Mishra(1993).
5. I have discussed this speech at some length in Ramesh (2017).
6. More than one person who worked with him and more than one of his close personal friends told me that Haksar had told Indira Gandhi that 'she must make up her mind whether she was Prime Minister of India or Sanjay Gandhi's mother'. That had got back to the young man with grave consequences for Haksar later.
7. Chagla (1985).
8. S. Chandrasekhar was offered the job at the suggestion of the physicist M.G.K. Menon. Haksar then himself suggested the name of sociologist M.N. Srinivas who, like him, had studied anthropology but at Oxford.
9. Dasgupta (2016).
10. Ramachandran (2013).
11. Dhar (2000).
12. Ghosh (2015).
13. The first three C&AG's belonged to the Indian Audit and Accounts Service (IA&AS). The fourth belonged to the ICS. There was pressure from the ICS network to have the fifth also come from that service but PNH told Indira Gandhi on 24 February that she should take note of 'intense inter-service rivalries and jealousies' and revert to the original pattern of an IA&AS officer becoming the CAG. He justified Bakshi's candidature on the grounds that   he was the senior-most IA&AS officer in service. He told the prime minister that Bakshi was an abrasive person but 'nobody has doubted his ability and integrity. If he has any vices, they consist entirely of his virtues.' After Bakshi's retirement in 1978, the C&AG has always been from the IAS, the successor service to the ICS.

14. Patel (2002).
15. Email correspondence of 24 December 2017.
16. 'Foreign Relations of the United States, 1969-1976', Volume E-7; Documents on South Asia, 1969-1972, Louis J. Smith (ed.), (Washington: Government Printing Office, 2005), Document 30.
17. Sharada Prasad (2002).
18. Ibid.
19. Pathak was also to chair a committee which comprised private sector executives, as well, to revamp public sector management. The committee's recommendations led to the creation of a Public Enterprise Selection Board and other changes in the way government ran these companies. Unfortunately, the exit of Haksar in early-1973 and the death of Kumaramangalam in May 1973 robbed Pathak of two of his greatest supporters at the highest levels and he himself left the country in January 1975 for medical reasons.
20. This is also corroborated in Kaul (1991).
21. Bernal (1939).
22. Parthasarathi (2007).
23. Dhar (2000).
24. Nayak (2011).
25. Haksar had better luck pushing the candidature of Choudhary Tayyab Husain from the seat of Gurgaon in Haryana.
26. On 23 January 1971, Haksar had recommended to Indira Gandhi the name of either Trilochan Singh or Shashi Bhushan for the New Delhi seat but clearly he changed his mind soon thereafter.
27. Raghavan (2013).
28. Bass (2013).
29. Mitra (2007).
30. Sobhan (2016).
31. Hasan (2004).
32. Aijazuddin (2002).
33. 'Foreign Relations of the United States, 1969-1976', Volume XI, South Asia Crisis, 1971, Louis J. Smith (ed.), (Washington: Government Printing Office, 2005), Document 91.
34. Mendes France (1972).
35. Sparrow (2017) is a wonderful new biography of Paul Robeson, an African-American who was a global icon particularly in the 1940s and 1950s for

his outstanding cultural accomplishments and fearless political activism. Nehru and Indira Gandhi too were enthralled by him and Nehru's plans to celebrate Robeson's 60th birthday in 1958 invited the wrath of the Eisenhower administration.

36. In the same letter Haksar told Chatterjee: 'I trust Tikki [T.N. Kaul] told you that you are on one year's extension. Sardar Swaran Singh resisted it a great deal. When I cross-examined him, he let fall a remark that the Speaker [of Lok Sabha] Dhillon apparently did not think highly of you. I flared up in the presence of the Prime Minister and said something to the effect that I personally did not think much of the Speaker as I had seen him busily engaged in buying bottles in London and Paris airports and that he even sought my assistance to have them cleared from Customs ... Anyhow please do let me know what really happened between you and Dhillon.' This reveals much of how Haksar functioned.

37. Telephonic conversation with Shankar Bajpai at my request 24 January 2018.

38. Email correspondence on 27 December 2017.

39. This conversation was revealed by Natwar Singh in whose house the meeting took place. He wrote about it in his review of Haksar's autobiography in *India Today*, 15 March 1990.

40. Gerberg (2008).

41. On 10 June 1971, Haksar would tell the Prime Minister: '... I am exercising extreme self-restraint on what Shri Romesh Thapar writes to P.M. from time to time. All that I would say is that he should not readily assume that the Government of India consists of cretins who do not know what is going on. P.M. should find some position for him so that his vast energies and creative impulses could be channelled and transmuted into recognizable shapes and forms. I often have had the melancholy duty to point out to him that since he never has had to work hard for anything in his life, he has become incapable of sustained effort to achieve anything and is thus reduced to being an Oracle. P.M. might some day ask him if he is prepared to assume responsibility for an area of his choice. If he succeeds in identifying one, he could be tried out provided he gives an undertaking that he would not chuck it all up within a year's time and revert to his role of an Oracle.' Thapar was reputedly part of Indira Gandhi's kitchen cabinet during the late-1960s and Haksar himself was close to him. After his exit from the

prime minister's Secretariat, in January 1973, Haksar would write once in a while for Thapar's monthly publication titled *Seminar*.

42. 'Foreign Relations of the United States, 1969-1976', Volume E-7, Documents on South Asia, 1969-1972, Louis J. Smith (ed.), (Washington: Government Printing Office, 2005), Document 151.

43. 'Foreign Relations of the United States, 1969-1976', Volume XI, South Asia Crisis, Louis J. Smith (ed.), (Washington: Government Printing Office, 2005), Document 311.

44. 'Foreign Relations of the United States 1969-1976', Volume XI, South Asia Crisis, 1971, Louis J. Smith (ed.), (Washington: Government Printing Office, 2005), Document 134.

45. Rasgotra (2016).

46. Named after the plot of Akira Kurosawa's 1950 film *Rashomon*.

47. Raghavan (2013).

48. Dasgupta (2016).

49. By a curious coincidence Qian Xuesan, the father of the Chinese space programme, had also completed his doctorate at Caltech and was on the faculty when Dhawan was there. They overlapped by two years but were not known to be particularly close.

50. In a tribute to Satish Dhawan, one of his closest colleagues A.K.N. Reddy at the Indian Institute of Science, recalled that 'Satish Loomba talked Dhawan into the chairmanship of ISRO' (Reddy, 2002). Haksar and Loomba, of course, were part of the same ideological circle. Dhawan's daughter, however, believes that it was the letter from Indira Gandhi to him that was responsible for making up his mind. He may have spoken to Loomba in April 1972 about it but by then he was committed to accepting Indira Gandhi's offer. Loomba's wife recalls conversations between her husband and brother, in which both were vehemently against military control of the space programme and this was one reason why Dhawan overcame his initial reluctance and accepted Indira Gandhi's request.

51. Email correspondence on 15 December 2017.

52. Palkhivala (1994).

53. The building was the official summer residence of the British governor of Punjab and was originally built by an Englishman called Mr Dane, who predicted that Simla town would come up around his creation. However, as his prediction was proved wrong the building came to be known as Dane's Folly.

54. Bhasin (2012).
55. Dhar (2000).
56. Gandhi, Rajmohan (2000).
57. Kaul (1979).
58. Sattar (2006).
59. Haksar (1988).
60. Lal (1986).
61. This means that only the strictest and most literal interpretation will be permitted.
62. Sharada Prasad (2002).
63. Although inexplicably in a 1998 TV interview he denied describing her in this manner.

IX. A Prime Minister's Special Envoy

(1973–1974)

Haksar left the prime minister's Secretariat on his own volition on 15 January 1973. He was not shunted out as all biographers of Indira Gandhi have written. For the next two years, Indira Gandhi would utilize his services as her special envoy. He would continue to meet her and be very actively involved with matters relating to nuclear energy, space and industrial research. This is also the time when he began to take on a more public role—in speaking and writing.

Haksar with President Bhutto, Islamabad, July 1973.

By now, it was known to many that Haksar was going to leave the prime minister's Secretariat. Haksar received a letter from P.B. Gajendragadkar, former chief justice of India and then chairman of the Law Commission. Capturing the sentiments of those who knew Haksar, the well-known jurist wrote:

> I know that, once you have made up your mind to retire, no one can dissuade you, because your decisions, both in personal and public matters, are, I have come to know, the result of deep and mature consideration. However, I am still hoping that, besides using your talent, culture and ability to produce creative literature, the P.M. may, in course of time, be able to persuade you to join politics a member of the Lok Sabha or Rajya Sabha whichever may suit you.

Haksar had already given notice to Indira Gandhi that 15 January 1973 would be his last day in the PM's Secretariat as principal secretary to prime minister. But he kept up the barrage of notes to her till the last day. Andhra Pradesh was in the grip of agitation with the Jai Andhra movement calling for the coastal districts of the state to separate from the Telangana region of the state. This was after a Jai Telangana movement in the late-1960s.[1] There had been convulsions in the Congress Party itself with Chief Minister P.V. Narasimha Rao under attack. Haksar sent the prime minister this assessment four days before retiring once and for all:

> I wonder how many more cardinal errors will be committed before the Andhra situation is brought under control. Yesterday's exercise of setting up a new PCC [Pradesh Congress Committee] is as fatuous as it is dangerous. It is like erecting a structure on a debris. Instead of clearing the debris and making proper assessment of correlation of forces, identifying the healthy elements and on that basis erecting the structure of PCC, we have gone the other way round. No good can come out of it. The predictable result of the new PCC would be harnessing of forces against it. The Chief Minister provides focus for agitation; whereas formerly we had one point, now we have provided them with the second rallying point. That is all very sad. But, obviously, someone is working to make things worse before they might hopefully become better. It may sound dramatic, but it will be a good thing if the Union Cabinet were to repair to Hyderabad, sit there and try gradually to bring back sanity after talking to everyone. Such a drama is better than the ugliness of the situation which prevails in Andhra Pradesh today.

The prime minister must have been relieved that very soon such discomfiting advice would cease coming to her on a daily basis. She noted in her own hand below Haksar's note almost immediately after she had seen it on the same day:

> How else could the party function? The Committee is not a solution but a forum [for] Congressmen.

But obviously she had been stung. She sent Haksar another note a few minutes later explaining her action. She need not have but this was Haksar, even though he was not a Congressman and even though he was soon to depart from her Secretariat:

As I have stated under your note, the purpose was not much a new PCC as to have a political forum which could try and build a base for whatever next step has to be taken. There is a clamour for President's rule but unless there are some political people who are functioning at that time, President's rule by itself will not get us anywhere. This Committee is not confined to the people whose names have been mentioned. It can be expanded. But our effort was to try and include those people who have some following. Originally, we had hoped to have Brahmananda Reddy himself but he declined. However, he and others can join when the situation improves.

At this moment, the initiative is entirely with our opponents. I would certainly have gone there except for a feeling that this would worsen and not improve the situation.

President's Rule was imposed in Andhra Pradesh on 11 January 1973. The next day Haksar was at it again:

I had respectfully submitted to P.M. yesterday that the new PCC set up in Andhra Pradesh is not likely to make a dent on the ugly situation prevailing there. I had submitted that we should first of all clear the debris, rescue such healthy forces as there still might be and thereafter create the political structure of a new PCC. I had proceeded on the assumption that the present Chief Minister and the present Government of Andhra Pradesh having proved their incompetence to rule the State would give way to the President's Rule. *The Hindu* of today carries an editorial and I invite P.M.'s kind attention to it. It is well argued and I think it is sound.

It might be argued that the President's Rule will make the confrontation between the Union and the agitators more direct. My contention is that it is already direct and that every passing day the agitation is not so much against the Chief Minister as against the Centre and the P.M. Indeed the Chief Minister indulges in all his hobby horses in the name of P.M. Therefore, it is erroneous to say that President's Rule will add any new dimension to the confrontation that exists. On the contrary, if there are Congressmen who have been driven by exigencies of local politics to support the agitation purely as a measure of keeping themselves alive politically, vis-à-vis the Jan Sangh and Swatantra, then President's Rule will provide just the right kind of escape for them to rally round and re-form their ranks within the existing Congress.

The chief minister in question was P.V. Narasimha Rao, who was an acknowledged failure in the state but was a transformed figure when he became prime minister 18 years later. Haksar would have a small role to play in Rao becoming prime minister as I will highlight later.

∾

On 15 January 1973, Haksar finally bid farewell to the prime minister. He had been at her side for five-and-a-half years. She would soon discover that 'a Haksar with power is not the same as power without Haksar', as the nuclear scientist Raja Ramanna was to put it almost three decades later. But for now, in an unusual gesture reflective of the huge respect she continued to have for him, she insisted that he continue as a member of the Atomic Energy and Space Commissions and as vice president of the Council of Scientific and Industrial Research (CSIR) which was an executive job.

A day later he was interviewed on All India Radio where he said that 1971 was a year of great importance for India 'when the collective wisdom of the civil servants, armed forces and politicians acting in fine coordination with each other that had brought the country out of an extremely difficult time'. Of course, he kept quiet on his own pivotal role that year. When asked what he planned to do next, Haksar's reply was, 'I will think a little, recuperate my health which is not good, and if any energy is left in me, I would like to use it for some wider purpose'.

On 17 January 1973, he wrote to Govind Narain, the union home secretary—one of the ICS officers he was genuinely fond of, and with whom he would remain in touch for another two decades:

Dear Govind:
You spoke to me over the RAX [restricted telephone line] yesterday morning and asked me, with a rare sense of delicacy, if I would accept the Award of Padma Vibhushan for the Republic Day of 1973. You said that it was P.M.'s desire that I should do so. You were good enough to give me some time to think it over. And this I have done. *May I, first of all, say that the very thought that I should be given an Award is by itself a*

great reward for whatever services I might have rendered as a public servant. I am grateful for this to P.M. However, I have a difficulty in accepting the award: All these years I have often said to myself that one should work so that one can live with oneself without regret. This gave me a measure of inner tranquility and even courage. Accepting an award for work done somehow causes an inexplicable discomfort to me. I hope I will not be misunderstood. I repeat I am grateful for the thought that my services should be recognized. For me this is enough. I would beg of you not to press me to accept the award itself. I shall be grateful if you kindly convey to P.M. my deep and abiding gratitude for the privilege I had to serve under her. [italics mine]

This letter has everlasting relevance and should guide anybody in public life at any point of time. There have been a few people who have refused such awards but only after they have been announced. I really cannot think of anyone else who has politely and *quietly* declined at the offer stage itself and that too with such high-minded sense of values.

Actually, this does not seem to be the whole story on these coveted awards. The nation's highest honour—Bharat Ratna—is usually decided by the president in consultation with the prime minister. Other national awards including the Padma Vibhushan are announced every year but the Bharat Ratna is rare and there is no annual ritual associated with it. After India's magnificent victory in the war with Pakistan in December 1971, President Giri had decided to award the Bharat Ratna to Indira Gandhi—an honour which she undoubtedly deserved for her remarkable leadership that year. One of Haksar's colleagues in the prime minister's Secretariat, B.N. Tandon, who maintained a daily diary from November 1975 until August 1976, was to write on 17 January 1975:[2]

> When Haksar saw this [Giri's letter] he said that Giri should not have done so. He advised her to tell Giri that she should not be awarded the Bharat Ratna. But the PM did not like this advice one bit and she remained annoyed with him for a few days…

Indira Gandhi did get the Bharat Ratna on 26 January 1972, at a special ceremony. But Haksar was able to extract one concession from her. Fifteen days earlier, he had told the prime minister that 'there should be no citation unless President himself do desires. Such a citation should be a brief one.' There was to be no citation read out on the occasion.

Even though Haksar had finally exited from her daily side, Indira Gandhi was not done with him. A few days after refusing the Padma Vibhushan, Haksar was in Iran as the prime minister's special envoy to help build a new bilateral relationship. But before he left for that country, he was to receive a letter from a colleague who had retired and who was to occupy Haksar's position in April 1977 after Morarji Desai replaced Indira Gandhi as prime minister. V. Shankar, who had retired as defence secretary in 1970, wrote to him on 20 January 1973:

> Ever since I read in the newspapers the news of your retirement in terms which left no doubt of its finality I have been wanting to write to you but some of my preoccupations and outings have not made it possible. *My purpose was just to pay my humble tribute, as an ex-colleague to the devotion, dedication, competence and skills with which you have served the country during the last so many years and to send you my best wishes on the occasion.* I know how difficult and onerous your responsibilities were and how critical and exacting the times were in which you had to serve loyally and wholeheartedly a great lady occupying a unique position not only in office but also in history ...
>
> During the last so many years I have held aloof from Govt. circlesv... *But I would like to assure you that notwithstanding the aloofness I have been following with silent and distant admiration the many activities, pronouncements and decisions of Govt. in which your hand was unmistakable* ... [italics mine]

Soon after his retirement, Haksar was inundated with letters from his friends and colleagues expressing both surprise and shock that he had chosen to go away. People who had never known or met him also wrote to express their sense of anguish at what he had done. Some, however, applauded him, and this letter of 15 January 1973 from the governor of Maharashtra, Ali Yavar Jung, was typical of this sentiment:

I see you have retired today. I am sorry but I appreciate your reason and, in fact, admire you.

Haksar's visit to Iran was choreographed by two Indian businessmen with intimate links to the royal establishment in Tehran—G.P. Hinduja and his brother S.P. Hinduja. Haksar met the Shah of Iran in Teheran on 24 January 1973. The Shah had been to Pakistan in January 1972 and President Bhutto had returned the visit some months later. Then in mid-January 1973 itself the Shah was again in Pakistan. Clearly, Iran and Pakistan were moving to formalize a closer economic, political and military partnership. India had to do something and hence Haksar's visit. His conversation lasted one hour and 17 minutes and was to have a profound impact on Indo-Iranian relations before the Shah was overthrown in February 1979. Haksar has left behind a 30-page record of his visit to Iran and of his conversation with the Shah. The conversation covered not just bilateral relations but also covered other regional issues, particularly the Soviet Union, Iraq and Pakistan. After the initial pleasantries in which the Shah expressed surprise that Haksar had retired and hoped that he could continue to be the emissary 'between our two countries', the serious talks began:

> Shah: ... Tell me, quite frankly, is India even remotely interested in the break-up of Pakistan?
>
> PNH: I do not know how I should answer the question put by His Majesty ... I have the added difficulty of not knowing the extent of trespass I could commit on His Majesty's time.
>
> Shah: Oh! I have set aside the whole evening if it be necessary to talk. We must talk. We have not talked for a long time. I must get to know what your Prime Minister and your country really feel ...
>
> PNH: I wonder whether His Majesty has ever asked the question: Who is a Pakistani and what are the contents of the word called 'Pakistan'? An Iranian, for instance, is a person who has lived in Iran, participated in its civilization, recites its poetry, speaks the language and altogether has a sense of belonging, not merely to the country called Iran, but the whole

cultural complex which goes by the name of Iranian civilization dating back to Cyrus the Great. An Indian has a similar feeling ... Such a thing is lacking in Pakistan [which] is merely a label attached to those portions of India carved out on the sole criterion that the majority of inhabitants in these areas were allegedly united by allegiance to a common culture, a common language , a tradition, a civilization, but merely to a religion ...

Shah: You are absolutely right. How many times did I caution Ayub and Yahya Khan against their ways. Ayub was a wiser man but Yahya was just too stupid. In 1971, I wrote to him several times asking him to release Sheikh Mujibur Rahman but he paid no attention. I am sorry I interrupted you. Please continue.

PNH: ... *What is surprising is not that the people of Bangladesh revolted but that they took so long to revolt. We in India could have sat back and relaxed to witness the spectacle of the break-up of Pakistan with calm detachment if the grim tragedy took place in some far-off country, but it was taking place within almost the heart of India ... And yet my Prime Minister waited not for a week or days, but for months on end ... Therefore if East Pakistan broke away from Pakistan, it was not due to Indian intervention.* It broke away because the minds and hearts of millions of these Bengalis were wholly alienated from Pakistan ... We could have continued the war, but on the very day that the Pakistanis surrendered in their thousands in Dacca, my Prime Minister offered an unilateral ceasefire. Our Chief of the Army Staff too agreed that it was pointless to go on fighting on the western front. And so, we had a cease-fire ... It was because of our stake in a stable Pakistan that my Prime Minister at Simla took the more difficult course of withdrawing of our forces from the territories of Pakistan which had penetrated deep into it specially in Sind and even in Punjab, displacing about a million people ...

Shah: ... What is the state of Sino-Indian relations?

PNH: Intrinsically, there is no real conflict between China and India. However, they developed their relations with Pakistan with the avowed object of putting pressure on India and making India fight on two fronts as the last Chinese Ambassador warned us. The events of 1971 embarrassed the Chinese a great deal because the second front collapsed ... normalization of Sino-Indian relations may not be, from the Chinese point of view, a top priority ... They know we do not constitute a threat to them, although they are constantly talking about our alleged nefarious deeds in Tibet ...

Shah: We must have more dialogue with each other, talk to one another ...

PNH: ... There should be no conflict of interests between good Indo-Iranian relations and equally good Iran-Pakistan relations ... Pakistan often accuses us of having aggressive designs ... *But at Simla Conference we made a very sincere effort to the Pakistanis that since they felt that we might engage in acts of aggression, we should have arrangements through Joint Inspection Teams where Pakistanis could see our military installations and we could see theirs. My friend Aziz Ahmed summarily rejected this offer on the ground that Pakistan had, what he described, a right to 'equal security'. I asked him several times to define this concept of equal security but he wouldn't ...*

Shah: ... Please convey to your Prime Minister my warmest regards and best wishes. I have the highest regard for her. It is quite extraordinary how she is grappling with the problems of the country of the size of India ... [italics mine]

This is a highly condensed version of the conversation between Haksar and the Shah of Iran. I have extracted at length from the transcript for a variety of reasons. First, as far I know, this is the first time the record of the conversation is being brought into the public domain. Second, this is perhaps the only place where Haksar talks unreservedly about the events of 1971 and 1972. Third, it gives a good idea of Haksar's own worldview and the manner he saw India's foreign policy in a private meeting which meant he could speak more freely. Haksar's tête-à-tête with the Shah of Iran was to bring about a major change in the political and economic ties between India and Iran. The major symbol of this transformation was the Kudremukh iron ore project for which Iran committed $630 million over a five-year period at a time when India's foreign exchange reserves were around $2 billion. His visit paved the way for Indira Gandhi's visit to Iran in April 1974 and the Shah's return visit to India a few months later. In April 1975, Haksar saw the Shah a second time in Tehran. No transcript of that conversation is available, but many years later in a speech at Calcutta University on 25 November 1987, Haksar recalled this second chat with the Shah:

I was involved with negotiations with Iran in 1973 and 1975 and had the opportunity to talk to the great Shah-en-Shah. I used to observe that the large number of Iranian students dispersed in Europe and America were constantly in agitation against the regime of Shah-en-Shah. And I asked this to His Majesty: I said, "May I, Your Majesty have the liberty to ask a question which troubles me because I am very anxious to establish good relations between India and Iran?" He said: "Yes, Mr. Haksar please go ahead". I said: "How is it that in your country which can boast of 12 to 14 per cent growth of GNP, which has no oil problem, which has no foreign exchange problem, how come that your intelligentsia is alienated?" To which His Majesty's answer in 1975 was, "Mr Haksar, in every society there are a handful of people who are alienated for some reason or other and our intelligentsia belong to that but we took good care of them". In 1979, the question was who take care of whom?

On 6 February 1973, Indira Gandhi addressed the One Asia Assembly in New Delhi. This was a conclave of 'distinguished editors, economists and governmental leaders from many countries of Asia and of other continents'. Her speech had been drafted by Sharada Prasad and must be perhaps the first of the ones not to have been seen or worked upon by Haksar beforehand. In the course of the speech, she referred to the war in Vietnam, Laos and Cambodia and asked a question: 'Would this sort of war or the savage bombing which has taken place in Vietnam have been tolerated for so long, had the people been European?'

This statement created a huge flutter in the Nixon Administration. The next day, the US State Department's spokesman Charles Bray said that Indira Gandhi's question was 'inconsistent with the messages from the Government of India expressing gratification for the peace which has been achieved in Vietnam. It contradicts recent communications from New Delhi suggesting a desire to improve the relations between our two countries.' Going one step further, US Secretary of State William Rogers hinted that the departure for India of the US Ambassador-designate Daniel Moynihan might be delayed.

Indira Gandhi immediately went on damage control mode, and on 9 February 1973, while speaking at the Nepal Council of World Affairs in Kathmandu, made a reference to her Vietnam remarks and said that they 'are not against any particular country. They were an assessment of what I think the future should be ... The remark I made was in no sense a criticism of the Vietnam Accord. But I only tried to point out that there are dangers which face all of us in the future events in South-East Asia.'

The US State Department welcomed this 'retraction' and said that 'the mini-crisis has blown over'. Moynihan was sworn in as ambassador and India's own Ambassador in Washington, L.K. Jha, declared the whole episode closed.

In the Haksar archives there is a handwritten draft of an article that he obviously intended to get published. It recounts this entire episode from the beginning till the very end and says:

> Although the "mini-crisis", we are assured, has blown over, several questions puzzle Indians and friendly foreigners alike: Was it necessary for Smt. Gandhi to appear to retract from here statement of February 6? Should she have taken notice of the spokesman of the US State Department or even of Mr. Rogers? Even if some gloss had to be put, could not the Ministry of External Affairs in New Delhi have been chosen as the appropriate channel? Is US Administration dictating to us total abstinence from any public criticism of American policies and purpose? *Is the price of improved Indo-US relations total surrender on our part?* [italics mine]

The article was never published and Haksar never went public with his concerns. But it would have been clear to him that with his departure from the sanctum sanctorum of Indira Gandhi's establishment, there was a change which was already becoming evident. Had he been around that 'retraction' would not have been issued.

ॐ

In early-April 1973, Haksar was again the prime minister's special envoy and this time to Bangladesh. This was part of an Indian initiative to deal with 'humanitarian' issues left unresolved at Simla and that required all three countries—India, Pakistan and Bangladesh—to be on board. Pakistan had yet to formally recognize Bangladesh and, therefore, what could have been dealt with bilaterally under normal circumstances between Pakistan and Bangladesh had necessarily to be coordinated by India. These included issues related to prisoners of war held by India and also those prisoners of war whom Bangladesh wanted to put on trial for war crimes. Bangladesh was also understandably very concerned about the fate of some 400,000 Bengali nationals stranded in Pakistan. Also included in Haksar's brief were the next steps needed to deepen the economic and political relationship between India and Bangladesh. He spent three days in Dacca meeting Prime Minister Sheikh Mujibur Rahman from 2 April 1973. Foreign Minister Kamal Hossain was his main interlocutor from the Bangladesh side. This was to be the beginning of shuttle diplomacy for Haksar since Bangladesh had to be brought around on the war crimes trial matter with India wanting to close the chapter and wanting the three countries to move ahead in a positive frame of mind.

On 10 July 1973, External Affairs Minister Sardar Swaran Singh informed his Pakistani counterpart that the 'Indian delegation to the talks would be led by Shri P.N. Haksar, who has the status of Minister of State'. Clearly this had been Indira Gandhi's doing. A letter from Lord Mountbatten[3] to Haksar of 17 July 1973 says much:

> ... I met Mrs Gandhi and we had a talk in which she mentioned she was using you for high-level negotiations, and, although this must be difficult for you, I thought it was a very wise move on her part ...

Haksar went first to Rawalpindi and Islamabad and then to Dacca. Although the talks were between him and Aziz Ahmed, the Pakistani minister of state for defence and foreign affairs, at every step he had to keep Bangladesh in the picture as well, and ensure that its concerns were addressed to its satisfaction. Haksar was thus, actually negotiating on behalf of both India and Bangladesh. The first round of negotiations took place in Rawalpindi and Islamabad from 24 July 1973 to 31 July 1973. Haksar had called on President Bhutto at the latter's residence in Islamabad on 27 July 1973, and at the end of the conversation, this exchange took place:[4]

> Haksar: Finally, if you permit me, Mr President, I would like to say something most respectfully. I am not a historian. (Pointing to the picture of a Buddha on the wall). What do you feel about the picture? Is, or is not that a part of Pakistan?
>
> President Bhutto: I respect Buddha.
>
> Haksar: Then, Mr. President, May I humbly ask, why do you talk of confrontation of thousand years? Are you in conflict with your own history? Is Pakistan in conflict with its own personality? To talk of confrontation has impact on the minds and hearts of people in India and Pakistan. It will be picked by the wrong type of people in India. Is that a contribution to durable peace in the sub-continent ... You said Sindhi language is 5000 years old. Is there a confrontation in Sind between the last one thousand years and the previous 4000 years? I beg of you, Mr. President, to think it over the implications of the pronouncements about confrontation of a thousand years ...
>
> President Bhutto: I will say less of it in future (President looked embarrassed and confused and said "it was for internal ..." but did not complete the sentence).

Then Haksar went to Dhaka for discussions with Sheikh Mujibur Rahman from 15 August 1973 to 17 August 1973. The record of discussions held on 16 August 1973 with Sheikh Mujibur Rahman and his colleagues had this to say:

> Mr Haksar stated that he was one of the most brutally frank civil servants. His approach to problems was to speak up his mind and to give his clear advice to the political leaders with whom he worked. After giving such advice, it was his practice to carry out whatever instructions he received to the best of his ability. Mr. Haksar expressed the hope that Sheikh Saheb would give him the same liberty to be as frank as he has always been with his own Prime Minister ...
>
> Sheikh Saheb said that he was aware of the tremendous problems that India was facing today and added that much of it was because of the

sacrifices that India made in 1971 and 1972 for Bangladesh. Mr. Haksar stated that Sheikh Saheb should not mention anything about sacrifices. Whatever India did was on the basis of shared ideals with the people of Bangladesh. Mr. Haksar added that apart from the magnitude of the problems that India is facing, the Indian leadership has to resolve them by democratic methods. To work a democracy is problematic. A leader ruling by democratic methods should have "three hearts, two brains and six kidneys". But somehow India will meet these problems ...

Sheikh Saheb then requested Mr. Haksar to give his assessment of the domestic political situation in Pakistan. Mr. Haksar said that the situation in Pakistan is fluid ... [and] called Sheikh Saheb's attention to the theory of historical evolution propounded by the historian Mr. E.H. Carr who, in a dissertation entitled 'What is History' had stated that history consists of the interplay of forces of change and continuity in any society. This is happening in Pakistan. Bhutto desires change but he is a prisoner of the forces of continuity ...

Aziz Ahmed came to New Delhi on 17 August 1973 and presented a Pakistani draft of the agreement six days later. On 24 August 1973, Haksar presented an Indian draft. On 28 August 1973, Haksar and Aziz Ahmed finally signed the agreement that took the Simla Accord forward. The verbatim transcripts of Haksar's discussions in Rawalpindi, Islamabad, Dacca and New Delhi, reveal Haksar at his supreme strategic and tactical best, mindful at every step of the national interest of two countries (India and Bangladesh) but always looking for avenues for mutual accommodation. Minutes after the agreement had been signed, Indira Gandhi sent this letter to Haksar:

> Neither of us care for formalities. But I must express my deep appreciation of the manner in which you have handled the whole delicate business of talking with the Pakistani delegation. The going was often tough and exasperating and entailed a great deal of hard work. The result has justified all the effort which you and your colleague have put in. I sincerely hope that the implementation will go smoothly and that the Agreement does in fact lead to peace and better relations in our sub-continent. I should like to thank you on my own behalf and on behalf of the Government.

Earlier, when the negotiations had resumed in New Delhi and the talks meandered along, Indira Gandhi had written to Haksar on 25 August 1973:

Dear Haksar Saheb:

I have been wanting to speak to you for some time but waited for the Pak delegation to return to their country. However the talks are dragging on. Hence this hurried note.

I am a little worried about the Algiers Conference [4th Non-Aligned Summit]. I foresee all kinds of pressures and currents and I do not know if the delegation that is proposed is really equipped to give any kind of lead ...

The thought struck me that your being in Algiers would make an enormous difference to India's role. I always hesitate to put such thoughts to you. But this too important an occasion not only from the point of view of what happens in Algiers but also the reaction in India and interestingly when far too many people are anxiously awaiting bad news, real or imagined slight to India and so on—for her not to speak up.

Will you at least think about it? I do sincerely hope that you can come.

This letter shows that Indira Gandhi may well have been in awe of Haksar. But her postscript to the letter is even more amazing. She added:

It will mean a great deal to me ... [italics mine]

A hint of emotional blackmail is perhaps evident here on the part of the prime minister. But that one sentence is reflective of the true nature of the Indira Gandhi–Haksar relationship in those years. Haksar obviously had no option but to agree and was in Algiers for the summit between 5–9 September 1973.

This was the year Haksar was to lose two of his closest ideological compatriots known to him personally for over three-and-a-half decades. These two were also amongst the closest advisers of Indira Gandhi.

First to depart was Pitambar Pant in February 1973, at the young age of 52. Haksar had ensured Pant became a member of the Planning

Commission in 1967 where he would pioneer perspective planning. Thereafter, Indira Gandhi had made him chairman of the National Committee on Environmental Planning and Coordination (NCEPC) which laid the foundations of environmental appraisal and analysis in the country.

Next to go was Mohan Kumaramangalam, who perished in an air crash on 31 May 1973 in New Delhi. He was a communist who became a Congressman. In 1964, he had first submitted a document called 'A Review of the Party Policy since 1964' to the leadership of the CPI. It had been buried then, but in early 1969 he once again submitted the document with a postscript. This has come to be known as the 'Kumaramangalam thesis',[5] which argued that the CPI should work closely with the Congress to achieve its revolutionary goals but in a democratic framework. Following that submission, many CPI members like Kumaramangalam himself, Chandrajit Yadav, K.V. Raghunatha Reddy, K.R. Ganesh, Rajni Patel, R.K. Khadilkar and Nurul Hasan had joined the Congress. They were all well accommodated in positions of power by Haksar with the enthusiastic backing of Indira Gandhi.

Kumaramangalam was not doctrinaire as a minister. He had masterminded the creation of SAIL and the nationalization of the coal industry. But, as Haksar wrote in a tribute to him a few days after his death:[6]

... Mohan was the only one in the ruling party, be he a Chief Minister or a Central Minister who raised his hand against the take-over [nationalization] of foodgrains trade.

Haksar and Kumaramangalam had also been carefully calibrating a policy towards foreign investment, as this note prepared by the latter after their discussions and sent to P.N. Dhar on 6 June 1972 for Indira Gandhi's consumption reveals:

We must take a quick look at the problem and also act with some boldness. It is necessary to take into account the need to secure rapid economic growth with a view to provide minimum essential goods and services at reasonable prices to the vast millions of our people below the poverty line. Adverse effects on the development of indigenous

technology, undue outflow of foreign exchange, ill-effects of foreign
management control—these should, of course, be guarded against,

- Allow foreign equity even in areas like steel provided GOI
  [Government of India] stake is at 51%.
- Adequate safeguards to ensure management control, training of
  Indian personnel and uninterrupted supply of spares.
- Prevent excessive repatriation of capital through high dividends.

Twenty-six days before his death, Kumaramangalam finished writing a
slim monograph called *Judicial Appointments: An Analysis of the Recent
Controversy Over the Appointment of the Chief Justice of India* that was
published a few months later.[7] And just three days before his demise in the
plane crash, Kumaramangalam completed a tract called *Coal—Prospects After
Nationalisation* which too came out later in the year.[8] These monographs
mirror Haksar's views as well and, in all probability, the two must have
had long discussions while they were being written. Kumaramanglam and
Haksar were exceedingly close going back to 1936. Both could speak up to
Indira Gandhi and there can be little doubt that her decline began when
both Haksar and Kumaramangalam departed from her side within a few
months of each other in the first half of 1973.

Haksar was a now a free citizen but continued to keep in close touch with
Indira Gandhi who would keep consulting him on various matters. He
would send her notes on whatever was bothering him. One such missive
went on 16 July 1973:

> I am recording this note under sheer compulsion of my nature and I may
> be forgiven trespassing on PM's time and attention.
>
> It might be useful to recall the Congress Party under Prime Minister's
> leadership sought the mandate of the people of India for a strong Centre
> and for mitigating, to some extent, the poverty that prevails in our land.
> The people of India gave this mandate in a full-throated manner [in 1971].
> In 1972, P.M. led the Congress Party again to the polls for electing State
> Governments. The central slogan was that the people should vote for

stable State Governments as against the state of affairs which prevailed between 1967 and 1972. The people once again responded beyond expectation of the usual run of Congress politicians.

These Congressmen have totally forgotten the history of the last 18 months and are now engaged in factionalism totally divorced from any principle whatsoever. Andhra was bad enough. This was followed by Bihar which for sheer maladroitness of handling takes the cake. Gujarat followed suit. I do not know the results of the election of the leader. However, I can predict that neither Chimanbhai Patel nor Kanitilal Ghiya nor indeed anybody else has either the character to command the unabated loyalty or even loyalty of overwhelming majority of legislators. They are all small men strutting about with the manners and accents of self-styled leaders. And now we are in the midst of a thoroughly disreputable crisis in Madhya Pradesh. I do not regard Shri P.C. Sethi as cat's whiskers. However, from all accounts, he has the merit of having given a clean administration in a State notorious for its moral depravity and corruption. *However, the time has come for P.M. to summon all her resources and energies to cry a halt. Thus far and no further ...* I feel that the Congressmen must be called to discipline and I would submit, with great respect, that the General Secretary of the Congress Party, preferably Shri Chandrajit Yadav, might be asked to make a statement somewhat along the lines of a hurriedly prepared draft I am attaching. [italics mine]

It does not appear that Haksar's draft was ever issued. But that very day, Chandarjit Yadav speaking in Gauhati warned against growing factionalism in the Congress party and called for a serious and urgent review of the party's functioning. In later years, Haksar would point to the crisis in the Congress itself—generated ironically by Congressmen themselves—that played a role in fuelling a sequence of events, particularly in Bihar and Gujarat, that ultimately culminated in the Emergency.

Now that Haksar was no longer in the government, he felt free to do things he couldn't have done when he was in the seat of power. Thus it was that Haksar wrote an article in a high brow monthly called *Seminar* that was edited by his friend Romesh Thapar. The article 'Commitment: A

Dirty Word?' appeared in August 1973 and described Haksar's philosophy of governance. Critics of Haksar have accused him of propagating the pernicious (in their view) of a 'committed" bureaucracy' and a 'committed' judiciary, thereby undermining the independence of both these institutions. That is what makes this article significant—if only it had appeared some years earlier, perhaps Haksar may not have been attacked so much. In a fine essay, he wrote:[9]

> … Civil servants, politicians, members of the judiciary and of other professions are often found accusing each other of either lacking commitment or of forcing the other to change his commitment. Behind this smoke–screen of controversy lies the grim reality of the lack of inner coherence in our entire social, economic, political and cultural existence. No dominant value system has yet emerged and the past broods heavily on the present. Some day perhaps, the imperatives of modernization of our economy and our society will create the new value system.
>
> … Secularism in thought and action, honesty, integrity and hard work as ethical compulsions, austerity, national pride, sustained by intellectual and spiritual self-reliance and some regard for the scientific temper: these are some of the essential elements of the new value system.

Many years later, Haksar spoke at length to Granville Austin, the eminent historian-scholar of the Indian Constitution and based on that conversation, Austin was to write:[10]

> To the gentlemanly Haksar, the word [commitment] meant commitment to the social revolutionary ideals of the Constitution, especially by his fellow civil servants, who should act with integrity and honesty, giving advice, not taking personal advantage and not caving in to politicians.

Without doubt, Haksar was genuine in asserting that to him commitment meant upholding and advancing the noble values and provisions enshrined in the Indian Constitution. He was also genuine in holding that there should be no conflict between what bureaucrats personally believe and that what they are duty bound to perform. But there was another dimension to commitment in Haksar's worldview that he did not articulate: that loyalty to Indira Gandhi was essential if commitment to the Constitution was to be achieved since she alone was in a position to implement the agenda of socio-economic transformation that India badly needed. This was because of who she was, the legacy she had inherited and also because she transcended 'particularism of one sort or another be it rooted in religion, language, region or caste'. Not everyone was a Haksar who could reconcile loyalty to Indira Gandhi with being brutally frank with her to her face. It was inevitable that when Haksar faded away, commitment came to be seen as unquestioning personal loyalty to the Indira Gandhi.

In October 1973, Haksar was asked to take over as chairman of the Governing Council of the Indian Statistical Institute (ISI) that had been started way back in 1931 by India's most eminent statistician P.C. Mahalanobis. It was amongst the earliest to be declared 'an institution of national importance' by an Act of Parliament in December 1959. The ISI had made significant contributions to Indian planning in the 1950s and the early-1960s but then had fallen into difficult days. This was both because of Mahalanobis's own management style and also because of the turbulence that swept Calcutta in the 1960s and early-1970s.[11] Three review committees in a decade had not been able to improve the work environment and morale.

Haksar had been in close touch with Mahalanobis till the latter's death. He was well aware of the state of affairs in the ISI and had been reluctant to get involved, but it appears his old friend Ashok Mitra, with some assistance from P.N. Dhar, had prevailed upon him. His appointment was welcomed by everyone in ISI—perhaps amongst the few things that everyone was agreed upon. Academics hailed him and the technical and non-scientific staff also issued statements praising his appointment. Haksar had allowed himself to be persuaded in spite of the grave difficulties ISI was going through because of the deep respect he had for Mahalanobis. Haksar's initial term was for two years but he was to remain chairman of the Governing Council for 25 years, a record that will most probably never even be even remotely equalled, let alone surpassed.

Towards the end of the year, in mid-December 1973, Indira Gandhi pressed Haksar into 'special envoy' mode again and asked him to lead a small Indian team for a high-level Indo-French colloquium in Paris. That this was to be more than a mere talk session was clear from the fact that B.D. Nag Chowdhury, the scientific adviser to the defence minister accompanied Haksar. He was then fully occupied with giving shape to India's nuclear test which was to happen in May 1974, and also to India's missile production plans.

ॐ

On 21 April 1974, Haksar has written to his close friend B.K. Nehru with whom he shared a unique relationship—poles apart ideologically but bound together personally, not the least because of their common sense of 'protective custody' as far as Indira Gandhi was concerned. Haksar wrote:

> I trust Fori [B.K. Nehru's Hungarian-born wife] and you have settled down and that you do not curse me for having suggested that it might be a good idea for you to be in London at this time.

Indira Gandhi had asked B.K. Nehru to be India's high commissioner in the UK but he had been unwilling until Haksar persuaded him to go—the persuasion was at Indira Gandhi's bidding. This was much like what had happened in 1972 when Indira Gandhi decided that T.N. Kaul should be India's ambassador to the US but he too had been most unwilling till Haksar was asked to intervene to get him to go.

Haksar had been invited by Lord Mountbatten to deliver the Sixth Nehru Memorial Lecture in London that was scheduled for 16 May 1974. One day before the lecture, Haksar sent a cable to the prime minister that read:

> PND must have informed you that I have come here to deliver the 6th Nehru Memorial Lecture and to speak on India's foreign policy at the Royal Commonwealth Society. I shall thus be adding to the cacophony of present day communication. However, there is some comfort in the knowledge that the world will not materially alter after I have spoken.
>
> *The day before I left, Homi* [Sethna] *came to see me. He looked very distraught fearing postponement of things. He asked me what I thought about*

it. I told him that since the decision had been taken there was hardly any
point in delaying its implementation.

I was shown a page and a half of a draft announcement. I suggested
to him that it might be advisable to say nothing more than a couple of
sentences without any explanation or revealing any details of the location
or magnitudes. I sincerely hope that this would be done and that we shall
then possess ourselves with patience and watch how the world reacts. I
devoutly hope that no one will take a press conference.

I strongly feel that after the event but before making the proposed
brief announcement, we might send for the Soviet Ambassador in New
Delhi and let him have a feeling that he was the only one to receive prior
information. I am suggesting this only because the Slavs take their love
and hate seriously.

Finally I would beg of you most earnestly to consider weaving the event
into a pattern of political and economic ascent from where we find ourselves
at present. The successful withstanding of the quite unconscionable demands
of railway unions might well be the commencement of the process of change
in the mood and temper of the country ...

I would have very much liked to say some thing about Bangladesh
and the way we are handling our relationship with that country. Even our
Mission in Dacca is being made quite incoherent and there is no central
point in New Delhi where problems get dealt with. Instead, there is a
wide dispersal of things in the various Ministries and Departments. I am
afraid that if we don't change our methods we shall pay an unnecessarily
high price. For different reasons, Iran too needs to be dealt with in a
special sort of way; otherwise, the present euphoria will soon vanish ...
[italics mine]

India's first 'peaceful nuclear explosion' took place in Pokhran on 18 May
1974. It is obvious that a decision to go ahead with such a test had been
taken at least 18 months earlier, in the final weeks of Haksar's tenure in
the prime minister's Secretariat. Sometime in 1972, Nag Chowdhury had
identified the site and Haksar, had made sure that the Indian Army was
fully on board. Even after his retirement Haksar was amongst the five or
six people involved in discussing the test and its operational details, and
its implications for economic and foreign policy. He gave an interview to

the weekly *Blitz* that appeared on 10 August 1974. His entire approach to Indian science was to be summed up in this answer of his to a question:

> ... It must also be borne in mind that India having missed the First Industrial Revolution cannot afford to miss the Second Industrial Revolution of the twentieth century by not mastering certain areas of science and technology just because it does not fit into the outlook of some countries ...

He ended the interview by declaring that:

> The Rajasthan explosion has sharply posed the problem that the world cannot live in safety in a system which seeks to freeze the development in the field of nuclear energy only in favour of advanced countries. If one has a sense of history, one instantly recognizes that advances in science and technology cannot be circumscribed by the negative concepts which underlie the Non-proliferation Treaty.

In retrospect, one criticism can certainly be made of this interview. When asked for his response to President Bhutto's famous statement that if India got the bomb Pakistan too would get it, even if her people had to eat only grass in the process, Haksar replied:

> If by eating grass one can produce atom bombs then by now cows and horses would have produced them. But, of course, the people of Pakistan under the great and charismatic leadership to which they are now exposed might produce a bomb on a diet of grass. Talking more seriously, India, at any rate, is not interested in forging nuclear weaponry and I doubt very much if Pakistan can force India into a nuclear arms race.

Pakistan certainly acquired a nuclear weapons capability by the late-1980s, if not earlier which, in turn, forced India to revisit its traditional aversion to the use of nuclear energy for military purposes.

In 1972, Haksar had played a crucial role in the nationalization of IISCO in Burnpur in West Bengal that had been bleeding because of mismanagement.

He had also been behind the establishment of SAIL in the same year. On 31 July 1974, Haksar wrote to his successor P.N. Dhar:

> I was recently in Calcutta. Aurobindo Ray of IISCO came to see me. I was utterly saddened by his plight. Since I feel some responsibility for persuading him to give up the highly lucrative job in Metal Box ... I felt I must write to you. If he has to go because Wadud does not like him, then we should arrange that he goes with his reputation in tact. Frankly I do not understand what is against him. Even under the most favourable circumstances it would have been difficult to manage the affairs at IISCO and give to them some shape within the short time during which Ray has been Administrator ... If Wadud has something against Ray then the only appropriate thing for him to do is to meet Ray under your auspices and sort out such fears and suspicions which might have grown up quite illegitimately. Indeed I would suggest the same procedure for sorting out the differences that exist and are now openly expressed between Wadud and K.D. Malaviya. These differences could easily be sorted out if PM were to arrange a meeting with Wadud and Malaviya together and with your active association. *What I fear is that if these things are not sorted out, then very soon SAIL will collapse. And if SAIL collapses, there is hardly any future for a rational organization of our public sector.*
>
> *You might legitimately ask why I should worry about these matters. It is because I feel sufficient sense of responsibility to write to you privately than to agitate publicly. I hope you do not mind my saying so. It might appear cruel but I do feel that you have to actively intervene in this matter and overcome old ideas, habits and modes of thought* ... As I see it Wadud has to learn that one has to carry on with a variety of men and that in our set up one has to take the Minister along. And Malaviyaji has to learn that Public sector industries cannot be run as departmental undertakings and that any self-respecting executive must be allowed to function within a broad framework of policy. [italics mine]

The supreme irony was that all the men named in this letter—Ray, Wadud Khan and Malaviya—belonged to the same ideological school as Haksar and Kumaramangalam. They were all fine men each in their own way but clearly they needed a ringmaster for them to function cohesively together.

By background and temperament, Dhar could not fulfill that role—only Haksar could. Haksar's frustration with Dhar is palpable. Many years later in an interview to Katherine Frank, Haksar would call Dhar 'spineless', even though they were the best of friends and PNH was especially fond of Sheila Dhar, a delightful personality in her own right.

∾

Haksar would continue to write to Dhar on various matters. Thus, on 9 September 1974, Haksar informed his successor about a problem that had arisen in relation to the Goa church. Various Catholic leaders had meet Haksar in Bombay and what he had heard incensed him:

> During my recent visit to Bombay I came across a number of Roman Catholics. The story they had to tell left me depressed. I am really amazed at how our government functions. We liberated Goa [in 1961] but now we cannot liberate ourselves from the tyranny of foreign missionaries who play havoc with us ...

The problem was this: the Archbishop of Goa continued to be an ethnic Portuguese who operated out of Lisbon. The delegation that met Haksar wanted an appointment of an ethnic Indian as archbishop of Goa before the Exposition of the body of St. Francis Xavier took place in Goa in December 1974. It also wanted the Government of India to pursue the matter with the Vatican.

As it turned out the first Goan was appointed Archbishop of Goa in January 1978. Haksar's letter to Dhar may have got the ball rolling and got the Government of India to tell the Vatican that an ethnic Indian should be appointed as archbishop of Goa.

As I talked to knowledgeable people, it turns out that Haksar had actually been lobbied by one small breakaway group of Catholics in Bombay which split from the Goa congregation and reunited many years later. Haksar may not have been made fully aware of intra-Catholic rivalries. To him, the matter was simple and straightforward: Thirteen years after liberation Goa had no business having a Portuguese archbishop exercising his authority from Lisbon. He was totally irreligious. To him, this was an issue of nationalism, plain and simple.

∾

The Spanish Civil War of the late-1930s had evoked the sympathy and support of Indian students in the UK like Haksar, Kumaramangalam and Rajni Patel. Krishna Menon himself was in the forefront mobilizing support for the republican cause and had taken Nehru to Spain in 1938. Nehru had written about the Spanish War in his autobiography and the impact it had on his thinking. Indira Nehru also was very much part of that youthful pro-republican brigade.

On 7 September 1974, Haksar sent a note to the prime minister's private secretary, N.K. Seshan:

> I am afraid it is rather difficult to answer the questions without knowing who the author is and what he is seeking to do in the book he is writing on the Spanish Civil War. I understand that Andre Malraux thinks well of the author. This gives some assurance.
>
> I must point out that question no. 4 can be answered in a variety of ways. The particular answer I have suggested is the one I am prepared to defend.

Indira Gandhi had been asked four questions on the Spanish Civil War and she had turned to Haksar to provide the answers which he did. The first question dealt with Nehru's thinking of that conflict and the next two with the causes for the defeat of the republicans. The last question–answer to which Haksar drew attention was this:

> Q 4. What are the main lessons of what has been called the Spanish tragedy?
>
> Ans: I do not know if history teaches lessons; in my view it only raises questions. And the question which the Spanish tragedy raised was: Can fundamental social, economic and political changes be brought about through democratic means without being overwhelmed by forces of dark reaction? In the newly independent countries of Asia and Africa,

the question is of contemporary relevance. The re-enactment in Chile of the tragedy of Spain shows how tenacious are the forces of reaction.

On 6 October 1974, Haksar's earliest mentor Krishna Menon passed away in New Delhi. They had known each other for some 40 years going back to the Indian League in the late-1930s. Krishna Menon had been responsible for Haksar's first London stint. They were extremely fond of each other and Indira Gandhi would send Haksar to Krishna Menon whenever she felt that the latter was having any problem or was feeling out of sorts—which was, actually, quite often. Haksar went on air the very night Krishna Menon passed away and publicly acknowledged what he owed him, by saying:

> What little I learnt about the art and science of diplomacy, it was at his feet. From him I learnt the art of negotiation, I learnt from him that in diplomacy the most important thing was courage, a non-negotiable sense of dedication to the interests of one's country; a capacity to see what your opponent has in mind and to discern whether there was a basis for linking your opponent's concern with your own.
>
> … I am not saying that Krishna was man without flaws. He had them but these were nothing compared to the extraordinary qualities he possessed …
>
> I have examined over a period of years the physiognomy of his critics. There were those who could not bear his proximity to Jawaharlal Nehru. Basically, these men and women lacked confidence in themselves and appeared tall because they walked on stilts of office or something else. There were other who turned against him after being beneficiaries of his kindness and patronage; and finally there were those, mostly foreigners, who called him "abrasive", "anti-West", "Fellow traveller" and "Communist", because he refused to play the diplomatic game according to the rules made by others.
>
> I had occasion to see Krishna in recent years without the halo of office. I found him without rancour … He was at peace with himself and that is what most of us would like to feel whenever our days are numbered.

This could well have a tribute to Haksar himself.

In 1973, Haksar had convinced T.N. Kaul that he should accept the offer of being India's ambassador to the USA. He had also prevailed upon B.K. Nehru to be India's high commissioner in the UK. Now it was the turn of the USSR. Shelvankar had already spent three years there and had done all that he could do. But relations between India and the USSR were not all that cordial as it seemed. It was sometime in November 1974 that Haksar persuaded D.P. Dhar to start his second innings in Moscow. On 19 November 1974, Haksar told the prime minister:

> I hope that Government of India have a proper appreciation of the evolving international situation so that our foreign policy remains firmly rooted in realities. In view of the matter, the quality and character of representation in Moscow must receive careful and anxious consideration; the more so because Shelvankar's assignment, largely because of the irrepressible character of his wife, has been negative. If Shri D.P. Dhar is now being entrusted with the task not merely of resuming the threads of our many-sided and complex relations with the Soviet Union but also mending the damage done to our relationship during the last three years, then it is obvious enough that we cannot send him to the Soviet Union after having maimed and battered him. And this is precisely what has been done in recent weeks by the kinds of reports and speculations which have appeared in the press. We should try, to the extent possible, to mitigate the effect of this and I submit that we proceed as follows:
>
> (i) Secretary to P.M. should send for the Soviet Ambassador. He should inform him, on behalf of Prime Minister and on her specific instructions, about Shri D.P. Dhar's assignment to Moscow ...
>
> (ii) After the Secretary has spoken to the Ambassador, he might take him for a few minutes to Prime Minister; all that P.M. need say ... is that she would like to convey to the highest leadership in the Soviet Union Prime Minister's personal involvement in the selection of Shri D.P. Dhar for this important assignment ... I would also recommend that at this meeting P.M. should also give some indication of her intention to visit the Soviet Union. A decision on this needs to be taken now ...
>
> (iii) On the day Secretary to P.M. and P.M. convey to the Soviet Ambassador information about Shri D.P. Dhar's assignment, the

Ministry of External Affairs should seek agre'ment to the proposed assignment.

(iv) As soon as agreement is received and a date for announcement is fixed, the formalities connected with the resignation of a Cabinet Minister should be completed, so that when an announcement is made, the resignation is linked up with the new assignment.

The announcement should specifically mention that Shri D.P. Dhar will continue to retain the rank of Cabinet Minister.

Haksar had no official position at that time and here he was telling the prime minister herself what to do down to the last detail. He was undoubtedly trying to assuage D.P. Dhar's hurt ego and feelings but the note also reflects the tremendous importance he placed on Indo-Soviet ties. The only intriguing feature of this note is the reference to Shelvankar and his English wife Mary, who was herself a great admirer of Stalin. Indira Gandhi and Haksar knew the Shelvankars very well since the late-1930s. They had appointed Shelvankar as consul general in Hanoi in 1968 and it was their decision—nobody else's—to appoint him to Moscow three years later. It is baffling that both Indira Gandhi and Haksar allowed him to continue for there for so long, knowing full well the damage that was being inflicted on bilateral ties by Mary Shelvankar's contretemps.[12] As far as a visit to the USSR was concerned for which Haksar had recommended that 'a decision needs to be taken now', Indira Gandhi would make the trip the very next month.

Sometime towards the end of 1974, Haksar was asked to contribute to a volume on the public sector being published as a tribute to his friend and colleague, Mohan Kumaramangalam.[13] His essay 'Public Sector: Hope or Despair' was a damning indictment of the system which he had been a part of. He had tried, in his own way along with Kumaramangalam to reform the functioning of public sector companies, but for the first time publicly he expressed his failure. He spared nobody:

... The boards of management groaned under the weight of a totally irrelevant and miscellaneous assortment of men. And to compound the offence, remote control from the Secretariat in New Delhi was exercised by men, both politicians and civil servants, who had no knowledge, and even less experience, of running enterprises of any sort, unless self-advancement could be legitimately called an enterprise ... The various political parties, from the Right to the Left, spawning their own trade union movements, made the public sector a happy hunting ground for promoting their self-interests. Efficiency, productivity, profitability and a sense of involvement of those who worked in these enterprises in their management, became so many dirty words. It seems as if someone was interested in establishing the proposition that the public sector just could not work.

Of course, he continued to hope for the public sector but his despair was very evident. And, quite remarkably, for someone who had worried so much of the growth of monopolies when he was in power, Haksar confessed that 'while a great deal of misguided effort has been directed towards restricting monopolies, practically nothing has been done to save the poor consumer from price rigging and restrictive trade practices'.

Notes

1. I have discussed this at length in Ramesh (2016).
2. Tandon (2003).
3. Incidentally, Mountbatten had been worried about his funeral arrangements for a long time. He had written to Haksar about it in 1971. He would broach the topic again when the two met in May 1974 in London and the conversation went something like this as recounted by Haksar later:

   Mountbatten: Parmeshwar, I am planning my funeral arrangements to the extent that I can. Some months back I had asked Indira to arrange for a couple of Indian air force planes to come to London at the time of my funeral and dip in salute. She promised she would look into this but I have not heard anything either from her or from the Indian air force.
   PNH: Oh, Lord Louis I am sure there is no disrespect intended! We Indians are a superstitious lot and do not like to think of your death. We hope you

have many more years of life ahead of you. That is why you have not heard from us.

Mountbatten: Oh I see! That explains a lot. I am really very touched.

Mountbatten would be killed in a bomb explosion in November 1978. There would be no Indian military participation in his funeral. Indira Gandhi was out of power then and Haksar was in retirement.

4.   Bhasin (2012).
5.   Singh, Satinder (1973).
6.   Haksar (1979).
7.   Kumaramangalam (1973a).
8.   Kumaramangalam (1973b).
9.   Haksar (1979).
10. Austin (1999).
11. Rudra (2000).
12. After her visit to Moscow in late-September 1971, Indira Gandhi had written to Mary Shelvankar: 'I do want to say "thank you" for your thoughtfulness, your gifts and for being yourself. But naturalness and spontaneity worry a lot of people who are not used to them. So many people waste a lot of energy putting on an act. Although, perhaps, it is just as well that they hide their real nature!' Quoted in Masani (1975).
13. Dutt and Nigam (1975).

X. The Planning Commission Years

(1975–1977)

Haksar was persuaded, much against his wishes, by Indira Gandhi to return as deputy chairman of the Planning Commission—a position with Cabinet rank—in January 1975. He was to play a critical role in the formulation of the 20-point programme of the prime minister, and also in gradually rebuilding the economy. He would enhance the prestige of the Planning Commission considerably. But there would be a permanent rupture between his family and Indira Gandhi because of the Emergency. Morarji Desai would succeed Indira Gandhi as prime minister in March 1977. Resisting the new prime minister's efforts to continue with him, Haksar resigned from all his official positions in May 1977 bringing to an end to his full-time, three-decades-old association with the Indian state.

Haksar (in a tie) at the Vikram Sarabhai Space Centre, Trivandrum, probably mid-1975. A young A.P.J. Abdul Kalam explaining the intricacies of the satellite launch vehicle with Satish Dhawan in-between Kalam and Haksar.

ON 4 JANUARY 1975, HAKSAR REPLACED D.P. DHAR AS DEPUTY CHAIRMAN of the Planning Commission although news of this possibility had been in the public domain since mid-November 1974. A few days earlier, he had replied to a congratulatory letter from one of his colleagues, Rikhi Jaipal, by saying that the new assignment was 'going to be a foolhardy misadventure'. Two years before his death, Haksar was to write to one of his successors many times removed as principal secretary to the prime minister, T.R. Satish Chandran, that he had allowed himself to be persuaded to rejoin the government full-time for what he termed 'wholly illegitimate reasons'.

Somewhat ironically the vacancy in the Planning Commission may well have arisen because of Haksar himself. B.N. Tandon, his colleague in the prime minister's Secretariat[1] and M.L. Fotedar,[2] then a Congress leader in J&K have both written that Haksar had been unhappy with

D.P. Dhar. I asked Dhar's son whether Haksar and his father had some sort
of a falling out that may have prompted D.P. Dhar being sent off to
Moscow yet again. Vijay Dhar smiled and said: 'Yes, there had been some
falling out over Sanjay Gandhi. My father's attitude towards the Maruti
car project was that "if Sanjay wants to do it, let him do it".' To this I
would add that Haksar had been miffed with D.P. Dhar for being
responsible for the fiasco in 1973 over the nationalization of wholesale
trade in wheat. He was also unhappy that Dhar had been unable to provide
effective leadership in the Planning Commission and had failed to bridge
the differences that had cropped up between the two economist stars of the
Planning Commission—Sukhamoy Chakravarty and B.S. Minhas—which
had led to Minhas's resignation.

B.N. Tandon's diary for this day—4 January 1975—has the following
entry:

> A noteworthy point today is the appointment of Haksar as the deputy
> chairman of the Planning Commission ... I can say without the slightest
> hesitation that in my entire career I have met only two or three such able,
> dedicated and patriotic officers ... The success that the PM achieved in
> 1971 was due to Haksar. India's policy towards Bangladesh, its subsequent
> liberation and the ensuing agreement with Pakistan in 1972 were all
> due to Haksar. Sometimes the PM and her senior colleagues would
> hesitate to take his advice but purely on the strength of his ability and
> deep understanding he would carry the day. But in spite of all this, his
> influence began to wane since the middle of 1972. The main reason for
> this was that he did not want to witness the decline and eclipse of the
> institution he had built. He did not approve of the sort of people who
> had begun to acquire a hold over the PM ... As far as I know he tried
> to explain all this to her on several occasions ... *The great thing about
> Haksar is that while others hesitate to speak their minds to the PM even over
> the smallest things, he expresses himself frankly, at times brutally which he
> knows would not be liked...*
>
> *... It would not be wrong to say that Haksar did not leave the PM's
> secretariat under happy circumstances. But he and PM remained in contact
> and she continued to consult him on several issues ... No other person was
> trusted by PM as much as Haksar was ...*

Even after he had retired, there were some attempts to re-induct him into government in some capacity or the other. But these were not successful because Haksar didn't want to come back to government. So everyone is surprised that he has now agreed to do so. After a lot of analysis, the only conclusion seems to be that he has come back under pressure from leftists ... *But the truth is that Haksar was turning into a silent critic of the government* ... The PM hates criticism and if a person like Haksar turned into a critic, it would have done her great damage. That is why it had become necessary for her to get Haksar into the machinery of government. He was not ready to join the ministry. That left only one option—to make him deputy chairman of the Planning Commission. [italics mine]

This is one of Tandon's longest entries in his diary. He had worked with Haksar in the PM's Secretariat on a daily basis between 1969 and 1973, and had continued to keep in frequent touch with him. The entry reveals much of what Tandon thought of the prime minister and her fluctuating equation with Haksar. But the diaries reveal that all through the period when Haksar was supposed to be in enforced hibernation, Indira Gandhi continued to consult him on various issues. The diary entries show that in November and December of 1974 Indira Gandhi had been talking to Haksar on the possibility of advancing the elections that were due in early-1976. We don't know what advice Haksar gave but what we do know from the diaries is that Haksar opposed some suggestions being made to postpone those elections to some later date.

Tandon's explanations for Haksar's return to the Planning Commission are not wholly far-fetched. PNH had indeed been writing to P.N.Dhar, voicing his growing discomfort at what Indira Gandhi was doing—or not doing. It could also be true that Haksar's left network wanted him back, more so since Kumaramangalam and Pant had passed away and D.P. Dhar was being sent to Moscow as ambassador. Who might this left network have been? Possibly Nikhil Chakravarty, G. Parthasarathi and Aruna Asaf Ali. In the Haksar archives there is an undated handwritten note written to him by P.N. Dhar which read as follows:

Haksar Sahib:

Having slept over it, I don't think Ashok Mitra's ideas on the subject of Deputy Chairmanship is all that crazy. You condemned it as a non-starter. I beg to differ.

I am thinking of mentioning it to PM today or tomorrow whenever I get an opportunity. I hope you are not too wildly reacting to it.

PND

Could it be that Ashok Mitra who later was to famously declare 'I am a Communist, not a gentleman' was behind Haksar's appointment as deputy chairman of the Planning Commission? Haksar had been Mitra's patron when the latter was in government during 1967–1972 and the two had worked very closely together in 1971 with Haksar meeting Bangladeshi 'freedom fighters' in Mitra's house. Mitra had also persuaded a reluctant Haksar to become chairman of ISI's Governing Council in October 1973.

In his diary entry, Tandon mentions Haksar's aversion to joining Indira Gandhi's cabinet as a minister. This is quite curious. He had drafted numerous speeches for Indira Gandhi to deliver in forums of the Congress party. He had drafted numerous resolutions that were adopted by various conventions of the Congress party. He moved in political circles. Yet, he avoided an overtly political role—although as a civil servant he was as political as could be and even more. Haksar was to allude to this dichotomy in his thinking in a letter he wrote on 28 October 1987 to Gisella Bonn, the German cultural figure who had been close to both Indira Gandhi and him. He confided:

> ... One fixed invariable principle I have always followed. It is not to enter the political arena under any circumstances.

Six years earlier to this letter while delivering a lecture at the JNU in New Delhi he had said:

> Most of my working life has been spent as a member of the bureaucracy. And I remain an unrepentant bureaucrat ... I have of course some understanding of what politics is about. Sometimes, I even flatter myself with the thought that I understand the essence and substance of political processes. I have also some feeling for history. *But when I contemplate the*

aggregate behaviour pattern of politicians in general and, more specially, of politicians in our country, I have a desire to fight even more strongly for my identity as a bureaucrat. [italics mine]

In many ways Haksar's life demonstrates how to be intensely political in the best, ideological sense of the term without necessarily being a full-time elected politician—which was Haksar's for the asking.

There could well have been one more reason for Haksar to rejoin the government full-time and this is alluded to in Tandon's diary entry of 19 March 1975. He writes:

> Seshan said ... [Haksar] had agreed to become the Deputy Chairman of the Planning Commission on the specific condition that the PM would rein in the activities of the coterie at her house.

N.K. Seshan was one of the key private secretaries to Indira Gandhi and had been with Nehru as well. To be sure, it would have been Haksar who would have told Seshan this, since it couldn't have been the prime minister herself.

Haksar got hundreds of letters from all over the country on his appointment. People from different walks of life congratulated him. L.K. Jha wrote from Srinagar on 9 January: 'You have taken over the stewardship of the Planning Commission at a most critical time ... I know that you will devote yourself to this task with the same dedication that you have tackled so many other problems.' A few days later he received a letter from Bombay:

> I have read just now about your appointment as Deputy Chairman of the Planning Commission. Teji and I are happy at your return to active life after your temporary retirement. A useful man is never allowed to retire ... We expect something original and practical and beneficial for the country from your past experience in various fields and your efficiency and responsibility. We know you will be able to do more than expected from you ... I must also congratulate the P.M. on her wise choice.

This was from his friend from Allahabad days and one-time colleague in the Ministry of External Affairs between 1955 and 1960—Harivansh Rai Bachchan, the father of the Bollywood superstar Amitabh Bachchan.

The job of deputy chairman of the Planning Commission itself was tailor-made for Haksar and it was no longer necessary for him to remain in the background. He used the 'bully pulpit' that the position offered to travel across the country and speak to different audiences on issues close to his heart. These included deepening land reforms and expanding irrigation, strengthening scientific and technological capabilities, building scientific temper, stimulating growth in poor states like Uttar Pradesh and Bihar and accelerating industrial development through better management of the public sector. I think that while he may have enjoyed the power of the prime minister's Secretariat, he really came into his own in the Planning Commission. He worked with only two members—Sukhamoy Chakravarty, widely regarded as India's pre-eminent economic theorist and B. Sivaraman, who had played a key role in making the Green Revolution a reality. He encouraged a number of younger economists to work in the Planning Commission and some of them were to go on and make a name for themselves—Yoginder Alagh, Vijay Kelkar and Nitin Desai being three such persons. Arun Shourie almost became a fourth. People who worked in the Planning Commission then recall that one of PNH's main achievements then was to protect the institutional integrity of the Planning Commission and make it more responsive to the requests being made by state governments. There is evidence to show that the public investment programme in key sectors like infrastructure began a revival from the mid-1970s onward. Quite apart from all this, his office and home became a meeting point for all those opposed to the Emergency. Arun Shourie wrote to Haksar from Washington DC on 26 November 1975 sending him a paper he had written that was extremely critical of the Emergency saying:

> I am sending it because of the esteem in which I hold you and because I look upon you as one of the last dykes, as one of the last influences for restraint and civility.

ॐ

On 12 February 1975, a little over a month after he had assumed charge in the Planning Commission, Haksar was back in the Allahabad High Court after a gap of 28 years. But this time the role was different—he was now a witness appearing on behalf of Indira Gandhi in an election petition that had been filed against her four years earlier. Indira Gandhi had won her seat by a huge margin in the 1971 mid-term elections but her opponent, Raj Narain, had taken her to court on various grounds of corrupt electoral practices. After some twists and turns between the High Court and the Supreme Court, the case was back in the High Court and hearings had begun. The verdict was finally pronounced by Justice Jagmohan Lal Sinha on 12 June 1975 and it was this verdict that was to result in the imposition of the Emergency a fortnight later. It has since been described as 'The Case That Shook India'. Ironically, on 25 February 1972, Haksar had advised the prime minister to clear Sinha's appointment as a judge of the Allahabad High Court along with six others.

It is now all but forgotten that Justice Sinha actually acquitted Indira Gandhi of four charges but held her guilty of two violations of the law. First, that special rostrums had been constructed special power connections had been provided by state government officials for the use of Indira Gandhi in her election meetings. Second, that a government official in her Secretariat, Yashpal Kapoor, had assisted her in her election campaign. Prashant Bhushan, the noted lawyer attended the hearings (his father was appearing for Raj Narain) and has written a book on the case based on the proceedings that took place.[3] Much of what I have to say about Haksar's role is from Bhushan's account supplemented by entries in Tandon's diary.

Haksar was directly concerned with the second charge. The facts are complicated but I have tried to simplify them. Kapur was an officer on special duty in the prime minister's Secretariat who met Haksar on 13 January 1971 with his resignation letter seeking immediate release. Haksar accepted the resignation orally and Kapoor started campaigning. But the office order, accepting the resignation with effect from 14 January 1971, was issued only on 25 January 1971. Justice Sinha held that Kapoor's resignation was effective only from 25 January 1971 and so he was guilty of campaigning for Indira Gandhi for a period of 11 days while drawing a salary from the Government of India.

In his testimony Haksar revealed that he had taken charge as deputy chairman of the Planning Commission on 4 January 1975 on a verbal order of the PM—meaning that the actual office order was issued much later after he had joined. He said that accepting resignations or making appointments orally was not uncommon for temporary government servants—the former definitely more so than the latter. On cross-examination by Shanti Bhushan, Haksar replied that 'he was not aware of any rule under which it was permissible to make appointments by word of mouth, but claimed that it was known that every appointing authority could appoint a person and terminate his services orally'.

What does Tandon have to say about Haksar's testimony? His diary entry of 24 February 1975 has this:

> ... Some problems have cropped up in the PM's election case after the evidence tendered by Haksar who has deposed that he was authorized to accept Yashpal Kapoor's resignation. He said that he did not, therefore, consider it necessary to consult the PM and accepted the resignation. But this is not the correct position and it has to be rectified ... It would be dangerous to place all the papers relating to the Kapoor resignation before the court as that would weaken the PM's case ... Kapoor's resignation had actually been sent on 25 January but it was shown to have been received on the 13th or the 14th ...

His entry for 17 March 1975 continues with the matter:

> ... She [Indira Gandhi] is preparing for testimony at home ... I was entrusted with the task of drafting a reply for the PM about Kapoor's resignation keeping in view Haksar's testimony [which] was wrong ... After a lot of thinking we prepared an answer as follows:
>
> > 'I do not know the procedural technicalities. Ministers can choose their personal staff either from the service or from outside. Sometime in early 1971, Shri Kapoor sought my permission to resign from the post of OSD. I allowed him to do so and asked him to contact the secretary for further action.'
>
> We were told later that the PM's lawyers had accepted it.

Indira Gandhi herself testified on 18 March 1975 and part of her cross-examination by Bhushan was as follows:

Counsel: Can you recall any instance in which you have asked any person to take charge of any post before an order appointing him to that post was made in writing and signed by the relevant authority?

Mrs Gandhi: I do not recall any such instance.

Counsel: Are you aware of any rule authorizing the Secretary-in-Charge of your Secretariat to appoint a person as officer on special duty in your Secretariat?

Mrs. Gandhi: I am not aware of any rule investing such authority in the Secretary, but I am also not aware of any rule contrary to it. I have always functioned on the basis that my Secretary was competent to make such appointments.

Indira Gandhi further revealed that Kapoor was paid his salary only for the period ending on 13 January 1971 and that he did not attend the Secretariat from 14 January 1971 onwards. She also confirmed that Haksar had told her that Kapoor had resigned on 13 January 1971.

However, all this did not impress the judge one bit and Haksar's oversight in not accepting Kapoor's resignation in writing at the very moment it was submitted doomed Indira Gandhi. Some months later, on 15 June 1975, Tandon was to record this in his diary:

> The truth is that Kapoor had submitted his resignation only on 25 January but had backdated it to 13 January. Action was taken on it only on the 25th. The official noting makes it clear that there was nothing to suggest that its acceptance had been mooted before the 25th. The noting is followed by the signatures of two officials and then by Haksar's. He accepted the noting and if the resignation had been accepted on the 13th-14th, he would have written so on the file. But he wrote no such thing and signed the file.

A case could be made for perjury as well by Haksar to defend Indira Gandhi in light of Tandon's diary entry. How could a man with such high standards of personal probity do such a thing? That Haksar was defending Indira Gandhi goes to the heart of the relationship between him and her.

But this was not all. Tandon's diaries also have an entry dated 9 December 1989 in his second volume which he has incorporated in his normal entry of 26 September 1975, and which he also mentions in the introduction to the first volume. It makes for depressing reading:

> After a long time I went to meet Haksar Saheb in his house. He was sitting alone in his room ... When he heard a sound and asked who is it, I told him my name upon which he became emotional and standing up, embraced me. When we were talking Siddharth Shankar Ray's wife Maya Ray walked in ... Haksar was in a mood to talk. He talked about Maya Ray's father (who was a doctor in London). Then the talk came around to Indira Gandhi and Rajiv. Haksar began to criticize them very unhappily ... He said, 'Maya I have seen the mother and son hitting their own wickets'. But I am mentioning this meeting in the Diary for a totally different reason. There is an indication in various places in the Diary that the judges of the Supreme Court had been approached by Indira Gandhi's side in her case. The general belief is that either Haksar or Gokhale [law minister] did it. Today, Haksar himself confirmed it to Maya Ray. He told her 'Maya this was really not necessary. Indira Gandhi had herself disposed of the case against her through amendments to the Constitution [that Haksar had opposed in the Cabinet as recorded by Tandon]. But I was forced to go to every judge'.

Tandon's diary entry that Haksar suborned judges at Indira Gandhi's behest was to be confirmed by A.G. Noorani who reviewed Tandon's first volume.[4] On 7 November 1975, five judges iof the Supreme Court led by chief justice A.N. Ray unanimously overturned Sinha's judgement, exonerated Indira Gandhi of the two corrupt practices and upheld her election. Noorani mentions that Haksar had told him about this. This is indeed most troubling and casts Haksar in poor light. One of the five judges incidentally was M.H. Beg, who had been with Haksar at Lincoln's Inn between 1938 and 1941 and had stayed in close touch sharing the same ideological beliefs. Beg himself was to become chief justice under controversial circumstances in January 1977.

Even from the Planning Commission Haksar would continue with his old habit of bombarding Indira Gandhi with notes on various topics. On 26 February 1975, he sent one such 'missile' to her:

I have some knowledge about the character and competence of Administrative Service (IAS) officers in the cadres of the various States of India and though I avoid taking interest in transfers and postings of officers, quite a few officers tend to come and see me ... In the course of one such recent meeting, I was alarmed to learn that a very unhealthy situation is being allowed to develop around the question of who should be the Chief Secretary of Gujarat. I could understand if the controversy were to centre around the capability and character of the officers concerned; unfortunately, the controversy has been political and it is being argued that the State Government of Gujarat should have a Gujarati Chief Secretary ...

Indian Administrative Service is an All India Service. If we examine the composition of various State cadres, we would find that in every State there is a fair mix of people. This is as it should be. Otherwise, we might as well abolish the All India Services and have only State services. Therefore, if one advocates that Gujarat must have a Gujarati Chief Secretary, he should understand the implications of such an advocacy to the maintenance of integrity of All India Services ...

May I take this opportunity of reminding PM that Bihar continues to fester and that MP is about to become explosive. Urgent attention needs to be given to both these States. [italics mine]

On 22 March 1975, Haksar sent another one of his brainwaves to the prime minister which was to trigger a process of transformation of one of India's oldest scientific organisations. The Indian Meteorological Department (IMD) had been started by the British in 1875 and some great names had been associated with it. But IMD had fallen on lean times. Haksar got interested in the revival of meteorological research, telling the prime minister:

I hope P.M. would let me invite attention, from time to time to certain basic problems which, though not strictly connected with planning, impinge upon our capacity to plan. This note is concerned with a sadly neglected area, viz., of Indian meteorology ...

Meteorology has been congealed in a governmental department—the Indian Meteorological Department. This year the Department will be 100 years old. This is, at present, under the Ministry of Civil Aviation and Tourism. Why? Obviously, because, historically speaking, while providing information for aircraft operations, meteorology provided the necessary data on winds at various altitudes, thunder-storms, visibility near ground, etc. Whatever the reasons there might have been for linking the Department of Meteorology with the Ministry of Civil Aviation, these are no longer valid ...

Today, the science of meteorology is growing very fast all over the world ... In the context of the requirements of our country, the Department of Meteorology must concern itself with agriculture, hydro-electric systems and with floods, droughts and cyclones ...

We need to achieve greater understanding of the operations of our climatic and weather systems which has such a vital impact on the need for increasing food and energy demands for our growing population. *Indian meteorology must study in depth the possibilities of climatic changes with possible serious repercussions on a great variety of aspects of our economic life* ... [italics mine]

Haksar was thus concerned with 'climatic change' way back in 1975. It is no exaggeration to say that the process of restructuring the century-old IMD and giving it the latest scientific and technological thrust began with this note, but the process took very long. It was to culminate in its transfer from the Ministry of Civil Aviation to the Ministry of Science and Technology and in its acquisition of high-power computing facilities by the mid-1980s.

On 3 April 1975, Haksar was informed that he would chair a committee to look at the defence expenditure plan for the next four years 'in the light of threat perceptions and the economic situation of the country'. The committee was unusual in its composition having as it did the cabinet secretary, secretary to the prime minister, foreign secretary, finance secretary, the air force, army and navy chiefs, apart from a few others like G. Parthasarathi, who was then chairman of the Policy Planning Division of the Ministry of External Affairs. Since time was of the essence, Haksar volunteered to submit the committee's recommendations at the earliest. On 9 July 1975, he wrote to Defence Minister Swaran Singh, sending him the report:

... In the course of very detailed studies conducted by the Committee, I personally became aware of several problems affecting our defence and I am taking the liberty of mentioning these to you ...

As much as 60 per cent of the expenditure on our Armed Forces is consumed by salary, rations, clothings, etc. In the course of my discussions with the Chiefs of the Defence Services, I expressed my anxiety about such a dysfunctional system. The firepower and the manpower do not get integrated in a cost-effective manner. I was encouraged by the fact that the Service Chiefs were not insensitive to the problem ... I trust this matter will be pursued ...

In the body of the Report we have expressed no doubt sotto voce, our concern at the state of defence production. I am not inhibited in this letter in saying that our country's economy cannot live with the way defence production is organized. Something urgent needs to be done about it. And what applies to defence production, applies equally to the defence R&D. *I shall also be failing in my duty if I did not record my sense of horror at the way we have been handling the entire field of aeronautics and missiles. This sense of horror is, if anything, heightened by the knowledge that we have in this country men of extraordinary competence and talent who are dispersed all over the place and are, therefore, wasted.*

Although the Report faithfully reproduces the concept of "subsidiary threats", frankly I have not followed its relevance, Either these threats are real enough to be taken into account in our defence preparedness or they are in the nature of padding for jacking up the demands of our Navy and of our Air Force ... The only problem which these so-called subsidiary threats pose are in the realm of diplomacy and I have no doubt that appropriate effort would be made to neutralize such threats ... [italics mine]

Swaran Singh expressed appreciation for Haksar's efforts at producing the report in just about three months. On 19 September 1975, the Cabinet Committee on Political Affairs gave its approval to the report and also discussed Haksar's letter to Swaran Singh. Reorganization of defence production and defence R&D was to be taken up in right earnest immediately after that. That the prime minister continued to trust Haksar's judgment on defence matters is also evident from a letter that the chief of the air force, Air Chief Marshal O.P. Mehra, had written to him a little while earlier on 9 March 1975:

> I called on the PM on Friday 7 March 1975 and mentioned a few points. She wants me to discuss the same with you.

∼

In April 1975, Indira Gandhi moved decisively to integrate Sikkim into the Indian Union. Inevitably, she was both applauded and criticized for it. P.N.Dhar was to have a chapter on it in his account of his tenure with Indira Gandhi,[5] but he failed to mention that Haksar had started serious thinking on the future of Sikkim way back in 1970 itself. On 28 November 1970, Haksar had sent a note to Foreign Secretary (FS) T.N. Kaul while keeping the prime minister informed:

> I had suggested to F.S. that we should carefully consider and review the underlying assumptions of our policy in Sikkim. We have had several meetings. Broadly, two points of view have crystallised themselves:-
>
> (i) *that our economic, social and political policies must be designed to involve the people of Sikkim, so that they feel that their destiny lies with India. Our instruments for such a policy should also be carefully chosen ...*
>
> (ii) that having regard to our policies in the past and what we have done in Bhutan, there is really no escape from leading Sikkim to a stage where it becomes a sovereign, independent State tied up with India.
>
> My own preference is for the first alternative. Be that as it may, we have to deal, for the time being, with the Chogyal. He is going to impress upon us the need to let Sikkim exercise greater autonomy and responsibility. He will stress as his reasons: the restiveness of his educated classes, particularly the young, under the influence of the spirit of our times and India's own anti-colonial ideals; the infectiousness of developments in Nepal and Bhutan; and the dangers of resentments growing if the natural aspirations of the Sikkimese to do more on their own is denied ...
>
> The pressures for change really centre around him and are sufficiently

manageable without any basic concessions on our part. P.M. might take the following line with him …

The existing relationship has been as helpful to Sikkim as to India. Where we have been found insufficiently considerate or overly restrictive, we are prepared to have a fresh look and meet all genuine grievances not only sympathetically but also generously. But grievances should not be manufactured or harboured till they become disproportionate—least of all by those elements in Sikkim, the ruling hierarchy, who owe their whole position to the Indian presence. We have an impeccable record of not interfering in Sikkim's domestic politics, and we have relied scrupulously on him alone. We always wish to do this and he should look upon us as his active supporter. The pressures he feels from his educated elite are very understandable and we should like to help him meet them. They cannot be met by giving in to illusions about Sikkim becoming free, prosperous and neutral like an Asian Switzerland if only India would relax its hold …

… We should exhort the Chogyal to create a feeling of mutual trust and confidence instead of subjecting us to one manoeuvre or another and to pressures of various kinds … [italics mine]

Without doubt, this note was to trigger a change in Indira Gandhi's approach to the Chogyal. He had been a protégé of her father and she herself had a fond personal relationship with him. But she could be unemotional when larger national interests were involved.

Two years later, Haksar was to take this forward and fire a second salvo that was to lead to Indira Gandhi's actions in April 1975. This is what he had told the prime minister on 14 March 1972:

I try to keep track of the goings on in the Ministry of External Affairs. The Foreign Secretary had spoken to me about his visit to Sikkim. But I have long felt that we really have no policy in regard to Sikkim except to wait upon Chogyal's varying moods. The Foreign Secretary says that he found him "in a chastened mood". With great respect, this makes no sense to me …

There was a time in 1947 when the people of Sikkim were with India. Thereafter, we developed great fondness for the Sikkim Darbar and now we wait on his frowns and on his smiles…

I tried at one stage to organize some serious thinking about our policy towards Sikkim. Nothing came out of it. The basic question is what are sanctions behind "Permanent Association" or "Protectorate" or anything else? In this later half of the twentieth century, a sanction behind any political framework has to be people if that framework is to prove durable. And we have totally alienated the people of Sikkim…

We had a similar sort of policy towards Nepal of alternating between Pro-consulars's stances and abject subjection to His Majesty. Until about a year and a half ago, we succeeded in restoring to our policy in Nepal a semblance of rationality …

We must not delude ourselves. The Chogyal wants independence, a membership of the United Nations and he is gradually eroding our will…

My own view is that until such time as P.M. has made up her mind, she should not see the Chogyal in order to put a seal to the so-called "Permanent Association". *In my view, we are not so utterly helpless. We can make a new beginning. We can establish contact with the people of Sikkim, develop relationship and earn their goodwill and use that as a real lever against the vagaries of the Chogyal. If we decide on such a policy, I have no doubt that in the space of two years we shall get the Chogyal running to us for protection against his own people. Otherwise, he will be taking us out for a ride all the time.* [italics mine]

In this cold-blooded note, Haksar was wrong on the time it would take for the Chogyal to change his approach. It was not two years as Haksar had predicted, but it took three years. But, by that time it was too late and he had burnt all his bridges with Indira Gandhi. For the moment, the prime minister agreed with the broad approach that Haksar had delineated. Three months later he was at it again and, on 1 May 1972, he made his views known once again to the prime minister before a meeting of the Political Affairs Committee of the Cabinet:

> … It is true that we do not like having the only Protectorate in Asia, and it might well suit our interests to meet the aspirations of the Sikkimese people. It is, however, doubtful whether they want independence rather than democracy. The latter would endanger the Chogyal's position, while giving him independence would endanger the people's aspirations for democracy. He has always shown absolutist tendencies …

... The Chogyal has been very careful not to support us on our problem with China in a way that might antagonize Peking. Even on Pakistan, his support to us has been very lukewarm ... Such caution in relation to China and Pakistan indicates a desire to play off these Powers against us as Nepal has been doing.

... P.M. has repeatedly advised the Chogyal to mend his anti-Indian ways, but I am not aware of any improvement. Partly this is our fault, since the Dewan we have given him plays the courtier instead of giving him good advice, but essentially it is the Chogyal's own approach to extract concessions by creating difficulties for us. Before we agree to any treaty revision, therefore, we should first try to prevail upon him to create a more harmonious working relationship.

At this stage we should tell him we are not averse to the type of changes he has suggested, and would be glad to help him achieve Sikkimese aspirations, but these must be based on two realities:

(i) *Sikkim is militarily vulnerable without India's military presence; and*

(ii) *Sikkim also has domestic stresses which only an Indian presence can contain.*

These weaknesses expose Sikkim to interference from China and possibly Nepal. Since such interference would harm his interests more than India's, we both need to maintain a relationship which allows us to protect Sikkim from external military pressure and domestic political instability. We need assurance that a partial revision of the treaty would not lead to a further demand a few years hence for a total revision which would exclude us totally from Sikkim ... If he does not agree, we should tell him that we are working over his draft to try and make it safeguard our rights and interests against unilateral erosion ... [italics mine]

In the face of this reasoning by Haksar, the Ministry of External Affairs's proposal to review the 1950 Treaty between India and Sikkim stood no chance of acceptance. Haksar proved to be an early hardliner on Sikkim when many in the government and outside were urging Indira Gandhi to find a way of accommodating the Chogyal. But on three occasions—once in 1970 and twice in 1972—Haksar would have none of it, and contributed profoundly to Indira Gandhi's thinking on this subject. In his approach to Sikkim he had been influenced by Shankar Bajpai, who was India's political officer in the kingdom for four years beginning September 1970, and who was always in close contact with Haksar. Their relationship was personal as well. Shankar Bajpai's father Girija Shankar Bajpai had recruited Haksar into the IFS in 1948.

Although he was in the Planning Commission, visiting dignitaries would call on him even if their visits were purely political. Thus it was on 19 May 1975, that a Pakistani delegation headed by Agha Shahi, the foreign secretary, came to meet Haksar. The record of that meeting has this:

> Mr. Shahi began the talks by saying that since he was leaving for Pakistan next morning, he wanted to pay his respects to the man who was the prime mover at Simla for the new Indo-Pak relationship as embodied in the Simla Agreement.
>
> Mr Haksar said that he was merely an instrument chosen by the Prime Minister. He said that he remained deeply committed to the conviction that internal conditions and external circumstances leave no choice for India and Pakistan to have any relationship except that of normalization and that of growth of trust and confidence on an objective basis.

After the initial pleasantries, Shahi got down to business and said that Pakistan was herself deeply disturbed by the Indian prime minister's statement that 'Pakistan is terrorizing Afghanistan', and the Indian foreign minister's statement that 'Pakistan is being belligerent towards Afghanistan'. Haksar responded initially in somewhat polemical fashion by noting that if Pakistan believes that India had nothing to fear from it, surely India is justified in telling Pakistan that it should be relaxed about Afghanistan. But continuing in a more serious way, he denied that India was encouraging or supporting Afghanistan in any manner as far as self-determination questions are concerned. Reiterating that India was for a bilateral negotiated solution of the problems between Pakistan and Afghanistan, Haksar continued:

He [Haksar] referred to Pakistan's pre-occupation with the question of self-determination in Kashmir. He said that there was a firm understanding at Simla about Kashmir but that it is now being said that the internal opinion in Pakistan cannot get reconciled to that understanding ...

Mr. Shahi ... said it is difficult for the people in Pakistan to forget 1971 when half of Pakistan was lacerated. Shri Haksar responded that ... India paid a heavy price for Pakistan's lacerations. He added that India added no salt to the lacerations but at Simla applied a healing balm of these lacerations. Even on the delicate issue of POWs India went out of her way to accommodate Pakistan.

The conversation covered other areas of bilateral concern. This was to be the last time Haksar interacted with an official Pakistani team from an official position. Although he was no longer directly in the foreign policy loop, the fact that Agha Shahi had requested to meet him reflected Haksar's special position vis-à-vis Indira Gandhi, and the perception was that he still counted for something.

12 June 1975 was a horrible day for Indira Gandhi and Haksar. It was not only the day that Justice Sinha's verdict came but the morning had begun with the death of D.P. Dhar in New Delhi at the age of 57. Pant had gone at 52 and Mohan Kumaramangalam had died at 55, both in 1973 and within three months of each other. Haksar's immediate 'left' circle in government seemed to have been jinxed.

The Emergency was declared, on 26 June 1975, and civil liberties began to get curtailed drastically. Much has been written about it and I will not add to the literature.[6] What is of direct relevance to this book is what happened less than a month later—on 15 July 1975 to be precise. This was the day when Haksar's 82-year-old uncle Inderbhai, who had been his benefactor since the 1930s, was arrested most decidedly on the orders of Sanjay Gandhi. A decade of pique at Haksar's well-meaning advice given in London to continue studying, five years of fury at Haksar's well-intentioned advice given to his mother to get him to abandon his car project and five months of anger at Haksar's testimony that had got his mother into serious legal trouble finally must have given Sanjay Gandhi enough cause for hitting at Haksar where it hurt most.

Urmila Haksar was to later write a book describing what Haksar and his family had to go through for over two years.[7] It makes for sordid reading even 40 years after the episode. Pandit Brothers had started in Chandni Chowk in New Delhi in 1927 and had later opened a showroom in Connaught Place in New Delhi. Initially it was a dealer for products made by Bombay Dyeing, an old and well-known Bombay-based textile company. Later Pandit Brothers had diversified into home furnishings and other such material; 80 per cent of Pandit Brothers was owned by Haksar's uncle, 10 per cent by Haksar's sister and 10 per cent by his wife.

On the morning of 15 July 1975, Haksar's uncle and 78-year-old brother-in-law had been arrested on the grounds that Pandit Brothers had been indulging in malpractices. D.P. Singh, a Rajya Sabha MP from Bihar and an intimate part of Haksar's circle met Indira Gandhi at around 10:35 am. She initially told him that the arrests must have had happened due to some valid reason. After a few minutes of Singh's entreaties, she spoke to the lieutenant governor of Delhi, Kishan Chand, and assured Singh that the prosecution would not oppose bail in this case. After considerable tension and drama both in the police station and in the court, by 4:30 pm the two elderly gentlemen were released on provisional bail for 24 hours. All through the day, Haksar sat in the Planning Commission office refusing to intervene in any way, leaving the entire matter in D.P. Singh's hands.

The next morning, the newspaper headlines had news of the arrest for 'gross violation of price tagging system on the items in their shop'. However, D.P. Singh went to court and succeeded in getting the provisional bail extended indefinitely. That same evening Urmila Haksar wrote:

> My husband came back from office looking tense and angry. He dropped down in a chair. "There was a Cabinet meeting. I am coming from there straight. I was sitting just opposite Mrs. Gandhi and all through the meeting I was staring at her. She would not meet my eyes and kept her gaze averted."

But while indefinite bail was given, the tax authorities swung into action immediately and reopened the income tax returns of Pandit Brothers for the past eight years. In addition, Pandit Brothers was being booked under the Monopolies and Restrictive Trade Practices (MRTP) Act, 1969 that, ironically, Haksar had helped make a reality. On 25 August 1975, Urmila Haksar as one of the partners was to be arrested. Haksar was away in Geneva attending a meeting of the International Civil Service Commission of the United Nations membership of which his old colleague, Foreign Secretary Kewal Singh, had with the prime minister's backing, literally cajoled him into accepting.[8]

Even if PNH were in New Delhi he would have been of little use since he had steadfastly refused to intervene in the travails of Pandit Brothers. Again, D.P. Singh came to the rescue and went straight to Indira Gandhi and told her that Haksar's wife may refuse to take bail and prefer to sit in Tihar Jail. The prime minister got the arrest stalled but Haksar's residence was searched twice. He bore all this with stoic silence attending Cabinet meetings chaired by the prime minister and opposing proposals coming to the Cabinet to amend the Constitution to consolidate the Emergency, and pass laws to deal with the consequences of Justice Sinha's verdict, as Tandon's diary entries of 20 July and 30 July 1975 reveal.

On 1 July 1975, just five days after the Emergency was declared, Indira Gandhi broadcast to the nation and announced a 20-point programme that 'promised to use the government's sweeping new powers to enforce longstanding policies for basic social change'. Ideas and suggestions had come from various quarters, including political parties like the CPI, and Haksar had been involved in the discussions. Unlike in 1969 when he was the pivot, this time around Haksar was just one of the many participants. But on one controversial issue, his views prevailed. The original 20-point programme had included nationalization of the textile industry as part of its agenda. This idea had come from the CPI and some Congressmen. What happened to it has been described by Mohit Sen, then very much a part of the CPI:[9]

> She [Indira Gandhi] had sent a copy of the address she planned to make
> to announce the twenty-point programme to Bhupesh Gupta and Haksar

in which the nationalization of the textile industry was included. The CPI leaders decided to consult Haksar privately. Rajeswara Rao [CPI general secretary] and Bhupesh Gupta met him in R.K. Garg's house. I was taken along by the General Secretary ... As far as I remember, P.N. Dhar was there ... Haksar dominated the proceedings and vehemently opposed the nationalization proposal. He said it would only add economic adventurism to political adventurism which the Emergency was. Rajeswara Rao supported the proposal ... In the end it was decided that the two separate responses in the names of those who made them should be sent to Indira Gandhi. It was Haksar's opinion that eventually prevailed.

Haksar had opposed nationalization of the textile mills way back in 1967 as well showing that he was not a dogmatic ideologue. He was certainly one of the prime movers of the nationalization of the general insurance, coal and oil refineries in 1972 but his approach was nuanced. As far as the CPI was concerned he could be wicked as well: when it had supported non-Congress coalitions called Samyukta Vidhayak Dal in some states after the 1967 elections, he told Mohit Sen that the CPI was then going through a 'Samyukta VD' phase.

Actually, there is very strong evidence to suggest that Indira Gandhi's 20-point programme had been derived in large part from a note of Haksar that had been sent to her a day *before* her announcement. In this note of 30 June 1975, Haksar told the prime minister:

> ... I would submit that the Prime Minister to send for the Chief Ministers and place before them the following programme with all the earnestness and authority that she commands:
> 1. Revision of agricultural wages.
> 2. Moratorium on private and non-institutional debts and debt-obligations of the rural poor—small and marginal farmers ands landless labour.
> 3. Abolition of Bonded Labour.
> 4. Declare that no tenant or sharecropper need vacate the land held in his possession whether such possession is recorded or unrecorded.
> 5. Direct all states to summarily evict ineligible encroachers on

government vacant land, gaon samaj land and other vested land and assign the released land to the landless poor.

6. Confer complete security of tenure in respect of homestead lands on which scheduled castes, artisans and agricultural labour have built dwellings.

7. Direction to States to implement the new round of ceiling legislation, passed after 1971, in a time-bound and once-for-all manner.

8. Special measures to strengthen peasant economy and new institutional assistance to small and marginal farmers.

9. Creation of a separate agency for providing credit and other development assistance to scheduled castes, scheduled tribes, and other sections of the rural poor.

10. Expansion of public distribution through better procurement of cereals and increased coverage of vulnerable sections.

It is indeed ironic that a man so deeply opposed to the Emergency, and who was soon to be its victim as well, had contributed so heavily to Indira Gandhi's very first major initiative after the declaration of the Emergency. Incidentally, Haksar was not present at the Cabinet meeting at 6 a.m. on 26 June 1975, when Indira Gandhi merely informed her ministerial colleagues that the Emergency was being imposed. He was away in Himachal Pradesh on his way back to Chandigarh that day. Would he have known about plans to impose the Emergency? This question is difficult to answer. It is true that his close friend Siddhartha Shankar Ray was the principal author of the move but the entire operation was executed secretly. Would he have opposed it in the Cabinet meeting? He would, most probably, have done so and made his views known but would not have resigned, as later events demonstrated.

The Emergency has been in force for about three months. Haksar had undergone considerable humiliation in that period. But while his family had been harassed, he had steadfastly refused to intervene. On the morning of 10 September 1975, Tirath Ram Amla, a senior and respected Congress leader from Jammu and Kashmir, had met the prime minister. His daughter was married to D.P. Dhar's son. What had transpired in that meeting was recorded that very night by Tandon in his diary:

> Tirath Ram said he had explained to the PM that the rigours of the Emergency should be lessened step-by-step and at an appropriate moment a programme should be worked out to do away with the Emergency altogether. She should take the assistance of an exceptionally capable man to complete these tasks. In this connection, he suggested the name of Haksar. The PM reacted adversely. She criticized Haksar and said that he made no efforts to understand other people's point of view. He was too rigid in his likes and dislikes. He would not be suitable for this task. Tirath Ram inferred from the PM's talk that Haksar was not in agreement with the Emergency and therefore the PM did not want to turn to him for assistance.

Clearly by then, even though Haksar had access to Indira Gandhi and attended Cabinet meetings where he spoke his mind freely and boldly, and even though she would call in him for conversations, a huge trust deficit had arisen between the two. He was certainly heard but not listened to and his advice not acted upon, unlike the early years of her prime ministership.

The tenth convocation of the ISI took place on 21 December 1975 in Calcutta. Haksar's old boss Subimal Dutt was elected president of the institute in place of Satyendra Nath Bose of Bose–Einstein statistics fame who had passed away. Haksar continued to be chairman. After the convocation was over, Dutt and Haksar had a quiet conversation which was recorded by the former in his diary that remains unpublished but that was made available to me by his grand-daughter:

> I had a quiet talk with Haksar. He said he was not consulted by Mrs G on matters of policy. ("If any impediment was placed in my way as Dy Chairman of the Planning Commission I would immediately resign"). Mrs G's principal concern is her own personal position. She wants 200 percent loyalty—not hundred percent from everybody and had surrounded herself with men of straw like Bansi Lal, P.C. Sethi.

Everybody, whether a politician, civil servant, businessman or industrialist will be judged by personal loyalty to herself.

Altogether it was a depressing account.

∾

In February 1976, Indira Gandhi had set up a committee of the Congress party to suggest further amendments to the Constitution to meet socio-economic challenges. In the background was also the debate that had been generated on the need for switching from a parliamentary system to a Presidential form of government. The debate had been triggered by B.K. Nehru, and political leaders like A.R. Antulay and V.P Sathe had taken up the cause. The committee was headed by veteran Congressman Swaran Singh and had all the leading lights of the left brigade as its members—Rajni Patel, A.R. Antulay, V.P. Sathe, K.P. Unnikrishnan, Siddhartha Shankar Ray, D.K. Barooah, and others. One member was D.P. Singh, a daily visitor at PNH's house and the man who had intervened on his family's behalf with the prime minister when they were being harassed in July and August 1975. It is through Singh that Haksar would keep in touch with the committee's deliberations.

One issue that particularly bothered Haksar related to Article 226 of the Constitution which gave authority to High Courts to issue writs. This was seen by many, including the PM, as a hindrance to the faster implementation of 'progressive' policies and programmes. Influential members of the Swaran Singh committee argued for complete deletion of Article of 226 but the final report was cautious and 'recommended leaving intact their [High Courts' authority to issue writs for the protection of citizens' fundamental rights but removing their authority to issue prerogative writs for "any other purpose"'.[10] This was approved by the Congress Working Committee in May 1976 and thereafter remitted to the government for further action. In the Cabinet, there were still voices arguing for doing away with Article 226 altogether, and on 23 August 1976, Haksar revealed his thinking to the prime minister:

Naturally, I have no vested interest either in retaining Article 226 or in amending it one way or another. However, I do have interest that whatever decisions are taken are based firmly on facts and supported by logic.

The kind of discussion we have had on Article 226 left a very strong impression on my mind that not everyone has understood the problems involved and had not devoted time and attention to study the matter in depth.

It was, for instance, argued that since every law provides some remedy, a citizen should be left to pursue that remedy and that, consequently, there was no need for arming the High Court with writ jurisdiction. I had submitted that I could document cases after cases where, if a citizen were left to pursue the so-called "ordinary remedies", he will be driven completely crazy. *Also, if the baffling variety of executive functionaries which exist in our country were to know that their decisions can only be called into question by prolonged processes of law, then arbitrariness, vindictiveness, personal animus and variety of those numerous failings which erode every society would have a field day.* [italics mine]

Haksar told the prime minister that while he was 'not unaware of the fact that in matters of social legislation, the powers of the High Court should be limited so that the process of social change is not thwarted', elimination of Article 226 would severely impinge on the welfare of millions of ordinary citizens of the country. Putting two and two together, it was evident that he had used his close friend D.P. Singh to ensure that the 'hawks' like Antulay, Patel, Barooah and Ray in the Swaran Singh committee did not get their way in having Article 226 deleted altogether.

∾

By far the most important role Haksar played internationally in the year was as the Indian chairman of the India–USSR Joint Commission that had been set up to deepen the economic relationship between the two countries. Normally, a senior minister would have been appointed as the Indian chairman but Indira Gandhi asked Haksar to chair it to signal the personal importance she gave to Indo-Soviet ties.

Haksar was in the USSR in early-April 1976 for a series of meetings with various Soviet leaders, including Premier Alexei Kosygin and Nikolai Baibakov, Stalin's oil commissar and then head of Gosplan, the Soviet planning agency. The records of these meetings reveal the special warmth and respect Kosygin and his colleagues had for Indira Gandhi. The interaction with Kosygin was on 5 April 1976 and was conducted in a very personal manner.

> Mr. Kosygin: How is the Prime Minister?
>
> Shri Haksar: Very well ... Prime Minister has asked me to specially convey to you her warm regards ... She is keeping very well.
>
> Mr. Kosygin: We are expecting her visit to the USSR ... She expressed her intention to come in May ...
>
> Shri Haksar: When I was in Delhi, she was enquiring about spring in Moscow. I told her May would also be spring.
>
> Mr. Kosygin: At the end of May the temperature is more or less normal. Of course, sometimes nature pays no regard to wishes of Prime Ministers and Presidents. And then now no law really governs nature's behaviour.
>
> Shri Haksar: If I know my Prime Minister, she is not much bothered by climatic conditions.
>
> Mr.Kosygin: I know that. She wears very light clothes and shoes even when it is cold.
>
> Shri Haksar: She walks very fast.
>
> Mr. Kosygin: Yes, it is a good quality.
>
> Shri Haksar: But most of us who are lesser mortals have difficulty keeping pace with her.

After this banter, the discussion became substantive and ranged over a wide variety of subjects. Haksar admitted that in 'considerable parts of the country ... agrarian relations have not been modernized and that this is the central thrust of the prime minister's recent programme which emphasizes the need for land reforms, reduction of indebtedness, and prevention of fragmentation of land'. Kosygin on his part reassured Haksar, saying 'We see the constraints of the Indian economy. We have been trying to do our very best to help. And we would continue to do so ... We shall do our best.' The details of the bilateral relationship were dealt with in Haksar's meeting with Baibakov and they went over different sectors of the economy. Here too, there were bouts of informality, especially when Haksar told Baibakov that 'To be connected with planning in India requires nerves. That is my input—not competence but nerves.' The conversation ended with Haksar confessing 'I try hard to be a philosopher but cheerfulness keeps bursting through. Cheerfulness is an antidote to the depression of planners.' Baibakov couldn't have agreed more.

Haksar was able to negotiate Soviet support for the two steel plants at Bhilai and Bokaro as well as for an oil refinery at Mathura and for manufacturing mining equipment in India. He was very keen on getting the Soviets involved in building the aluminum industry in India and some progress was made in Moscow. But that did not go far, since a few years later India signed an agreement with a leading French company to develop the rich bauxite reserves in Orissa.

On 4 April 1976, when Haksar was in the USSR, the *New York Times Sunday Magazine* carried a long article titled 'India is as Indira Does'. It was written by J. Anthony Lukas and described the situation prevailing in India 10 months after the Emergency had been imposed. Lukas spoke of the rise of Sanjay Gandhi and how Haksar was Sanjay's 'particular rival'. He wrote:

> There has been bad blood between the two men for years, dating from the days when Haksar had to get Sanjay out of several youthful scrapes involving drink, cars and women. Most recently, Sanjay blamed Haksar for hostility to the Maruti project and for refusal to backdate a letter which would have legalized one of his mother's disputed election practices.
>
> So after the Emergency was declared, Sanjay and his associates decided to "send Haksar a message". The message was delivered by way of Haksar's uncle, Pandit Haksar who owns Pandit Brothers, a well-known New Delhi dry goods firm. One day, Government inspectors descended on the store's branch in Connaught Circus and conducted rigourous searches for improperly priced goods. When they failed to find anything,

they moved on the store's branch in the Chandni Chowk district and there, on the balcony, discovered some bed sheets with no price markings. On this technical violation alone, they promptly arrested 85-year-old Pandit Haksar and his partner. Only after strenuous protests from their friends, did Mrs. Gandhi herself get the pair released on bail. But P.N. Haksar got the message.

Haksar was outraged when he saw this article that was sent to him by Rikhi Jaipal, India's permanent representative to the United Nations in New York. He sent a long rejoinder taking great umbrage that Lukas had not spoken to him for his article. The rejoinder was published on 16 May 1976:

J. Anthony Lukas has reported that the judgment delivered by the Allahabad High Court against Prime Minister Indira Gandhi might have been different if a certain document had been backdated and that I refused to do so. There was never any question of doing this. I was myself a witness in the case and there was never any doubt about the validity of the resignation of the employee in question. Mr. Lukas might do well to study the judgment of the Hon. Mr. Justice Beg of the Supreme Court, who went into the facts of the case in detail.

There is another piece of gossip which Mr. Lukas retails when he mentions the alleged escapades of the Prime Minister's son [Sanjay] and my alleged involvement in getting him out of situations. I am amazed at such fictional writing without any substratum of truth.

Mr. Lukas also refers to the case of my uncle [who was arrested on a minor technical violation]. That matter was dealt with under the due process of law. And in one matter the Supreme Court itself gave a judgment in his favour; the counsel for the Government conceding the case in his favour. There was never any question of sending me a "message". I continue to perform my duties as the Deputy Chairman of the Planning Commission without any fear whatsoever of the Prime Minister as its Chairman.

During the long period of my service under both Jawaharlal Nehru and Mrs. Indira Gandhi, I have always had, and continue to have, the privilege of expressing my views with utmost freedom. So no "message" was sent and none has been received. [italics mine]

Lukas responded to Haksar's reply:

> Given the exigencies of life in India's new dictatorship, Mr. Haksar's
> denials do not surprise me. He could scarcely do otherwise if he wants
> to hold on to his job. I stand by the facts as reported in my story.

Lukas had obviously not done his homework on Haksar properly. Haksar
had to be coaxed into taking the Planning Commission job and his public
silence on the Emergency had nothing whatsoever to do with wanting to
'hold on to his job'. Whatever Haksar had to say to Indira Gandhi, he
would say to her face and he had been doing that for years.

The National Development Council (NDC), a deliberative body chaired
by the prime minister and comprising all chief ministers and some union
ministers, was having one of its periodic meetings in New Delhi in
September 1976. A few weeks earlier, Haksar sent Indira Gandhi a couple
of notes on Uttar Pradesh and Bihar—the states he said were crucial for
India's progress. These highlighted the development challenges as also the
political and administrative inadequacies there. He pointed to rampant
financial mismanagement which was stifling growth in these two most
populous states of the country. At the NDC meeting itself, on 25 September
1976, Haksar took a position that would not have been expected from a
left-wing ideologue that he was purported to be. He spoke of reducing
losses in power and irrigation projects which, in itself, was nothing out of
the ordinary. But he also went on to make a special plea for raising water
and power rates that were an anathema to the doctrinaire socialists in the
Congress. And once again, he harped on tenancy legislation and land
reforms. Haksar was an inveterate socialist but on financial matters he was
a conservative and believed in fiscal prudence as far as the exchequer was
concerned, as indeed Indira Gandhi herself did.

1977 was to be Haksar's last year in government and bring to an end three
decades of public service from within government in various capacities. He

had started life as a very junior official in 1947 and was to leave as someone who had enjoyed the rank of a full-fledged cabinet minister.

On 18 January 1977, Indira Gandhi had stunned everybody by announcing that elections would be held two months later and that some of the provisions of the Emergency were going to be lifted. This was completely unexpected as much as it was welcome. A couple of weeks later, in early-February 1977, she met with Haksar and the conversation between the two has been recounted in I.K. Gujral's memoirs based on what Haksar had told him on 19 March 1977. According to Gujral's account:[11]

> When she asked him what she should do under the circumstances [her senior colleague Jagjivan Ram had just left her to join the Opposition ranks, so this meeting must have been around 4 or 5 February 1977], Haksar had first suggested: *'Indiraji, first you get rid of this Emergency; it is of no use to you but it continues to be an uncomfortable issue'*. She had surprised him when she said in response: 'All my friends and supporters feel that there would be hardly any hope of [winning] the elections without the fear of the Emergency'. And his [other] suggestion was *'Please ask him [Sanjay] to live separately ... Now I say it once again, please send him away'*. Quoting from the epic Ramayana, he had pointed out: 'After all, even Ram had to stay in exile for fourteen years before he ascended the throne...' Haksar added: 'To all this her response was as expected: Everyone is attacking him [Sanjay] and nobody comes to his defence. All sorts of false stories are circulated about him'. Haksar had then clarified: 'The fact that ... such stories are afloat proves my point that he is a drag on you'. He then told us: 'But she did not accept my advice and the meeting ended unpleasantly'. [italics mine]

Elections were held in mid-March 1977 and by the late evening of 20 March 1977, it was clear that both Indira and Sanjay Gandhi had lost and that the Congress was faring very badly. The next day all the results were out and on the morning of 22 March 1977, Indira Gandhi resigned as prime minister. Two days later, Haksar wrote to the new prime minister, Morarji Desai:

My dear Morarji Bhai:

Let me first of all convey to you my warm felicitations on the occasion of your assuming the high office of the Prime Minister of India ... Your vast experience, knowledge and record of service to this nation will no doubt help in steering the ship of our State to a safe haven.

I assumed charge of the Planning Commission as its Deputy Chairman on January 4, 1975 ... The time is fast approaching for addressing oneself to some rather extraordinarily complex problems of our socio-economic transformation with many baffling structural problems ... *In order to enable you to proceed in this matter smoothly, I hereby submit my resignation from the Deputy Chairmanship of the Planning Commission ... I would wish to be relieved as soon as possible ...*

I have been Member of the Space and Atomic Energy Commissions for now nearly 10 years and I should like to be relieved of this membership as also of the Vice Presidentship of the Council of Scientific and Industrial Research ...

At the instance of the out-going Finance Minister I had assumed responsibility for giving shape and form to the newly created National Institute of Public Finance and Policy ... I hereby submit my resignation from the Chairmanship [of this Institute].

I have also been the Chairman of the National Labour Institute from its inception ... I, therefore submit my resignation from the Chairmanship of this Institute as well.

... I happen to be the Co-Chairman of the Indo-Soviet Joint Commission. The Commission was to meet in New Delhi in March. Might I suggest that a message be sent to the Soviet Co-Chairman both about the new Indian Co-Chairman as well as about the date on which the postponed meeting could be held.

... I would deem it a great favour if you would kindly let me have an early intimation of the acceptance of my resignation from the various posts I have mentioned. [italics mine]

Haksar had masterminded the sacking of Morarji Desai as finance minister on 16 July 1969. He had even drafted the letter that Indira Gandhi had sent Morarji Desai that day:

As a disciplined soldier of the party you lent support to the resolution which was adopted, even though I know that in regard to some of the basic issues that arise, you entertain strong reservations and have your own views about the direction as well as the pace of change. You have expressed your views clearly in the Working Committee and on other occasions. I have given deep thought to this matter and feel that in all fairness, I should not burden you with this responsibility in your capacity as Finance Minister, but should take it directly upon myself.

But Haksar had great personal respect for Morarji, even though ideologically they were poles apart. That respect must have been mutual, for the prime minister replied to Haksar on 28 March 1977:

I have your letter of March 24, intimating to me your desire to resign from the Deputy Chairmanship of the Planning Commission and from the various other offices you hold. While I appreciate the reasons which have prompted you to take this step and understand the situation in which you would like to be relieved as soon as possible. I am sure you will realize how sorry I am to have to deal with this problem so soon after assuming my new responsibilities. The variety of positions that you have held with such distinction does not make it easy for me to decide on alternative arrangements and I do hope you will agree to continue for a few days more to enable us to make suitable alternative arrangements ...

Haksar replied to the prime minister two days later:

I have your kind and gracious letter of March 28, 1977. It greatly touched me.

I am more than conscious of the tremendous burdens which this country has placed on you. And I would not wish in any way to add to it. Therefore, a few days more or even a month, as you say, will not inconvenience me. Even if it were to, such inconvenience must be borne in the larger interests of the affairs of State being run in a smooth and orderly manner ...

May I take this opportunity to thank you warmly for all the kindness, courtesy, and consideration you have shown to me personally?

But almost a month had elapsed and Haksar had heard nothing from the prime minister. The reason becomes apparent from a letter dated 23 April

1977 that Haksar wrote to Sukhamoy Chakravarty, who was then spending a year at Erasmus University in Rotterdam on leave from the position of member, Planning Commission:

> ... It is now almost end of April and I have not been told yet who precisely will take over from me [as deputy chairman of the Planning Commission].
>
> ... *He* [Morarji Desai] *asked me to continue in an indirect sort of way but I told him that my continuation would be in the nature of a defection and indicative of some differences I might have had with the former Prime Minister. This could not now be encashed by me.* I felt he understood my position which, I told him, was non-negotiable. I am free to confess that he was extraordinarily nice and gracious ... [italics mine]

Not having heard anything from the prime minister till mid-May 1977, Haksar sent him a note on 16 May 1977:

> I apologise for troubling P.M. once again in respect of my personal matters. However, I do feel strongly that if the Government desires to use Planning Commission as an institutional mechanism for planning, the time has come for ending the uncertainty that surrounds it.
>
> I propose, subject to P.M.'s approval, that I definitely relinquish charge as Deputy Chairman of the Planning Commission as well as the Vice Presidentship of the C.S.I.R. on 31st May, 1977 ...

In December 1972, Haksar had walked away from Indira Gandhi at a time of his choosing. In May 1977, he walked away from Morarji Desai, also at a time of his choosing. He had served the 'Indian State' as he would often call it for 30 long years. He had seen years of influence and power. He had also seen years of 'benign neglect' and some periods of 'malign intent'. But he had persevered almost without doubt because of his intellectual admiration for Nehru and his personal loyalty to Nehru's daughter.

As far as Morarji Desai was concerned, his attitude towards Haksar was itself quite remarkable. Haksar was to later recall to a close friend that Desai had paid rich tributes to him in his final appearance in a Cabinet meeting and that the way Desai had treated him was markedly warmer and affectionate than the way Indira Gandhi had dealt with him in later years.

Before leaving, Haksar sent the prime minister a note on what he considered to be priorities for the new government. In this communication of 16 May 1977, he called for more disaggregated agricultural planning, a sharper focus on 100 of the most backward districts of the country, emphasis on better utilization of scarce land and water resources and, above all, overriding priority to employment planning particularly in small towns and rural areas. Many of these themes were to become essential features of development policy in the years to come.

∾

On 30 April 1977, Haksar received a hand-written letter from his old compatriot R.N. Kao. The two had worked together to set up India's external intelligence agency R&AW nine years earlier. Kao wrote:

> My dear Babbobhai:
> As discussed with you, enclosed is the draft of a note which you might wish to use as you think best. I have tried to include in it only the most important points to avoid making it too long.
>> Yours ever,
>> Ramji

Kao had sent a draft of a note to be sent by Haksar to the prime minister. I am not sure whether Haksar actually sent the note or discussed it orally with the PM. No copy of the note that he may have sent to Morarji Desai is available in Haksar's archives but Ramji Kao's draft is, and it says much:

> *During the last few weeks, there has been a series of articles in newspapers and journals, making various speculations about the Research & Analysis Wing and Shri R.N. Kao, Secretary in charge of that organization, presently on leave. All of them are ill-informed, which is understandable, because the R&AW was formed as a secret organization to deal with foreign intelligence. In these publications, gross and serious charges have also been made against Shri Kao as well as the R&AW accusing them of going beyond the charter of their duty and interfering in internal politics ...*
>
> *... In my capacity first as Secretary to the then Prime Minister and later as her Principal Secretary, I was closely associated with and was aware of the decisions taken regarding the structure of R&AW and its working*

... When the decision was first taken by the Government in 1968, to establish a separate organization to deal with external intelligence, the idea was to be set up a secret agency, as different from the Intelligence Bureau, which was well-known ... From this decision, flowed certain ideas regarding its structure and working procedures, as also to give it a cover name and to disguise its head by giving him a designation similar to that given to officers of corresponding rank in the main Secretariat of the Government of India ...

... It was decided that for the sake of maintaining proper co-ordination with all the ministries concerned it would be logical to locate R&AW within the Cabinet Secretariat. *It was also agreed that the head of the organization would, in operational matters, and those affecting assessments, have direct access to the minister concerned, i.e, the Prime Minister.*

... Bearing in mind the extreme sensitivity of the whole field of foreign intelligence work, the then Prime Minister decided that the head of R&AW should exercise all the administrative and financial powers admissible to officers of his rank in the ministries and departments of the Government of India ...

It is within my personal knowledge that in the first briefing, which the then Prime Minister gave to Shri R.N. Kao, regarding the guidelines on which he was required to set up the new external intelligence organization, he was specially asked by her not to create in the R&AW another police organization, which should be only a copy of the ...

... 1971 was the year of the first test of R&AW which was very closely involved with the Bangladesh and Pakistan operations. The results achieved during this period justified the decision of the Government to set up a new foreign intelligence organization on modern lines. In the years that followed, there came further consolidation, and the R&AW was asked to undertake new responsibilities... The R&AW has also been rendering another valuable service by maintaining secret liaison with other friendly foreign intelligence services in matters of common interest ...

My object in writing this note the Prime Minister is not to try and give a certificate to Shri Kao ... but only to point out the grave danger involved in dismantling and crippling the new organization dealing with external intelligence which was for the first time established on modern lines here in 1968. It ... deserves to be protected from slanderous political baiting. [italics mine]

This draft reveals many things. It shows how Haksar and Kao had worked in tandem to set up R&AW and get it going. It also shows how Kao believed that Haksar still carried some credibility with the new prime minister for him to convey what Kao wanted to be conveyed to Morarji Desai. Unfortunately, Kao's own archives at the Nehru Memorial Museum and Library are closed. There have been a couple of books on R&AW[12] but they are all silent on the Haksar–Kao partnership. Haksar talked of many things but never of his association with Kao. Even after he had left the prime minister's Secretariat, Haksar would be visited by Kao almost every other night—with nobody other than immediate family knowing. What they would have talked about, alas, will never be known.

31 May 1977 was the last day of Haksar in government service. Before departing, he wrote to Morarji Desai:

> ... Problems connected with science and technology require constant review. For instance, for over hundred years, our meteorological organization was never looked into. I had caused it to be reviewed by a Committee which consisted, among others, of the present Cabinet Secretary and Dr. Raja Ramanna. I believe the review has been useful. I think that the time has come to review the functioning of the Atomic Energy Commission ... I believe the whole area of medical research and engineering research in our country needs a review. In the meantime, we have to take a view of the precise relationship between the planning process and the growth of science and technology ...

Haksar's argument was that the existing institutional structure in government was not bringing about a match between 'demand' and 'supply' as far as science and technology was concerned. He was not 'empire building' since he was leaving the Planning Commission but his experience had convinced him that it is only through this body, suitably strengthened that India's science and technology effort would get a meaningful thrust. Morarji

Desai acted on some of the recommendations of Haksar's very last note and attracted tremendous criticism from the scientific community for his decisions. Nobody knew that these decisions emanated from someone who had been the strongest champion of and advocate for that community for almost a decade. When Indira Gandhi returned to power in January 1980, she reversed these decisions which had mostly to do with the transfer of research laboratories from the CSIR umbrella to their 'user' ministries as Haksar had envisaged.

Notes

1. Tandon (2003).
2. Fotedar (2016).
3. Bhushan (2017).
4. Noorani (2003).
5. Dhar (2000).
6. The literature on the 1975 Emergency is voluminous. Dhar (2000) and Tandon (2003) and Tandon (2006) are valuable insider accounts.
7. Haksar, Urmila (1978).
8. Haksar was elected as India's representative by the U.N. General Assembly. The Commission was to function till 1980 and make far-reaching recommendations on the terms and conditions of employment in the UN system.
9. Sen (2003).
10. Austin (2000).
11. Gujral (2011).
12. Raman (2007).

XI. The Sage of Shantiniketan
(1977–1998)

On retirement in January 1973, Haksar had moved into his house in a colony called Shantiniketan in New Delhi. From 1 June 1977 onward till his death on 27 November 1998, Haksar was to hold no official position. He would chair important committees, guide academic and research institutions (like the Jawaharlal Nehru University, Giri Institute of Development Studies, Centre for Research in Rural and Industrial Development and the Indian Statistical Institute), serve as patron of many worthwhile public causes (like the Delhi Science Forum and the Zaheer Science Foundation), write regularly about national and international issues mostly in the monthly journal Man & Development, publish a number of books, serve as friend, philosopher and guide to many civil servants, activists and NGOs and become a leading public intellectual. In late-1982 he would lose his left eye and by mid-1989 would become completely blind.

The Years of Estrangement (1978–1984)

Indira Gandhi with Haksar and T.N. Kaul, early-1980s; occasion and location unknown.

THE MORARJI DESAI GOVERNMENT HAD SET UP A COMMISSION OF INQUIRY under the chairmanship of a retired Supreme Court judge, J.C. Shah, to investigate the excesses of the Emergency. On 8 February 1978, the case history on the raids on Pandit Brothers and subsequent events concerning Haksar's uncle and brother-in-law was presented to the Commission. It quoted Kishan Chand, the lieutenant governor of Delhi during the Emergency as saying that the real motive behind the drastic action against Pandit Brothers and its partners was actually to embarrass Haksar. Chand admitted that he was satisfied that there was actually no justification whatsoever for the raids and the arrests. The case history also provided graphic detail of how R.K. Dhawan, the additional private secretary to the prime minister, called Chand's secretary, Navin Chawla, to have the raids and arrests carried out making it clear that Sanjay Gandhi wanted them done immediately.

The very next day, R.K. Garg, an eminent and widely respected lawyer, one-time CPI member and close friend of Haksar, wrote to Justice Shah giving a chronology of all that happened in the Pandit Brothers case since July 1975. Garg's letter ended thus:

> It is in my knowledge that Mr. P.N. Haksar was always of the view that the Prime Minister's son must not sponsor or promote Maruti Limited and the Prime Minister must make a choice between the son and the Nation. How Sanjay Gandhi took it was his concern. Mr. P.N. Haksar tried to maintain high standards of integrity in every office of trust that he occupied. I know of no other reasons that could have invited the indignities and injustice for the venerable old man Mr. R.N. Haksar, who happened to be his uncle ...

On 15 April 1978, Haksar himself deposed before a Commission of Inquiry that had been set up on 30 May 1977 to investigate all affairs connected with Maruti. The Commission was chaired by a Supreme Court judge, A.C. Gupta. But, in his deposition Haksar held firm and said that 'I don't think what happened to Pandit Brothers had anything to do with Maruti. If you say it is within my knowledge whether the two are connected, the answer is may or may not be connected. It is a matter of speculation.' But he did not equivocate when asked about his opposition to the small car project, saying that his opposition had been consistent from 1966–1967, 'when the government was considering whether to sponsor such a project or not'. His opposition to the Maruti project, he revealed, was 'based on the fact that the country needed an efficient public transport system and backing the small car project would be squandering resources'. He also revealed that all papers related to Maruti stopped coming to him after September 1970 itself. He denied having ever spoken to Sanjay Gandhi about the project, declaring that:

> My duty was to discuss matters with the Prime Minister and not with his or her son.

He admitted that had made his views known repeatedly to Indira Gandhi and that her reaction was that 'the government and the cabinet had decided upon it'. He lost his cool once when he was questioned by the government counsel and retorted to an insinuation made by saying:

> I was not serving the family. I was a government servant. To say that I was serving the family of Indira Gandhi is atrocious.

In spite of all evidence to the contrary, Haksar insisted on denying any link between what happened to Pandit Brothers and to his close relatives and his stance on the Maruti project. He was, in his mind, being loyal to Indira Gandhi. But that loyalty would come under new strain a year later and Haksar would, for the first and only time, criticize Indira Gandhi by name for something she would say about him.

On 23 April 1979, Haksar's mother who had been living with him passed away. Haksar had been much closer to his mother and somewhat distant from his father. The next day Indira Gandhi asked Usha Bhagat, who had worked with her for well over two decades, to accompany her to Haksar's house—the same house which had been searched twice by tax authorities in 1975 during the Emergency. Bhagat writes in her book:[1]

> … It was quite hot, and on reaching Mr. Haksar's home we did not find anyone waiting for us. I was surprised. We rang the bell but no one appeared … After some time the front door opened and an elderly lady peeped out sleepily, no doubt wondering who was disturbing them during their afternoon siesta. She was Mrs Mushran, Haksar Sahib's sister, and she took us to Haksar Sahib's study. Haksar Sahib must have been resting as well because he took some time to come. By then I had realized that no prior intimation about our visit had been given. There had been some strained relations between Mrs Gandhi and Haksar Sahib. *When Sanjay's Maruti car project had become controversial, he had spoken and advised Mrs Gandhi frankly, as only he could, and had been sidelined.* However, Mrs Gandhi being a very correct person wished to pay her condolences … Mrs Gandhi did not speak a word. Mrs Mushran sat staring coldly at Mrs Gandhi. During the early periods of the Emergency, Pandit Brothers, a firm owned by Mr. Haksar's uncle and his brother-in-

law, Mr Mushran, had been raided, allegedly at the behest of Sanjay and both the gentlemen had been taken to the police station in handcuffs. Mrs Mushran had obviously not forgotten the humiliation suffered by her husband. To cover the embarrassment, I talked incessantly with Mr Haksar. I was quite amused by the whole episode. [italics mine]

Usha Bhagat may have felt quite amused but for Haksar's family it must have been a torture. While he had kept up his relationship with Indira Gandhi, Urmila Haksar and Saraswati Mushran had become her sworn enemies from that fateful day of 16 July 1975. They neither forgave nor forgot.

Indira Gandhi had never spoken publicly about Haksar after their estrangement in 1975. He had been a member of her Cabinet till March 1977. Thereafter, contacts between them had declined sharply with Indira Gandhi expressing her annoyance with Haksar in private conversations for his stance during the Emergency. But, whatever she felt she shared only with some friends like Mohit Sen of the CPI. But this was to change in September 1979 in an interview of hers published in *The Illustrated Weekly of India*. She had spoken to an American academic, Mary C. Carras, and attacked Haksar's integrity. Haksar was away from India for a month from mid-August 1979 and it was only after someone drew his attention to it, did he see the interview and the sensational charge hurled at him by his erstwhile boss. He wrote to the editor on 4 October 1979 and his anguish is palpable:

In your September 9-15, 1979 issue, you had published an interview given by Smt. Gandhi to one Mary C. Carras. At page 23, there is sub-heading titled "People like Haksar had land". How criminal of me!! This headline had apparently been provoked by *an answer given by Smt. Gandhi to a question put to her ... She was asked: "Wasn't property given to him [Sanjay Gandhi] by Bansi Lal?". To this question, Smt. Gandhi, without any provocation whatsoever, brings in my name. She says: "The difference is that, in most places, they are poor people; here people like Haksar had land. And I am not sure of the figure because I have never talked about this* to Sanjay or anybody, but somebody told me that he (Haksar) bought the land for only Rs 6000/- and he got over Rs 26,000/- for it". Frankly, I do not know what Smt. Gandhi is trying to establish or even to say.

I certainly bought land in the village of Mulahera situated in … Gurgaon. The land … is equivalent to 2 acres … I paid for it by a cheque for Rs 30,800 drawn on my account with the Grindlays Bank bearing the date 1.12.1969 … Unknown to me this land was acquired by the Government of Haryana … On or about the 10th of July I received a cheque of Rs 20,930/- by way of compensation for the acquisition of the land … This was the situation on the date Smt. Gandhi was giving her interview on the basis of unascertained facts testifying to the wisdom of the proverb that if facts are against you so much the worse for the facts.

Against the order of the Land Acquisition Collector, large number of persons affected filed appeals in the Court of Additional District and Sessions Judge … Towards end of January this year [I was informed] that Additional District Judge had enhanced the compensation … I said that I was not interested in making a fortune out of this and that I would be happy to receive whatever [additional] compensation that was due. Only a few weeks ago I received the enhanced compensation for land amounting to Rs 14,080 together with the usual solatium at 15% and 6% interest rate from 10.7.71 to 13.12.78. These are the facts.

Smt. Indira Gandhi could have left me alone and I too would have maintained my self-imposed silence but I cannot allow gossip tainted with malice to be purveyed as facts to your readers. [italics mine]

Haksar was clearly incensed even though this had been an old charge hurled at him going back to the years when he had opposed Sanjay Gandhi's Maruti venture. The canard had been spread by Bansi Lal, the chief minister of Haryana, that Haksar was opposing the venture because he had lost his land. This charge was absurd, since Haksar's opposition pre-dated his buying that two acres of land and his objection was on grounds of principle: that India did not need a small car at that point of time and even if it did, the prime minister's son without any resources of his own should not be the person producing these cars.

This was the first and last time Indira Gandhi and Haksar went after each other in public. We don't know what she thought of Haksar's riposte. Soon thereafter, elections were announced and she got busy with campaigning. On 30 November 1979, Haksar wrote to Arjun Sengupta, the noted economist who was then at Oxford University and who would join Indira Gandhi's office two years later:

> Mrs. G's platform is very simple. All that she is saying is that "you have seen Janata rule and you have seen the Lok Dal rule and you know neither of them can govern. I can govern and so try me again". And so the people of India will certainly try her again. Thus, 1980 will come. Even [if] she secures a clear mandate for herself, she will be faced with increasing inflation, a vast deficit budget, a politically divided country, regional turbulence. This should lead to assembling together under her banner all those yearning for order and discipline …

Even before opinion polls showed her return to power, Haksar was telling Arjun Sengupta that Indira Gandhi was going to become prime minister again.

C.B. Muthamma was the first woman to clear the civil service exams in 1948 and the first woman to join the Indian Foreign Service in 1949. She was known to be an efficient officer but she had been overlooked for promotion. In the late-1970s, three persons junior to her had been appointed to the highest grade in the service ignoring her claims. She then approached Haksar who supported her strongly, and got his friend D.P. Singh to argue her case in the Supreme Court. The Supreme Court gave its verdict on 17 September 1979 and upheld her contention that not only was injustice done to her unjustifiably, but that the criteria for promotion in the Ministry of External Affairs were opaque and blatantly discriminatory against women. It was a landmark judgment that would have major implications for women diplomats. Three days later, she wrote to Singh from The Hague, where she was then India's ambassador, saying 'the success of the case is due entirely to you and Mr. Haksar who advised me in the first instance, including the advice to hand over the case to you'.

Indira Gandhi made a spectacular comeback and was sworn in as prime minister a fourth time on 14 January 1980. Two days later Haksar wrote to her:

> No one contemplating our national scene with clinical objectivity can fail to rejoice at your second coming. And I rejoice at it even more because I sensed it way back in April 1977 after having attended the first Cabinet meeting presided over by Morarji Desai. In the monologue I inflicted on you on April 13 of that year, I said that people were already feeling contrite. Sitting in the Planning Commission and surveying our national scene on the eve of November 19, 1976 [when Indira Gandhi turned 59], I felt and wrote to you [letter not available] that you were in your person the single most important element in our nation's future and that you should carefully weigh both the pitfalls as well as the opportunities. The people of India have come to the same conclusion.
>
> The question is: Where do we go from here? I am so glad that you have used the words "the healing touch". These words, when translated into a series of policies and programmes, could create the proper atmosphere. And it is this atmosphere which is of crucial importance. After all problems of economic development, agrarian reforms, creation of employment, abolition of poverty, etc. cannot be achieved in a decade or even two. But one can endeavor to create an appropriate national consensus. One can create a sense of national purpose. *As in war, so in peace, the art always lies in either winning over the enemy or destroying him completely. Historical experience shows that there are greater rewards for the art of reconciliation than of annihilation.*
>
> As I am writing these few lines to you, my mind is full of all kinds if feelings and emotions… However, I won't burden this letter with all that and would conclude it by wishing you all the very best. [italics mine]

In 1975, Haksar's family and he were harassed at the express orders of Indira Gandhi's younger son. In 1979, she had publicly seemed to question his integrity. And yet, Haksar wrote this letter. Coming from anybody else these words would sound 'sycophantic' or be seen as a 'job application'.[2] Haksar could most certainly not be accused on both these grounds. He was neither an applicant nor a supplicant—he had never been one nor would he ever be. He always said what he felt. Indira Gandhi and he went back decades. He had been an acolyte of her father. She had plucked him from relative obscurity in the diplomatic service and installed him right next to her. This could be one reason why he continued to be loyal to her even amidst all the knocks he received. It is also clear that he genuinely believed that she was the only political personality who embodied all the values so dear to him—secularism, socialism, democracy (the Emergency notwithstanding), scientific temper and a global worldview.

Indira Gandhi's reply is not available. But many years later, Mohit Sen was to write in his memoirs regarding this letter:[3]

> He [Haksar] showed me his letter to her [Indira Gandhi] when she returned to power. It was affectionate, intimate and expressed the hope as well as the wish that she would be more than just another Prime Minister or words to that effect. He signed the letter using his nickname. He also showed me her reply beginning by calling him 'Dear Mr. Haksar', stating that good wishes were always welcome and signing off as 'Indira Gandhi'.

That must have hurt enormously but like always Haksar would take it in his stride.

On 25 June 1980, the *Times of India* carried a longish discussion on Afghanistan between Haksar and K. Subrahmanyam, India's leading strategic analyst and then the director of the Institute of Defence Studies and Analysis in New Delhi. Moderating that conversation was the newspaper's editor Girilal Jain. Haksar was to make a number of references to Pakistan, Bangladesh and China as well. For the first time he confessed that in Simla 'we made one concession after another to Pakistan to get one thing—to make them accept the need for durable peace and the doctrine of bilateralism as the means to achieve that peace'. The cornerstone of Simla, he went on to add, 'was founded on the recognition that all our mutual problems in the past were aggravated and shall certainly be aggravated in the future if we allow third-party interventions'. On Bangladesh too, perhaps for the first time he allowed himself to comment:

It used to be said, for instance, that India brought about Bangladesh. Many people said that there had been some conspiracy. In fact the people of Bangladesh were in revolt. We did not bring it about. I used to tell my Pakistani friends especially Mr. Aziz Ahmad, that he was the founding father of Bangladesh. If the Pakistanis had not insisted that Urdu should be imposed on the Bengalis, the trouble would not have begun.

Haksar would have an important role to play seven years later in the reconciliation with China. He gave a preview into his thinking in the discussion with Subrahmanyam and Jain when he said:

I believe that China and India should work towards promoting mutual understanding, mutual cooperation and mutual comprehension as both a short-term as well as a long-term objective for its own sake. However the past cannot be forgotten since it forms part of our historical experience. *The most important thing in our relationship, according to me, is not the border issue though it is an important one, it is this dimension of confidence and trust which has been destroyed.* The process of building that trust has to be a gradual one ... We should not yield to the temptation of trying to pull something like a rabbit out of a hat. [italics mine]

It was in this conversation that Haksar expressed his admiration for an earlier generation of American diplomats like George Kennan and Averell Harriman while calling his old interlocutor of 1971, Kissinger, and his successor Zbigniew Brzezinski 'rootless adventurers'.

The establishment of the Nehru Centre in Bombay was a tribute to his hero by the lawyer who had been a communist in his youth along with Haksar and had later become the boss of the Congress party in the country's commercial capital. Nehru had written about the young and adventurous Rajni Patel in the *National Herald* and had also brought him to the attention of Mahatma Gandhi and Sardar Patel.

Two years before he passed away, Rajni Patel organized a colloquium on 'scientific temper' that was attended by a number of scientists and others. Haksar presided over the four-day conclave at Coonoor between

22–25 October 1980 in which 'what needed to be done and to halt the process of decay of reason and rationality' was discussed and debated. Nine months later, a statement was issued that had among its signatories, apart from Haksar himself, his old colleagues from the scientific world, like Raja Ramanna, Satish Dhawan, Y. Nayudamma and C.N.R. Rao, K.N. Raj the economist, Shyam Benegal the film-maker and other noted public personalities. The statement created quite a stir when it came out.

The statement bemoaned that despite Nehru's persistent advocacy of a scientific temper, 'we are witnessing phenomenal growth of superstitious beliefs and obscurantist practices'. But it also cautioned that 'the emphasis on the method of science does not imply that science and technology have solutions to all human problems at any given time'. It pointed out that 'the role of reason is to apply scientific knowledge to problems, to grapple through the method of scientific inquiry'.

Two years later, in January 1983, the Nehru Centre was to organize another symposium to take the idea of a scientific temper forward. The theme this time was on science and spirituality and it was to embroil Haksar in an argument with Raja Ramanna of all people. Swami Ranganathananda of the Ramakrishna Mission was present and Haksar expounded his usual theme that spirituality as practiced in India had given rise to backwardness of all types and that religious orthodoxy had become the bane of Indian society. Swami Ranganathananda took the view that there was no conflict between science and spirituality, if spirituality is seen, as Swami Vivekananda had done, in the spirit of Vedanta. Raja Ramanna's own views happened to converge with that of Swami Ranganathananda. Then followed an angry but affectionate exchange of letters between Haksar and Raja Ramanna. Needless to say, both stuck to their positions.

◦◦

Indira Gandhi wanted Haksar to help her out on some national issues. Maybe the absence of Sanjay Gandhi who had died in an air crash in June 1980 emboldened her in this regard. Sometime in May 1981, she sent word to Haksar that he should take some interest in Kashmir. Not sure how Haksar would react, she sent the message through Rashpal Malhotra, who was very well-known to her as well as well as to Haksar. The exact date is not known but Haksar's response survives and reads thus:

> Rashpal has delivered your message. I share your concern about Kashmir. I would like to help but it seems to me that matters have become far too complicated. I have to think deeply about them. Modalities have to be most carefully planned.

This may looked like a brush-off but Indira Gandhi would not give up and a while later asked Rashpal Malhotra to find out whether Haksar had done anything about looking into the matter of Kashmir. Again, Haksar sent a message back to her through the same channel:

> On thinking it over, I find it embarrassing to undertake the mission behind the back of the Governor and in derogation of his authority and position. The Governor of the State is an important institutional prop. One would not wish to undermine it. While initial essays can be of a purely personal encounter, the subsequent developments cannot take place behind his back.

It is clear that Indira Gandhi wanted Haksar to be sort of a secret and special envoy to deal with Kashmir but without the governor of J&K, B.K. Nehru, knowing it. It was actually quite a bizarre idea but it was clear that the governor did not enjoy her fullest confidence even though she had herself handpicked him for that sensitive post.

Haksar had already opened a line of communication with Sheikh Abdullah, who he had first met in February 1948 when they were both part of India's delegation to the United Nations. He wrote to the J&K chief minister on 20 May 1981, after Indira Gandhi's first message conveyed through Rashpal Malhotra. A copy of that letter is not available but the Sheikh's reply of 1 June 1981 is, and reads thus:

> Thank you very much for your letter of May 20, 1981. *Your genuine concern over the unfortunate developments that of late have taken place, no doubt prompted by your love and affection for me and the overall national interests, has deeply touched me. I need not tell you that I have great love,*

regard and esteem for you not only as a sincere friend but also as a highly emancipated and intellectually honest person.

I hope you will agree that not unoften things get distorted if reported out of context. When personal communication breaks down misunderstandings crop up and more so when rantings of power-hungry politicians and vested interests are given credence and falsehoods are allowed to befog realities. That is why I have always believed in personal liaison which leaves no room for misunderstandings … This really explains the genesis of the unhappy turn of events in our relationship …

I wish we could meet soon to have a heart to heart talk, for sometimes written words fail to express the feelings and emotions one wishes to convey. I would, therefore, be indeed happy if you could make it convenient to spend some time with us. There should be no mental reservations about spending a holiday in the Valley as my personal guest. Rest assured I can afford to be a host to a valued friend like you...

I very much wish that you continue the arrangement regarding visiting Professorship at Kashmir University who very much like to benefit from your erudition and wisdom accumulated over the years … [italics mine]

Haksar went to Srinagar in September 1981 to give some lectures at the University of Kashmir. He met Sheikh Abdullah twice and with members of the Kashmiri Pandit community. On his return, he thanked the Sheikh on 19 September 1981:

… I am so glad that I was able to talk to you and that you were so generous with your time. I have now some understanding of the problems. None are basically so intractable as to defy proper handling. As an ordinary citizen of India, it would be my endeavor to try and help to the extent I can. Our public life in India is so full of hatred and animosity that we cannot really work out any reasonable and rational solutions. Some healing touch and generosity are necessary …

Then he wrote a 'Dear Induji' letter to the prime minister on 16 October 1981, setting out the conclusions he had reached after the long conversations with Sheikh Abdullah and his wife:

1. The 1953 episode [his arrest] haunts Sheikh Saheb. And it haunts Begum Sahiba even more. Sheikh Saheb was nursed back into some rationality when the processed of restoration began which culminated in the act of restoration.

2. The trauma of '53 surfaced in 1977 when the Congress decided to withdraw support to him. Even at that time I had told Makkhan Lal [Fotedar] that the Congress was acting in a mindless fashion. The net result was that Sheikh Saheb felt exempted from the limits of constraints imposed by any sense of noblesse oblige.

3. There is no visible erosion of Sheikh's position in the Valley. Consequently, the reasons for the Sheikh to be where he is are as valid today as they were in 1975.

4. Neither the Sheikh nor, indeed, Begum Sahiba, contemplate their future outside India.

5. The only circumstance in which the people of the Valley of Kashmir and, therefore, their leaders might find Pakistan attractive would be if the country were to become not only democratic but also succeeds in evolving an appropriate state structure which would take into account the identities called the Sindhis, the Baluchis, the Pathans and even some of the Punjabis ...

6. *In the short term extending to the next few years, the question we have to ask ourselves is: Can we handle Sheikh Saheb? And the second question is: Who will handle him? It can only be done by someone who must, of necessity, be a person visibly of your choice and, equally, visibly carry your authority.*

7. Political organ grinders, contractors, hoteliers, Cinema proprietors, are all esteemable people. But their perceptions are refracted through the prism of self-interest and varying fortunes.

8. In any scheme of handling of Sheikh Abdullah, Begum Abdullah as well as Farooq, one has to think of the stature, background and the experience of those who seek to lead the Congress in the Valley. It is unwise to leave Mir Qasim maimed, bruised and distraught.

9. I found Sheikh Saheb had a completely cock-eyed view of the state of international relations. I tried to help him see things in a different light. This is going to be a continuous task which someone will have to perform ... [italics mine]

After laying out these broad impressions and emphasizing that he had no axe to grind, Haksar told Indira Gandhi:

> ... I was horrified to learn in Srinagar that Sheikh Saheb had included my name, without my consent, in the list of persons he thought would be appropriate for appointment as Governor of J&K. It was an atrocious thing to do. Everyone has his dreams. I had mine too. At one time, it included being an engine driver. But being a Governor has never been part of my dream.
>
> ... It is now for you to decide the broad framework within which you wish to deal with the Sheikh today, tomorrow and the day after. And Mir Qasim too!

Eleven months later, the Sheikh was dead. He was to be replaced by his son Farooq Abdullah, who had an extremely close personal relationship with Indira Gandhi but he woud soon end up antagonizing her.

❦

It appeared that Haksar was finally getting around to writing some sort of a memoir when on 24 December 1981, he wrote to his old colleague P.N. Dhar, who was then working at United Nations in New York:

> I am in the process of recollecting things and putting them down. It is my hope that some day it might take the shape and form of a book. And even if it does not, it would at least be a truthful account of what happened to me. In one or two matters, I need your assistance.
>
> I once mentioned to you about that meeting we had together in my house where we thought we would find some elegant solution to the Maruti problem. Amongst those present from us were T.A. Pai, D.K. Barooah, Siddharth Shankar Ray and Om Mehta. I know there were others but I cannot recall ...
>
> *The other thing is about the Simla Agreement. You would recall that you and I went to see the Lady and she lost her temper. And I beckoned to you to withdraw. Then I quietened her down. But what was the provocation? Also about the last evening ... what is your recollection? Would you consider helping me?* [italics mine]

Most unfortunately P.N. Dhar's answer to these queries of Haksar is not available. But in his memoirs, Dhar was to shed some light on the second incident on whiuch Haksar wanted some elucidation. He writes:[4]

> I was therefore for the return of the POWs [prisoners of war]. But I was strongly opposed to the immediate return of the territories ... I made these points in a briefing session which Haksar and I had with Indira Gandhi. Before I could finish she grew impatient and flew into a rage. I was puzzled by her loss of temper. My hunch is that she was under pressure—this could only have been from the Soviets—to return the occupied territories. But this is only a hunch. I wasn't personally aware of any such pressure. Perhaps Haksar was. He signaled me to withdraw and I left the room. He told me soon after that he 'had quietened her down' and that she wanted to meet members of political affairs committee of the cabinet ... At that meeting Indira Gandhi asked Haksar to brief her cabinet colleagues on the stage that negotiations had reached and explain the reasons for the possibility of our returning occupied territory ...

1982 was to be a terrible year for Haksar. First, his beloved uncle Inderbhai, who had sustained him financially in Allahabad in the 1930s and 1940s and with whom he was exceedingly close, died on 8 January 1982 at the age of 89. Haksar received a very large number of messages and letters from family and friends showing how popular his uncle had been. No condolence letter from Indira Gandhi to Haksar is available in his archives but one unusual letter of 2 February 1982 from somebody else is and reads thus:

> ... I had the privilege of knowing Panditjee [as PNH's uncle was called] for about a decade. He was really a grand old man: having refined manners and catholicity of outlook; kind and considerate; at the same time he was not prepared to compromise on his principles and had the strength of will to resist what he considered to be wrong. I know, I think many of us know, the onslaught he had to face for some time in his old age. But he did not give in and continued to put up a fight. I remember his remarks full of wit and humour. Even in the worst gloomy situation his comments and apt couplets were such as would make every one laugh and dispel the gloom.

He was always kind and affectionate to me and his passing away has been a great loss to me personally.

The person who had sent this letter was Indira Gandhi's arch political rival— Atal Bihari Vajpayee, who went on to become prime minister of India.

A little less than a month later, Haksar's brother-in-law K.P. Mushran, who had been arrested along with Inderbhai in July 1975, died on 4 February 1982. Mushran had retired as member of the Railway Board and while he and Haksar were personally fond of each other, they were poles apart temperamentally. Mushran was a 'systems man' and felt that Haksar was a bit too ideological and concentrating too much power in the prime minister's Secretariat. They would have arguments but never heated ones.

∾

Still getting used to life without his uncle, Haksar dashed off a letter to Indira Gandhi on 24 January 1982 after reading reports of a speech made by Foreign Minister Agha Shahi of Pakistan:

…I hope that our Ministry of External Affairs as well as PM's Secretariat have carefully read Agha Shahi's speech at the Majlis-i-Shoora in which he sets forth with considerable skill Pakistan's foreign policy … Pakistani regimes, he argues, may change, but relations with China remain the cornerstone of the successive governments. Equally immutable are the Islamic links. Pakistan's passion for non-alignment is underlined … He underplays quite effectively the revival of the American connection and presents Pakistan in a somewhat heroic role of being able to get American assistance on Pakistan's own terms …

Agha Shahi says nothing which might be construed as hostile to the Soviet Union. On the contrary, he darkly hints that Pakistan is cultivating the Soviet connection …

I devoutly hope that we have worked out both the strategy and the tactics of our response. The ease with which Pakistan obtained the maximum propaganda advantage from their offer of no-war pact makes me uneasy about the way we are going to handle the forthcoming negotiations.

... I also hope that those who engage in the negotiations will ensure that ... we always appear to be inspired consistently with the vision of durable peace. Above all, we must never allow ourselves to appear in the eyes of the people of Pakistan as a belligerent party ...

Finally, we should be ready to discuss the so-called Kashmir question within the framework of Simla agreement ... This brings me to urge once again a somewhat clinically objective view of the situation in the Valley. *If National Conference and the Congress cannot reach a modus vivendi and thus hang together, they will assuredly hang separately and Jamaat-i-Islami will be the gainer. Diplomacy after all is an art of science of reducing the number of one's opponents and not increasing them.* [italics mine]

Unfortunately, the rest of this letter is not available. There must have been something else of a personal nature for Indira Gandhi to respond the way she did on 6 February 1982 while on a flight from Gorakhpur to New Delhi:

Thank you for your letter. It was good of you to write about the talks with Agha Shahi. I shared your letter with the Foreign Minister.

Why should you think I might be offended? As you know, I always welcome suggestions and views and have said so repeatedly in private and public. In this way I get many useful ideas from different kinds of people and you are experienced and knowledgeable.

Indira Gandhi was clearly confusing Haksar's report of Agha Shahi's speech as his talks with the Pakistani diplomat. That apart something that Haksar had written in his usual self-deprecatory style must have irked the prime minister to make her as defensive as she appears in her reply. She was matter-of-fact and showed no sign of their past bonhomie and camaraderie.

Indira Gandhi and Haksar had gone through a harrowing time with the USA between 1969 and 1973. After Haksar's departure in January 1973 bilateral relations hadn't really improved, although Kissinger had visited New Delhi in October 1974. After she came back to power in January 1980, her approach towards the USA began to change. But the man who was with her when she met President Nixon at the White House on 4 November 1971 still harboured old suspicions. Haksar wrote to the prime minister on 9 July 1982, and it is obvious that she had completely ignored him while planning for this important visit:

> You would be going to Washington. I do not know what we are seeking to achieve by the visit. And I am wondering if any specific area of possible agreements between ourselves and the US have been delineated. Reagan is beleaguered and besieged. And in November, he faces a mid-term election. How will he fare? Shouldn't one have waited and watched?
>
> *As far as I can see, the timing of the visit is not propitious. To get something out of the United States, we also have to give. I do not see what the United States can give which would be meaningful to us. And what could we possibly concede?* Of course, it is always possible to have conversations seeking to understand how Reagan's mind works—assuming, of course, Reagan has a mind ...
>
> Be that as it may, Reagan is for the time being the President of the United States. Therefore, one has to deal with him. We could have dealt with him if the visit to the U.S. was preceded by visits to Japan, Germany, France and U.S.S.R ... [italics mine]

Sadly, the rest of the letter is missing in the archives, as is Indira Gandhi's reply. But what is available of the letter shows that Haksar appears frozen in time. It is almost as if he was writing out of pique but that certainly was not it. He genuinely believed in what he was saying. He made the same mistake that many in America and elsewhere made of severely under-estimating Ronald Reagan. Not that he was starry-eyed of the USSR for sure. In a 'Letters to the Editor' in the *Times of India* of 29 July 1982, he took issue with an interpretation of the themes contained in his book *Reflections on Our Times* by Sham Lal, and said:

> Since I have never experienced the emotions of looking upon the Soviet Union either as Mecca or a god, I never felt the need to write an elegy on the god that failed ...

Granted that Western economies were going through troubled times in the early-1980s, viewed retrospectively, Haksar's pessimism regarding the

US and what it could do for India appears misplaced. No doubt he felt that there would be a quid pro quo that the US will demand from India but to say that Indira Gandhi should not have embarked on that trip was being highly negative. Indira Gandhi, whom he had tutored in her initial years, had moved on and acquired the confidence to deal with the US on her terms. Sadly, Haksar seems to have failed to recognize this reality.

From Haksar's standpoint Indira Gandhi was soon to make amends. By August 1982, Haksar had lost his left eye completely and his vision in the right eye was beginning to get impaired. But that did not stop him from publicly supporting Indira Gandhi's visit to the USSR in September 1982 when its utility was being questioned in certain circles in New Delhi. Haksar took the view that 'there was no need to be shamefaced about friendship with a country which had protected our interests in international forums in vital matters'. India, he believed, 'should have the courage of conviction to own up its friendship with the Soviet Union'. In a dig at those who wanted to play coy about this relationship, given India's growing proximity to the USA, Haksar announced that he had 'discovered an illicit aspect of our relations with the Soviet Union. Otherwise, why would one try to cover the friendship with apologetic phrases.'

Haksar had a vast circle of official and non-official contacts in many countries, including Pakistan and Bangladesh. He would keep getting information from them which he would pass on to his friend R.N. Kao. Sometimes he would approach the prime minister herself, as he did on 15 January 1983:

> I enclose a note on the situation in Pakistan. I have, of course, no means of ascertaining the accuracy of the analysis made. However, I have met during the last few years a variety of Pakistanis, both officials and private individual, who left me with an impression that today's Pakistan is, more than ever, a witch's cauldron. It can boil over and not just simmer ...
>
> *I should really have handed over the note to Ramji [Kao]. But then I thought that without higher political direction neither he nor the relevant*

organization [R&AW] can deal with the vital questions of forging links with a wide variety of political tendencies in Pakistan.

What applies to Pakistan equally applies to Bangladesh. During the last few years, I had occasions to meet a variety of people from Bangladesh. Not all are Awami Leaguers. I got the impression that Bangladesh can put India in an extremely awkward situation.

The more I contemplate the political situation in our sub-continent, the more I am driven to the conclusion that we need to actively promote contacts, links, conversations etc. between serious-minded Pakistanis and Bangladeshis in order to work towards the concept of durable peace in the sub-continent *which, in effect amounts to working for a de facto confederation of India, Pakistan and Bangladesh ...*

In order that we may pursue the strategic goal to which I have referred in the previous paragraph, we would need to take stock of our own situation with clinical objectivity. Given such an objectivity, one could, I feel still work out a more assured future. That is why I had taken the liberty of suggesting, several months ago, the need for a reassembly of all those Congressmen who had gathered together in 1969. When Antony [A.K.] joined the Congress in Kerala, it could have been made an occasion for launching the process in a dramatic sort of way. If atomic fission produces energy, atomic fusion produces even greater energy.

I know that anything that I say has long been treated as suspect. And yet I must persist. [italics mine]

The last two lines of this letter were quite a pathetic cry of helplessness from her one-time alter ego and mentor.

Indira Gandhi's reply of 2 February 1983 did not help matters much. It was curt and impersonal, and read:

I cannot remember if I have acknowledged your letter of January the 15th.

There is no question of anybody being considered suspect. I value the opinion of others.

I have been in touch with the situation and already had most of the information which your informant gives. But there were some points which had not been brought to my attention earlier.

She chose to remain quiet on the suggestion for a call from her to re-unite all Congressmen who had left the party because of the Emergency and because of Sanjay Gandhi.

ॐ

1983 was to bring China back in Haksar's life through his classmate at the LSE, Fei Hsiao-tung. The two had been fellow students of Malinowski at the LSE in 1938 but had lost track of each other after that. One had returned to India and become a top civil servant and the other had gone back to China and become an eminent academic. Fei was a professor at the Institute of Sociology of the Chinese Academy of Sciences and also the vice-chairman of the Chinese People's Political Consultative Conference. On 8 June 1983, Fei wrote to Haksar:

> It should be a nice surprise to have a note from a old friend when we were all in the twenties. For so many years, we did not hear anything from each other. Only last year, when I met a delegation from India, I was so much excited in hearing that you had asked your friends to locate me in China. From them I got your address ...
>
> There is so much to tell you about the forty years of our separation. I do not think I could do so through writing. My friend, Mr. Zhu Chun, now working in our Embassy in New Delhi may spend some of your leisure time to tell you the story of one of your old friends, who had so much been impressed by your personality as young energetic patriot from the East. Now we all got old, but our memory of those days may still revive our spirits.
>
> May I hope sometime in the future, we shall shake our hands and embrace each other once more.

In 1982, a delegation of the Indian Council of Social Science Research (ICSSR) led by its chairman, G. Parthasarathi, had visited China. Haksar had asked S. Gopal and P.C. Joshi—two members of that delegation—to find out Fei's whereabouts and if possible meet with him as well. As things turned out, Fei was present in one of the official engagements of the delegation.

To say that Haksar was pleasantly shocked to receive this letter would be an understatement. In a state of excitement, he immediately wrote to Indira Gandhi on 26 July 1983:

> My last encounter with the Chinese was in Korea. That was way back in 1953-54. Since then, I have not met any Chinese. And now, suddenly out of the blue, I received a letter from the Military Attache of the Chinese Embassy in New Delhi. It is curious! Isn't it? I enclose a copy of the letter together with a copy of my reply.
>
> Fei along with Jomo Kenyatta and another Chinese called Francis Hsu were my good friends in LSE. Jomo, of course, is dead. Francis is teaching Anthropology somewhere in California. But Fei has re-emerged from the limbo of history.
>
> I have been of the view that we in India have just not taken the trouble to understand the Chinese ... All our scholars in India have invariably been wrong in their assessments. Our foreign office is no better ...
>
> I was so struck by Fei's attempt to revive our old friendship that I thought I should inform you about it ...

Indira Gandhi's reply was brief but encouraging:

> Your letter of the 26th July was given to me last evening.
>
> It is an excellent idea for you to renew your old contacts. I agree that we do not have a good understanding of our neighbour and the world situation is such that this as becoming increasingly crucial.

Haksar then replied to Fei on 2 August 1983:

> Your close friend and former student Mr. Zhu Chun, came to see me at my residence on Saturday July 30 and handed over to me your letter of June 8. I read it. I re-read it. And I read it time and again in an effort to bridge the time-gap of 44 years and more. So many images of you passed through my mind—your calm and contemplative visage; your tremendous sincerity and integrity, your warmth and your deep commitment to the future of your great country. My last recollection of you is of my visit to your digs in Regents Park Road on top of a shop ...
>
> As you say it is rather difficult to write out in a letter the history of our times as we have seen it through our lives. Many of our dreams

have been fulfilled. Many have turned sour. And yet, I continue to have faith in humanity. When we are no more, we must leave this faith as an inheritance for those who will come after us—better and more sensitive human beings, altruistic and inspired by a wider vision …

I too have a hope and aspiration that some day, some time, somewhere we would meet and bridge the gap of time and its tortures by embracing each other.

Haksar and Fei were to meet sooner than they expected. In March 1984, Fei came to New Delhi to attend a conference to which Haksar also had been invited. They finally met up with each other and this was to lead to Haksar's first ever visit to China in November 1984.

Haksar turned 70 on 4 September 1983. It must have felt like old times when he received a 'Dear PNH' letter after a long time from his friend and former boss. Indira Gandhi had greeted him thus on that day:

I have just heard that it is your 70th birthday.

I send my greetings for this day and for your work with continuing commitment to the causes which we hold dear.

With good wishes,

Indira

But by that time, in spite of the fact that they would meet and she would consult him from time to time, Haksar had become somewhat cynical about her. He wrote to P.N. Dhar on 2 November 1983:

Ages ago I gave up noting the obvious landmarks in one's life measuring the passage of time. I was therefore taken aback a little by the reactions to my 70th birthday. Even when I was in Geneva, a telex came from Aruna Asaf Ali. The message was prefaced by the remark that the Prime Minister had told her on telephone that September 4 was going to be my 70th birthday. Then followed the message exhorting me to continue to want to live for doing "great things". As the message came through our Embassy in Berne, it created curiosity and excitement which was quite embarrassing to me. *When I returned on the 10th, I found a letter awaiting*

*me from Prime Minister herself in which she exhorted me to prolong my life
that I could "serve the cause which we had always believed in". I did not
really know what to say to all this. I do not even know what cause we held
dear.* [italics mine]

Earlier in the year, on 19 May 1983, Haksar had been particularly cynical
about the prime minister when he wrote to Dhar:

> ... Since almost all the Indian economists have been mobilized, I should
> imagine that very soon all our economic problems would be sorted out.
> I am now waiting for all the political scientists to be mobilized so that
> we can solve our political problems. In the meantime, Punjab and Assam
> continue to fester. Probably J&K would be added to the list. What a
> pity that a modus vivendi could not be worked out with the old man
> [Sheikh Abdullah] while he was still living. Now there is no one big
> enough to do it.

Indira Gandhi and Haksar had been through much together. They went
back at least to almost 50 years. They had seen times of glory. They had
seen times of setbacks. He had been extraordinarily close to her and she
had depended on him like on nobody else. But he had also been through
a lot of pain and anguish because of her son and she, in a rare moment
of anger, had lashed out at him and questioned his integrity. Haksar had
been prepared to forgive, if not forget. However, it was clear that by 1983,
Haksar had begun to wonder about his friend—what she really stood for
and what she really believed in.

Thomas Abraham was Haksar's Foreign Service colleague and they had
known each other well since 1952. The families had come to be very
intimate. Abraham had worked closely with Haksar during the Bangladesh
crisis, and had also served as India's high commissioner to Singapore
and Sri Lanka, and later was ambassador in Switzerland. He carried on
a correspondence with Haksar frequently. In November 1978, Abraham
had hosted Haksar and his wife in Colombo and on 27 November 1978,
Haksar had thanked him:

Our first visit to Sri Lanka was highly educative. My notions of that country, I discovered to my horror, were so primitive. So small an island is really so extraordinarily complex, sociologically speaking ... I did not know that the Sinhala people regard themselves with such deep passion and conviction that unlike the Tamilians, they are the proud descendants of the Indo-Aryans. *I used to feel a sense of regret that Buddhism did not strike roots in our country, but looking at the Buddhist church and the hordes of monks roaming all over Sri Lanka, I felt relieved that we in India did not have the problem of meeting organized religion.* [italics mine]

In 1983, G. Parthasarathi was appointed as the prime minister's special envoy for Sri Lanka following the carnage of Tamils that had taken place in Colombo and other places in July of that year. On 30 September 1983, Haksar wrote to Abraham:

G.P did tell me that he was going to meet you at the airport in Geneva. From little bits of conversation I had with him, I just could not gather the broad framework with which he has conceived his mission. However, the public image is of a Tamilian missionary speaking for Tamilians and on behalf of Tamilians. This might be a good thing for our domestic politics which I seriously doubt ... I am not sure whether anyone has worked out in detail the consequences of promoting Eelam.

Two months later, Haksar expanded on this theme to Abraham on 2 November 1983:

Frankly, I do not know the framework within which we are 'intervening' in Sri Lanka. The choice of the Envoy, the persons who were found visibly to be around him when he first visited Colombo, the noises we have made in Tamil Nadu could only be interpreted that our concerns are not "Indian" but narrowly Tamilian; that the Sri Lankans en masse are ranged against us. They may well be but it is not in our interest to make it appear so. India should be or ought to be concerned with the well-being, contentment of all the peoples of that fair island. We should search for allies amongst the Sinhalas who are not infected by the politics of incitement pursued by both the Tamilians and by Sinhalas. I do not know from where have the Eelam boys got the message that the next time massacres take place, we shall occupy part of Sri Lanka as the Turks did in Cyprus. I am not even certain whether the Jaffna Tamilians are so well oriented towards us in political terms ...

As it is not my custom to speak until I am spoken to, I keep whatever I might have to say strictly to myself or share it with you. It serves no useful purpose to be a volunteer, more specially when one's approach is so very different from those driving the chariot of the Indian State ...

In any negotiations, it is elementary to ask oneself what cards one holds. Even from this point of view, I do not know what is it we are offering in consideration of which Jayawardene and company would concede something. [italics mine]

What a precipitous fall for someone who had himself driven the chariot of the Indian state for so long with such distinction. He was really in deep freeze as far as Indira Gandhi was concerned. And being the man he was, he did not see it fit to tell her that her policies on Sri Lanka were wrong. Haksar was to unburden himself to Abraham on two more occasions. On 25 December 1985, he was to write:

... My first instinct that we should not get involved at all as a mediator between the Tamils and Sri Lanka and that we should appear at all times to be well-wishers of the inhabitants of the island, was not too wrong. That is why I suggested your name to Mrs G. But at that time [1983] she was far more concerned about the political effect on the Tamils in India and she thought that she should be seen visibly as a person acting on defence of their interests. The wily Jayawardene has outmanoeuvred us. The result is that all the world now thinks that it is India's failure to bring the Tamils around to a 'reasonable' position which is the root cause of the problem in Sri Lanka.

Three years later, on 21 January 1988, Haksar was to confess to Abraham:

I have a peculiar sense of satisfaction when I contemplate the whole mess in Sri Lanka. I had advised Indira Gandhi, if you recall, that India should not assume a mediatory role and certainly not under the "Tamil flag". I must also confess that the ideological flag unfurled by Jayawardene and company which was frankly 'racist' was bound to create a mess. We have compounded it by pathetic reliance on MG Ramachandran and the

LTTE. Apparently our intelligence had no clue whatsoever. And I really do not know how we can extricate ourselves with dignity and honour. I really feel sad about our army being involved in this thankless task. The children of those who are dying do not know what their fathers are dying for. [italics mine]

∾

For quite some time Indira Gandhi had been very unhappy with the governor of Jammu and Kashmir, B.K. Nehru. Her main grouse was that he was too close to the new chief minister, Farooq Abdullah and was not sufficiently mindful of the Congress's interests in the state. B.K. Nehru had been asked to resign and he had sent in his resignation sometime in late-December 1983 but it had been kept pending. On 23 January 1984, Indira Gandhi chaired a fateful meeting which has been described in some detail by B.K. Nehru himself in his memoirs:[5]

> The meeting started at 9.30 pm with the Prime Minister presiding. The two ministers present were Messers R. Venkatraman and Pranab Mukherjee, the Defence and Finance Ministers respectively. Neither had any direct connection with, or knowledge of the affairs of Kashmir. In addition were present Messers M.L. Fotedar, G. Parthasarathi, Rajiv Gandhi, Tikki Kaul and Babboo Haksar ... Virtually everybody agreed, some vociferously, some less noisily and some by keeping silent, that Farooq was no good and should be gotten rid of. They also agreed that as the only obstacle in getting rid of Farooq was the Governor, there was no alternative but to get rid of him also. *The only person who seems to have disagreed, at least openly, was Babboo Haksar who said that as we have a perfectly good Governor in Kashmir we should follow his advice. He seemed to have influence over Farooq; the best course would be to permit him to use that influence in the direction in which we wanted Kashmir to move. The only person who had supported Haksar was Rajiv saying that he thought that Haksarji was right.* [italics mine]

Indira Gandhi had wanted Haksar to be present at this meeting but was not sure how he would react if she spoke with him directly. She asked T.N. Kaul to bring Haksar along. Nehru's account is corroborated by one of the participants at that meeting. M.L. Fotedar's memoir[6] has External Affairs Minister P.V. Narasimha Rao and Head of R&AW R.N. Kao also in attendance in the meeting and says:

> Haksar Saheb spoke for 50 minutes and succeeded in persuading the Prime Minister that Nehru should not be shifted. Venkatraman and Mukherjee raised some questions ...

But, as Fotedar admits, Haksar had saved the situation only momentarily, because on 27 March 1984, Farooq Abdullah announced in the State Assembly that B.K. Nehru was being shifted shortly. On 22 July 1984, Farooq Abdullah himself was dismissed by the new governor, Jagmohan, and a government headed by his brother-in-law G.M. Shah was installed. Two years later, on 24 March 1986, in an interview given to K.K. Katyal of *The Hindu*, when asked what he thought of the events of July 1984, Haksar said:

> I can only describe the decisions taken and the events flowing from these decisions as tragic and perverse based on totally false perceptions of reality ... The lesson to be drawn is obvious enough. Decisions must be taken on the basis of ascertained and ascertainable facts and not on the basis of pride and prejudice. And this applies not merely to Kashmir but to the whole of the country.

Asked further on Farooq Abdullah, Haksar went on:

> The most important fact to note about Dr. Farooq Abdullah is that he has emerged as the leader of the National Conference and legitimized himself through the elections. He is, from what little I know of him, inclined to be somewhat impetuous. But his kind of impetuosity could have been easily managed. As to his alleged immaturity, all I can say is that our election laws while prohibiting insane people from contesting elections, have no provision for 'immature' person. Also, there is no way of measuring immaturity as there is a way of ascertaining insanity. We must, in my view, not allow our prejudices to get the better of us and warp our judgment of the central fact that Dr. Farooq Abdullah won the last elections and we should have respected the verdict of the people.

This was a rare public indictment of Indira Gandhi and her political colleagues who had egged her on to get rid of both B.K. Nehru and Farooq Abdullah, decisions that only Haksar had the courage to oppose to Indira Gandhi's face.

∞

The crisis in Punjab was hurtling towards its denouement. On 20 March 1984, Haksar sent Indira Gandhi a long note through R.N. Kao, stressing that:

> The solution to the Punjab problem must be achieved through the political process and this political process, in turn, must form part and parcel of the general process of renewing the hopes, faith and credibility. Prime Minister, in her person, is still the cornerstone of our national edifice. Prime Minister must be seen to be bending over backwards in starting the process ...

He then went on to spell out specific steps that he had in mind in revitalizing the political process for solution to the problems in Punjab that he said 'must be seen as part of a process affecting the rest of India':

(i) P.M. should address a letter to each of the leaders of the political parties in India (I have suggested a possible draft). The same letter should be sent to all Chief Ministers

    (a) The tone and the temper of the letter needs to be sustained by the P.M. and everyone else speaking on her behalf;

    (b) P.M. might consider making a national broadcast on the Punjab situation enlarging on the theme of the letter, maintaining its tone and temper;

    (c) I am assuming that those who have been arrested recently for the violation of our Constitution would be released. Either P.M. or someone authorized on her behalf should explicitly state that this is done as an act of reconciliation ...

(ii) Simultaneously, a letter from the Prime Minister should go to a fairly large number of Indian citizens who have in recent months issued statements on the situation in Punjab and invite them to a meeting with the Prime Minister ...

The meeting with the opposition parties should be held separately from the meeting suggested at (ii) above ...

It is my hope that the first meeting [with the opposition parties] would yield a consensus. That consensus would centre around the following propositions.

    i Chandigarh to become the Capital of Punjab.

    ii A new capital to be built for Haryana.

    iii The allocation of waters to be decided by a Commission in accordance with the well-established norms governing the rights of riparians.

    iv. The border areas between Haryana and Punjab including Fazilka and Abohar should be redefined taking into account the following three criteria.

        a. Village as a Unit

        b. Linguistic composition of the population of a village

        c. Territorial contiguity

At the very end, Haksar added in his hand:

If you have to enter the Golden Temple some day, the steps I have suggested are the necessary pre-condition. [italics mine]

Indira Gandhi was to enter the hallowed Golden Temple on 24 June 1984 in completely different circumstances than Haksar would have ever imagined.

Haksar met Indira Gandhi on 8 May 1984 and Punjab was discussed, because 19 days later he was to write to her again, expressing his disappointment that his suggestions had been ignored:

I am more reinforced in my conviction that there can be no viable or durable solution to the Punjab problem unless the processes involved in solving it involve the rest of India. There has, therefore, to be a design—an architectural design. I had taken the liberty of suggesting a design in my note of March 20. If that design or some variant of it had been put into operation in the month of March 1984, we would have by now created an environment in the whole of India which, in course of time, would have created the minimum condition for solving the problem of Punjab. The design, by very definition, is an integrated system. The release of Akalis was part of that design. Outside the design, it becomes a more discrete event. And I fear that the expectations of what would happen in releasing the Akali leaders would be belied.

Politics is concerned with bargaining and in order to bargain, one always pitches one's claim high and so, the Akali leaders who have been released would be involved in the logic of appearing to take a hard line so that they do not lose their bargaining position.

I should like to reiterate once again that in my view, the extremists in Punjab, objectively speaking, are sustained by the ideology of Khalistan with all its nuances and ramifications. If my hypothesis is correct, their aim would be to create conditions for migration of Hindus, more especially from its urban areas and their withdrawal from trades, commerce, industry and property-holding.

There was one important matter which I wanted to mention to you. I did not because I had already taken an hour of your time. It concerns the way we are handling the three Indo-China states [Vietnam, Laos, Cambodia] ...

As for China, I had submitted that India-China relations need to be studied in depth. Our system, as we have operated, does not enable us to do so ... [italics mine]

China was always on Haksar's mind and he would badger Indira Gandhi on it. And the letter shows the range of subjects he would raise with her when they met. And as for Punjab, as Haksar had anticipated, the Akalis continued to take a hard line. Events moved rapidly thereafter and Operation Bluestar was launched on 1 June 1984 by the Indian Army to rid the sacred Golden Temple of the hundreds of armed militants hiding and operating from within its precincts. Seven days later, speaking at a meeting organized by a group dedicated to opposing communalism, Haksar called on all secular and democratic parties not have any association or relationship with parties based on religion. Mixing politics with religion, Haksar warned, was a sure route to the disintegration of India. For the first time, in public he appealed to Indira Gandhi to give up her approach of confrontation with the Opposition but balanced that by asking the Opposition to also abandon its kneejerk 'Remove Indira' attitude. And, speaking like a Marxist that he was, he drew attention to economic factors that he said were fuelling divisive tendencies and movements—the main such factors being unemployment and inequality.

On 14 June 1984, Haksar wrote a 'Dear Induji' letter again:

I cannot remember who wrote it. But the feeling those two lines expressed acquire a poignancy of their own when I contemplate our country. To the best of my recollection, those two lines were:

> "Getting and spending we lay waste our hours,
> Is there nothing in this world which is ours"

From time to time you speak feelingly about things. You spoke of the 'healing touch' in 1980. It just failed to get translated into action. You have spoken again about a healing touch ... I was just wondering whether it is beyond the capacity of the Birlas, the Modis, the Tatas, the Mafatlals, et al who have lived off the fat of the land to gather together in response to your call for a healing touch, to bring sustenance, succor and support to those families—be they in Bhiwandi or Punjab, who have suffered ...

The newspapers this morning carry headlines about the discovery that the terrorists were inspired by Khalistan. This is a welcome discovery. But it means that millions of Sikhs have to be rescued from the poisonous emanation of this ideology ...

Finally, I am wondering whether any political strategy would inform and inspire the process of interrogation of those taken into custody; or would they be left to be handled by the Police and/or the Military. [italics mine]

ॐ

J.R.D. Tata, the doyen of Indian industry turned 80 on 29 July 1984. He and PNH had been close friends for over three decades. This friendship was independent of the relationship that Tata had with the Nehru family. Both of them had been together as members of the Atomic Energy Commission in the 1970s and Tata had invited Haksar to address Tata executives in Poona in 1971. On 1 August 1984, Haksar wrote to him:

Dear Jeh:

... I missed the news that you are now 80 years old. Soli Godrej who visited me the other day told me about it. How wonderful? Please accept my warmest felicitations and best wishes for continuing your innings, the scoreboard reading: 100 not out.

Now that you are 80, isn't it time for you to reflect creatively and constructively on the state of our country? I hope you will do this. I have always been intrigued by one question: How is it that leading members of Indian bourgeoisie just did not measure up to their counterparts in Europe and Japan? I am omitting America largely because it is not a country with any significant history ... We on the other hand are over-burdened with history. In that sense, our evolution and our problems correspond more nearly to the problems of Europe, Japan and China.

Haksar's letter obviously unleashed pent up furies in J.R.D. Tata, for he was to send a very long reply on 26 September 1984. After apologizing for the long delay 'to thank you for your charming letter', Tata let fly:

Dear PN:

You have asked me whether it is not time for me to reflect creatively and constructively on the state of our country. I have done so, and for a long time ...

I was a little puzzled by your own puzzlement ... I don't know by what criteria you compared us ... with our European and Japanese counterparts, and what you would expect from them, but if it is initiative and creativeness in their field of activity, I would imagine that ... men like Jamsetji Tata and his sons fully measured up to their counterparts elsewhere in the world, including America, In a smaller way, men like the Wadias who built men-of war for the British Navy, or the Sarabhais for their contribution to science and culture, also measure up ...

The advent of independence brought a dramatic change in the situation which would normally have provided the same vital base as in other countries for great projects, ventures and adventures by Indians. An essential pre-requisite, however, would have been freedom of choice, of investment and of action ... Instead of releasing energies and enterprises, the system of licences and all-pervasive controls imposed on the private sector of the country, combined with confiscatory personal taxation, not only discouraged and penalized honest free enterprise but encouraged, and brought success and wealth, to a new breed of bribers, tax evaders and black marketeers ...

The nationalization, on expropriatory terms, of insurance and banks, conveniently created a state monopoly of investible and lendable funds, while fiscal policies, combined with the use made of the Companies Act, the Industries (Development and Regulation) Act, the Monopolies and Restrictive Trade Practices Act and innumerable other enactments, regulations and administrative decisions effectively concentrated all economic power in the hands of the politicians in power and the bureaucracy. Under such conditions, efforts at promoting and bringing to fruition large projects, however desirable, became nightmarish and time-consuming one, or ended in outright rejection. I need only cite the example of the great Tata Fertiliser Project of 1967 which would have brought immense benefits to the Indian economy but was rejected outright on the ground that Tatas were already too big ...

I am sorry to inflict this long tirade on you, for which my excuse is that you, albeit innocently, provoked it yourself by your question: *I began my 55-year career as an angry young man because I couldn't stomach the foreign domination of our country ... I end it as an angry old man ... because it simply breaks my heart to see the continuing miserable fate of the vast majority of our people, for much of which I blame 35 years of ill-conceived economic policies of our Government.* [italics mine]

J.R.D. Tata certainly had been provoked. In his counter-blast, Tata had referred to 'the great Tata Fertiliser Project of 1967'. This was a gigantic fertilizer project planned at Mithapur in Gujarat based initially on imported raw material, but whose use was expected to decline over time. The project had strong supporters and opponents within the government. Leading the brigade opposing the project was the minister of shipping and transport, the distinguished economist Dr V.K.R.V Rao. Haksar would be later accused of having this project shot down but the records show otherwise. On 26 July 1968, he told the prime minister:

I understand P.M. wanted to see papers about the Tata Fertiliser Project ... Having seriously considered the matter over and over again, I have reached the conclusion that this is a very well-conceived and comprehensive project. Its scale is such as to give us an assurance of low cost. The project must be seen as a whole, which some of its critics are not doing. The building of the port, for instance, is an essential element in the cost. It is no use arguing in abstract that this port could be situated elsewhere.

On 1 January 1969, Haksar sent the prime minister an unusually detailed 27-page note based on his consultations with various people and that systematically addressed all the objections that had been raised against the project. On 1 May 1969, he told the prime minister that 'it is not good enough merely to shut out the Mithapur project, but those who do so must provide concrete alternative proposals which are practicable and can produce the necessary amount of fertilizer in an identifiable period of time'. It is clear both the prime minister and he wanted to find a way out to get the project moving. But Rao's objections, coming at a time when concentration of economic power had become a big political issue, elicited strong support in the Congress party and in Parliament as well. The Planning Commission and its deputy chairman, D.R. Gadgil, had also weighed in against the project. Ultimately, the Tata proposal was shelved.

Haksar responded to that Tata's reply on 3 October 1984:

I have your letter of September 26. It moved me deeply. It moved me because you wrote it with such passion, sincerity mixed with compassion for the "continuing miserable fate of the vast majority of our people".

Please do not misunderstand me. It was not part of my intention to enter into polemics. Problems of our country, howsoever one may view them, are much too complex to yield to an attempt to score debating points.

Is the essence of what you say is that all these years, following our Independence, the government policies have brought us to the present situation? Apparently, a simple-minded Adam Smithian policy would have done the trick in India. But even this proposition needs to be worked out. It is not so self-evident in India. And even Adam Smith before he set himself out as some sort of an Economist, had a very strong feeling for morality ... *It is true that Jamshedji Tata along with men like Walchand Hirachand or Ambalal Sarabhai articulated the deeper urges for modernization of our social, economic and political order. No such urge is visible today at the collective level of our industrialists and men and women engaged in trade and commerce.*

Be that as it may, the sole object of my raising the question which I did was to invite your attention to the fact that the entire process of historical transformation of an ancient society such as ours, where human beings are deeply enmeshed in all kinds of valid or invalid traditions, thought processes, social structures, etc., cannot be subsumed within a category called 'Economic Policy', howsoever conceived ...

Might I conclude this letter by saying that I deeply respect your anger, but from what little experience I have of life, anger has always been a bad counsellor. [italics mine]

Other than Tata, Haksar had some others also in the world of business and industry whom he respected and stayed in frequent contact with—men like Keshub Mahindra, Bharat Ram, S.P. Godrej, H.P. Nanda, Neville Wadia,[7] K.A. Hamied, D.L. Shah and Amrut Mody. Mahindra had written to Haksar on 6 January 1975 on his taking over as deputy chairman of the Planning Commission:

My dear Haksar Sab:
Knowing that you could have opted for any position in government, you picked the most difficult one. How true to your character and convictions. May I join many to wish you much luck and wish also for you a little more contentment and lots of happiness.

In an earlier generation, Haksar was much enamoured of Walchand Hirachand to whom he paid handsome tributes in a public lecture.[8] What was common to all these people was not just that they were successful businessmen but were businessmen with a larger sense of social purpose and commitment. A trust founded by Shah was to reprint Haksar's autobiography in the early-1990s.

Haksar's first ever visit to China had, by then been finalized, and on 1 August 1984, he wrote to the person who had invited him—his former classmate Fei Hsiao-tung:

My very, very dear friend Fei:

I have been thinking of writing to you ever since we met together here in Delhi. Both my wife and I shall carry the memory of our meeting at the lobby of the Ashoka Hotel and your subsequent visit to our house. It was one of the most joyous occasions for us. It was a deeply moving experience to meet with you and to feel that though the world has changed, certain values still abide ...

All the contemporary conflicts in our world stem from false perceptions, false consciousness and false history. As we turn towards the 21st century, the only thing worthwhile for each one of us to do, both as individuals and as organized states is to consciously sublimate our individual and collective energies to bring happiness, well-being, enlightenment, a spirit of cooperation among our respective peoples and organized states...

Both my wife and I are intensely looking forward to our first visit to your great country and to learn something about it firsthand.

Later in the year, on 27 October 1984, Haksar accompanied by his wife left for his long-planned China visit. They were going to spend 10 days in Japan first before proceeding to China. He was in Tokyo when Indira Gandhi was assassinated on 31 October 1984. He cancelled his engagements and isolated himself for a day or two and then continued with his visit. On his return, he would write to Fei on 13 December 1984:

I meant to write to you soon after our return ... But I could not. While we were away from our country, a tragedy of vast dimensions was enacted on October 31. And when we returned, it took us quite some time to treat it as a part of the tortured history of human kind ...

I have come back with the deep conviction that our two countries must interact with each other continuously at every point of our national endeavor so that we can banish for ever the very idea of conflict between us ... The characteristic feature of our age is the vast explosion of not merely science and technology but of human consciousness. And our two countries together represent a very large segment of humanity. Don't we have to set new patterns of international relationship?

∾

Haksar's good friend, brother of one his chums from the late-1930s and someone who had worked with him in the initial years of Indira Gandhi's prime ministership, General P.P. Kumaramangalam, wrote to him on 12 November 1984:

> The events of the last twelve days must have shaken you as much it has done me. Whatever my reservations on certain actions of Mrs. Gandhi, she nevertheless had done good in many fields and had kept our country's image up in the world. Knowing how close you had been to her and what confidence you had put into her in the early days of her premiership, I have no doubt you are feeling sad over the way she was assassinated. It was typical of her, following in her father's way of thinking, that she insisted Sikhs were in her security personnel in spite of warnings. My sympathies go to you on this occasion as knowing you, I know you will feel her loss deeply ...
>
> The little I know of the present PM ... I am certain he is a person of integrity. My fear is his inexperience and from what I have heard of his advisers (or whiz kids) does not give me much confidence. I hope therefore he will call for your advice and also other elders like you. I understand that unlike his brother, he holds no bitterness towards you ...

A few days later, on 9 December 1984, the general again wrote to Haksar:

> I do not know Rajiv [Gandhi] at all well. His grandfather had the intellect and after a long and severe period of trial, he had made himself eminently fit for the role he had after independence. His mother had not her father's exceptional intellect, but she had the goodwill of many elders like Padmaja [Naidu] whom she could turn to for advice with trust (as also good friends like Mohan [Kumaramangalam] and GP [G. Parthasarathi]) and this helped her in the start of her career as Prime Minister. *On top of it all she had you as Counsellor and friend who had no personal ambition to be either a grey eminence or to usurp her power.*
>
> I am happy that we will have a young man with fresh ideas who will take over the helm but he has not the experience and I do not think he has any elders whom he can trust and whose advice he will take. *Someone like you will be necessary to help him through his initial phase. I hope he bears no resentment to you as did his brother. I hope he will realize*

what you did for his mother and therefore confide in you on important
matters ... [italics mine]

Rajiv Gandhi certainly held no bitterness towards Haksar as Sanjay Gandhi
had, which the general so correctly pointed out. But Haksar did not become
the 'elder statesman' that Kumaramangalam was praying for, although Rajiv
Gandhi would meet Haksar from time and time and certainly give him a
patient hearing.

What did Haksar really think of Indira Gandhi? We will never know
for sure since he never did say anything about her in public. But he seems
to have spoken to a few people. Indira Gandhi's biographer Katherine
Frank spoke to him extensively in the mid-1990s, and in one place quotes
him as follows:[9]

> Haksar's opinion of Indira at this time [1966] was that she was intelligent
> but out of her depth. He felt that 'basically she was not a political person,
> that she didn't grasp the complexities and problems of political situations'.
> In short, she needed guidance, but she had real potential. *Her most*
> *valuable gift in Haksar's eyes was her ability to connect with the people, an*
> *extraordinary bond he always believed to be genuine.* [italics mine]

But, by 1977, he seems to have become embittered for, I.K. Gujral writes
in his memoirs that on 19 March 1977, Haksar unburdened himself to
him in the presence of their mutual friend, Syed Mir Qasim, the former
chief minister of Jammu and Kashmir, and said:

> You too have known her for a long time. Let us accept that she is a
> mediocrity who achieved great heights while her complexities forced
> her to prove time and time again that she could not survive without
> crutches ... He then recounted how different were Pandit Jawaharlal
> Nehru's qualities of head and heart, which had remained deeply ingrained
> in his mind.

Clearly, by 1977, Haksar had become wiser and was no longer starry
eyed about her. Too much had happened between them to embitter the
relationship, if not end it permanently. Sanjay Gandhi and Haksar's poor
opinion of him was undoubtedly the main reason for the rupture. But

it is also true that Haksar, by comparing her with her father, was being somewhat unfair to Indira Gandhi.

Mohit Sen was a communist leader who was for years in the CPI and later left to be part of the United Communist Party of India, which had a short life. His brother had been in London with Haksar in the late-1930s and Sen himself was a regular visitor to Haksar's house. He would, after the mid-1970s, become an ardent champion of Indira Gandhi and his memoir,[10] is full of praise for her. He recalls:

> On an altogether different plane was the relationship between her and P.N. Haksar. She told me very little about this relationship though she did mention very appreciatively his guardianship of her two sons when they were students in England. She also spoke more than once about his deep wisdom, his pride in India and his integral vision that was a rearticulation of that of her father's. Also, more than once, however, she added, both mischievously and wistfully, that she did not think he thought much of her!
>
> Meeting P.N. Haksar during the Emergency and after she had returned to power, I could not but be struck by the bitterness with which he spoke about her ... He accepted her capacity to mobilise the people but, as she had put it, did not think highly of her intelligence ...

B.K. Nehru recounts in his memoirs how he met Haksar sometime at the end of 1975, and told him that he would tell Indira Gandhi what Sanjay was doing.[11] He records Haksar's response:

> He said to me that it would be the greatest mistake to say anything critical in the slightest degree about Sanjay. She was absolutely blind as far as that boy was concerned; she regarded him as perfect, he could do no wrong ... If ever I said anything which implied any criticism of Sanjay, the immediate effect would be that access would be denied ... What little good I could do and was doing by injecting ideas into her thinking and suggesting actions to be taken would no longer be possible.

Haksar certainly felt Indira Gandhi's loss deeply, and also for the horrendous killings of Sikhs that followed her assassination. He was uncharacteristically dispirited. On 5 December 1984, he wrote to his close friend M.R. Vyas in Bombay:

… What happened on October 31 and that which followed it are utterly, utterly shameful for our country. And the shame of it all came as an unbearable agony when one was confronted with the national endeavour and the passion behind it of countries like Japan and China [from where he had just returned]. So words like tragedy, trauma etc. become all very routine … Despite 75 years of struggle for freedom and nearly four decades of independence, even a simple idea like secular nationalism has not found its naturalization in Indian habitat. It wanders around like a strange animal in a hostile jungle to be devoured by the wild beasts of Hindu, Muslim and Sikh revivalists. And there is no end to it all.

The Rajiv Gandhi Years (1985–1990)

Haksar receiving the Indira Gandhi Award for National Integration from Prime Minister Rajiv Gandhi, New Delhi, November 1989.

IT TOOK HAKSAR A WHILE TO GET BACK TO NORMAL LIFE AFTER INDIRA Gandhi's killing, and as soon as he did on 1 January 1985, he wrote to Natwar Singh:

> Ever since Urmila and I returned back to New Delhi on November 22, you and Hem have been out. A few days ago I telephoned your home. Your brother was there and I left with him a message saying that I had telephoned. All this activity on my part was inspired by a desire to communicate with you largely because, as you can imagine, I have been bottled up within myself since October 31. Anyway the past now forms part of history. The present and the future beckons us.

On 8 January 1985, Haksar had met with the new prime minister, the son of his former boss and someone who he had known for years. He had discussed the continuing crisis in Punjab with Rajiv Gandhi and had recalled the advice he had given the prime minister's late mother—which, unfortunately, had not been taken. He reiterated what he had told her: that the prime minister should launch a massive outreach programme to reach out to people from different walks of life, especially Sikhs from outside the state and proceed with the healing process in Punjab. He also wanted Rajiv Gandhi to explain to the nation the continuing significance of 30 January 1948, the day of Mahatma Gandhi's assassination, and announce that it would be marked solemnly every year.

On 18 January 1985, Haksar received a letter from the newly appointed defence minister of India, P.V. Narasimha Rao, who, six years later, would become prime minister himself:

> Thank you for your letter for the New Years Day. Coming as it does as a departure from your normal inclination, your message of felicitation is of special value and encouragement to me.

This reply was a bit unusual and I wanted to know what lay behind it. Fortunately, one of Narasimha Rao's closest aides remembered the background and recalled:

> PNH at that time had developed a deliberate, almost ascetic, aloofness from power or the powerful. A new year letter was extraordinarily thoughtful, made all the more so by its total absence of precedent. PVNR [P.V. Narasimha Rao] was very moved although that was not an emotion he carried on his sleeve as you know. PVNR was trying to find a more positive term for the disinclination that his [Haksar's] customary, and by no means malign, distance suggested ...

This aide was to move to New York in 1986 by which time Narasimha Rao had become minister of human resource development. He called on Haksar before leaving and recollects being advised thus:

> He [Haksar] told me to spend one Saturday afternoon each month at the Strand used books store and buy enough to keep me intellectually

occupied for the month in that otherwise "cerebrally arid" city. He asked me how PVNR had taken to HRD [human resource development] and I replied that I thought he was excited by the opportunity to really create something that would be his own. PNH replied: "Yes, I can see that. The man has a mind." He paused, took a sip of his drink, and continued, "A mind can be a dangerous thing in politics."

On the occasion of her first death anniversary, the Indira Gandhi Memorial Trust (IGMT) that had been formed had decided to bring out a volume of recollections of and tributes to her. Naturally, Haksar was also asked for his contribution and he replied on 30 April 1985 to Sharada Prasad who was then the secretary of the IGMT:

> I have your letter ... asking me to contribute something to a volume of tributes and reminiscences to be published on the first death anniversary of our former Prime Minister Indira Gandhi. As you can imagine, it is not an easy thing to do. Perhaps my doubts and hesitations could be overcome if I could talk to you and I shall be only too glad to come over at any time which may be convenient to you either in your office or in your home. I hope you will sympathise with the predicament in which you have placed me.

As it happened, the impressive volume comprised some 200 contributions from political leaders, scientists, artists, authors, musicians, civil servants, intellectuals and a whole host of others from across the world. But, the man who had, perhaps, been closest to her and helped the most in creating her iconic image was missing in the compendium.

Ironically, a few years later, Haksar was to encourage Sharada Prasad to do what he himself had been unable to do, and Sharada Prasad was to respond in a similar fashion on 30 September 1993:

> I am guilty of grave neglect in not having replied to the letter you wrote last month. I was away in Bangalore for a month and returned only a few days ago and saw all the letters that had arrived in my absence. But even after my return I have delayed writing to you. The real reason is a

dilemma I am in. You have a right to ask me to put down my memories of some of the historic events and processes we have been through and of that *unfathomable* person we worked for. But remembrance of things past makes me very uncomfortable and also the thought that history is perhaps made by adventurers abetted by cowards and confused people. A further contributory factor is the medical problem that impaired my memory, because of which what were once uncertainties have become uncertainties. I can only explain this to you when we meet. Therefore, please do not ask me to jot down memories. [italics mine]

Alas, the two people who knew her best—or, at least, as much she allowed herself to be known—Haksar and Sharada Prasad never wrote anything about Indira Gandhi and about their times with her.

Haksar began the new year by writing wistfully to the prime minister. It was a cry of a deeply hurt man. He told Rajiv Gandhi on 1 January 1986:

> The calendar has inexorably revolved. Today is the first dawn of a New Year. For some strange reason, I thought of you and Sonia and, of course, of the children. Perhaps it was one of those phenomenon of stream of consciousness. There has remained in my mind some memories of the past. That might have been the reason for my thinking about you and yours ...
>
> I saw you last on January 8, 1985. Almost a year has rolled by. Several times I thought of seeing you and talking to you. However, constituted as I am, I could not convince myself that I would be justified in making trespasses on your time and, even more, on your attention. *In fact, I wrote to you twice without evoking a response. This is not by way of any complaint, but I shall be failing in my duty if I did not say that there are a few things which are worrying me. And, at my age, the worries are not on my own account. They centre around our country and, naturally, around you as our Prime Minister.* [italics mine]

The prime minister too had been thinking of Haksar. The National Integration Council (NIC) was set up by Jawaharlal Nehru in 1962 to find 'ways and means to combat the evils of communalism, casteism, regionalism, linguism and narrow-mindedness, and to formulate definite conclusions in order to give a lead to the country'. On 24 February 1986, Prime Minister Rajiv Gandhi wrote and invited Haksar to be a member of the Council. Haksar replied on 8 March 1986:

> … I feel, within myself, a sense of inadequacy in contributing anything worthwhile to the deliberations of the NIC. I find myself totally ill at ease when impassioned speeches replace serious thinking. And the problems of National Integration Council are, if anything, more intractable today than they were in the earlier years of nation-building in our country. In my view … national integration is the end-product of processes involved in nation-building …
>
> I have no doubt that the reconstitution of the National Integration Council could not have been undertaken with the sole purpose of traversing the ground already so laboriously traversed during the period of more than two decades. It is in this hope that I warmly and sincerely welcome your efforts to search for some fresh approaches … I find myself duty-bound to accept your kind and gracious invitation.

The NIC got moving quickly and, on 24 May 1986, Haksar received a letter from Home Minister Buta Singh:

> You may kindly recall that the National Integration Council in its meeting of 7th April 1986, had set up a Standing Committee of 21 Members under Shri Jagjivan Ram as Chairman. The Prime Minister has now set up a Punjab Advisory Group from amongst the Members of the Standing Committee which could report to the Home Minister. The Group can also report directly to the Prime Minister on any matter that they may consider appropriate because of its extreme urgency or utmost importance.
>
> The Prime Minister has been pleased to nominate you as a Member of the Group.

This group also had the BJP leader L.K. Advani as one of its members. Two days later, Haksar told Buta Singh what he really thought of this initiative of the prime minister:

... I sincerely hope I will not be misunderstood, but quite frankly, I really fail to see how such a group can tender advice on a matter like Punjab which is one of extraordinary complexity and has implicit in it political and security dimensions of utmost sensitivity ...

As an outside observer of the scene ... it would seem that a part of our country called Punjab is face to face with a problem whose outward manifestations consist of young men engaged in killing ... We have also witnessed the scene when a group of people came from somewhere and then disappeared after unfurling the flag of Khalistan. This raises a question whether there is any relationship between the movement and the ideology of Khalistan and the young men described as extremists and terrorists? We also know that for more than a decade, people calling themselves Khalistanis and having even constituted the government of Khalistan, moving about freely in Great Britain, Canada and in the United States, and all these countries are supposed to "friendly" countries ...

The same day as Haksar was pouring cold water on the prime minister's request, he was approached by a group of eminent citizens on New Delhi to get involved in their efforts to find a solution to the crisis in Punjab. I.K. Gujral approached Haksar on behalf of this group. While regretting his inability to attend the first meeting of the group, Haksar told the future prime minister of India:

... I share your anxieties. The question before our country is whether the whole of India, including governments and political parties, can be persuaded to see the dangers to our very national existence. Either we do this on a national scale or we, inexorably drift once again to a state of anarchy and disintegration. *Neither the situation in Punjab, nor the situation in Kashmir nor in the North East can be dealt with within the calculus of everyday politics that we play. That politics has brought us to the present stage ... All political parties, including, of course, the Congress , are busy playing the game of politics as usual and we simply must get out of this miasma of politics* ... Nothing else will do. [italics mine]

It would have been particularly anguishing for Haksar to say the things he said in this letter which were, in many ways, a severe criticism of Indira Gandhi. Like the NIC initiative, the Gujral initiative too ended up nowhere.

Two years later, Prime Minister Rajiv Gandhi would invite him for two meetings on Punjab with a small group—the first on 28 March 1988 and another a month later, on 25 April 1988. There is unfortunately no record of what Haksar said at these meetings.

∽

On 23 April 1985, the Supreme Court had passed a judgment on an appeal filed by a divorced Muslim woman called Shah Bano and directed that her husband pay her a maintenance allowance for the rest of her life as mandated by law. The judgment was immediately attacked by Muslim clerics and religious organizations on the grounds that it went against Muslim personal law. The prime minister welcomed the verdict but pretty soon began to get lobbied by a number of his own colleagues—both Hindu and Muslim—and by Muslim religious organizations with a demand that he do something to rectify the verdict. In February 1986, he finally gave his approval to a Bill to be introduced in Parliament that would nullify the Supreme Court's decision. A few days after it had been introduced, Haksar wrote to Gopi Arora—one of Rajiv Gandhi's top aides—on 28 February 1986:

> I am unable to understand the political compulsion behind the proposed Bill in Parliament. All historical experience shows that attempts to accommodate reactions masquerading in religious, racial and political garbs feeds and strengthens darkest political reactions. One just cannot fight communalism in India—Hindu, Muslim or Sikh—by seeking accommodation. Such attempts only vets appetite of enemies and discourages friends.
>
> I devoutly hope a sober assessment would be made. A joint select committee would be a nice place to give a burial to the Bill ...
>
> I have a hunch some third rate politicians ... are suggesting that the proposed Bill may win them Muslim votes ... Some so-called wise politicians scared Smt. Indira Gandhi that the whole Bangladesh affair was losing her Muslim votes in Bihar. But she took a firm stand and no Muslim votes were lost in Bihar in the 1972 elections.

Arora gave a perplexing reply the next day, saying: 'A relevant radicalism, of which fight against communalism will be a major element, is the need of the hour. But the entire structure of the political economy stands in the way of such radicalism. Voluntarism can only go so far and no farther. I am not advocating helpless surrender to what is. One must do what one ought to. At this juncture, your guidance is absolutely crucial.' But, whatever guidance Haksar was giving when asked was obviously leading nowhere because the prime minister with his brute majority in the Lok Sabha was able to steamroll the Bill through. As if to mollify Hindu sentiment, the locks at the Babri Masjid-Ramjanmabhoomi complex at Ayodhya were opened on 1 February 1986. These two events were to change the entire discourse of Indian politics and lead to the rise of the BJP.

The last President of the USSR, Mikhail Gorbachev visited India twice in two years—in November 1986 and November 1988. On both occasions, Prime Minister Rajiv Gandhi called in Haksar both individually and as part of a small group of eminent people to brief and advise him. Haksar had been taken up with Gorbachev especially after his summit with President Reagan at Reykjavik in October 1986, when nuclear weapons came tantalizingly close to being abolished. After his first visit he wrote an editorial in *Man & Development*:

> Mikhail Gorbachev has shown extraordinary tenacity of will and purpose even in the midst of the rigor mortis of the Soviet political and State apparatus. However, it would be wrong to think of Gorbachev as an accidental or random phenomenon. He has woven together the trends of Soviet society which were expressed by Lenin, Luncharsky, Maxim Gorky. Khrushchev, Kosygin, Andropov and Marshal Ustinov. Gorbachev's own contribution no doubt is distinct, more specifically in formulating with great precision the tasks facing Soviet society in the context of the real world today. Among all the political leaders in the world, he alone has pinpointed the one single source of human tragedy which lies in men

and women, including politicians perceiving reality as refracted through the prism of past thought structures.

Haksar is usually associated with his political, diplomatic and educational contributions. But he was to leave his mark in the field of culture as well. On 20 January 1987, he received a letter from P.V. Narasimha Rao, minister of human resource development that was to open yet another chapter in Haksar's life. The letter read:

> You would be kindly aware that we have three Akademies functioning as autonomous Bodies. These were brought into being many years back and were constituted as Registered Societies to look after the disciplines of Lalit Kala, Sahitya, Sangeet and Natak.
>
> In a meeting of the National Council of the Arts, India's apex Advisory Body on cultural matters presided over by the Prime Minister himself, it was decided to carry out a review of the activities of these Akademies and to suggest structural and thematic changes in their functioning ... *The Prime Minister feels that this important body should be headed by a person of your eminence ... I shall be grateful if you would kindly accept to head this Review Committee.* [italics mine]

The six-person review committee that Narasimha Rao mentioned in his letter was to be finally constituted on 24 March 1988, with the National School of Drama also added to its scope of review. The delay was caused by Haksar's reluctance to accept the prime minister's offer because he was not convinced that the government would take his recommendations seriously. It took a lot of cajoling by the prime minister's information adviser, Sharada Prasad, to finally bring Haksar on board.

On 21 January 1987, an extraordinary event took place at a press conference being addressed by the prime minister. In response to a question, Rajiv Gandhi blurted out 'you will soon be talking to a new Foreign Secretary'. The-then foreign secretary, A.P. Venkateswaran, was sitting in the front row

when his sacking was announced. Haksar was shocked. He had known Venkateswaran very well over the years. Most recently, Venkateswaran had hosted him in Beijing in November 1984. He wrote to the prime minister on 27 January 1987:

I have heard some vague rumours that the Government of J&K is proposing to set up a Committee with a specific terms of reference on Jammu's autonomy with Balraj Puri as its Chairman. Must we go on compounding errors of judgment?

I am seriously disturbed about the fall out of L'affaire Venkateswaran.

There is one other matter which is causing me even more serious concern. Way back in 1975 I had funded a very sensitive project. It is being totally messed about. This is serious.

I would suggest that you authorize someone enjoying your confidence, but possessing total integrity, to speak to me and report back to you.

My sense is that the 'very sensitive project' that Haksar lamented about was the company to make high alloy and special steels called Midhani which had been set up in Hyderabad to meet the needs of the nuclear, space and other industries. Three weeks later, on 28 February 1987, Haksar wrote to the lady who was occupying the seat that he had adorned 15 years earlier, Sarla Grewal:

When I had the pleasure of meeting you the other day, I had mentioned that one of the ways in which our Prime Minister could smooth things out following the Venkateswaran affair might be to offer him a suitable appointment within the country. It had then occurred to me that, perhaps, a Membership of UPSC [Union Public Service Commission] might be the right sort of thing. UPSC was meant to be and should remain a highly prestigious body ...

... I do not know what is the tenure of the present Chairman of the UPSC, H.K.L. Capoor who worked under me in the Planning Commission ... I cannot say he is of the same calibre as the Chairmen I have known since our Independence. I cannot therefore recommend Venkateswaran's appointment as a Member of the UPSC if he is to be one of the rather indifferent gentlemen who now occupy the exalted position.

However, if there is any possibility of restoring to UPSC its true image, then Venkateswaran could well be considered as the Chairman. [italics mine]

The prime minister did, in fact, offer the membership of the UPSC to Venkateswaran as Haksar had suggested but Venkateswaran was firm on not accepting any 'compensatory largesse' from Rajiv Gandhi.

The Venkateswaran episode had saddened Haksar. But there were other issues bothering him. Old hands in organizations he had dealt with while at the helm of power used to meet him and complain of governmental apathy. Thus, it was that on 26 February 1987, he wrote to Gopi Arora:

> ... *I expect from you, as usual, utmost objectivity and still more objectivity. In the governance of the country at the level of the Prime Minister and his aides, there is nothing more important than that the people should know that matters would be handled objectively and justly.* I have no doubt that you share my sentiments and would do the needful. I have some knowledge of skullduggery which goes on in various places, including BHEL—an organization about which [Robert] McNamara had once told me that "India could justly be proud of it". But it has been reduced to an extremely unhappy state.
>
> This observation of mine applies with equal vigour to the family of the Atomic Energy Agency. I am not concerned about who the Chairman is, but I am deeply concerned that the entire organization should be so sick and should run fever ... For more than ten years of my life, I had been involved in nothing more than trying to sort out personal maladjustments. There was a time when Homi Sethna and Raja Ramanna were in a state of war which affected the morale of BARC [Bhabha Atomic Energy Centre] seriously. Earlier still, there was lack of proper communication between Vikram Sarabhai and Homi Sethna ... BARC has grown too large. It is too miscellaneous that there is no inner coherence. It has become an umbrella organization and needs urgent repair ...
>
> *So far as I am concerned, some of the recent actions of the government seem to be predicated upon the assumption that things should be allowed to get worse before they get better. I have often expressed this feeling to you in our personal conversations* ... [italics mine]

Clearly, Haksar was already becoming disillusioned with the new regime. He would keep writing to the prime minister and keep meeting him and his aides but obviously that was because he felt a deep sense of obligation. He had thought of himself as a sentinel when he was serving the Indian state on a day-to-day basis and that self-perception had not disappeared.

○

Kallol Bhattacharjee, a journalist working with *The Hindu* came out with a riveting book in 2017 called *The Great Game in Afghanistan: Rajiv Gandhi, General Zia and the Unending War.* The book tells the story of an attempt by President Reagan to involve the Indian prime minister in trying to find a solution to the Afghanistan imbroglio in 1987, making use of Gandhi's excellent rapport with Mikhail Gorbachev. The channel of communication between Reagan and the Indian prime minister was the then-US Ambassador to India, John Gunther Dean. But, Bhattacharjee did not know about Dean's meetings with Haksar.

On 26 March 1987, Dean called on Haksar at 4 pm. What happened then was recounted by a hugely miffed Haksar in a letter to Rajiv Gandhi on 11 April 1987:

> Even in the midst of pain, anguish and vast amount of turmoil caused by the murder of my own niece as well as her husband, I am gathering myself together to write this letter to you because of my fear that unless things are handled with care, concern and circumspection, we might land ourselves in a mess. I simply hate being reduced to the status of being unprofessional. In my time, I have been entrusted with extremely difficult and sensitive tasks and I know all the perils of crossed wires entangled with cross purposes ...
>
> *Gopichand Hinduja accompanied by his brother Ashok Hinduja turned up to see me on March 26th ... They came with some sort of a 'mission' and that 'mission' was that I should agree to receive the American Ambassador Dean in New Delhi, whom I had never met. The Hindujas said that I could be of very great assistance in sorting out the Afghan problem in which the Americans are extremely keen to have India's involvement.* The American Ambassador called on me in company of G.P. Hinduja and Ashok Hinduja on the morning of 27th March at 9.30 am. He was with me for half an hour. He did not mention anything to me about Afghanistan

but merely said that he would like to see me again if I would agree to do so. Accordingly I gave him time to call on me on March 31 at 4 pm.

When he [Dean] called on me at the appointed hour, he read out to me some message which Ambassador Dean had apparently conveyed to you personally. It was a message from Ronald Reagan on Afghanistan. Thereafter he read out to me a long communication from an interesting but well-known character called [Armand] Hammer [owner of Occidental Petroleum] who is known to be a go-between between the State Department and the higher echelon of the Soviet leadership. The central idea was that the Americans were ready to carry out serious negotiations with the Russians and were even prepared to have some transitional arrangements for the withdrawal of Soviet troops. India could act as some sort of catalytic agent. When I asked him what made him think that I could play a role, Ambassador Dean mentioned that when he had met you the previous day, he had mentioned to you that he would talk to me and that you had not discouraged him from doing so. I must say that I was somewhat taken aback by this ...

In the arena of international affairs, it is perfectly legitimate to practice deception provided one does not fall victim to it oneself. If it was your intention that Ambassador Dean should be softened up, it would have been only proper and appropriate and less dangerous if I would have been informed beforehand that he was seeing me with your knowledge and approval. Frankly, I do not know what to do and I also do not know what sort of response you have sent to Ronald Reagan to the message of which Ambassador Dean had delivered to you ... [italics mine]

The prime minister must certainly have mollified Haksar for Dean was to call on him a second time on 21 April 1987. This was to be a longer meeting. Haksar prepared, in his usual meticulous style, a record of that 90-minute conversation. Basically, Dean had told Haksar that India enjoyed the confidence of the Soviet Union and could play a significant role in search of a settlement in Afghanistan. Dean also argued that a settlement in Afghanistan could never be reached in terms of victory or defeat of one side or the other and that the settlement must take into account Soviet pre-occupations. He admitted that it would not be easy to find a solution but that it was important to be seen to be engaged in search of a solution. In the absence of such a search, Dean pointed out, the situation around Afghanistan would certainly deteriorate, involving Pakistan too in a manner which would openly undermine that country's non-aligned position. Haksar recorded:

> He [Dean] expressed the hope that the impending visit of our Foreign Minister to Kabul, about which I know nothing, could begin the process. He also referred to the conversation between the Minister of State, K. Natwar Singh and various members of the US leadership, both in Government and Congress. (I devoutly hope that the goings on is not another example of far too many cooks engaged in spoiling the broth, a la Sri Lanka).

Dean also told Haksar that regretfully the US aid to Pakistan would have to continue but that India should not take objection to it and should enhance cooperation in a variety of spheres with the USA. To this Haksar replied that 'the interests of the US were not served and will not be served by the present paradigm within which the US is operating its relationship with Pakistan and that it was not even good for Pakistan'.

To Haksar's comment that 'since the Afghan situation had been allowed to fester for such a long time, I should imagine that it was part of US calculation that time was on their side', Dean surprised Haksar by confessing that he did not think time was on US's side. That is why the US was hoping that India could play a 'creative, constructive and mediatory' role even without necessarily achieving results.

Haksar ended the record of the conversation by saying that Dean let fall a sentence to the effect that India's excessive pre-occupations with the danger from Pakistan had made India insensitive to the dangers from China, and cryptically remarked that there were lot of indications that China might engage in some border conflict with India.

Haksar sent the record to the prime minister the very next day, on 22 April 1987, and told him:

> I am not yet able to firmly come to any definitive conclusion about the precise aim which Ambassador Dean has in mind in exhorting us to play the part which he is ever so anxious to assign to us. I cannot fail to observe

that the principal contenders in Afghanistan are in contact with each other at a fairly high level. Yaqub [foreign minister of Pakistan] has been to Moscow and Shultz [US secretary of state] was recently there. During these visits, they could not be exchanging jokes. Surely Afghanistan must have appeared prominently in their conversation. There is also proximity talks periodically held in Geneva under the auspices of the representative of the UN Secretary General. The consultations between the Afghans and the Soviets must be constant and continuous. The question therefore is where precisely do we come in ...

So far, most of the talking has been done by Ambassador Dean and I have listened to what he had to say with an air of sympathy. If you agree, I can now probe him further. But I should like to know what is the purpose of the mission to Afghanistan which Ambassador Dean told me our Foreign Minister is undertaking.

After this, the prime minister's Office took over but pretty soon as Haksar had feared the Indian initiative fizzled out as Bhattacharjee describes in his book.

Since 1983 Haksar's interest in China had been heightened and he had been to that country in November 1984. Two years later, purely as a private enterprise on his part, he got the Krishna Menon Memorial Society to invite a Chinese delegation to India in November 1986. This delegation had been led by Li Beihai, a council member of the Chinese Association for International Understanding and a senior Communist Party official. Haksar also kept up correspondence with Chinese academicians. On 12 February 1987, he wrote to the prime minister about a Chinese scholar, Professor Wei Fung Chiang. Haksar said:

> The distinctive thing about him is that he was the first Chinese scholar who came way back in the 30s of the Century to study in Shanti Niketan when Tagore had established the China Bhavan under the leadership of Prof. Tan Yun-Shan ...
>
> I understand that the China Bhavan will be celebrating its Golden Jubilee in April this year. Prof. Wei Fung Chiang is desperately anxious

to be invited on this occasion as the first Chinese student who studied in China Bhavan. I would beg of you to kindly arrange this ... The distinguished scholar is at present engaged in writing two volumes on "Tagore as my Teacher...

The prime minister, who was also chancellor of Visva-Bharati University, started at Santiniketan by Tagore and also where Professor Wei Fung Chiang studied, complied with Haksar's request. But this was the easy part. More complex matters were to follow very soon. On 11 April 1987, Haksar wrote to the prime minister saying that the matter of China was agitating him. He wrote:

> ... It is a perfectly sound idea to carry on unadvertised and confidential negotiations with the Chinese. There are far too many complex issues to be sorted out in our mutual relationship. This task is not made any easier by our not knowing the various fallback positions in the course of prolonged negotiations. When you were good enough to receive me sometime ago, I had mentioned to you that we should set up a small confidential group to study the various aspects of Sino-Indian relations. My impression was that you had agreed with this idea. So far as I am aware, nothing seems to have been done.

Two days later, Haksar again wrote to Rajiv Gandhi:

> On the question of dealing with China, I devoutly hope that the Chinese will not get the impression that we are hard pressed. This would be the impression on the minds of the occupiers of the Middle Kingdom if several dignitaries arrive at their Court paying homage and carrying tribute from their Indian counterpart. That is why I had cautioned against crossing of wires when it comes to making choice of diplomatic agents. I am bound to say this so that we do not clutter up any new start or new initiatives.

The early part of 1987 seemed to be ill-starred for normal relations between the two countries. Rajiv Gandhi had announced full statehood for Arunachal Pradesh and army chief General K. Sundarji in a daring move had positioned Indian troops to confront the Chinese army in the Sumdorong Chu Valley in Arunachal Pradesh. It was in this background that Rajiv Gandhi sent Haksar to China in May 1987 as his special envoy for high-level discussions with Chinese leaders. But barely a week before he left, Haksar wrote a stinker to Rajiv Gandhi's top aide Gopi Arora on 18 May 1987:

> Today is Monday, the 18th of May. There is barely a week left ... And yet we have done nothing to discuss so that we have a firm answer to the questions: What is to be done? What is the strategy? Having regard to the past, these are not easy questions to answer. And each one of it is fraught with serious consequences ... Negotiations must inevitably involve give and take. Also, one has to be extremely careful about the framework within which one gives and also takes ... We have not even come round to discussing even the Agenda ...
>
> ... I should like to caution you against the perils of an exercise marked by an exchange of verbiage even in poetic language. But, in international relations, soft words butter no parsnips any more than harsh words break any bones. There are a very large number of detailed questions to which I should like to have answers. And the answers should be given to me, if I may say so, at the highest level. It is quite easy for me to fall sick and even to enter a hospital which will be a way out for you. But ad-hocism and dilettantism are fraught with grave consequences.

But this letter was *not* issued since Arora met Haksar that very day. C.V. Ranganathan who had just then joined as India's ambassador in China has written:[12]

> ... the visit made a significant contribution in conveying a clear political message. This was that India desired good relations with China and was prepared to adopt a forward looking policy without being mired in the past.

Nine years later, on 7 October 1996, while writing to one of his closest friends Dwarka Chatterjee, who had retired as India's ambassador to France, Haksar was to recall this visit:

> ... I personally do not agree with the view that China should be regarded as a permanent enemy. I am saying this not because of any historical insight which I possess, but because I spent ten days in the month of

May 1987 in persuading the Chinese to the acceptance of the formula I had invented which was to the effect that despite our differences on the border issue and other issues, we should endeavour to renew and reconstruct the totality of Sino-Indian relations in the field of trade, industry, technology, agriculture, etc. etc. ... Tactically speaking, it is necessary to give the message across the chanceries of the world that they should not rely on Sino-Indian animosities.

In May 1987, Haksar had been accompanied by V.V. Paranjpe, a foreign service officer widely acknowledged even by the Chinese to be amongst the most fluent of Mandarin speakers. He was, in fact, the official interpreter from the Indian side during Nehru's visit to China in 1954. In the final years of his life, Haksar had written to Paranjpe to find out whether he had kept any record of the discussions they had with the Chinese but he did not hear back, because by then Paranjpe himself was very ill. But, Haksar has left some clues behind.

On his immediate return, Haksar did not sound very optimistic that he had achieved much, as he confessed to T.N. Kaul on 10 June 1987:

Urmila and I returned from our visit to Peking early in the morning of June 2. It was one of those visits that had no particular focus. My own reaction is that we need to have an un-biased and fresh look at the state of relationship between our two countries. Nobody has the time or the inclination to do this. In the absence of this, one merely reacts and sometimes over reacts. Sino-Indian relations cannot be handled in this way.

A few days later, Haksar invited the attention of Gopi Arora to a report that had appeared in the *Indian Express* of 20 June 1987, saying that Defence Minister K.C. Pant had declared in Tawang in Arunachal Pradesh that India would not yield an inch of its territory to China under any circumstances. Haksar wrote to Arora on 22 June 1987:

... I think one has to make a very conscious and concerted move within our own government to coordinate the pronouncements of our Ministers if Defence and External Affairs. The Defence Minister could have spoken about safeguarding the territorial unity and integrity of India rather than harking back to that ill-fated Parliamentary Resolution of 1962 about India not "surrendering an inch of our territory". What was the use of spending hours in trying to send a brief to our Foreign Minister [who had made a stop-over in Beijing on 10 June 1987 on his way back from North Korea] when that brief is contradicted in words and spirit by our Defence Minister? Even otherwise, it should be a well established principle that soldiers take over only when diplomacy fails. The Defence Minister is taking over even before the Foreign Minister has failed. Problems of foreign policy need to be handled with greater care and professionalism than that is being displayed by us.

Arora replied that very day that he shared Haksar's ire over the press reports of the defence minister's visit to Arunachal Pradesh and that Haksar's letter was being placed before the prime minister so that 'a more coordinated view of our China policy will emerge, sooner rather than later'.

A month later, Haksar was at it again, writing to Arora on 11 July 1987:

I had long been sensing that there is one other conspiracy afoot seeking to throw a spanner in our attempts to think afresh about Sino-Indian relations … The Dalai Lama and his supporters continue to be active. You would have noticed that they got together a group of 100-odd MPs in support of their cause.

I have received reports that a German Television outfit has recently made a film on Dalai Lama. The BBC has carried out a series of broadcasts on the Himalayas. I hope you will send for the text of these broadcasts and see the mischief behind them. More recently, some 30 to 40-odd so-called scholars from Western Europe, Britain and America assembled together under the auspices of the Institute of Advanced Studies in Simla to discuss Tibet and Buddhism. I am sure that your own intelligence agencies keep you fed with the great variety of activities which are going on right now.

Finally, I should like to invite your attention to an article published in the Indian Express of July 3, 1987. On page 6 of the issue, you would find an article (dateline LONDON), under the title: "India has upper hand on Border issue". I am enclosing a clipping of it for your perusal.

It is not necessary for me to spell out the mischief and it is entirely for you to see how you can combat it. The border issue is difficult and complex enough and if we had to do the reopening of the Tibetan question, we can settle down to endless conflict with China …

I have a very uneasy feeling that I committed a mistake in engaging myself in the Mission to China. [italics mine]

Three days later, Arora replied, saying that 'Efforts to prevent, indeed smother, any fresh thinking on Sino-Indian relations are continuing, both at home and abroad'. He also promised to 'come over and discuss with you developments subsequent to your visit'.

Haksar's visit had, in fact, paved the way for Rajiv Gandhi's truly historic visit to China in December 1988. Two major agreements on the border were to be signed thereafter, the first in 1993 and another in 1996. With the benefit of hindsight, therefore, Haksar sounded different when he wrote on 27 November 1996 to T.R. Satish Chandran, principal secretary to Prime Minister H.D. Deve Gowda, regretting his inability to be present at a lunch being hosted for the visiting Chinese president. Haksar told Satish Chandran:

I do not know whether you are aware of the fact that way back in 1987 in the month of May, I made a special journey to China at the insistence of the then Prime Minister Shri Rajiv Gandhi to negotiate with the Chinese the concept I had of renewal and reconstruction of Sino-Indian relations in its totality despite our differences on the border question …

During my visit to China I carried on one of my life's hardest negotiations with my Chinese counterpart, Mr. Fu Hao. The entire verbatim record of these conversations is, I am sure available both in the Prime Minister's Office as well as in the Ministry of External Affairs. At the end of my negotiations with Mr. Fu Hao, I was given a special audience by H.E. [His Excellency] Mr. Zhao Ziyang …

I am sorry to inflict this letter on you, but I felt it is my duty to inform you about the critical element and background of Sino-Indian relations which took place in 1987 with my visit to China. It was on my part a labour of love. As you are no doubt aware, politics may change, but geography does not. So we are landed with China as our neighbor and have a frontier with that country extending to several thousand miles. This should provide a background to enlarging interactions between

China and Indian every field, social, cultural, scientific and technological, agriculture, education diplomacy, security and so on ... [italics mine]

Unfortunately, I found it impossible to get hold of the record of discussions that Haksar had in China. Haksar's visit had a very important domestic context as well. Not everyone in the Congress Party and outside was entirely convened about the necessity for India to take the initiative for a full rapprochement with China, given the Chinese 'betrayal' of India in 1962. There was one school of thought which believed that the Chinese could never be trusted because they were responsible for humiliating Nehru and hastening his demise in May 1964. There were others loosely called the 'Soviet lobby' who thought that India should wait for some Sino-Soviet breakthrough before trying for a Sino-Indian rapprochement. Natwar Singh in his memoirs writes that during his stint as the junior minister in the Ministry of External Affairs in 1985 and 1986, his own senior minister, P.V. Narasimha Rao, was averse to any big Indian leaps as far as relations with China were concerned. G. Parthasarathi, one of Indira Gandhi's key foreign policy advisers and who had been India's ambassador in China when the 1962 war erupted, was another influential voice not enamoured for accelerating that pace of normalization of India's relations with China.

Haksar was the 'patron saint' of the left in India. He was respected hugely in this community and, if he could advocate a new approach to China, Prime Minister Rajiv Gandhi must have believed that part of the domestic opposition could be overcome. Before Haksar's visit to China, his diary for 1987 shows he had a series of meetings with Congress leaders, as well as with CPM leaders like E.M.S. Namboodiripad and Harkishan Singh Surjeet, apart with Gopi Arora.

Did Haksar come to a new approach to China late in life? The evidence suggests otherwise. Writing in 1988, Sharada Prasad—normally the most reticent of men and not given to hyperbole or exaggeration of any sort—writes that in the early hours of 3 July 1972 after the Simla Pact had been signed between Indira Gandhi and the president, Haksar, P.N. Dhar and he were driving back to the cottage where they were staying. In Sharada Prasad's words:

I remarked to Haksar and P.N. Dhar that it was, all in all, a day India could be satisfied with.

I recall what Haksar said in reply: 'Ah, not until there is an agreement also with China.'

What Haksar had mentioned in July 1972 was to happen in December 1988 when Rajiv Gandhi met with Deng Xiaoping in Beijing. Haksar's visits had paved the way for that breakthrough by helping mute domestic criticism and by conveying to the Chinese India's desire for a whole new approach to bilateral relations. Credit is given to Deng Xiaoping for being pragmatic and creating an opening. In reality, this is exactly what Haksar had been advocating for years—keep the border issue aside and start cooperating in other areas.

Elections had been held in Jammu and Kashmir and the National Conference–Congress alliance had been swept into power. Haksar wrote to the prime minister on 11 April 1987:

> *I feel redeemed by the election results in Kashmir. How tragic was the decision taken [by Indira Gandhi] to remove Farooq Abdullah in total defiance of the advice I had tendered to Induji in your presence!* However, the recent victory of the National Conference alliance should not give way to the tendency of "business as usual". The Muslim United Front has, for the first time in the last 40 years, acquired some sort of mass base in Kashmir. But who will do the fighting against the kind of feelings, emotions and sentiments which the MUF has managed to crystallise in the Valley? And not to fight it would be to invite disaster. My premonitions have so far never been proved wrong *and I would urge with all the strength at my command that one can no longer play around with secular ideology. Also, one ought not to be allergic to the word 'ideology'.* All human affairs are motivated by ideology ... [italics mine]

Actually, these elections were to mark a turning point in the Valley. Haksar had mentioned the Muslim United Front (MUF). It is generally believed that the MUF's ambitions were deliberately thwarted at the ballot box and that this played a role in fuelling the subsequent militancy in Kashmir.

∾

The National Integration Council, at its meeting held on 12 September 1986, had set up another five-member group to submit to the Council 'proposals for discussion on matters affecting or pertaining to National Integration'. Haksar was to be the convenor of the group which had as its member, senior journalist Prem Bhatia, the noted film-maker Shyam Benegal, the artist M.F. Hussain and the space scientist Yash Pal. The group addressed itself to three issues: the meaning of national integration, its importance and measures to promote it. Haksar's report was discussed with the prime minister and others on 23 June 1987. At this meeting, there was an intervention by the BJP leader L.K. Advani which was thus:

> References have been made in para 12 of the Report: "… freeing politics from symbolism and rituals of religion". *I would think that far more important is freeing politics from the influence of organized religion.* Symbolism is a very minor part of it. For example, in Punjab we have confronted a situation where the State or the Government or politics is sought to be controlled by organized religion. That is far more dangerous for the concept of secularism and the concept of national integration. [italics mine]

In light of how Advani was to take the BJP to new heights later, these observations of his have a certain sense of irony.

∾

On 7 April 1988, the prime minister called Haksar for a long, informal conversation. On 27 July 1988, Haksar wrote again to Gopi Arora giving his responses to some of the questions that the prime minister had raised with him:

> *As I understand it, PM is, if I may say so, rightly concerned about our living from day to day without any effort to come to grips with the changes taking place or likely to place in the future* … I entirely agree that in the fast-

changing world of today, failure to analyse and to understand how things are shaping up or likely to shape up can be , and often is, disastrous for any nation.

... We ought to carefully study the evolution of the world around us ... I am convinced that this cannot be done and ought not to be done within the framework of the government. In the Soviet Union as well as in the United States, institutions have been created outside the government who are charged with the responsibility of continuously studying, in great depth and in great detail, the evolution of foreign policies, economies, etc. of other countries. Some of the universities are also involved in such studies.

When the Indian Council of World Affairs was set up, the inspiration was drawn naturally from Britain. It was hoped that the Indian Council of World Affairs would be like Chatham House. I need not comment on what happened to this hope ... If the government could ... rescue the Indian Council of World Affairs, it could be the centre and the nucleus for futuristic studies on the evolution of our foreign policy in the midst of the changing patterns of international relations ... Existing institutions, human resources as well as financial resources could be optimized through the Indian Council of World Affairs acting as a catalyst ...

... Might I conclude this letter by exhorting the Government of India to continuously and unrelentingly pursue the logic of a dialogue with China within the broad framework with which I began more than a year ago. To get diverted from it is to commit a very serious error of judgment. [italics mine]

Arora, had by then moved as secretary in the Ministry of Information and Broadcasting but would continue to be consulted by the prime minister on various issues. He replied on 27 July 1988:

While the need for a diversified institutional base for study and research is not disputed ... PM's concept was that this institutional base should be linked to a mechanism within the government so that studies, analyses and research papers become a crucial input into decision-making. An institutional device within the government is perhaps required to continuously review issues, policies and programmes impinging on national security ... *We look to you to head an organization with a clearly defined structure and linkages with concerned governmental agencies. I would earnestly request that you give thought to this aspect* ... [italics mine]

It is clear that the prime minister wanted to get Haksar back into the governmental system but that was not to happen. Meanwhile, Haksar continued to be concerned with some of the prime minister's actions as this intensely personal letter of his to Rajiv Gandhi of 1 September 1988 reveals:

As I have known you all these years, I have always felt that you were sensitive, loving, tolerant and introspective. However, the messages which come out tend to contradict your real nature. This is sad indeed. And I am in state of deep anguish when I contemplate the latest message which comes out of government's attempt to amend the law relating to criminal defamation. I wonder who could have given advice that such a law should be enacted. The art and science of politics is the art and science of enlarging one's supporters and not the other way round. The new law on defamation is ill-conceived. It contradicts the fundamental premise of criminal jurisprudence. There should be serious rethinking on it. False pride and impatience are cardinal sins. And one should always appear to pay homage to democracy and public opinion.

I do not know how you would respond to this letter of mine. But, I must go on doing my duty. [italics mine]

A defensive prime minister responded two months later, on 9 November 1988:

… I entirely understand and appreciate your genuine concern. As you know, we have decided not to make the Defamation Bill, 1988 into law. Nevertheless, our legal provisions and procedures are such that it becomes almost impossible for an ordinary individual to seek redressal against defamatory writings. I do hope that there will now be a wide ranging public debate and discussion on the issue of defamation, so that there is some remedy evolved against scurrilous and defamatory writings.

Rajiv Gandhi was embarking on his epochal visit to China on 24 December 1988. A week before that Haksar wrote to him:

I am suffering from acute bronchitis for the last 8-9 days. But for this, I would have endeavoured to see you on the eve of your departure to China: *Prior to my departure for China on May 25, 1987, there had been as*

*many as 8 rounds of official level talks between our two countries devoted
to the border problem. Nothing came out of these talks except mutual
exasperation. In the meantime, a tense situation had developed along our
border in June 1986. It was in this context that I was sent by you as a
Special Emissary.* The broad theme of my mission was to "reconstruct
and renew" Sino-Indian relations ... On my return to Delhi I saw you
briefly. I had then expressed the view that "reconstruction and renewal"
of Sino-Indian relations required a great deal of detailed work. I hope
that this has been done during the last one year or more. Be that as it
may, one has to convey to the Chinese with great deal of passion and
conviction that you are deeply committed to the processes of renewal and
reconstruction which would require detailed examination of potentialities
of cooperation in the fields of trade, commerce, industry, science and
technology, education and culture as well as for our working together for
a nuclear-weapon free and non-violent world ... Incidentally, the Chinese
did participate in the international seminar we organized recently on this
theme in New Delhi ...

On your return to India, the Press would naturally ask you (a) the
border question, (b) Tibet and, possibly (c) Kashmir. I have no doubt
that you have firm and clear answers to these questions. In 1961, G.
Parthasarathi and R.K. Nehru quite unnecessarily raised with Chou
En-Lai the question of Kashmir. This was a folly. One doesn't go to a
foreign country to discuss with them matters pertaining to integral part
of India. As for Tibet, there is no reason to depart from the Principles
underlying the Treaty of 1954.

On the border question, it has been my view that the frontiers
between India and China need to be demarcated on the ground in
terms of objective criteria e.g., Watershed Principles, River valleys,
administrative control etc. *I am still hoping that some day China and India
could agree to announce that neither side has any claims on the territory
of the other side and that they would determine their frontiers in terms of
principles commonly accepted.* [italics mine]

Rajiv Gandhi's visit was an outstanding success. He could justly take credit
for the rapport he struck with Deng Xiaoping who was almost double his
age. Haksar had played his role in making that breakthrough happen.

∾

The Indian National Congress had instituted the Indira Gandhi Award for National Integration in 1985. The first three recipients of the honour were: Swami Ranganathananda of the Ramakrishna Mission, with whom the late prime minister had enjoyed a particularly close association; Aruna Asaf Ali, who as a young woman had unfurled the national flag in Bombay on 9 August 1942 which was to mark the beginning of the historic Quit India movement; and Bharat Scouts and Guides. The fourth awardee for the year 1988 was Haksar. It took some cajoling from the prime minister himself to get PNH to agree to accept the award, named after someone with whom his name would be inextricably linked for posterity. Ultimately, he went along. In later years, Satish Dhawan, Sharada Prasad and M.S. Swaminathan would also be the recipients of this award.[13]

Rajiv Gandhi presented the award to Haksar on 31 October 1989 and it was only appropriate that he recalled Haksar's role in advising Indira Gandhi 'during her most difficult and successful years'. There could be nobody better placed than him to highlight this role having seen it from within the-then prime minister's family. He, of course, also highlighted other contributions of Haksar as a 'distinguished civil servant, diplomat and intellectual and a constructive and practical thinker'.

Earlier in the year, on 24 February 1989, writing in the *Times of India*, Haksar's old colleague P.N. Dhar appeared to have anticipated what the prime minister said about Haksar while conferring the Indira Gandhi award on him. Dhar had written:

> The new Prime Minister [Indira Gandhi] faced a two-fold challenge. The first was to establish her pre-eminence in the cabinet and the second to forge a set of policies and develop a credible political stance. To meet these challenges the Prime Minister could not depend solely on cabinet colleagues. Some of them were her political rivals who believed that, as a Prime Minister on probation, she should abide by the judgment of party elders. She also needed aides who were not her colleagues and who could give her professional assistance and advice. In the circumstances prevailing in the country, Mrs Gandhi did not need dispassionate, on-the-one-hand-and-on-the-other type of aides. She had to be an activist to be a successful Prime Minister. For that she needed a one-handed secretary to head her office which would provide the necessary inputs for such a

role. *This was undertaken by the PMO during the crucial years of 1967-1971 under the leadership of Mr. P.N. Haksar who perceived the prevailing political tensions as aspects of the more basic economic and social changes. He reorganised the work of the office and raised its calibre and potential for assistance and advice.* [italics mine]

This remains the best description of the background to Haksar's assuming office in the prime minister's Secretariat in May 1967 and what he accomplished in the next five years.

Less than a month after Haksar got the Indira Gandhi Award, on 29 November 1989, Rajiv Gandhi resigned as prime minister following the election results which saw the Congress lose its majority. But Haksar's mind was elsewhere for that very day his wife Urmila Haksar passed away. She and Haksar had been a pair for over half a century. They had defied tradition and convention by being together for well over a decade before marriage. She was an intellectual, activist and author in her own right but unfortunately she got overshadowed by her husband. She had studied both in India and abroad, and had taught when it was not common for women to do so. She had become a communist in 1942 without ever joining the Communist party. If Haksar was Indira Gandhi's ideological compass during 19670–1973, Urmila Haksar remained Haksar's ideological soulmate for decades.

In the 1970s, her distinctive identity had been recognized by Indira Gandhi herself when she was made a member of the first-ever Committee on the Status of Women in India. She contributed considerably to the Committee's landmark report that was submitted in 1974. But by mid-1975 she had become Indira Gandhi's bitter foe and never reconciled to the humiliation that Haksar's family had been subjected to during the Emergency. For seven years from 1982 onward, Urmila Haksar was Haksar's 'reader' of books, newspapers, magazines and letters since he had lost his left eye completely and his right eye was fast degenerating. In her demise, therefore, Haksar was to lose more than a wife. She was literally his life-support.

The review committee of the national cultural bodies headed by Haksar submitted its report in July 1990. It had slogged for almost two years during which Haksar's wife had expired. Haksar and his fellow members met some 900 cultural personalities in 18 states and submitted a report that proved to be hugely controversial. The report, for which Haksar wrote the introductory chapter, pleased nobody. It castigated both the government and the cultural bodies themselves. It decried the 'mindless frenzy of cultural extravaganzas in the country', 'the rash political intervention into culture', 'the reduction of folk art and culture to museum exhibits to satisfy exotic interests', 'the excessive Delhi-centric activities of the cultural bodies' and said that 'the approach to culture must encourage regional diversity and not merely tolerate it'. It called for breaking the stranglehold of vested interests in the three Akademies and the National School of Drama and for bringing about greater accountability and transparency in their functioning.

On 10 November 1990, two Myanmarese students hijacked a Thai jetliner on its way to Bangkok to Yangon. The students used a fake bomb made out of soap and got the flight diverted to Calcutta. They were demanding the release of Aung San Suu Kyi and other political figures and also called for end to martial law. Haksar's residence had become the refuge for pro-democarcy activists from that country who had fled to India. His daughter was also very closely involved with their cause and she took up the case of the student-hijackers and could get access to top political leaders in West Bengal, thanks to her father's reputation and connections. She fought a long battle and finally, on 3 July 2003, one of the hijackers Soe Myint was acquitted by a court in Calcutta (the other had returned home while out on bail). In the meanwhile Soe Myint and others had been running a news agency virtually out of Haksar's house. The news agency Mozzima is still running out of Myanmar's capital and Soe Myint recalls his association with Haksar who he called Papa thus:

> For the Burmese refugees like us, Papa's home was our shelter. It was so great to listen to him, whatever he talked about—from politics, history, India-Burma relations, India's foreign policies, to food and literature.

He had great memories and knowledge on every subjects we discussed. I remember Papa one day reciting Shakespeare by heart to me. I was so surprised he remembered each and every word. I remember Papa cooking for us for the dinner ... Those dinners were always delicious and very homely.

I remember Papa smoking passionately. Papa would close the door of kitchen sometimes when he cooked so that we got surprised of what he was cooking for us. Politically, he was a great supporter of Burma's movement for democracy and for the Burmese democracy activists in India. We used to request him to speak at the events on Burma's struggle for democracy. We used to ask him who should be contacted for such and such political gathering. He was one of the members of the committee that awarded Daw Aung San Suu Kyi with the Jawaharlal Nehru Award for International Understanding in 1993. He introduced us to many political leaders in India so that we could lobby them for their support for democracy in Burma ...

Haksar had a connection with Aung Saan Suu Kyi many years earlier. Michael Aris, her husband, had written to him on 22 September 1972:

Lady Gore Booth has explained to me about the kind assistance you have given us in the matter of clearing our personal effects through the Calcutta customs. I cannot tell you how grateful my wife and I are for the trouble you took in this regard. We had, I must admit, nearly given way to despair at one stage and are now overjoyed at the successful venture. This, I feel sure, we owe entirely to your kind efforts and we are truly grateful.

My wife and I are presently employed by the Government of Bhutan and expect to continue here for some time to come. It would give us considerable pleasure if we should have the opportunity of meeting you should you ever come to Thimpu.

The Lonely Years (1991–1996)

*Haksar speaking at an informal get-together on his 80th birthday,
New Delhi, September 1993.*

ON 21 MAY 1991, RAJIV GANDHI WAS ASSASSINATED IN THE HOLY TOWN
of Sriperumbudur. The very next day Haksar wrote to his widow:

Sonia dearest:
*It is just not possible for me constituted as I am, to make public demonstration
of my personal anguish and grief.* I cannot even find words to convey to
you the intensity of my feelings. I know the state of your mind and heart

452

and of Rahul and Priyanka. I also cannot forget the way Rajiv and you stood by me and gave me sustenance. A mother's heart full of love and compassion alone can give meaning to life. And the children certainly would need it to provide a healing touch. So, dearest Sonia, I wish you Bon Courage. You should of course know that I am still around if that is of any use to you.

I saw Rajiv in his mother's lap in 1945. I have so many images of him and then you and him together. I just bring myself to believe that he is no more. It is a cruel fate that fathers have to attend the funeral of their children.

No words of mine, I know, can bring you comfort. But I was under tremendous pressure of inner urge to communicate something to you, howsoever inadequately.

With love to you and dear children

Yours in grief [italics mine]

Rajiv Gandhi's funeral was on 24 May 1991. What happened after the funeral is described thus by Natwar Singh:[14]

After the funeral there was intense political activity … Sonia Gandhi herself refused to be the President [of the Congress Party] when it was suggested to her. I told her that the time had come for her to indicate her preference for the role; whoever she chose would naturally become PM. For so momentous a decision I suggested she ask P.N. Haksar for advice. She said she would let me know … The next day she asked me to bring Haksar to 10 Janpath. Haksar's advice was to offer the post to Vice President Shankar Dayal Sharma. He suggested that Aruna Asif Ali and I should sound out the VP … Aruna Asaf Ali conveyed Sonia's message to the VP. He said he was touched and honoured by Soniaji's placing so much trust in him. What followed staggered Arunaji and me. The VP continued. The prime ministership of India is a full-time job. My age and health would not let me do justice to the most important office in the country. Kindly convey to Soniaji the reasons for my inability to take on so awesome a responsibility.

After hearing the VP's refusal I asked Sonia to once again send for P.N. Haksar, who advised her to call P.V Narasimha Rao. Thereafter the Congress Working Committee met [on 29 May 1991] and unanimously elected P.V. as Congress President. [italics mine]

Haksar and Shankar Dayal Sharma had been close in the late-1960s and early-1970s. Sharma was a fellow Lincoln's Inn alumni, erudite and well read, a one-time socialist and a die-hard Indira Gandhi loyalist—all plus points as far as Haksar was concerned. But he was 73 and, as he himself admitted, not in the best of health. Narasimha Rao was three years younger but he too was not totally fit. I asked one of Narasimha's closest aides what is perception was of the relationship between Haksar and Narasimha Rao. He replied:

> [There was] a measure of reciprocal but distant respect. I am sure PVNR knew that he was not PNH's first choice for recommending as possible PM and I suspect there was a history in both his perception of PNH's role in his removal from the Andhra CMship and the uneasy equation they must have had during the Emergency when PVNR was a loyal General Secretary.

Ideologically and personally, Haksar was closer to Arjun Singh than to Narasimha Rao. In his memoirs, Arjun Singh has written:[15]

> I had, in the late 1960s and early 1970s developed close personal relations with P.N Haksar, principal secretary to Prime Minister Indira Gandhi and one of her important advisors during these turbulent times. Haksar possessed a clear and methodical mind and was totally in favour in restoring the ascendancy of the prime minister in all national matters. His long association with Jawaharlal Nehru created an aura around his personality and gave weightage to his opinions, observations and suggestions ...

It was Haksar's association with Arjun Singh which had enabled Anil Sadgopal to launch his trail-blazing experiment in science education in primary schools in Madhya Pradesh in 1972. Sadgopal was, like Satish Dhawan, a doctorate from Caltech (in biochemistry and molecular biology), and had returned to India in the late-1960s. He gave up his research career at the Tata Institute of Fundamental Research in Bombay, and with some like-minded colleagues started Kishore Bharati in Hoshangabad district of Madhya Pradesh in 1972. Haksar had supported the initiative and also helped to establish it.

Inspite of this proximity to Arjun Singh, however,[16] Haksar suggested Narasimha Rao's name. This shows that Haksar did not always automatically canvass the case of those in his circle, just because they happened to be his friends. He must have weighed the relative merits of Narasimha Rao and Arjun Singh dispassionately and rooted for the former.

Narasimha Rao became prime minister on 21 June 1991 and immediately appointed Dr Manmohan Singh as finance minister. Some days later, on 9 July 1991, Haksar wrote to congratulate the new finance minister:

> I met PND [P.N. Dhar] the other day. He told me that you were working past midnight. I can understand the intense pressure in which you have to work. But please do take care of yourself.
>
> I do not engage in the formality of felicitating you on your becoming our Finance Minister. I think the Congress Party needs to be felicitated for having put the entire burden on you. *You are, perhaps, our only economist who is sensitive to complexities of the real problems of 'economic development'. As your friend and admirer, I can only send you my best wishes.* [italics mine]

The finance minister replied in a somewhat emotional vein eight days later:

> I have been greatly moved by your letter of 9th July 1991. *You are the one who brought me into the Government* and the best I can do to justify your confidence and deep affection is to dedicate myself to work sincerely for the realization of ideals and objectives so dear to your heart.
>
> I owe it to you and our people that I will perform my duties with firmness, determination and dedication that the current situation in our country warrants. [italics mine]

Dr Manmohan Singh had the highest regard for Haksar and was the first to reach Haksar's residence on his demise in 1998.

Meanwhile, as had happened in 1985 in the case of Indira Gandhi, Haksar now faced a similar situation in regard to her son and successor as prime minister. On 11 July 1991, he wrote to Natwar Singh who had succeeded Sharada Prasad as the secretary of the Indira Gandhi Memorial Trust:

I have your letter of 17 June. You have put me in the same embarrassing situation in which Sharada had put me when he asked me to contribute an article to a book dedicated to the memory of Smt. Indira Gandhi. In terms of purely personal relations, I have deepest affection for Rajiv. And, I believe, he gave me his affection and also respect. However, writing about Rajiv as Prime Minister is another matter. Also, being old-fashioned, I subscribe to the wisdom contained in the Latin proverb *Mortus nil nisi bonum*. [Don't speak ill of the dead]. So, you will understand my perplexity and dilemma generated by your letter. This is a purely personal letter to you as you will understand what I am trying to say.

Ever since his China trip of May 1987, Haksar had become increasingly involved with meeting Chinese diplomats and academics visiting India. He had been invited in 1991 and again in 1992 to return to China, but because of his health he could not accept these invitations, although he made arrangements for others to go under the aegis of the Krishna Menon Memorial Society. In February 1992, he spoke at a joint India-China seminar in New Delhi organized by the Nehru Memorial Museum and Library. This was to be one of the few occasions when he elaborated on his views on bilateral ties between the two countries in public:

> Naturally in the process of interaction between China and India, we have to be conscious that there has to be language for communication. Even if we carry on our dialogue through the English language, there must be a realization that the more we learn about each other's history, language and civilization, the more direct and intimate will be the process of communication. I realized this in the course of six months I spent in Panmunjom in Korea when I had to deal with almost every day with Chinese representatives. Very often we found our communications snarled up due to inadequacy of translating Chinese into English and vice versa ... We should have studies of Chinese language, culture and civilization in as many universities as possible ...
>
> *We have equated Sino-Indian relations with the border and predicated the reconstruction of relations between India and China on the settlement*

of the border. We have exaggerated, I think, because it should be the other way around. If I have a dispute along the boundary with my neighbour it is more likely to be solved when my neighbour and I have mutual trust and confidence than by some formula for the boundary ...

We must not acquire a vested interest in conflict. Unfortunately, we are all subjected to too much propaganda. Earlier ... there was the Peking versus Delhi thesis. There was also Neville Maxwell, a great defender of China, whom I once called the legitimate widow of Comrade Mao Zedong to the annoyance of a British friend. But it is true that we Indians have looked at China through Western eyes and research done in the West presented in the English language ... And I am sure the same is true of the Chinese looking at India as well ... We have to have a direct approach. [italics mine]

Neville Maxwell, a noted British journalist was the author of *India's China War* which came out in 1970 and had painted India as the villain and China as the victim in the 1962 conflict. Three years before the book came out, when a friend wrote to Haksar on an article that Maxwell had written on Indian politics in the London Times on 5 May 1967, Haksar had replied:

... Neville Maxwell is beyond redemption ... My own view is that Neville faithfully reflects the poisonous sources of his information who are mostly our own compatriots.

1992 was to reveal a feature of Haksar that had become pronounced after his retirement. Even in service, he would raise his voice against what he felt was wrong but this became even louder when he was no longer serving the Indian state. He would write constantly to those in power on behalf of people who would come to him seeking help to redress their grievances. For instance, on 19 February 1992, he wrote to Home Minister S.B, Chavan:

All these years you have treated me with kindness. At any rate that is my feeling. It is this feeling which has emboldened me to *write to you about a very sad and tragic case of prosecution of two young men of great idealism namely Irfan Engineer and Vir Singh Patel. All over our country such young men are engaged in democratic and peaceful work to safeguard the interests of tribal people.* I used to know one such person called Neogi who worked in Madhya Pradesh and was done to death. And now Irfan Engineer and Vir Singh Patel have been lodged in two jails—Baroda Central Jail and Bhuj Jail respectively. They were both working among the Dangs. Long time ago the Home Ministry conducted a very detailed survey of agrarian tensions and conflicts. I even recall during Indiraji's Prime Ministership, we had a Cabinet meeting to which we had invited some leading Indian sociologists to participate. Obviously no sustained work is done at the political level to defuse such tensions and conflicts within a peaceful democratic framework. [italics mine]

Haksar's sense of anger and outrage is obvious. The home minister promised 'to look into the matter very soon', and a few weeks later the young men who had been incarcerated under the National Security Act were indeed released.

Some months, after pleading the case of the two young men with the home minister, Haksar was on to another minister on 30 November 1993—this time it was A.K. Antony:

I have heard that you are anxious that well-off sections of our society who can afford to buy wheat, rice and sugar in the open market should not rely on the public demonstration system. I have heard that you are anxious to even enact a law on this subject and that you are naturally wondering what should be the cutoff point in terms of income groups. It occurred to me that even if you have a law you would require an enforcement agency and you may also have difficulty in having the cutoff point. I am wondering why since our Independence our politicians do not appeal to the conscience of our people and stimulate the Gandhian technique ...

As I started writing this letter I thought I should surrender to you my own ration card. Of course, it contains the name of my wife which should have been deleted as she passed away in 1989. I might have therefore committed a technical breach of the law for which I am prepared to pay such penalty as you may impose.

Naturally I would beg of you to keep whatever I have done in surrendering my ration card as confidential between you and me. I would not seek any advertisement. [italics mine]

Clearly Haksar did things not for self-promotion but because he believed in them. Over two decades later, Prime Minister Narendra Modi would appeal to the better-off sections of society to voluntarily give up their subsidies for cooking gas. Haksar had quietly shown the way much earlier.

ॐ

The C. Achutha Menon Foundation had invited Haksar to contribute to a souvenir being released on 13 January 1993 to mark the 80th birth anniversary of the Kerala communist leader who had been chief minister of the state from 1972 to 1977. He and Haksar had got along famously and both had worked together, in the face of bureaucratic and political obstacles, to give shape to the Sree Chitra Medical Centre in Trivandrum.[17] Haksar used the occasion to dwell on the issues of fundamentalism and secularism that had acquired new importance in the wake of what had happened at Ayodhya on 6 December 1992 when a rampaging mob had demolished the Babri Masjid:

> ... If the words secular, secularism and secularization are to be understood as part and parcel of a universal process of secularization of the human mind, then we have inflicted enormous damage on the nation-building process in India, by totally unacceptable and false translation of the word secular and secularism by equating them to the doctrine of religious tolerance expressed in the words like *Dharma-nirpekshta* and *Sarva Dharma Samabhava*. These translations have produced great schizophrenia in our politics which, in time, has produced the situation with which we are now actually confronted in Punjab and Kashmir ...
>
> There is one more question which needs to be answered: What is the relationship between religion, howsoever defined, and processes of secularization. Is this relationship inherently antagonistic? The answer is no. The process of secularization merely leads to finding the domain of each, both at the level of the individual and of society and state. That is why the word "Secular" ... means "concerned with affairs of this world, not "spiritual or sacred". *It is to be hoped that if the Republic of India is not to degenerate into a state of anarchy, the time has come to come to grips with the real meaning of such words like "secularism" and "fundamentalism".* [italics mine]

459

This is a supreme rationalist not denying religion but saying religion is a private matter and not for something for the state to get involved with. Like Nehru, Haksar is drawing a distinction between a multi-religious society and a secular state. But that he differed with Nehru in some respects became obvious a few months later. A group of civil society activists in New Delhi had set up a Citizens Tribunal on Ayodhya with three retired judges and a number of intellectuals as members. The idea was to gather evidence of what had happened in Ayodhya and in other places after the demolition. Haksar was invited but did not attend saying that he was not an eye-witness to any of the events that the Tribunal was investigating. On 2 July 1993, he wrote to E. Deendayalan who had invited him:

> We have also added to confusion by saying that to be secular is to give equal respect to all religions. This is totally false. That we should respect all religions equally is the duty of all human beings who call themselves civilized for it embodies the meaning and substance of the word 'tolerance'. Also there is a misconception about the relationship between the words "secular" and "religion". *One can be deeply religious and yet be secular when it comes to matters relating to the public domains. And politics is concerned with matters of the public domain ...* When you mix the two domains in the name of religion, you have the phenomenon of rise of fundamentalism of one sort or another.
>
> *I have also a feeling that despite my deepest respect for the life and work of Jawaharlal Nehru, it was a grave error to codify Hindu laws instead of having a uniform civil code.* If we have one criminal law for all the citizens of the Republic of India and one law in respect of Income Tax, transfer of property etc., there is no reason to have separate codes for the Hindus and Muslims. All these distortions are the products of our not being able to think clearly about our past, present and future. [italics mine]

Haksar was a quintessential Nehruvian. But he was not an uncritical devotee as his letter to Deendayalan reveals.

❧

Haksar turned 80 on 4 September 1993. His friend, the industrialist J.C. Kapur, wrote to a number of people who had known Haksar and asked them for a short two-page recollection of the man, preferably handwritten. This was then compiled and presented to Haksar. Diplomats, civil servants, politicans, industrialists, scientists and cultural and literary personalities contributed to this mini-*festschrift*. J.R.D. Tata wrote to Kapur, saying:

> ... Being myself on the threshold of attaining 90 years, I am not terribly impressed by someone's completion of 80! ... While I hold Mr. Haksar in high regard for his accomplishments and his services to the country, I have had some differences with which, I am sure, Mr. Haksar would himself remember and which, though not affecting my personal esteem for him, make me hestitate to contribute to the commemorative volume ...

India's future prime minister, I.K. Gujral, recalled the morning of 15 July 1975, when Haksar's uncle and brother-in-law had been arrested at the behest of Sanjay Gandhi:

> I recall the morning that had caused revulsion alround in the city. It was sickening evidence of a ruthless era. I met Haksar Sahib in his Planning Commission office. The hand shake of that morning communicated more than his words could. After a pause and with a determined voice he said, "They want to bend me. I would rather break!" The ring was solemn. It is this P.N. Haksar I respect most.

Jaswant Singh was later to be India's minister of external affairs and finance minister. He belonged to a party which was bitter critic of Indira Gandhi. He wrote in his tribute:

> It does not often come to human beings to be able to influence events through the strength of their ideas. P.N. Haksar is one of those exceptions to whom the Almighty granted an opportunity of giving shape to the ideas he has held for a life-time. *Certainly for almost a decade between 1967 and 1977, no other single Indian, other than the late Mrs. Gandhi had such a profound influence in the shaping of events as did P.N. Haksar* ... He has, all his life, been the composer; the musical score has been written by him, others have merely conducted the orchestra ... A man of peace, yet ironically he sculpted independent India's most signal feat of arms in the defeat of Pakistani Armies in the then East Pakistan. Yet in its wake he crafted the Simla agreement; a rare combination and a rarer achievement ... [italics mine]

B.K. Nehru, Indira Gandhi's cousin, administrator and diplomat went down memory lane:

> Baboobhai Haksar and I come from exactly the same background. We are both Urdu speaking Kashmiri Pandits belonging to the expatriate Kashmiri community. We have also been educated in the same institutes of learning, at Allahabad University, the London School of Economics and the Inns of Court. We share the same birthday and further to emphasise our affinity, I have followed his bad example by getting myself the same eye disease as he has …
>
> Both of us, having been educated in England in the 1930s came out of Academia with strongly leftist ideas and enthusiasms. It was probably our different experiences thereafter which led us to different points of view. Baboobhai remained a believer in the socialism which believes in State ownership of the means of production and distribution and consequently an admirer of the Soviet Union … In spite of our differences of opinion and my disapproval of some of the appointments he made—or, to be technical, were made by the Prime Minister on his advice—and to many of the policies she followed, equally on his advice our personal relations remained as close as ever …

Arundhati Ghosh, who was then India's ambassador in Cairo, echoed the sentiments of many when she sent in her tribute:

> Paying tribute to one's 'guru' by a 'chela' would seem to smack of presumption but since Mr. Haksar has never demanded the 'gurudakshina' that is his by right, one may perhaps presume however reluctantly to try and express in words on this special occasion of his 80th birthday the bonds of affection, respect and trust that he has built with so many of his younger colleagues in the foreign service … More fancifully, in ancient India, Mr. Haksar would have been the Rishi in whose ashram we would all have been students.
>
> Almost 30 years ago I met Mr. Haksar as a raw recruit to the IFS— the operative word being 'raw'! It was at his hands that I received my initiation; throughout my career it has been a touchstone, a basis for actions and decisions. It was from Mr Haksar that I learnt to see India as a whole, a totality, a single complex entity, beyond my service, class, community and other definitions of my Indianness.

Three years later, Ghosh was to hit international headlines for her feisty defence of India's position on the Comprehensive Test Ban Treaty (CTBT) Conference at Geneva which was applauded and supported very strongly by Haksar in his editorial in *Man & Development*. She was one of many younger IAS and IFS officers who kept in touch with Haksar till his passing away.

༄

A few months later, one of his closest friends for some six decades turned 80. Nikhil Chakravarty and Haksar had both been part of Feroze Gandhi's circle. Unlike Haksar, however, Chakravarty could never get himself to become part of Indira Gandhi's orbit. On 3 November 1993, PNH wrote to him:

> … We have travelled long together. May that journey continue with me leaning on your shoulders so that I do not tumble down by taking a false step. As someone who saw the light of the day two months earlier than you did, may I send you and your partner my love and best wishes. For love is something which "looks upon the tempest and is never shaken". The inventor of class struggle could not help writing poems and falling in love with Jenny von Westphalen. That is how I felt when I visited for the first time in my life the cemetery at Highgate.

The inventor the class struggle was, of course, Karl Marx who had brought Haksar and Nikhil Chakravarty together in the first place in London in 1936. The ex-communists were romantics in their own way.

In July 1992, India was rocked by a huge stock market scandal and Harshad Mehta had become a household word. There was a furore in Parliament, and a Joint Parliamentary Committee (JPC) had been set up a few months later to investigate the gigantic fraud that had taken place in which banks were hopelessly involved. This was to lead to an unusual admission from one of the key architects of bank nationalization in July 1969. Haksar wrote to Dr Manmohan Singh on 23 December 1993:

> *How I wish I had been called as one of the witnesses to the JPC. I would have been then able to tell them the tragic history of the way nationalized banks*

were operated. Two of the most ugly expressions were the extravaganzas of loan melas and almost criminal way in which the cultural value that one should pay one's debts was subverted. The underlying idea that the nationalization of banks to a finely tuned credit planning was frustrated. Also, the RBI was always treated as an attached and subordinate office by our politicians. Most of the RBI Governors of the past did, of course, nothing and were quite content to enjoy the sinecure. The only person who wanted to do something was Jagannathan. But neither the Prime Minister nor the Finance Minister paid any attention. Then during the Emergency a man who knew nothing about banking was transferred from LIC and made the Governor and Deputy Governor in charge of banking was chosen ... [He] was a very subservient type officer of Indian Revenue Service. If I recall correctly his name was Luthra and a man of great integrity like Hazari was replaced. However, it is too much to expect that our politicians as a class possess either a feeling for history or a sense of history. They do not even ask the basic question of historiography, namely, how and why things have happened as they did. Anyway, I do hope that this country would continue to have the advantage of your leadership. [italics mine]

Twenty-four years after orchestrating bank nationalization virtually overnight and in the greatest of secrecy, was Haksar having second thoughts? I don't believe so. His regret was not with nationalization per se but with how the political class had hijacked it and subverted in many ways the original intent behind the radical move. But surely Haksar could have anticipated this? Did he really think there would be no political interference? Yes, as long as he was around he kept the politicians at bay. But surely he could not have thought that he would be a permanent fixture? What Haksar told the finance minister in 1993 had become painfully to him just five years after nationalization itself. Ashok Mitra had written to Haksar way back on 5 July 1974:

Since people assume these days you have all the time in the world, you cannot escape the role of Uncle Confessor! This time it is D.N. Ghosh, of the Department of Banking, whom you know. Ghosh has no personal problem, but would like to have a discussion with you on the drift of banking affairs in the country. He was feeling somewhat bashful, and wanted me to write to you. He will perhaps telephone you after a few days to make an appointment.

Ghosh had unburdened himself to Haksar on how the original high-minded sense of social purpose which had driven the two of them along with the prime minister to nationalize banks in November 1969 was being subverted by the extreme politicization of appointments in banks and financial institutions. This, Ghosh argued, was devaluing professional excellence and integrity.

∾

In 1983, Haksar had renewed his friendship with classmate at the LSE, Fei Hsiao-tung. He had been to China in 1984 and 1987. Since then he had continued to take keen interest in India–China relations. He had been invited a third time to visit China but couldn't go because of health reasons. On 14 February 1994, he wrote to Fei again:

> ... It was really wonderful to meet you again. It is because of that the Ashoka Hotel in Delhi has come to mean something to me. That is where my wife and I met you on your first visit to India ...
>
> I wonder is there is any way in which Chinese and Indian social scientists could exchange their experiences in respect of the problems arising in the course of transformation of very ancient societies and civilizations to what is called "modernity" ... I am sure the Chinese scholars are working in the "software" rather than the "hardware" of modernization. I should very much like to publish the articles by Chinese scholars in a journal which I have been editing for a very long time. It is called Man & Development ...

∾

Dr Manmohan Singh had just presented his fourth Budget. Each of the Budgets since July 1991 had revealed a side of the finance minister's personality that very few knew existed—his fondness for the poet Mohammed Iqbal. Haksar wrote to him on 2 March 2 1994:

465

I listened with rapt attention to your budget speech. I could not help rejoice at the fact that it was your 4th Budget in succession.

If I may borrow a word from the world of music, the overture was, indeed, poetic. I suppose the melancholy science of economics does need that sort of opening. It was also possibly a gentle reminder to your listeners that they have to seriously investigate the reason why India has survived the ravages of time even while as Iqbal said and whom you have quoted, the great civilisations of Greece, Rome and Egypt have perished. In contemplating this panorama of our country's history, *my own convictions got reinforced which I once publicly expressed long time ago that there is no such thing as good economics which is manifestly bad politics any more than there is good politics which is manifestly bad economics. And the only economics I understand is that one should live within one's own means,* hard work, have a feeling for quality and a sense of pride ...

I am grateful to you for devoting some part of your speech to science, technology as well as to statistics ...

If my memory does not fail me, I had taken the liberty of once mentioning to you that the government should undertake a sustained programme of explaining to the citizens of the country as to why they should pay tax in their own interest ...

I apologise for inflicting this letter on you. *But situated as I am, I am under some sort of a compulsion to communicate and I cannot find anyone to whom I can communicate except you.* [italics mine]

Haksar was not entirely happy with the economic liberalization programme unveiled by Dr Manmohan Singh in July 1991. But because it was Dr Manmohan Singh, he had supported it because he had full faith in the finance minister's integrity and impeccable credentials. His approach was 'if Manmohan says India must do this, I suppose there must be good reason for India to do so'.[18] He backed Dr Manmohan Singh wholeheartedly when it came to setting right the country's finances and cutting out subsidies enjoyed by the relatively better off sections of society. He supported the finance minister in his efforts to liberate Indian private enterprise from various types of controls. But he was unhappy that import liberalization was also taking place and felt that self-reliance was taking a back seat. Unbridled consumerism was also something that bothered

Haksar as an unfortunate consequence of what Dr Manmohan Singh had unleashed.

∾

Four years had passed since Haksar had submitted his report on the review of government-run cultural institutions. It had been a labour of love for him. He had written substantial portions of it. But the report had divided the cultural world. It has drawn support but also evoked criticism. The media had, by and large, welcomed it but to Haksar's great disappointment the government itself chose to bury it.

It must have been a surprise, therefore, for him to receive a letter from J.J. Bhabha, the newly appointed chairman of the Sangeet Natak Akademi. Jamshed Bhabha, the brother of Homi Bhabha, had been instrumental in setting up the National Centre for Performing Arts (NCPA) in Bombay which Indira Gandhi inaugurated in December 1969. He wrote on 18 June 1994:

> You write beautifully. Not only have I read the Haksar Committee report but I have spoken with admiration about its content and felicitous wording to my colleagues at the Sangeet Natak Akademi (SNA) and the NCPA. When I was asked, though totally new to the Akademi and its past proceedings, to "give evidence" regarding the SNA before the Parliamentary Enquiry Committee on the Ministry of Human Resource Development, I told the Members of Parliament in the course of my answers to questions about some of the recommendations of the High Power Haksar Committee Report, that it contained the finest and most eloquent definition of "culture" I had ever come across in my extensive reading on philosophy and the arts ...
>
> Please take care to keep well and active. The country needs men of the high quality of your mind, character and spirit.

Bhabha's encomiums were just the tonic that Haksar needed to unburden himself. On 4 July 1994, he replied:

> *... You are the first person to express appreciation of the so-called Haksar Committee Report ... I have long felt the agony and the anguish of our entire educational system being so completely immunized against being infected by*

467

the virus of culture. And so we have large number of persons who I can, at best, describe as educated barbarians. Our entire educational system is a mere linear expansion of Lord Macaulay's design for us Natives ...

We boast of our ancient civilization and culture which has survived the ravages of time. But how many primary school teachers are there in our country who can convey to our children what culture actually means. It is not surprising that intolerance, crime and corruption go on increasing ... Wealth production is no doubt important but there is no economic theory of love, compassion, tolerance, human response to dance, drama and music, etc.

If India survives today, it is because millions upon millions of people sustain themselves by their values inherited through cultural manifestations contained in our songs, in our dances and in our proverbs.

I apologise for unburdening to you in so unseemly a manner. But then I have remained unaffected by the 'stiff upper lip' culture despite the long years I spent in Great Britain. I am myself the product of interaction of several cultures... [italics mine]

On 16 May 1998, just six months before Haksar passed away, Jamshed Bhabha was to issue a farewell message on his resignation as chairman of the Sangeet Natak Akademi in which he thanked the president of India, various officials and well-known personalities like Girish Karnad, Vilayat Khan, Kapila Vatsyayan, Mrinalini Sarabhai, Sonal Mansingh and Yehudi Menuhin, among others. He also added:

This Farewell Message would be incomplete without recording my debt of gratitude to Shri P.N Haksar for his eloquent support of my efforts some decades ago to build up the National Centre for the Performing Arts, starting with its inauguration by Smt. Indira Gandhi, then Prime Minister of India and extending to the brief period of almost five years as Chairman of the Sangeet Natak Akademi.

∾

31 October 1994 marked the 10th anniversary of Indira Gandhi's assassination. Haksar had scrupulously avoided speaking or writing about her. The Narasimha Rao government had set up a large committee

of eminent personalities to suggest ideas for the occasion. It had, as its members, political leaders, scientists, cultural figures, intellectuals and many others who had worked closely with Indira Gandhi or had been her ardent admirers. Somewhat uncharacteristically, Haksar agreed to be a member of the committee which appears to have met just once on 15 July 1994. In that meeting, Haksar mostly kept quiet and spoke up only once when Narasimha Rao himself observed that 'the idea is to use the opportunity as a springboard for a comprehensive medium like a film to portray Smt. Indira Gandhi's personality'. Haksar's response to this was recorded as follows:

> Shri P.N. Haksar said this is a complex issue and a word of caution is necessary in that the observance should avoid alienation on that occasion and neither remotely remind nor reawaken old controversies. It would be better if existing programmes, namely eradication of poverty, etc could be integrated and revitalized and strengthened during this period.

As it happened, he and Sharada Prasad were the only ones in that like-minded group to even draw attention to the controversies that are an inherent part of Indira Gandhi's legacy.

Haksar continued to be active with the various academic institutions and causes with which he was associated. But this was inevitably going to be the time of departures of some of those with whom he had been closely associated for decades—personally and professionally.

First to go, on 1 April 1995, was G. Parthasarathi. Strangely, although he was at Oxford at about the same time when Haksar was in London, their association had not started in the late-1930s. It was only in 1949 when Parthasarathi was posted as the PTI correspondent in London when Haksar was in the High Commission there that the two became really thick with each other. The previous year Haksar had worked with Parthasarathi's father at the United Nations. Haksar was to recruit Parthasarathi's son as his aide in 1970. The two were poles apart in temperament: Haksar was voluble, Parthasarathi was taciturn. Haksar reduced everything to writing, Parthasarathi preferred oral conversations. Haksar appeared wise when he spoke, Parthasarathi appeared sagacious even when he remained silent. Haksar was the quintessential intellectual preferring a life of books, Parthasarathi had also played Ranji Tropy cricket. But both had been rebels in their personal lives when it was not the norm to be so, with Haksar marrying his cousin and Parthasarathi marrying a Parsi. Both had been part of Indira Gandhi's inner circle with Haksar wielding power and Parthasarathi commanding influence. Haksar was to write later of Parthasarathi:

> It was a measure of his greatness that though, at times, we had differences both of perception and understanding, he never allowed such differences to diminish in any way our friendship which I shall always cherish as long as I live.

These differences were, most notably, on China on which Haksar felt that Parthasarathi was a 'hardliner' long after it warranted to be a 'hardliner' and Sri Lanka on which Haksar's view was that Parthasarathi could not be an effective interlocutor with the Sinhalas given his strong Tamil connections.

Soon after Parthasarathi's death, JNU, the university of which he had been the first vice-chancellor, was rocked by agitation. Haksar had been appointed as its chancellor in April 1991. On the morning of 24 April 1995, the-then vice chancellor Yoginder Alagh sent a letter to Haksar that was delivered at his residence. Alagh reported to JNU's Chancellor:

> I regret to say that some of our students have blockaded the Library, Academic and Administrative buildings from this morning. Some political groups have threatened to gherao and use direct action to stop the proceedings of the Academic Council meeting scheduled today at 3 pm.
>
> The issue they say is privatization of JNU and an agenda item which presents views and papers on resource raising etc., should be dropped. I had a discussion with the Students Union where I gave them an assurance that there can be no question of privatization of JNU. I also told them that the discussion can begin with a statement from the President of JNU Students Union and this will be discussed in detail ...

The Rector and I have no option now, but to go on Satyagraha with immediate effect until coercion stops and a free discussion in the Academic Council is allowed. The Satyagraha will continue until the Academic Council meeting is held …

This was and remains unprecedented in India's university history. Normally, students, teachers or workers go on protest fast but here was a unique situation when the top management itself was doing so. Haksar's reaction was instantaneous and he issued a public statement within a few hours that went as follows:

August 24, 1995

AN APPEAL BY SHRI P.N.HAKSAR, CHANCELLOR OF JNU TO THE COMMUNITY OF TEACHERS, STUDENTS AND OTHER FUNCTIONARIES OF THE JAWAHARLAL NEHRU UNIVERSITY

If I had been in a better state of health than what I am this morning and not confined to my bedroom, I would have personally come with bended knees to appeal to you all to restore peace and tranquility in our campus. I would request each and every one personally to allow the meeting of the Academic Council to proceed in an atmosphere of free debate befitting our proud democratic traditions. I would equally appeal to the Vice Chancellor and the Rector to give up immediately their satyagraha. I can reinforce the assurance given by the Vice Chancellor that there is no question whatsoever of 'privatisation' of JNU. The Academic Council is discussing a report prepared by a Committee headed Prof. Raja Raman. I devoutly hope and pray that everyone will heed to my heart-felt appeal.

I would have liked to address this appeal individually to everyone concerned for the future well-being of our University, but obviously, in this particular moment of crisis, I cannot do this. I would once again go on bended knees without any false sense of pride to appeal to everyone to let the Academic Council meet and let there be a free discussion on each and every item.

The appeal was to have its desired impact.

Towards the end of 1995, Haksar had occasion to write on Kashmir. He had been to Kashmir for the first time in June 1968 and since then had kept in close touch with developments there. A leading political figure of Kashmir, Saifuddin Soz had asked Haksar to write a foreword to his edited volume *Why Autonomy to Kashmir?* This piece was to sum up Haksar's thinking on the issue and what he said is still very relevant:

> ... It is said of the Bourbons of France that they learnt nothing and forgot nothing. I would earnestly plead that we do not act as the Bourbons did. We must forgive and forget and we must also learn from history. It is only through this process that we can hope to heal the wounds inflicted in the state of Jammu and Kashmir ...
>
> ... In one corner of our country, namely the Valley of Kashmir, we can boast of a common heritage represented by Rajatarangini and Sufiana Kalam together with the soul stirring messages of Sufis and Rishis. Nature's bounty has made the valley a paradise on earth. The skills of its people have produced exquisitely beautiful products known all over the world. That valley now is the vale of broken hearts, tears, death and destruction ... *It is about time that we who call ourselves proudly the citizens of the Republic of India rallied in support of our fellow citizens from the Kashmir Valley ... I would assert that the overwhelming mass of people of Kashmir yearn for peace and tranquility ...*
>
> ... The present tortured condition of the state of Jammu and Kashmir can be restored to health by urgently reviving and deepening democratic processes and respecting the historical context in which the State of Jammu and Kashmir became part of the Union of India ...
>
> ... *The problem of Kashmir is not a problem of Hindus vs Muslims. To convert it as such is to jeopardise the prospects of fulfilling our dreams articulated by our poets, our writers and our great leaders of the past.*
>
> ... We have committed many mistakes in the past in dealing with the problems in Kashmir. It was, for instance, a mistake which led Sheikh Abdullah to live away from his home for a long time. However, this mistake was corrected. But then another mistake was made when in 1977 the Congress Party withdrew its support to the National Conference led by Sheikh Abdullah. I think we should have the courage and honesty of purpose to recognize these mistakes so that we do not commit them again ...

... If the autonomy already enjoyed by the State of Jammu & Kashmir within the Indian Union is insufficient, this could be debated and discussed in terms of facts and logic and not by means of death and destruction ... [italics mine]

The autonomy debate in Kashmir continues but, alas, not as Haksar had advocated 'in terms of facts and logic', but 'by means of death and destruction'. He believed that the original faith of the people of Kashmir in 1947 was that they were joining an India suffused and driven by 'pluralistic humanism' represented by Gandhi and Nehru. His message was that this faith which has been damaged must be restored both for the sake of Kashmir as well as for the sake of India itself.

The Last Three Years (1996–1998)

*Two old comrades together: Haksar and Union Home Minister Indrajit Gupta after the
former's Maulana Azad Memorial Lecture, New Delhi, January 1997.
The two had first met as young communists in London in 1936.*

HAKSAR'S FIVE-YEAR TENURE AS CHANCELLOR OF JNU ENDED ON 1 APRIL
1996. Newspapers reported that Satish Dhawan, the man Haksar had
picked 24 years earlier to build India's space programme was to be the new
chancellor. Haksar wrote to him saying that he was overjoyed with that
news since this meant he and Dhawan would meet a little more frequently
in New Delhi. But that was not be, since on 13 April 1996, Dhawan sent
a hand-written letter to Haksar:

My dear Haksar:
Thank you for your kind letter.
    I have not accepted the JNU Chancellorship and there is no way I
will change my mind. No one from the Ministry of Human Resource
Development or JNU considered or ascertained if I would accept—
some one in Delhi proceeded to make the decision and make it public.
Apparently it appeared in newspapers etc on April 5th or 6th. My wife and
I received some phone calls after that from friends and acquaintances who
were surprised—& some amused—to learn that the news was not true!

... Elementary grace in behaviour and attitude is evaporating fast in India's public life. Recall how JRD Tata was removed from Air India. Also recall Jawaharlal stopping his car and getting out to enquire the welfare of an old mali near Barakhamba Circle—the old man used to send red roses to Jawaharlal. I do not presume in the class of the two great Js but I do hold firmly the essence of civilized society lies in the dignity due to every human being

Please be rest assured that I am amused not peeved—but not easily diverted from what I believe I must do or not do. I will see you in Delhi whenever I land there—Be Well.

Warm regards,

Satish.

The letter reveals the principled man Dhawan was. Seven years younger than Haksar, he must have been the only person to call him 'Haksar' while others resorted to 'Haksar Sahib' or 'PN' or 'PNH' or 'Baboobhai'. A month later, on 15 May 1996, Haksar replied:

I read your letter of April 13, 1996 several times over. And, each time my anguish increased and my faith in the future of our dear country faltered. One tries to renew one's faith by recalling the memories of persons like Gandhi, Nehru and others. But I know that it is a mere dead ritual. Every year I am gripped with depression when the eminent worthies of our political life repair to the samadhis of Gandhi and Nehru to lay flowers or hang portraits and set up statues in Parliament house. Since I cannot derive any comfort by invoking divine will, or even entropy, I turn to you for receiving the precious gift of love and friendship. If I may say so, you have done the right thing in refusing to accept the Chancellorship of JNU in the circumstances of the case ...

In early-September 1996, Dhawan's daughter had got married and Haksar wrote to him on 11 September 1996 and went down memory lane:

... All my attempts to persuade you to write have failed. I am not going to ask you to write again until you have some inner compulsion within yourself to articulate your anxieties and concerns. At this stage, what I am interested in knowing from you is your perception of the circumstances which impelled you to leave California Institute of Technology; come over to India and take over the responsibilities of setting up a Space Commission of which you were the founding Chairman. Dear old Vikram [Sarabhai] had a vision. I could see he was least interested in atomic energy. He was always looking towards the sky. I do not know what strategy he had in mind for development of space research in our country. I know he set up PRL [Physical Research Laboratory] in Ahmedabad as well as the Thumba Equatorial Rocket Station in Kerala. There was no Space Commission. ISRO was but a name. You gave to all these things not only shape and form but also inspired on a systematic basis space research. What I want from you is your recollection of your return to India and what made you do so? ...

You might be wondering why I am bothering you with all these things and not leave you in peace. I must confess constituted as I am, I cannot live in peace and the only people whom I can turn to are my friends. And you are, if I may say so, the dearest and nearest one. Please do forgive this seeming sentimentalism. But I do really want you to send me a brief note.

... There is another matter which obsesses me. It arises out of the circumstance that I was associated with Atomic Energy Commission for several years. There was a sense of deep pride among those who worked for BARC. We were proud of the fact that we had developed our own calendria; we had developed our own leak-proof pumps and so on and so forth. At the moment I see that the entire Atomic Energy Commission in a state of not knowing where they are meant to go. Inevitably, there must be deep frustration. Have you any views on this subject? Everyday we have conferences inviting foreigners to invest in our "infrastructure". But we have infrastructure in our own country in terms of highly qualified, dedicated scientists, engineers, technologists, etc.

Enough of this nonsense. But please do respond if you can. It means so much to me at the age of 83. [italics mine]

Till the very last Haksar's magnificent obsession was self-reliance in science and technology. Here he was recalling events that took place a quarter of a century earlier, and even at the age of 83 as he put it, his memory was sharp and his observations incisive. He had no access to official papers. In any case, he could not see at all. Yet, he was able dictate minute details of space and atomic energy and he continued to worry about them, as much as he did when he was in a position of authority and power. Unfortunately, Dhawan's reply to this letter is not available either in his archives or Haksar's.

∾

The two old LSE classmates from across the Himalayas had kept in touch with each other. On 15 April 1996, Fei Hsiao-tung wrote to Haksar:

> I was deeply moved by your letter of March 13 [not available]. The dear friendship between old fellows is indeed very unusual. It seems that the letter you asked the Indian Embassy to pass on to me has not arrived yet, but it is also possible for me to leave it somewhere around since my memory is not so good recently. I have traveled a lot around the country and for this reason my life is not in good order ...
>
> ... I am sorry that I have some difficulties to express my ideas and feelings in English since I have not written in English for a long time. This is the reason I did not write to you to present my thanks after reading your book. I really enjoy your style of writing, with the logic of an abstruse philosophy and a good sense of humour ... You have always been my dearest friend, we both belong to the world and have tried to leave some ideas to the future generations. Our hearts are connected and we do not need any words.

Haksar replied to his Chinese friend on 10 June 1996:

> I just cannot find words to express the depths of my feelings when I read and re-read your exquisitely beautiful letter of April 15. This letter of yours shall remain my most precious possession.
>
> How I wish I could travel and be with you ... But having no eyesight for the past several years travelling even within India becomes quite a problem ...
>
> I find that though our two countries are bearers of distinctive civilization for several thousand years, there is very little interaction between our scientists in both social and natural sciences. I have been firmly of the view that China and India should set an example to the distracted world in creative cooperation and friendship based on the

famous five principle of peaceful co-existence which Jawaharlal Nehru and Premier Chou En-Lai elaborated at Bandung ...

In this letter, Haksar also requested Fei to send articles by Chinese scholars for *Man & Development* and suggested some topics as well: how China is dealing with the problem of collecting and disposing human excreta; the general approach in China in building urban settlements; and, dealing with environmental problems. He confessed that he still did not know what the phrase 'sustainable development' meant but he welcomed enlightenment on it from Chinese scholars.

∾

On 29 July 1996, another member of Haksar's intimate ideological and personal circle, Aruna Asaf Ali, passed away. Born Aruna Ganguly, she had shocked everybody by marrying Asaf Ali—a leading Congressman, 23 years her senior. Asaf Ali was a close compatriot of Nehru and had been India's first ambassador to the USA, and later was India's ambassador in Switzerland where he died in 1953. Other than being mayor of Delhi, Aruna Asaf Ali never occupied political office but remained steadfastly committed to progressive causes.

On 8 August 1996, Haksar wrote to Dhanraj Acharya who he had first recruited to the CPI way back in 1942. He was to recall his communist past vividly:

> You cannot imagine how happy I felt when you travelled all the way to Delhi and spent some little time with me. Bardhan who called on me for the first time mentioned to me that you have also seen him. And today the news is that he has become the General Secretary of the CPI. I have almost a photographic memory of your face, Bardhan's face, Kusum Paranjape's face. I still feel as if I was taking a class of young pupils. And now, Bardhan has graduated to the high post.
>
> I have long been of the view that those who call themselves "communists" and regard Marx as their Guru and interpret him according to their own predilections so that we have in India the privilege of so many political parties dividing themselves in the name of Karl Marx, should all

come together and call themselves the United Democratic Communist Party of India. *And they should think of not merely class struggles but also about maintaining the individual's integrity and pride of our common motherland and preserve its glorious diversity.* [italics mine]

Two years left in his life and he was thinking of how to give new shape and direction to the communist movement in India. But Marxism to him was no religion to be blindly followed; it was more a mode of intellectual inquiry and analysis, a way of looking critically at socio-economic phenomena.

A few months later, K.S. Shelvankar passed away in London on 19 November 1996, the 79th birth anniversary of Indira Gandhi. Haksar and Shelvankar had known each other for six decades. Shelvankar's book *Problems of India* which came out in 1940 by Penguin in London, had created a sensation when it was published and was promptly banned in India. It was to become standard reading of educated Indians of that generation. Haksar's 'Dear Shelly' and Shelvankar's 'Dear Hakki' letters had continued till the middle of 1996.

The Indian Council of Cultural Relations (ICCR) had instituted an annual memorial lecture series in honour of Maulana Abul Kalam Azad and Nehru had kicked off the series in 1960. Over the years many distinguished personalities from India and abroad had spoken at this forum. Haksar delivered this lecture on 4 January 1997. Sitting next to him on the dais and presiding was his old friend from the communist years in London and then the home minister of India, no less. Indrajit Gupta had been with PNH in the late-1930s in London but on his return remained with the CPI unlike Haksar.

The home minister's presence may not have been a complete surprise. But what took Haksar aback was the presence of someone whose ideology had been an anathema to Haksar all his life but with whom he had retained a warm personal friendship. This person was to become prime minister India some 18 months later. Atal Bihari Vajpayee was not the only future prime minister present. His successor Dr Manmohan Singh was also there to listen

Haksar regale the audience for over an hour extempore—like always—with Sanskrit slokas, Urdu couplets and English poetry while talking about the onset of the 21st century. His main themes were 'How India could retain its character and unique identity by tempering its scientific, economic and political determinism with culture and values', 'How everyone seemed to be concerned with environmental pollution while ignoring mental pollution' and 'How the exploitation of religion for political advancement would only lead to human suffering'.

R.N. Gurtu, a retired judge of the Allahabad High Court, was one of Haksar's closest friends going back to his youth. They would write to each other every month. Gurtu was a poet of sorts and Haksar would encourage him to have his poetry published. One of the very last letters from Haksar to him was on 20 February 1997:

> What a joy it was to receive your scribbled note and also read your poem … I thought the Greeks had all the wisdom but far from it. If they had it, their civilization would not have been destroyed. Despite all our follies and troubled times, the Indian civilization has survived. As for Plato's dialogue in which he says a person is wise if he says that he does not know is nothing original to me. It was written several thousand years ago when it was stated in Katho-upanishad that "apradnya iti pradnya" which means that the wisdom consists of saying one does not know. However, this is not to negate the fact that one knows quite a lot but not everything …
>
> I have now lived without eyesight for more than 9 years. It is sheer bloody-mindedness on my part to carry on as I am doing. But it is soothing and comforting to know that you are there.

Haksar was not a Hindu zealot or a xenophobe. He was a champion of science, secularism and modernity. Yet, his pride in Indian culture was unparalleled. It came from a deep study of ancient Indian texts, particularly the Upanishads which were his favourites. He was very much taken up with the character of the wise but under-stated Vidura in the epic *Mahabharata*, who is considered to be the very embodiment of 'truth, impartial judgment, dutifulness and steadfast *dharma*'.

Nine months before he passed away he would write to Katherine Frank on 4 February 1998:

The sacred books which we have inherited from India's ancient civilization are Vedas, Upanishads, Shastras and Puranas. In one of the Upanishads, there is a dialogue between a young man and the God of Death. The name of the young man is Nachiketas and the God of Death is called Yama. The young man pleads with Yama for immortality. With compassion, Yama tells the young man that he can give all kinds of things, but cannot give immortality ...

In the month of June 1997 I was caught hold of by my doctors and subjected to all kinds of tests in a hospital in Delhi called Apollo. The tests as well as the amount of money I had to spend reminded me of a Sanskrit verse which goes as follows:

"O Vaidyaraj (doctor), I bow to you as you are the twin-brother of Yamaraj (God of Death). The only difference between you (doctor) and Yamaraj is that while Yama only deprives you of your life, you Vaidyaraj takes away both my life and my earthly possessions.

After undergoing all the tests, the curiosity of the doctors was aroused and they wanted to fiddle around with me a little more. I had to recite to one of the doctors the verse in Sanskrit which I have quoted above. Then they let me off. I am therefore still alive though somewhat distracted by the bizarre goings on in our political arena. [italics mine]

Even as he was about to 'shuffle off this mortal coil', Haksar would not lose his sense of humour.

On 17 September 1997, Haksar wrote to Bakul Patel, the widow of his friend Rajni Patel, who he had first met in 1937 in London. The letter seems to repudiate whatever Haksar had done for half a century:

I wouldn't have inflicted this letter on you but for the way you have described me as Indira Gandhi's 'conscience keeper'. If you would turn to Oxford Dictionary to find out the meaning of the word 'conscience', you will find the following:

481

"the moral sense of right and wrong, especially as felt by a person and affecting his behaviour".

I could not become a 'keeper' of something which did not exist. If I were to briefly describe my own career in Foreign Service it could only be described as an errand boy during the Nehru years who graduated to become a valet. And as the saying goes: "no man is hero to his valet". A valet's perception of his master is quite different from those who come and visit the master and dine and wine with him. [italics mine]

A week later, after this uncharacteristic indictment of Indira Gandhi he would write to her biographer Katherine Frank:

I wonder how far you have proceeded with the writing of your story. Knowing a little bit about your sense and sensibility, I am sure that your book will be a fitting memorial to the life and work of Indira Gandhi.

On 2 April 1998, seven months before he passed away he again wrote to Frank:

I have read with admiration the way you are tracing the footsteps of Indira. Yes, I was in London from 1935 to 1942. Feroze was there too.

His very last letter to Frank was on 10 June 1998:

As I was contemplating my life and my time, as well your total involvement with Indira Gandhi's life and work, it occurred to me that you might consider meeting someone in the Rolls Royce factory where Sanjay spent a few years as an Apprentice. You may find out from them what they thought of him when he was working there. *After all, the story of Indira Gandhi is not the story of a character in fiction. She was a daughter; she was a wife; she was a mother; she was also the Prime Minister and possessed not only a body but also a soul.* [italics mine]

The letter to Bakul Patel therefore cannot be seen in isolation. True, in itself it is a harsh judgment of Indira Gandhi by Haksar. But his letters to Frank at about the same time are of a different nature and in Frank's biography of Indira Gandhi which came out in 2000, Haksar is on record both praising and criticizing the prime minister he worked for. He was not niggardly in praise and was not unsparing in criticism of Indira Gandhi. I would put down Haksar's letter to Bakul Patel to one of those moments especially in old age when you begin to think that your life has had no meaning. Stephen Greenblatt has pithily described this condition as 'late-life melancholy'.[19]

~

Haksar and Homi Sethna had remained in touch over the years. They would meet every once in a while and catch up with each other. Sethna had scrupulously avoided speaking on nuclear energy matters after his retirement. On 24 September 1997, Haksar wrote to him:

> ... It appears that PTI [Press Trust of India] has circulated an interview by P.K. Iyengar in which he says that the Department of Atomic Energy was all ready to explode a Hydrogen Bomb and that it was vetoed as a result of my advice to Indira Gandhi. It appears to me that P.K. Iyengar and his mentor Raja Ramanna have concocted all this. He doesn't seem to even know that by 1974 I was not even Secretary or Principal Secretary to Prime Minister. I finally quit the PM's office in January 1973. I do however recall what a hard time you had as Chairman of the Atomic Energy Commission in coping with Raja Ramanna. *I believe that Ramanna has written an autobiography in which he alleges that I was even opposed to Pokharan explosion. Frankly, I am distressed by reading all this. But I do not know what to do about it. So, I am turning to you for your advice and guidance.* [italics mine]

On 27 October 1997, Sethna replied to Haksar sending him a copy of a speech he had just delivered at the BARC. The speech was on advances in chemical engineering but Sethna used the occasion to also say this:

> ... You are aware that I was Chairman of the AEC [Atomic Energy Commission] when India took the decision to have its PNE [Peaceful Nuclear Experiment] in 1974 ... A lot of thinking had gone into arriving at a decision to go ahead with that experiment. But the Government was committed to one thing—that it shall use the experiment for peaceful purposes and for gaining knowledge in harnessing the tremendous potential of nuclear fission. I have said all these only to highlight the fact

that we should remain a peaceful country in the comity of nations and take lead in realizing a world without nuclear arsenals. A good friend of mine and an Adviser to Mrs. Gandhi wrote to me about two weeks ago asking me why I am not clarifying certain wrong untrue statements on India's intentions on exploding a hydrogen device following our PNE in 1974 appeared recently in the press. I wrote to him that it was not my intention to remain in the limelight forever by making sensational statements ...

A year later, and a few months before his death, Haksar would go on record for the first time on his role in India's nuclear test of May 1974.[20]

Haksar and Katherine Frank clearly enjoyed each other's company. He wrote to her on 4 February 1998:

I feel greatly honoured that you have enlarged the photograph of Indira Gandhi and installed her in your study. I wish I could have shown you a set of photographs I took of her in the course of 15 minutes and how the expressions of each phase was different ...

Haksar was justly proud of the photographs he had taken of Indira Gandhi which, as I have mentioned earlier, were taken while on a river cruise near Dacca in March 1972. They are indeed stunning.

On 17 March 1998, a grand function had been organized in New Delhi to celebrate the 78th birth anniversary of Sheikh Mujibur Rahman, and naturally Haksar had been invited as a special guest. However, he was very ill by that time and could not attend. But he made it a point to send a message from his sick bed.

MESSAGE FROM SHRI P.N. HAKSAR

My present state of health prevents me from being present at the Public Meeting jointly organized by the Friends of Bangladesh and the High Commission of Bangladesh this evening on the sacred occasion of the 78th Birth Anniversary of Bangabandhu, Sheikh Mujibur Rahman ...

I have had the privilege of interacting with Bangabandhu during the entire period beginning with his return to Bangladesh in the month of

January, 1972 and later on when I was assigned the task of conducting negotiations with Pakistan beginning with the Simla Conference and thereafter. Several critical questions were involved such as recognition by Pakistan of Bangladesh as a separate Sovereign State, repatriation of 93,000 prisoners of war as well as Pakistani nationals of Bihari origin numbering about two lakhs as well as the repatriation of Bangladeshis stranded in West Pakistan. All these questions were difficult in the circumstances prevailing at that time and would have been difficult to solve but for the wide vision and statesmanship of Sheikh Mujibur Rahman ...

I still feel the pain and agony of the tragic news I received in Geneva on the 15th of August 1975 when I heard Bangabandhu's life was cruelly extinguished. However, Sheikh Mujibur Rahman whom we lovingly called Bangabandhu remains an immortal part of the history of the South Asian sub-continent ...

Haksar's illness had prevented him from going to Dhaka for a symposium that had been organized by his friends and admirers. He was obviously deeply disappointed he could not go on what he called his 'last pilgrimage to Dhaka'. But this disappointment was compensated somewhat because at about this time the Bengali translation of his autobiography—*One More Life*—was published in Bangladesh with a foreword by Kamal Hossain, the former foreign minister of Bangladesh who had worked closely with Haksar in 1973. On 18 May 1998, Haksar wrote to Hossain:

You have given me a wonderful gift by publishing the story of my childhood and boyhood. How I wish I could read the book because I knew Bengali alphabets ...

In his foreword, Hossain wrote:

... I had heard from Mr. Tajuddin Ahmad and those who worked with the Provisional Government headed by him from March to December 1971 speak of Mr. Haksar's special role as Secretary to the Prime Minister in the inner councils of decision-making. Critical decisions during that period had involved the timing and level of support to be given by India to our liberation struggle, relations with the pro-liberation forces which had crossed over to India in the face of the military onslaught unleashed on 25 March 1971 and with the Provisional Government which had been established in Mujibnagar in April. 1971 is recognized as India's finest hour ... Mr. Haksar's contribution to that success is widely acknowledged ...

His visit of April 1973 had proved to be catalytic. He came with a constructive and problem-solving approach ... This approach enabled us—Bangladesh and India—to transcend the obstacles presented by delay in formal recognition [by Pakistan] and made possible the Joint Declaration of Bangladesh and India in April 1973 ... Deferring the issue of formal recognition, we had declared that we would take the initiative to pursue a solution based on a coordinated and simultaneous repatriation of stranded Bengalis to Bangladesh, stranded Pakistanis to Pakistan and a return of the prisoners of war, subject to the trial of a stipulated number. The responsibility fell on Mr. Haksar to conduct successive rounds of discussions in Islamabad and New Delhi. During these discussions, he maintained continuous consultations with us almost on a daily basis. These discussions bore fruit as they broke the deadlock and led to the agreement concluded in August 1973.

Mulk Raj Anand and Haksar went back to the London of the 1930s. They had remained in touch. On 19 March 1998, Haksar wrote to Anand:

... Delhi is a cruel city. Unless one has power, pelf and 'influence', one is condemned to live without experiencing the sensation of friendship. Your letter gave me that feeling of apnahat and somewhere from the dark recess of my mind, the following lines written by some poet whose name I do not recall, began emitting comforting sensations. The lines are as follows and I wonder if you know who wrote them:

> She gave me eyes
> She gave me ears
> Gentle cares and delicate fears
> And Love and Thought and Joy.

I began recalling our days in London before the war as well as during the war and, of course, 8, St. George's Mews.

I have always felt that if you were a white man instead of being a blackie, you would have by now got a Nobel Prize in Literature. The first thing I ever read of what you wrote was a short story titled "Lament on the Death of Master of Arts". In my humble opinion, apart from Untouchable, your novel titled "Two Leaves and a Bud" was very, very moving …

This morning I heard over the radio the swearing-in- ceremony of a new government. I wonder how a person like you, endowed with deep sensibilities and sensitivities, surveys our contemporary Bharat …

The noted author replied some weeks later, on 5 April 1998:

Of course, your rare note, dictated inspite of your eye trouble, made me feel that our affection is sustained.

Often when I hear or read news of what's going on, I know you that you must be feeling and reacting from the point of view of values you held dear when you were involved in Government.

In retrospect, inspite of the emergency, the first years of your time as adviser to Prime Minister Indira Gandhi, remain memorable. Not many know how much of our first policies owed themselves to your advice. But Sanjay's doings and the emergency brought stain to the good things Indira did in the first few years.

I wish, as you had dictated the first part of your autobiography, you might persuade yourself to put down what very few people know, how you conducted State affairs or rather how State affairs were conducted under your advice by the young lady who had matured in her father's house, but still needed help to run the country … [italics mine]

Haksar had heard on radio the swearing in of Atal Bihari Vajpayee as prime minister on 19 March 1998 as he had informed Mulk Raj Anand. The new prime minister must have remembered Haksar for on 3 April 1998, Haksar was to write to the man who now occupied the same position he once had. Haksar wrote to Brajesh Mishra, the principal secretary to the prime minister and a person he had interacted with closely on India's China policy in 1970:

It was really lovely of you to telephone me the other day. I am taking the liberty of requesting you to deliver the enclosed letter into the hands of the Prime Minister. I have written it in an intensely personal vein.

Looking forward to meeting you some time some day.

With my blessings and best wishes,

Alas, we will never know why Mishra telephoned Haksar. Was it just a courtesy call or were there some matters of state talked about? But the letter that Haksar wrote to the prime minister in 'an intensely personal vein' is indeed available and is also dated 3 April 1998:

> You have known me long enough to know that I seek nothing from the State called the Republic of India. I even refused to accept Padma Vibhushan which was offered to me in January 1972 [actually it was in January 1973]. I vowed to serve my country the best of my ability when I gave up my lucrative law practice in Allahabad and joined the Indian Foreign Service which was being created. Our mother land which has greater splendour than swarga is beset with large number of extraordinarily complex and difficult problems. You have undertaken to pilot the Ship of State through extraordinarily turbulent waters. As I [am] older to you by as many as 13 years, I can perhaps send you my blessings and best wishes for steering the ship to a safe haven ...

Haksar's July 1990 report on culture obsessed him. A new minister of human resource development had taken over. He happened to be a physicist and shared the same alma mater with Haksar—Allahabad University. On 3 June 1998, Haksar wrote to Dr Murli Manohar Joshi:

> In a few months time, I shall attain the age of 85 ... I am not too well. However, I am under some compulsion to write to you to invite your attention to a report I had submitted to the Government of India way back in 1991. That report was the product of my two years of travelling in our country in the course of which I penetrated into every nook and corner and interacted with thousands of creative people. The Chapter II of the report ... was inspired by "pluralistic humanism" which in my humble opinion constitutes the cornerstone of our ancient civilization ... In our country, culture is derived from word, viz., *Sanskriti* which means refinement. I have been a passionate advocate that our entire educational

system, from primary level right up to university has been completely drained of refinement both in terms of values as well as sensitiveness to creative arts.

I devoutly hope and pray that you will do me the honour of at least going through the report yourself ... We need to deeply ponder over the English word, viz., "pluralism". Bharat, Hind, Hindustan or India cannot survive without pluralism. We cannot weave pluralism into the fabric of our civilization of today and tomorrow without tolerance and morality.

∾

On 23 June 1998, Nikhil Chakravarty passed away. Haksar and Chakravarty had both been very close to Feroze Gandhi from their UK days but Chakravarty had drifted apart from Indira Gandhi and the Emergency snapped whatever links the two had. He edited *Mainstream*, a leading voice of the Left movement. Haksar would write for it often not surprisingly under the pseudonym 'Vidura'. Twelve days before Nikhil Chakravarty's demise and five months before his own, Haksar wrote to their mutual friend, Subrata Banerjee in Calcutta:

The suffering of Nikhil is quite unbearable. He is still lying in hospital. He does not seem to recognize anyone or speak anything. My own younger brother who is 14 years junior to me is lying dangerously ill. So far as I am concerned, I go about the business of living but my doctors have put me in a state of mental distress. I committed the mistake of going through various check-ups. There is some indication of malignancy in my right kidney ...

To be quite frank, I have long been in favour of India becoming a nuclear power. In the real world of politics, even in the countries which claim to follow Jesus or Buddha, moral arguments do not carry weight. Possessing nuclear weapons and then passionately advocating nuclear disarmament might carry some little weight. However, we have handled China rather badly. Our Defence Minister needles China unnecessarily. I am troubled by this ... [italics mine]

On 31 July 1988, Haksar opened up for the first time on his role in India's nuclear programme to Raj Chengappa, a noted journalist who was to write a racy, informative book on India's quest for nuclear weapon[21] It was uncharacteristic of Haksar and he actually went on record on his recollections. Did he get any premonition that he would not be around when the book would be out? In the interviews he was to reveal that he had many discussions with Indira Gandhi on the subject going all the way back to late-1967 and that both of them were convinced that India would have to conduct a nuclear test since China had already done so in October 1964. The theoretical work for the tests had begun then. He further told Chengappa while he had supported the need for tests, he was not entirely sure that May 1974 was the right time because as he recalled:

> I was also thinking about the future. We needed to prepare a little better. We needed to convert this explosion into a weapon. There was a lot of technical work still required ... What I was looking for was a series of explosions ...
>
> [But] I was also worried about keeping the whole thing secret. It was not easy and the real achievement was not the test per se but that the Americans didn't know about it. They always thought we were digging for oil or water at Pokharan. Also, having gone this far I felt we should now go ahead and acquire the competence.

It is true that initially Haksar wanted the test to be better timed politically so as to influence the elections which were due in early-1976. But he had quickly changed that view and the Chengappa interview provides an explanation for this change.

Sometime in very early-August 1998, the old warrior was diagnosed with malignant growth in his right kidney. But he soldiered on and wrote to Murli Manohar Joshi a second time, expressing his inability to attend a dinner to which he had been invited saying:

> ... I hope and pray that in the next 50 years of our country, viz., Bharat, Hind or Hindustan or India will become a shining example to the distracted world of today how we have succeeded in combining pluralism with humanism. This of course we cannot do unless we passionately

dedicate ourselves to combining shiksha with sanskriti as the cornerstone
of the process of India's renaissance ...

A fortnight later, on 19 August 1998, Haksar regretted his inability to
attend a function to commemorate the 54th birth anniversary of Rajiv
Gandhi to which he had been invited by Ram Jethmalani, the minister of
urban development saying:

> I have known Rajiv Gandhi almost from the day of his birth. There was
> a time when he was in London. I was, more or less, loco parenti. I still
> feel an ache in my heart when I recall the brutality of his murder.

Six days later, he chaired the Governing Body meeting of the Centre for
Research on Rural and Industrial Development (CRRID) in New Delhi.
He had been chairman of this Chandigarh-based research institution since
January 1980 and has also been editor-in-chief of its international quarterly
Man & Development for which he wrote erudite editorials regularly. These
editorials provided a forum for Haksar to let off his steam. In this very last
CRRID meeting of his, he was silent most of the time until, as Subrata
Banerjee who was present recalled:[22]

> ... towards the end, when a remark from Dr. Manmohan Singh provoked
> him. Haksar's criticism of the government's structural adjustment
> programme was incisive. I saw he was tired when we got back home.
> I chided him for exerting himself. He said he could not refrain from
> responding to Dr. Manmohan Singh's remarks ... That was the last time
> I saw Haksar.

Soon after Haksar's death, Dr Manmohan Singh would take over as
chairman of CRRID's Governing Body in January 1999 and continue in
that position till he became prime minister in May 2004.

Sometime in early-October 1998, Home Secretary B.P. Singh
called Haksar up to say that the prime minister had decided that three
distinguished civil servants who had served India so nobly for long—
Haksar, L.P. Singh and B.K. Nehru—should be decorated with the Padma
Vibhushan. Haksar was in the hospital. His daughter picked up the phone
and told Singh to 'let it be' and that 'her father would simply not agree'.

As it turned out, a few days later L.P. Singh, Haksar's contemporary from Allahabad University in the early-1930s, home secretary in the late-1960s and thereafter ambassador and governor, passed away on 17 October 1998. On the eve of the 1999 Republic Day, it was announced that the Padma Vibhushan was being conferred on B.K. Nehru and posthumously on L.P. Singh. Both Indira Gandhi and Atal Bihari Vajpayee had failed in having this honor conferred on Haksar.

On 16 October 1998, Haksar had occasion to write to Murli Manohar Joshi a third time in six months:

> I am truly grateful to you for your kind thoughts and good wishes on the happy occasion of Deepawali of 1998. With all my heart I reciprocate your kind thoughts and sentiments. I wish you success in creating a vision of India which will bring to life the dreams of all our saints, Sufis and poets like Rabindra Nath Tagore.
>
> The state of my health is keeping me wholly occupied with its problems. I have been in and out of hospitals and at the end of September I went through an extremely traumatic experience of having blood transfusion for two consecutive days each transfusion lasting for nearly 8 hours. I am now in a state of utter exhaustion, but I have gathered myself together to write this brief letter to you ...

Forty-two days later, Haksar's 'business of living' as he had put it came to an end. He had started his life admiring Dr N.B. Khare, a Congressman who then became president of the Hindu Mahasabha. His life was to end just after he had written to someone belonging to the same ideological brotherhood.[23] There could have been no greater irony for Jawaharlal Nehru's protégé and Indira Gandhi's alter ego.

Haksar was on his last legs—but obviously he didn't know that—when he wrote to R. Lakshmipathy, chairman of the PTI Board on 12 November 1998:

> Some time ago you wrote to me asking me to continue to be a member of the Committee of the PTI Board. I am in a state of dilemma. I should like to continue to do what I can to serve the Board. However, I am troubled about my present state of health. Be that as it may, for the time

being at least, I have pleasure in accepting your gracious invitation to remain a member of the Committee [the Board].

Fifteen days later, Haksar departed leaving behind not just 'his footprints on the sands of time' but also an incredible treasure trove of papers that has made this biography possible.

Notes

1. Bhagat (2005).
2. A very fawning letter of 15 January 1980 to Indira Gandhi from the second senior-most judge of the Supreme Court, P.N. Bhagwati, would soon come to light and he could never live it down during the rest of his distinguished career.
3. Sen (2003).
4. Dhar (2000).
5. Nehru (1997).
6. Fotedar (2016).
7. On 7 August 1996, Haksar would write to the industrialist Nusli Wadia: 'It was a source of great inspiration to me when I by accident of circumstance met your dear father in the company of my late uncle way back in 1968 or 1969. Thereafter I met him whenever he came to see me. Through him I learnt the beautiful story of the House of Wadias who were ship builders and even built ships for the British who used to boast about their ruling the waves in all the oceans of the world ...'
8. Haksar (1979).
9. Frank (2000).
10. Sen (2003).
11. Nehru (1997).
12. Ranganathan (2002).
13. Actually, this was the second exception Haksar would make to his policy of turning down accolades. He had agreed to accept the Soviet Land Nehru Award for 1987, along with noted writers—R.K. Narayan and K.M. George.
14. Singh, Natwar (2014).
15. Singh, Arjun (2012).
16. Urmila Haksar wrote about the day PNH's uncle and brother-in-law were arrested on 15 July 1975 in Haksar, Urmila (1978): 'My husband told me

that in his office (Planning Commission) one of his visitors at the lunch hour was Arjun Singhji (former Education Minister of M.P) … My husband told him briefly that his uncle and brother-in-law had been arrested that morning. He [Arjun Singh] turned pale and his face fell. He exclaimed "They are doing this to *you*". He got very upset and offered to go to the court. My husband calmed him and told him that there was nothing Arjun Singhjji could do. When Arjun Singhji went away he went to the small room attached to his [Haksar's] office room and sat there anxiously waiting for the news…'

17. Haksar inaugurated the Medical Centre in February 1976 and it became an Institute of National Importance by an Act of Parliament in 1980. Haksar's role has been described in Valiathan (2004). Valiathan writes that as Haksar was leaving Trivandrum after the inauguration, he gave Valiathan a piece of paper with a friendly wink and the remark 'here is a love letter for you'. It turned out to be a letter from a top CPM leader of Kerala who cautioned Haksar not to associate with the Sree Chitra Medical Centre which was a 'CPI show'. Achutha Menon belonged to the CPI which was then in alliance with the Congress in the state.

18. I have discussed the importance of Dr Manmohan Singh's background and personality in making the 1991 economic reforms widely acceptable in Ramesh (2015).

19. Greenblatt (2011).

20. A needless controversy has been created by a scholar Vivek Prahladan, who wrote in *The National Interest* in late-2016 that Haksar had been an unapologetic nuclear hawk all the time and that he had prepared a long note in 1968 on India's nuclear strategy. Prahladan likened this note to the American diplomat George Keenan's famous 8000-word 'long telegram' from Moscow to his bosses in February 1946 on Soviet intentions and how best to 'contain' them. Prahaldan has been dishonest to say the least. The note in the Haksar archives is unsigned and undated. There is nothing to indicate that Haksar was the author. Actually, it appears to be part of a manuscript of a book that somebody else was writing on India's nuclear policy. The manuscript ends thus: '… the areas where advantageous collaboration between China, Japan and India is possible are elaborated in the final chapters of this book'.

21. Chengappa (2000).

22. Banerjee (2017); Banerjee was one of Haksar's long-time acolytes and his wife Karuna had played the role of the mother in Satyajit Ray's *Pather Panchali* which had been shown at Cannes in 1956 because of Nehru's intervention at the instance of PNH.

23. In the final decade of his life, Haksar would carry on correspondence with K.R. Malkani, a leading light of the Deendayal Research Institute, named after an icon of the Jan Sangh. Malkani was clearly an admirer of Haksar although they were poles apart in terms of political ideology.

A Look Back

THIS THEN WAS THE LIFE AND TIMES OF A MOST UNUSUAL INDIAN WHO HAD not only a remarkable capacity to think but also was afforded an unusual opportunity to act. On rare occasions in history, a person finds his right niche at the right moment. Parameshwar Narain Haksar found his at an extremely critical period in India's recent history. He held public offices with unparalleled distinction and set standards in public and personal life which few can imitate and fewer still improve upon.

I have deliberately eschewed the temptation to be judgmental which is so easy to be with the benefit of hindsight. I have also not indulged in any form of 'psycho-history' to delve into the relationship that Indira Gandhi and PNH had enjoyed for almost five decades—a relationship that, sadly, got hugely bruised in the last decade of her life much to her detriment. Mine has been a straight-forward chronicle of a life of a most fascinating man, much of it in his own words; a man who, even when the times changed, remained steadfast to his beliefs, principles and ideology. He was different and made a huge difference.

I set out only to tell a story. Even so, some assessment I suppose is inevitable and expected.

Haksar contributed heavily to the making of Indira Gandhi, especially in the first six or seven years of her prime ministership. He ran her Secretariat with the 'protective instincts of a close friend and the privileged power of a trusted confidant'. They formed a awesome duo: she with her charismatic appeal, he with his intellectual gravitas. Ultimately, she took all the decisions no doubt, but she was influenced heavily by him at every turn. His loyalty to her remained undiminished even after the humiliation he had to suffer during the Emergency. And that loyalty was not in expectation of any reward or recognition.

He did make the prime minister's Secretariat a powerful body but, contrary to popular belief, did not centralize all authority. He dominated but was not domineering. He kept the Secretariat very small and encouraged youngsters. Ministries took their own decisions, some of which he supported and some of which he opposed. He got his way frequently but there were occasions when he did not get his way even after having had his say.

He did drive the prime minister somewhat crazy at times with his long and, at times, long-winded and verbose notes. But he felt the need to do so since he thought he was 'educating' a prime minister who needed to have the full facts before arriving at a decision. He belonged to a tradition which valued the written word and that believed that writing is a way of not just communicating but also clarifying one's own thoughts.

Haksar did promote his ideological cronies to positions of power and authority even allowing for the fact that many of them were part of Indira Gandhi's circle as well. But many of them were certainly worth promoting, having impeccable academic credentials. But he also canvassed the case of people whose ideology did not necessarily converge with his when he found them to be persons of capability and integrity.

It is true that in his eagerness to make Indira Gandhi a symbol of a definite ideology that he believed was progressive and was badly needed, Haksar by-passed the structures of the Congress party of which she was an indispensable part. Institutionally, the Congress party may well have suffered as a result. At times, he appeared to betray disdain for her colleagues believing as he did that she was the magic wand, in spite of all her infirmities.

He did demonstrate a great fondness for the Soviet Union but this was at a time when India needed that superpower on its side with the USA and China being hostile to it. But at all times he used the USSR to advance India's interests—political and economic. And these interests did get advanced. And he was an early advocate of a rapprochement with China and Pakistan

He did betray a fixation on the public sector and a bias against the private sector. But that was the prevailing orthodoxy then. However, that fixation was on a public sector that was run professionally and commercially. His obsession paid off in some cases and did not in others.

Could Haksar have done more to make economic policy more pragmatic in the mid-1970s when it was clear that India was in crisis? Decidedly so. There are two long notes suggesting bold economic reforms buried in his archives: one dated May 1973 and another dated October 1974, both prepared by the-then chief economic adviser in the Ministry of Finance, Dr Manmohan Singh. These would undoubtedly have been discussed but for some reason did not become a reality then.[1] But his pre-occupation with concentration of 'economic power' and with 'growing inequalities' continue to have significance today.

He did speak of a 'committed' bureaucracy and a 'committed judiciary'. But for him that commitment was to a value system that was enshrined in the Constitution and that was anchored in a recognition of the inequities that lie at the core of the Indian society. He didn't quite realize that such a commitment in the hands of lesser men and women could degenerate into a commitment to a single individual.

Haksar invested all his energies in building up one individual—Indira Gandhi—believing as he did that she was ultimately her father's daughter. Solicitous of her personal interests at all times, unflinching in his loyalty to her, he saw everything through her prism but he had the courage to speak truth to her face. What he perhaps had not bargained for is that in the process of building loyalty to her, he would create a large circle of sycophants who lacked his moral scruples and intellectual convictions.

He was undoubtedly opinionated and never shied away from expressing those opinions, both orally and in writing. But he was also open to new ideas and thinking and to listening to alternative points of view. He had a high sense of self-esteem, but curiously at the same time also displayed humility and was self-effacing in his heyday. There was always a larger social vision to whatever he did and 'whatever lapses might be associated with him, they were not of a personal nature'.

He remained an unreconstructed democratic socialist all his life, a democratic socialist who never repudiated his debt to the Marxist mode of intellectual inquiry; a Marxist deeply proud of Indian civilization and it ancient glories, profoundly irreligious but in awe of India's spiritual traditions, not wedded to any dogma but open to reason. The socialist values he espoused in public became his guideposts in private life as well.

He cannot be divorced from the spirit of his times, vividly reflecting as he did the *Zeitgeist*. Having spent 16 of his first 54 years in London, he reflected British left-wing traditions and thinking of that era with all its strengths and biases. Viewed in *today's* context, he was brilliantly wrong in some of his beliefs but he got enough things right which have served the country well. However, even where he was wrong, he had enough justifiable reasons for his stances.

Civil servants are judged by what they accomplish before they retire. In my view, that is a limited perspective. They should also be judged by how they adjust to their post-retirement life. Some continue to hold on to some office or the other. Some just wither away unable to handle the loss of office and power. P.N. Haksar was, and remains, one of the very few who served the Indian state for three decades with distinction and then, on his own terms, seamlessly became the conscience of Indian civil society for the next two. He stood tall by the manner of his exit from the very pinnacle of power. That is the true measure of the man, whose life, though now like an extinct comet, has continuing significance and deserves to be rescued from amnesia. During his heyday he was not a mere person but indeed 'a whole climate of opinion' anchored in the noblest of human values.

Note

1. Seventeen Congress members of Parliament, all avowedly socialist, had written to Indira Gandhi on 31 January 1975, protesting against a suggestion made by the-then minister of industrial development—T.A. Pai—to 'offload' 49 per cent equity in public sector companies to the private sector, workers and the public. This appeared to have the support of Haksar and P.N. Dhar but went nowhere. It was implemented by Dr Manmohan Singh in July 1991 with 'offload' being called 'disinvestment'.

A Note on Sources

THE MOST IMPORTANT SOURCE FOR HAKSAR'S NOTES AND LETTERS IS HIS extraordinarily rich archive at the Nehru Memorial Museum and Library (NMML). This covers the period 1947–1998. I have made only partial use of the collection. Many more books could be written based on it. I have not used any unsigned notes of which there are quite a few in his archive. There is, for instance, an unsigned eight-page note dated 11 November 1970 in PNH's collection arguing for the appointment of H.R. Gokhale as the next chief justice of the Supreme Court in the grounds that he was not only an eminent lawyer but also had impeccable 'progressive' credentials. Other names, including that of Mohan Kumaramangalam were discussed in the note. The note went nowhere and Gokhale became minister of law and justice in March 1971.

For the pre-1947 period I have depended on material available in the National Archives, Haksar's unpublished second volume of his autobiography and the published memoir of his childhood and boyhood *One More Life* (1989). The International Institute of Social History, Amsterdam is the source for his 1939 paper on the student movement in India.

The letter from Girija Shankar Bajpai to Jawaharlal Nehru is from the collection of K. Shankar Bajpai. Indira Gandhi's letters to Rajni Patel are from the special collections at the Penn State University Library, USA. Indira Gandhi's letter to Mrs Sasadhar Sinha is from the Sasadhar Sinha collection in the British Library, London.

Much of the primary material used in the 1971 and 1972 chapters is derived from Volume III of Avtar Singh Bhasin's comprehensive and extremely valuable documentary study of India–Pakistan relations between 1947 and 2007.

A number of Haksar's own anthologies of his lectures, articles and interviews have been an invaluable source of material. They are a delight to read even after all these years. Prominent among them are *Premonitions* (1979), *Reflections on Our Times* (1982), *India's Foreign Policy* (1989) and *Contemplations on the Human Condition: Vol II* (2002). These too have been indicated at the appropriate places.

The 75th birthday volume *P.N. Haksar: Our Times & The Man* (1989) has a collection of some very informative and insightful essays by a wide cross-section of his friends and colleagues which has helped me structure this book.

All volumes of *Selected Works of Jawaharlal Nehru* have been published by the Jawaharlal Nehru Memorial Fund (JNMF).

Acknowledgements

My greatest thanks are due to the Nehru Memorial Museum and Library (NMML). Jyoti Luthra was particularly helpful at all times. Jaya Ravindran's assistance at the National Archives was readily forthcoming.

Nandita Haksar, PNH's elder daughter, who gave away all his papers to the NMML with open access, thereby placing historians and other scholars in her perpetual debt, was always available to answer my questions.

Gopal Gandhi, Srinath Raghavan, Mahesh Rangarajan and T.C.A. Raghavan read the entire manuscript carefully and made very many valuable suggestions. I am deeply indebted to them. Srinath Raghavan's advice that the essentials should be differentiated from 'the ruminations of a wise man in his autumn' helped me to make the book tighter.

Four nephews of Haksar—Viney Mushran, Dipak Haksar, Sanat Kaul and Vinit Haksar—were of considerable help to me in understanding PNH the man and his family, as well as the interconnections within the Kashmiri Pandit community. Kadambari Kaul, grand-daughter of P.N. Sapru, one of Haksar's closest friends wrote out her memories of Haksar which I found of substantial use.

I am grateful to D.P. Dhar's son, Vijay Dhar and Satish Dhawan's daughter, Jyotsna Dhawan for their assistance. Bijoya Goswami gave me the 1939 group photograph of Indian students in London in which her father Snehangshu Acharyya and Haksar are present. Bakul Patel responded readily to my requests for material on Haksar and her late husband. Mrs Premila Loomba recalled in vivid detail the friendship that her brother Satish Dhawan and Haksar shared for almost four decades. Supriya Guha, Subimal Dutt's grand-daughter, generously provided me with her grandfather's diary entries.

Shankar Bajpai was a wonderful source of information on India's foreign policy and on IFS history. He spoke to Henry Kissinger on my behalf. Natwar Singh, too, was an encycolopedia whom I consulted often. B.N. Tandon, Moni Malhoutra and Salman Haidar, colleagues of Haksar in the prime minister's Secretariat, were generous with their time and recollections.

R. Gopalakrishnan put me in touch with Rajendra Narla who enabled me to get correspondence between PNH and J.R.D. Tata available in the Tata Archive. Rashpal Malhotra, founder of CRRID in Chandigarh, the institution with which Haksar was so closely associated, was an enormous fund of information.

The *Hindustan Times* provided me the originals of the two Sudir Dar cartoons. The Press Information Bureau (PIB) of the Ministry of Information and Broadcasting was the source for Haksar's photographs with Margaret Thatcher and the *Times of India* for the Indira Gandhi-Kosygin photograph of August 1968. I obtained the Haksar photograph with A.PJ. Abdul Kalam and with Krishan Kant from the *Hindu*. All other photographs are from the NMML. The photograph of Klugmann and Haksar is from Eric Hobsbawm's autobiography *Interesting Times*. Dhanraj Acharya's son Pramod Acharya shared his father's picture with Haksar.

Gita Kudaisya of the JNMF helped locate Nehru's correspondence with C.D. Deshmukh and B.G. Kher.

Ritu Vajpayi-Mohan served as sounding board, on matters small and big. Sayantan Ghosh helped improve the book in good measure.

A FEW PHOTOGRAPHS TAKEN BY HAKSAR

Indira Gandhi

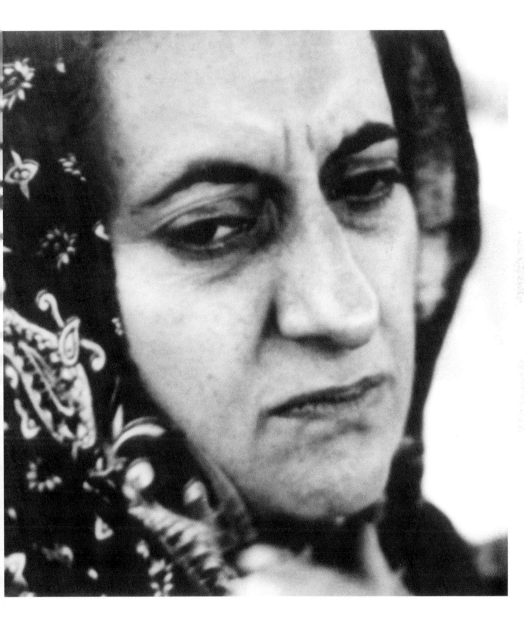

Sheikh Mujibur Rahman

R.N. Kao

J.R.D. Tata

Raja Ramanna

Select Bibliography

Aijazuddin, F.S., (ed.), *The White House and Pakistan: Secret Declassified Documents, 1969-1974*, Oxford University Press, 2002.

Anand, Mulk Raj, 'Memories of P.N. Haksar', *The Tribune*, 3 January 1999.

Andrews, Geoff, *The Shadow Man: At the Heart of the Cambridge Spy Circle*, IB Taurus & Co, 2015.

Austin, Granville, *Working a Democratic Constitution*, Oxford University Press, 1999.

Awana, Ram Singh, *Pressure Politics in Congress Party: A Study of the Congress Forum for Socialist Action*, Northern Book Centre, 1988.

Barnes, Robert, 'Between the Blocs: India, the United Nations & Ending the Korean War', *Journal of Korean Studies*, Volume 18, Number 2, Fall 2013.

Bass, Gary, *The Blood Telegram: Nixon, Kissinger and a Forgotten Genocide*, Alfred A. Knopf, 2013.

Bernal, J.D., *The Social Function of Science*, Routledge, 1939.

Bhagat, Usha, *Indiraji: Through My Eyes*, Penguin/Viking, 2005

Bhasin, Avtar Singh, *India-Pakistan Relations 1947-2007: A Documentary Study*, Volume III, Geetika Publishers, 2012.

Bhushan, Prashant, *The Case That Shook India*, Penguin/Viking, 2017.

Chagla, M.C., *Roses in December*, Bharatiya Vidya Bhavan, 2012.

Chakravarty, Suhas, *V.K. Krishna Menon and the India League, 1925-47*, Har-Anand Publications, 1997.

———, *Crusader Extraordinary: Krishna Menon and the India League 1932-1936*, India Research Press, 2006.

Chandra, Siddharth, Goran Kuljanin and Jennifer Wray, 'Mortality from the Influenza Epidemic of 1918-1919: The Case of India', in *Demography*, published online, 3 June 2012.

Chengappa, Raj, *Weapons of Peace*, HarperCollins, 2000.

Das Gupta, Amit, *Serving India: A Political Biography of Subimal Dutt (1903-1992), India's Longest Serving Foreign Secretary*, Manohar, 2017.

Dasgupta, Chandrasekhar, 'The Decision to Intervene: First Steps in India's Grand Strategy in the 1971 War', *Strategic Analysis*, Volume 40, Number 4, 2016.

Dayal, Rajeshwar, *A Life of Our Times*, Orient Longman, 1998.

Dhar, P.N., *Indira Gandhi, the 'Emergency' and Indian Democracy*, Oxford University Press, 2000.

Dutt, R.C. and K. Raj Nigam (eds), *Towards Commanding Heights*, Standing Committee on Public Enterprises, 1975.

Falk, Bertil, *Feroze the Forgotten Gandhi*, Roli Books, 2016.

Fotedar, M.L., *The Chinar Leaves: A Political Memoir*, HarperCollins, 2015.

Frank, Katherine, *Indira: The Life of Indira Nehru Gandhi*, HarperCollins, 2001.

Gandhi, Rajmohan, *Rajaji: A Life*, Penguin, 1997.

Gandhi, Sonia, *Two Alone, Two Together: Letters between Indira Gandhi and Jawaharlal Nehru 1922-1964*, Penguin, 2004.

Ghosh, D.N., *No Regrets*, Rupa, 2015.

Gerberg, Itzhak, 'The Changing Nature of Israeli-Indian Relations: 1948-2005', Doctoral dissertation in international politics, University of South Africa, 2008.

Greenblatt, Stephen, *The Swerve*, W.W.Norton & Co., 2011.

Gujral, I.K., 'P.N. Haksar: Governance with Social Purpose', in Subrata Banerjee (ed.), *Haksar Memorial Volume II: Reminiscences and Haksar Memorial Lectures*, Centre for Research in Rural and Industrial Development, 2004.

————, *Matters of Discretion: An Autobiography*, Hay House India, 2011.

Haksar, Nandita, 'On the 100th Birth Anniversary of Parmeshwar Narain Haksar', *Mainstream Weekly*, Volume LI, Number 38, 7 September 2013.

Haksar, P.N., 'The Challenge of India's Social and Cultural Transformation', Feroze Gandhi Memorial Lecture, 29 November 1976.

————, *Premonitions*, Interpress, 1979.

————, *Reflections on Our Times*, Lancers Publishers, 1982.

————, *India's Foreign Policy and its Problems*, Patriot Publishers, 1989.

————, *One More Life, Volume I: 1913-1929*, Oxford University Press, 1990.

————, 'The Gorbachev Phenomenon', in Subrata Banerjee, *Haksar Memorial Volume I: Selected Writings, Speeches and Letters*, Centre for Research in Rural and Industrial Development, Chandigarh, 2004.

Haksar, Urmila, *The Future That Was*, Sterling, 1972.

————, *That Case of Pandit Brothers*, Perspective Publications, 1978.

Hasan, Muyeedul, '1971: PNH in Bridging the Security Gap', in Subrata Banerjee (ed.), *Haksar Memorial Volume II: Reminiscences and Haksar Memorial Lectures*, Centre for Research in Rural and Industrial Development, 2004.

Hobsbawm, Eric, *Interesting Times: A Twentieth Century Life*, Allen Lane, 2012.

Kaul, H.N., *K.D. Malaviya and the Evolution of India's Oil Policy*, Allied Publishers, 1991.

Kaul, T.N., *Diplomacy in Peace and War*, Vikas Publishing House, 1979.

———, *My Years through Raj to Swaraj*, Vikas Publishing House, 1995.

Kiernan, V.G., 'Mohan Kumaramangalam in England', *Socialist India*, 23 February 1974 and 2 March 1974.

Kumaramangalam, Mohan S., *Coal Industry in India: Nationalisation and Tasks Ahead*, Oxford and IBH Publishing Company, 1973.

———, *Judicial Appointments: An Analysis of the Recent Controversy over the Appointment of the Chief Justice of India*, Oxford and IBH Publishing Company, 1973.

Lal, Air Chief Marshal P.C., *My Years with the IAF*, Lancer International, 1986.

Malhotra, Inder, *Indira Gandhi: A Personal and Political Biography*, Hay House India, 2014.

Masani, Zareer, *Indira Gandhi: A Biography*, Oxford University Press, 1975.

McKenzie, Kermit E., *Comintern and World Revolution 1928-1943: The Shaping of a Doctrine*, Columbia University Press, 1964.

Mendes-France, Pierre, *Dialogues avec l'Asie d'aujourd'hui*, Gallimard, 1972.

Mishra, Brajesh, 'The "Mao's Smile" Revisited: Sino-Indian Relations During an Important Period', *Indian Foreign Affairs Journal*, Volume 1, Number 4, October–December 2006.

Mishra, D.P., *The Post-Nehru Era: Political Memoirs*, Har-Anand Publications, 1993.

Mitra, Ashok, 'Dreams and the Man', in Subrata Banerjee (ed.), *Haksar Memorial Volume II: Reminiscences and Haksar Memorial Lectures*, Centre for Research in Rural and Industrial Development, 2004.

———, *A Prattler's Tale: Bengal, Marxism and Governance*, Samya, 2007.

Moraes, Dom, *Mrs Gandhi*, Jonathan Cape, 1980.

Nayak, Ranganath P., *Pangal Ramanath Nayak: His Life & Work*, published by Narayan Nayak, Ranganath Nayak, Amarnath Nayak, 2011.

Nehru, B.K., *Nice Guys Finish Second*, Penguin/Viking, 1997.

Nielson Jr., Howard C., Memorandum for the Files, US Department of Justice, Office of Legal Counsel, 5 August 2005, available at http://www.justice.gov/sites/default/files/olc/legacy/2009/12/30/aclu-ii-o80505.pdf.

Padgaonkar, Dileep, *Under Her Spell: Roberto Rossellini in India*, Penguin/Viking, 2008.

Palkhivala, Nani, *We, the Nation: The Lost Decades*, UBS Publishers, 1994.

Pant, Kusum, *The Kashmiri Pandit: Story of a Community in Exile in the Nineteenth and Twentieth Centuries*, Allied Publishers, 1987.

Parthasarathi, Ashok, *Technology at the Core: Science & Technology with Indira Gandhi*, Pearson/Longman, 2007.

Parthasarathi, G. and H.Y. Sharada Prasad (eds), *Indira Gandhi: Statesmen, Scholars, Scientists & Friends Remember*, IGMT/Vikas, 1985.

Patel, I.G., *Glimpses of Indian Economic Policy: An Insider's View*, Oxford University Press, 2002.

Prasad, H.Y. Sharada, *The Book I Won't Be Writing and Other Essays*, Chronicle Books, 2003.

Raghavan, Srinath, *1971: A Global History of the Creation of Bangladesh*, Permanent Black, 2013.

Rajimwale, Anil, *History of Student Movement in India (1920-1947)*, Manak Publications, 2001.

Ramachandran, G., *Walking with Giants*, New Horizons Media, 2013.

Raman, B., *The Kao Boys of R&AW: Down Memory Lane*, Lancer Publishers and Distributors, 2013.

Ramanna, Raja, 'Five Decades of Scientific Development: Memories of P.N. Haksar', in Subrata Banerjee (ed.), *Haksar Memorial Volume II: Reminiscences and Haksar Memorial Lectures*, Centre for Research in Rural and Industrial Development, 2004.

Ramesh, Jairam, *To the Brink and Back*, Rupa, 2015.

———, *Old History, New Geography: Bifurcating Andhra Pradesh*, Rupa, 2016.

———, *Indira Gandhi: A Life in Nature*, Simon & Schuster, 2017.

Ranganathan, C.V., 'Memories of an Indian Ambassador: 1987-1991', in Tan Chung (ed.), *Across the Himalayan Gap: An Indian Quest for Understanding China*, Indira Gandhi National Centre for the Arts, 1998.

Rasgotra, Maharajkrishna, *A Life in Diplomacy*, Penguin/Viking, 2016.

Reddy, K.N. Amulya, 'Remembering Satish Dhawan', *Current Science*, Volume 82, Number 2, 25 January 2002.

Rudra, Ashok, *Prasanta Chandra Mahalanobis: A Biography*, Oxford University Press, 1996.

Sarkar, Bidyut (ed.), *P.N. Haksar: Our Times & the Man*, Allied Publishers, 1989.

———, *The World of Satyajit Ray*, UBS Publishers, 1993.

Sattar, Abdul, *Pakistan's Foreign Policy, 1947-2012: A Concise History*, Oxford University Press, 2006.

Sen, Mohit, *A Traveller and the Road: The Journey of an Indian Communist*, Rupa, 2003.

Shaw, Graham, 'On the Wrong End of the Raj: Some Aspects of Censorship in British India & its Circumvention during the 1920s-1940s, Part 2', in Abhijit Gupta and Swapan Chakravorty, *Founts of Knowledge*, Orient Blackswan, 2016.

Singh, Arjun, *A Grain of Sand in the Hourglass of Time: An Autobiography*, Hay House, 2012

Singh, Khuswant, *Truth, Love & A Little Malice—An Autobiography*, Penguin, 2002.

Singh, K. Natwar, *One Life Is Not Enough: An Autobiography*, Rupa, 2014.

Singh, Satindra, *Communists in Congress: Kumaramangalam's Thesis*, DK Publishing House, 1973.

Sobhan, Rehman, *Untranquil Reflections: The Years of Fulfillment*, Sage, 2016.

Sparrow, Jeff, *No Way but This: In Search of Paul Robeson*, Scribe Publications, 2017.

Spinney Laura, *Pale Rider-The Spanish Flu of 1918 And How it Changed the World*, Jonathan Cape, 2017.

Tandon, B.N., *PMO Diary-I: Prelude to Emergency*, Konark Publishers, 2003.

———, *PMO Diary-II: The Emergency*, Konark Publishers, 2006.

Tandon, Prakash, *Punjabi Saga (1857-1957)*, Viking, 1988.

Valiathan, M.S., 'Shri P.N. Haksar I knew', in Subrata Banerjee (ed.), *Haksar Memorial Volume II: Reminiscences and Haksar Memorial Lectures*, Centre for Research in Rural and Industrial Development, 2004.

Index

Bharat Ratna awards, 311
Bhattacharjee, Kallol, 433, 436
Bhushan, Prashant, 347
Bhushan, Shanti, 348
Bhushan, Shashi, 102
Bhutto, Zulfikar Ali, 262–264, 266, 268, 319, 329
Biliankin, George, 63
Birendra, Prince, 135
Bombay Natural History Society (BNHS), 101
Bose, Satyendra Nath, 364
Bose, Subhas, 28
Bowles, Chester, 95, 101
Brandt, Willy, 249
Bray, Charles, 316
Brzezinski, Zbigniew, 389

C. Achutha Menon Foundation, 459
Carras, Mary C., 384
Carroll, Nicholas, 63
Caudwell, Christopher, 28
Central Bureau of Investigation (CBI), 141
Centre for Research on Rural and Industrial Development (CRRID), 491
Chagla, M.C., 98, 100, 130
Chakravarty, Nikhil, 32, 343, 463, 489
Chakravarty, Sukhamoy, 342, 346, 374
Chand, Kishan, 360, 381
Chandran, T.R. Satish, 341, 441
Chandrasekhar, S., 131
Chandy, K.T., 31, 44
Chaplin, Charlie, 58–59
Chatterjee, Dwarka, 214, 438
Chavan, S.B., 457
Chavan, Y.B., 140–141, 183, 230, 266, 272, 283–284, 290
Chawla, Navin, 381
Chengappa, Raj, 489
Chogyal of Sikkim, 354–355, 357
Choudhury, Moinul Haque, 280
Chou En-lai, 223, 228

Chowdhury, B.D. Nag, 106, 172, 327–328
Christian Free Church, 33
Committee on Public Undertakings (COPU), 177
Communist International (Comintern), 25
Communist Party of Great Britain (CPGB), 26
Communist Party of India (CPI), 17, 26, 32, 192, 322, 361–362, 384
Communist Party of India (Marxist), 32
Comprehensive Test Ban Treaty (CTBT), 463
Congress Forum for Socialist Action (CFSA), 102, 104, 115, 132–133, 139
Cornford, John, 28
Council of Scientific and Industrial Research (CSIR), 170

Dasgupta, Chandrashekhar, 241
Dasgupta, Sonali, 88–89
Dayal, Rajeshwar, 17, 70
De, Niren, 143, 254, 292–293
Dean, John Gunther, 433–436
Deng Xiaoping, 443, 447
Desai, Morarji, 101, 133–134, 139, 141, 144, 312, 371–374, 377–378
Desai, Nitin, 346
Deshmukh, C.D., 57–58
Dhar, D.P., 136, 171–172, 196–197, 206–207, 220, 227, 237, 253, 259, 265–266, 271, 294, 334–335, 341–342, 359, 364
Dhar, P.N., 8, 86, 141, 156, 322, 326, 330, 343–344, 354, 394–395, 403–404, 442, 448, 455
Dhar, Sheila, 331
Dharia, Mohan, 102, 132
Dhavan, S.S., 31
Dhawan, Satish, 106, 175, 242–245, 390, 448, 454, 474
dissolution of Parliament, 1970, 186–188

This

By S

T.N. KAUL

D.P. DHAR